In Solidarity

In Solidarity
Academic Librarian Labour Activism and Union Participation in Canada

Edited by Jennifer Dekker
and Mary Kandiuk

Library Juice Press
Sacramento, CA

Copyright 2013 respective authors.

Published in 2014 by Library Juice Press

PO Box 188784
Sacramento, CA 95822

http://libraryjuicepress.com/

This book is printed on acid-free, sustainably-sourced paper.

Library of Congress Cataloging-in-Publication Data

In solidarity : academic librarian labour activism and union participation in Canada / edited by Jennifer Dekker and Mary Kandiuk.
       pages cm
    Includes bibliographical references and index.
    Summary: "Provides a historical and current perspective regarding the unionization of academic librarians, an exploration of some of the major labour issues affecting academic librarians in a certified and non-certified union context, as well as case studies relating to the unionization of academic librarians at selected institutions in Canada"-- Provided by publisher.
    ISBN 978-1-936117-62-8 (alk. paper)
    1. Librarians' unions--Canada 2. Library employees--Labor unions--Canada. 3. Academic librarians--Faculty status--Canada. 4. Collective bargaining--Academic librarians--Canada. I. Dekker, Jennifer, author, editor of compilation. II. Kandiuk, Mary, 1956- author, editor of compilation.
    Z682.2.C216 2014
    331.88'1102770971--dc23
                          2014017726

Contents

Acknowledgements
  – Jennifer Dekker and Mary Kandiuk vii

Introduction
  – Jennifer Dekker and Mary Kandiuk 1

Part One: The Origins of Academic Librarian Labour Organizing in Canada
  Academic Status for Canadian Academic Librarians: A Brief History
  – Leona Jacobs 9

  Out of the "Library Ghetto:" An Exploration of CAUT's Contributions to the Achievements of Canadian Academic Librarians
  – Jennifer Dekker 39

Part Two: Case Histories
  A "Honey" of a Union Deal: Gender and Status in the Labour Action of Carleton University Librarians, 1973 – 1975
  – Martha Attridge Bufton 63

  Academic Librarianship: The Quest for Rights and Recognition at the University of Toronto
  – Harriet M. Sonne de Torrens 81

Ontario College Librarians' Campaign for
Parity - Networking for Social Change
— Robin Inskip and David L. Jones   107

Part Three: Current Issues and Experiences
Librarians as Teachers, Researchers and Community Members
— Meg Raven, Francesca Holyoke and Karen Jensen   127

Highs and Lows: An Examination of Academic
Librarians' Collective Agreements
— Marni R. Harrington and Natasha Gerolami   151

Librarians as Faculty Association Participants: An Autoethnography
— Justine Wheeler, Carla Graebner, Michael Skelton,
    and Margaret (Peggy) Patterson   171

The Quiet Librarian: Workplace Complaints and Collegiality
— G. Douglas Vaisey   185

Academic Librarians at the Table - Bargaining for Parity
— Mary Kandiuk   197

Part Four: Case Studies
From Certification to Strike - Academic Librarians &
Archivists at the University of Western Ontario
— Mike Dawes, Linda K. Dunn, and Aniko Varpalotai   221

The Mouse That Roared
— Christena A. McKillop   237

The Mouse That Didn't Roar: The Difficulty of Unionizing
Academic Librarians at a Public American University
— Stephanie Braunstein and Michael F. Russo   251

Collegial Self-Governance for Professional Librarians: The Establishment
and Evolution of a Library Council at Brock University
— Tim Ribaric   277

Notes   291
Contributors' Biographies   347
Index   353

Acknowledgements

We would like to take this opportunity to acknowledge our contributors and thank them for volunteering to share their valuable experience and knowledge. We would also like to extend our appreciation to Rory Litwin (Publisher) and Alison Lewis (Editor) at Library Juice Press for providing a venue for this work. Lastly a sincere thank you to Jill Flohil, our copy editor extraordinaire, whose skills and understanding of the value of librarians' contributions to union work has contributed in no small measure to this collection.

Jennifer is grateful to the collective of academic librarians; my peers allowed me entry into this profession; they mentored me (including Mary Kandiuk, who taught me what it means to stand up and be heard in the union, for which I owe a career's worth of gratitude); my colleagues motivate me to work hard and they sustain me. I wouldn't be involved in workplace issues at all if it weren't for them. Further, I'd like to acknowledge Susan Spronk and Jean-Daniel Jacob of the Association of Professors of the University of Ottawa who were enthusiastic and supportive of this project right from the start. Finally, my family: Brent, Maeve and Sylvia.

Mary would like to thank her co-editor, Jennifer Dekker, who is one of the most passionate defenders of librarians' rights that I know. It has been an honour to collaborate with her on this project. I would like to acknowledge and pay tribute to Brenda Hart, Executive Staff Associate, of the York University Faculty Association (YUFA) who provided York librarians with a political education and sat down with them many years ago to map the political strategy which brought them to the point they are today. I would also like to thank Brian Abner, former President of YUFA, for supporting librarians when they embarked on what proved a very long journey to improve their terms and conditions of employment. And finally, I would like to extend special thanks and appreciation to "my guys" (Bob, Alex and Nicholas) for their tremendous support through what is now approaching three decades of union activism and participation.

The Editors would like to acknowledge the financial support of the YUFA Faculty/Library Research Grant Fund (Article 19.29, YUFA Collective Agreement) for this project. Mary would also like to note the YUFA half-course equivalent release to support librarian research projects (Article 18.17f, YUFA Collective Agreement), coincidentally negotiated by her in the 2009-2012 round of collective bargaining, which facilitated completion of this work.

–Jennifer Dekker and Mary Kandiuk
June 2014

Introduction

Rights, Recognition, and Respect

Academic librarians in Canada are among the most heavily unionized workers. The Canadian Association of University Teachers (CAUT) Librarians' Salary and Academic Status Survey for 2010-11/2011-12 suggests that of the approximately 1,288 academic librarians who are members of CAUT, over 95% are part of their faculty associations.[1] In the US, the Bureau of Labor Statistics, in its 2014 release of the *Union Members Summary* states that "Among occupational groups, the highest unionization rates in 2013 were in education, training, and library occupations... (35.3% each)."[2] Librarians in both jurisdictions have been unionized for some 45 years and have been represented by various professional associations since the early 20th century. Despite these numbers, Kathleen de la Peña McCook notes that "the literature of academic library unionism is scant."[3]

In Solidarity documents the birth of labour organizing of academic librarians in Canada and to a lesser extent in the US. It offers specific instances of working conditions and workplace practices, analyses of collective agreements, tales of labour disruption; it describes the experiences of librarians on bargaining teams and even conveys one group's failed attempt at organizing. Although not the intention of the book originally, *In Solidarity* can be used as a textbook introduction to unionizing—not only for librarians but for other academic and public sector workers. A concept such as collegial governance is applicable to all academic staff; collective bargaining is universal among unionized employees; and the historical chapters will prove instructive for a great many workers. In this case, because many of the subjects involved were and are women, *In Solidarity* also documents the struggles of a largely female occupational group to gain control of their working conditions.

The chapters in the first section, *The Origins of Academic Librarian Labour Organizing in Canada*, chronicle the impetus and first efforts of academic librarians to organize from the late 1950s to the early 1980s. Leona Jacobs explores the key roles played by the Canadian Association of College and University Libraries (CACUL) and the Canadian Association of University Teachers (CAUT) in raising the issues of academic status, salaries and working conditions for academic librarians. Jennifer Dekker examines the lack of advocacy on the part of professional associations and the proactive role of CAUT in advancing the working conditions of Canadian academic librarians.

In the second section, *Case Histories*, Martha Bufton discusses the issues of gender and status at Carleton University in the broader context of the pursuit of equity in Ontario during the 1960s and 1970s. Harriet Sonne de Torrens describes the early history of librarianship at the University of Toronto, including the evolution of library education and the fight for recognition and status of librarians. Robin Inskip and David Jones describe the parallel movement in Ontario's system of community colleges, focusing on their struggle for academic equivalency to teachers and equal pay for work of equal value.

The third section, *Current Issues and Experiences*, explores current issue relating to the unionization of academic librarians. Meg Raven, Francesca Holyoke and Karen Jensen examine the workload responsibilities of teaching, research and service and the role of collective agreements in ensuring balance. Marni Harrington and Natasha Gerolami provide a comparison and analysis of collective agreements, illustrating their importance in controlling the trajectory of librarians' work. Justine Wheeler, Carla Graebner, Michael Skelton and Margaret (Peggy) Patterson use autoethnography to convey the experience of librarians participating in faculty associations, providing a compelling narrative of the impact on the participants and the communities they represent. Douglas Vaisey provides an overview of the complaint and grievance process and librarians' experiences of grievance. The section concludes with Mary Kandiuk's examination of the role of collective bargaining with respect to improving terms and conditions of employment and the issues and challenges experienced by librarians as members of minority groups within faculty associations.

In the final section, *Case Studies*, two chapters examine the strike by academic librarians and archivists at the University of Western Ontario, a pivotal event in academic librarian labour history. Mike Dawes, Linda Dunn and Aniko Varpalotai examine the issues of salary, academic status, and autonomy that led to the strike in 2011, while Christena McKillop focuses on the empowerment of librarians during their job action. The only chapter in the collection to present a US perspective, by Stephanie Braunstein and Michael F. Russo, depicts a very different labour environment at Louisiana State University and a stark difference in resolve between US and Canadian academic librarians with respect to unionization. The section concludes with an examination by Tim Ribaric of the issues and challenges of collegial self-governance for academic librarians at Brock University.

Readers will no doubt remark that most of the contributions are written by female authors. Is this surprising, given that the "marginalization of librarianship is due to the fact that it is a woman's profession" and that the "undervaluing of library work" is a "product of its gendered nature?"[4] Librarians—mostly female—mobilized early on to tackle issues of pay equity, academic status and professional autonomy. But other than unionization, what means were or are available to them? Professional associations? Friendly relations with library administrators? Frustrated by a lack of progress, librarians turned away from their professional associations and local library administrators and instead looked to the national academic labour organization, CAUT or in the US, the National Education Association, the American Association of University Professors or other unions, as well as their local faculty associations, to further their collective professional interests.

While striving for a balance in terms of representation of the US and Canada, we found that few American librarians were willing or able to share their stories. Therefore this collection is nearly entirely focused on Canada, where the percentage of unionized workers is, like in the US, slipping, but remains high for workers in the educational sector.[5] The Canadian context is of course smaller (in terms of numbers of librarians and numbers of universities) than the US. It might surprise American readers to discover that there are fewer than 100 universities in Canada and that they are nearly all publicly-funded.[6] Despite this, we believe that the historical accounts, pressing issues and case studies we have gathered can provide guidance to those who are interested in above all improving their workplaces, but also asserting their academic status, exercising their academic freedom, participating in collective bargaining and accepting the responsibilities that accompany all of the above, no matter where they are located geographically.

A Few Words on Academic Freedom...

Unfortunately no author responded to the Call for Proposals with a chapter on the issue of academic freedom for librarians, which we feel is one of the core—perhaps *the* core—issues of our time. In Canada, there have been recent and notable cases of tenured or permanent librarians being terminated for arbitrary reasons or sued for expressing professional opinions. The ability of management to limit speech through various sanctions, combined with the comparatively small size of the academic librarian job market, we suspect, has resulted in an environment where not many want to write or speak publicly about their experiences, while others are prevented from doing so by agreements governing the settlement of grievances. But silence erodes free expression, chips away at academic freedom (through the exercise of self-censorship) and ultimately, damages democracy itself. Bruce Barry writes, "The ability of these people (public employees) to speak freely and publicly about the agencies where they work is an important way of keeping tabs on the effectiveness of the critical services they provide, and by extension the effectiveness of open government in a democratic society."[7] This statement is particularly fitting in a time when it is vital to critique excessive managerialism, litigation and neoliberal politics in universities, and ensure that postsecondary education remains independent of business and government interests, and that citizens have the right and the ability to access higher education. Regarding the crackdown on freedom of expression, Henry Giroux states, in our universities "This loss of faith in the power of public dialogue and dissent is not unrelated to the diminished belief in higher education as central to producing critical citizens and a crucial democratic public sphere in its own right. At stake here is not only the meaning and purpose of higher education, but also civil society, politics and the fate of democracy itself."[8]

We have attempted to weave together chapters that speak to the various facets of academic librarian activism and union participation. Contributors describe the powerful role of unionization, collective bargaining and collective agreements in defining terms and conditions of employment. Motivated by a desire for justice in the workplace, they became active, not only in pursuit of their own interests, but in defence of those whose rights have been violated. The core values of academic librarianship—the belief in academic freedom, shared governance and equity—are all evident in the contributions.

We hope that *In Solidarity* encourages academic librarians to be more active in their unions, and to push for unionization or facilitate changes in their workplaces that replicate those of unionized libraries. But being unionized does not confer immediate benefits. Librarians must bargain for better working conditions. We must enforce that we have academic freedom and freedom of expression within our workplaces. Once gains are made, unionized librarians must ensure an employer's compliance with the collective agreement which can be more difficult than negotiating the agreement itself. Sustained effort is required to ensure that unionization, organization or other forms of workplace activism are not for nothing. It is also critical that academic librarians cultivate and express their collective voice. The story of academic librarian labour activism and union participation is necessarily about finding this voice and being heard.

There are many ways to be a workplace activist; working through a union is only one, but it is where we have focused. However, this book should not be seen as only for those librarians or libraries that are unionized; its goal is much broader: to bring about positive changes in our workplaces; to enhance the working lives of librarians; to educate librarians about professional solidarity; and to strip away some of the fear in asserting one's rights and making one's voice heard in the workplace.

– Jennifer Dekker and Mary Kandiuk[9]

Bibliography

Barriage, Sarah. "Library Workers Will Not be Shushed: 2012 Union Review." *Progressive Librarian* 41 (2013): 86-97.

Bruce, Barry. *Speechless: The Erosion of Free Expression in the American Workplace.* San Francisco: Berrett-Koehler, 2007.

CAUT. *Librarian Salary and Academic Status Survey, 2012 Part I: Salaries, Salary Scales and Academic Status*, Dec. 2012. Ottawa: CAUT, 2013.

Giroux, Henry. "Public Intellectuals Against the Neoliberal University." Truthout (Oct. 29, 2013). http://www.truth-out.org/opinion/item/19654-public-intellectuals-against-the-neoliberal-university.

Harris, Roma. *Librarianship: The Erosion of a Woman's Profession.* Norwood, N.J.: Ablex, 1992.

McCook, Kathleen de la Peña. "Unions in Public and Academic Libraries." *School of Information Faculty Publications.* Paper 108. (2010). http://scholarcommons.usf.edu/si_facpub/108.

Statistics Canada. Table 282-0078. *Labour Force Survey Estimates (LFS), Employees by Union Coverage, North American Industry Classification System (NAICS), Sex and Age Group, Annual (Persons).* (2009-2013). http://www5.statcan.gc.ca/cansim/a26?lang=eng&retrLang=eng&id=2820078&paSer=&pattern=&stByVal=1&p1=1&p2=38&tabMode=dataTable&csid=.

US Department of Labor. Bureau of Labor Statistics. Table 3. "Union Affiliation of Employed Wage and Salary Workers by Occupation and Industry, 2012-2013 Annual Averages." (2014). http://www.bls.gov/news.release/union2.t03.htm.

Part One

The Origins of Academic Librarian Labour Organizing in Canada

Academic Status for Canadian Academic Librarians:
A Brief History

Leona Jacobs[1]

Introduction

The Canadian Association of University Teachers and the Canadian Association of College and University Libraries believe that the professional staff of university libraries are partners with faculty members in contributing to the scholarly and intellectual functions of the university and should be accorded academic status and the rights and responsibilities of that status.[2]

Academic librarians[3] working in Canadian universities have been mostly informed about the concept of academic status by the predominantly American library literature that focuses on faculty status for librarians. Thus, when asked, many Canadian academic librarians assume that they have faculty status. However, the overwhelming majority of Canadian academic librarians do not officially have faculty status, the single documented exception being the librarians at Laurentian University.[4] Technically, faculty status equates to the status held by teaching faculty in terms of rights (entitlement to ranks, promotion, tenure,[5] compensation, leaves, and research funds), responsibilities (the same processes of evaluation and comparable standards for promotion and tenure), acceptance of the status by the institution as a whole, and participation in the governance of the institution.[6] Academic status, on the other hand, is recognition that the duties performed are integral to the academic mission of the institution but that all the rights and responsibilities associated with faculty status are not necessarily to be expected.[7] While the rights and responsibilities of librarians in Canadian academic institutions may approximate, to varying degrees, those of faculty, what the majority of Canadian academic librarians have is academic status and that, as it turns out, was by choice.

The sequence of events leading to academic status for Canadian librarians working in universities is not unlike that relating to the granting of faculty status for academic librarians working in the United States.[8] In Canada's case, the first step towards academic status resulted from the efforts by the Canadian Library Association (CLA) to develop and promote librarianship as a profession, and then from the persistence of the Canadian Association of College and University Libraries (CACUL), aided and abetted by the Canadian Association of University Teachers (CAUT) in the context of the Canadian labour movement and the establishment of public sector unions.

This is a story—a story that chronicles the formation of the CLA and of the CACUL, the role of the CAUT in putting meaning to the concept of academic status, and the push and pull of the debate around academic status, some of which persists to this day.

A National Organization for Canadian Librarians

Right from the beginning, the CLA was occupied with matters of standards, not only as these related to the delivery of library services, but as they also related to the salaries, the working conditions, and the perception of librarianship as a profession, or, in a word, status. In a paper delivered to the Alberta Library Association in 1945, the year leading up to the CLA organizing conference, Hazel Bletcher, librarian at Lethbridge Public Library, noted that one of the objectives of the proposed CLA was to raise the status of librarianship, commenting parenthetically, "We all know we suffer under the general idea that anyone can be a librarian if she can hand out a few books."[9] Bletcher went on to assert, "There is no doubt of the unifying influence of such an association and if there is anything in the much used phrase 'Union is Strength' we need the association."[10]

Prior to 1946, there was no CLA. Canadian librarians, lacking a formal national organization of their own, often joined the American Library Association (ALA). The earliest mention of a Canadian equivalent was at the ALA conference, held in Montreal, Canada, in 1900. It was there that nine Canadian librarians met and unanimously agreed to form a Canadian library association. However, by that fall, the enormity of establishing a nation-wide library association set in and it was decided instead that the first step would be to organize provincial associations.[11]

The issue arose again in 1925, when the ALA held an annual conference in Seattle where it was suggested that "this convention be marked by an innovation—a meeting of all Canadian librarians present, to discuss problems purely

Canadian in character."[12] This was followed by a second meeting in Vancouver, after which it was reported that, "while nothing was done in the way of creating an organization, much was accomplished in arriving at a clearer understanding of both needs and difficulties."[13] In 1927, with Canadian librarian Dr. George H. Locke as President, the ALA met in Toronto where two more meetings of Canadian librarians were arranged, the outcome being "a resolution to organize a Canadian Library Association, with the object not of competing with the American Library Association or with provincial associations, but of securing co-operation on all matters affecting the welfare of the library movement throughout Canada as a whole."[14]

Recognizing that a better understanding of library conditions and needs was required to inform the development of such an organization, a commission was formed, made possible with funding from the Carnegie Corporation and with the purpose of inquiring into the state of library services in Canada. The Commission's work was completed during the summer of 1930, culminating in a report, *Libraries in Canada: A Study of Library Conditions and Needs*.[15] Besides describing the Canadian condition regarding library services across Canada, whether these related to public, government, or academic libraries, the Commission expressed the belief that a national library association would speed progress in addressing deficiencies in library service, but not without paid professional staff. The Commission concluded, however, that help from the national government was unlikely and that the costs would be too great for library workers of Canada to finance. Thus, the idea of a Canadian library association was once again set aside until such time as "some Canadian of wealth, in search of a philanthropic investment . . . may see in this matter a suggestion and an opportunity."[16] In the end, it was American philanthropy that took up the suggestion.

The need for a Canada-wide library association remained a dominant theme of discussion whenever librarians gathered. In 1934, when the ALA once again met in Montreal, another small group of 11 Canadian librarians gathered and formed a Canadian Library Council but, as with previous attempts at organizing, this fledgling group withered before it could bloom into the much desired national organization.[17] It was not until 1940 when two quite independent lines of thought negotiated the great Canadian compromise. As it is reported, libraries had been left out of any discussions about library services to World War II armed forces because the invitation had only been sent to national organizations. Feeling the missed opportunity for librarians to "meet the responsibility that should be reasonably theirs,"[18] Margaret Gill, president of the Library Association of Ottawa, sent a letter to other library associations that November inviting an "expression of opinion on the proposal that a national association be formed during the coming year."[19] Meanwhile, the ALA struck the Committee of Canadian Consultants to address the same issue. The two streams of mutual concern merged in a meeting held in Ottawa in January 1941, where they decided to form the Canadian Library

Council, to be staffed by representatives from provincial library associations. The Council would also serve in a consultative role (under the name of the Canadian Library Advisory Board) to the ALA, aided financially by the Rockefeller Foundation and the Carnegie Corporation[20] and with the long term aim of establishing a "permanent and self-supporting Canadian Library Organization."[21]

The Canadian Library Council held its first meeting in October 1941 and officially incorporated under the Companies Act in December 1943. In May 1944, Elizabeth Morton was hired as the Council's secretary to begin the process of nation-building as far as library services were concerned,[22] the first order of business being to initiate publication of *The Bulletin*, a bi-monthly (at best) newsletter designed to keep all parts of the country informed of all things library and librarian.[23] Expectations for the Council were high; in November 1944, the Vancouver News-Herald reported, "Though officially incorporated only nine months ago, [the Council] has already . . . gathered into one stream various efforts and influences that hitherto have been unrelated and unco-operative, and channelled them into a united strength . . . . In the Canadian Library Council there is the promise of a base and a spearhead—a source of pooled and reservoired strength, and a springboard and bridgehead from which to attack problems that are the foundations of national intelligence and well-being."[24]

By April 1945, the Council met to discuss its future. Would it be a division of the ALA or would it become a Canadian organization? The provincial association representatives took the question back to their respective associations and returned to the October meeting with the answer: there was unanimous agreement to direct the Canadian Library Council to "proceed with the organization of a Canadian Library Association."[25]

Encouraged by the ALA, the CLA was formed in 1946 at the organizing conference held at McMaster University in Hamilton, Ontario. At a meeting immediately following the organizing conference, the Canadian Library Council met with the ALA as the Canadian Library Advisory Board (to the ALA), where it was agreed to disband the Board. As well, there was agreement to develop a new affiliation between the two Associations, to continue appointing Canadians to ALA committees, to invite the CLA secretary (i.e., Elizabeth Morton) to continue to serve as a corresponding member of the ALA Editorial Committee, and to continue the Joint Committee of the CLA and the ALA.[26] It would seem that the first step, formation of a national organization, was complete.

Focusing on Academic Librarians

Within the CLA, different interests started to emerge and members sorted themselves accordingly, whether by task, by audience, by type of service, or by type of library. Informal interest groups, formal committees and semi-autonomous sections formed to continue working on the details of furthering librarianship, libraries, and library services in Canada. University and college librarians formed one of these groups. Right from the beginning in 1946, college and university librarians requested the formation of a College and University Libraries Section. Instead they were encouraged by the governing CLA Council to join with the special librarians to form a joint section to be known as the Research Libraries Section.[27] It was not a suggestion immediately pursued, for they continued to meet informally as a special interest group until the 1949 conference when, under the leadership of Marjorie Sherlock, the group prepared a petition for the purposes of establishing the Research Libraries Section of the CLA,[28] a section subsequently approved at the 1950 conference.[29] The Research Libraries Section was active, as evidenced by summaries of their annual reports published in *The Bulletin* and then in the newsletter successor, *Feliciter*, and one might assume the Section served the purposes of the academic librarians as far as dealing with specific issues of library services to researchers. However, it apparently did not address the specific and unique problems of being a librarian in a post-secondary educational system as the college and university librarians continued to meet informally until finally achieving special committee status as the College and University Libraries Committee (CULC) in 1959.[30]

Meanwhile, the Research Libraries Section was being promoted as the section of choice for special librarians[31] and, at the Section meeting in 1960, there was a movement to establish closer co-operation with the Special Libraries Association and local chapters of the same.[32] By 1962, the Research Libraries Section was considering its future. In doing so, Douglas Lochhead, then chair of the Section, reiterated the original purpose of the Section as being "to act as a clearing house of information between colleges, universities, and research libraries, and to promote the interests of such institutions generally."[33] He went on to quote from the Section's Annual Report for 1960-1961:

> It is evident that the Section is failing to meet the needs of the libraries which constitute the bulk of its membership. In recent years a committee of university librarians has been formed to deal with their specific problems, and special librarians are calling for greater emphasis on those topics which are of particular interest to their group. Clearly there is a need for a revitalized programme which will satisfy the interests of those libraries for which the Research Section was originally founded.[34]

In fact, the Research Libraries Section was considering splitting into two new sections, one focused on special libraries and the other on university libraries.[35]

At the same time, and encouraged to do so by the Research Libraries Section, the CULC once again petitioned to form its own section within the CLA. As stated in the minutes of a meeting held on June 27, 1962, the CULC observed that:

> [t]he 1961-1962 report of the Committee on Committees reveals no less than four new committees have been established this year to dissect the

academic library field . . . . [C]ommunication between the committees is undirected and tenuous, and none of them has any direct representation of [*sic*] the CLA Executive. Besides these splinter groups exists the Research Libraries Section; but those of you who attended yesterday's meeting of the Section are aware of the feelings expressed at that meeting regarding the needs of college and university libraries.[36]

Attendees were asked to consider these observations in light of the size of the academic libraries segment within the CLA: the similarities (rather than differences) between college and university libraries, the similarities (rather than differences) between individual academic libraries, the lack of a direct communication channel to the CLA Executive, and the observation that: "[a]lthough comparisons are dangerous, and although the Canadian situation is not entirely similar to that prevailing in the United States, the relative success of the American Library Association's approach to the problems we now face would seem to suggest that the path taken by the A.L.A. is well worth exploring."[37] The minutes go on to recommend a resolution "urging the immediate formation of a College and University Libraries Section of the Canadian Library Association."[38]

It is not immediately clear what the path taken by the ALA actually refers to although, given the context (i.e., formation of a section specifically for academic libraries within the CLA), it might be assumed the reference was to the formation of the Association of College and Research Libraries (ACRL) as a division within the ALA and the role of the ACRL in addressing the issues of academic librarians. The annual conference in 1960 in Montreal, Quebec was a Joint CLA-ALA affair and the Research Libraries Section, including members representing the CULC, held joint meetings and sessions with the ACRL.[39] It is very likely that there was some informal (and undocumented) commiserating and sharing of strategies regarding furthering the issues of academic librarianship in Canada, perhaps including discussions about organizing their own section. The ACRL, in the case of the ALA, was organized as the ALA's first division in 1940 under the inaugural name of the Association of College and Reference Libraries.[40] In 1958, the ACRL's University Libraries Section established a Committee on Academic Status under the leadership of Arthur McAnally which, in 1959 (only the year before the Joint CLA-ALA Conference), formally endorsed faculty status for academic librarians as a policy and a right, a stand subsequently approved by the ACRL and the ALA.[41]

Formation of a College and Universities Section within the CLA required a petition with 50 signatures. Fifty-nine signatures were verified by the CLA Administration. On July 14, 1962, Elizabeth Morton communicated the success of this petition and the agreement by the Council of the CLA to form a college and university library section.[42] One year later, with the new Section's constitution in place, the CACUL was formed.[43]

In Search of (Academic) Status

To say that salaries and working conditions and professional status for librarians was a priority for the CLA would be an understatement. At the organizing conference of the CLA, on June 15, 1946, the following resolution passed unanimously, "Resolved that this Conference suggest to the Executive Committee that consideration be given to the setting up of Library Standards for Salaries throughout Canada."[44] It wasn't just about the salaries and working conditions of those already practicing librarianship. One of the main preoccupations for the CLA, in a post-World War II world, was recruitment into the profession of librarianship and a key strategy was to make it an appealing career choice by enhancing salaries and working conditions.

A salary committee was established in the fall of 1946 with Charles D. Kent as Chair. So began a series of surveys that compared the salaries and working conditions of librarians (generally) with the goal of establishing national standards. In that first year, there was no systematic tool for collecting the data; selected libraries, 64 in all, from the public, university, and special sectors, were asked to share their salary schedules as well as any information on pensions, cost-of-living bonuses, qualifications, holidays, sick leave, hours of work per week, and anything else that related to the well-being of librarians.[45] By the second year, a form had been developed to standardize and make comparable the requested information, but it was clear that getting such information from any library, save for public libraries, was going to be challenging, given that university, special, and legislative libraries were part of the larger parent organization.[46] Annual surveys of all libraries were conducted until 1951 when it was decided to do them triennially, starting with the 1952-53 survey and to begin, at that time, collecting information on the types of duties associated with the various salaries reported.[47] Such were the beginnings of work on position classifications and standards, standards which would come to be based on the size of the library.[48] In a 10-year status report on the activities of the CLA since its founding in 1946, it was noted under Part II, Activity 1 b) *Standards of Librarianship* that:

> [t]hese standards are in progress. A standard now exists on salaries for public libraries. A preliminary compilation has been released regarding practices for the welfare of librarians. A classification of positions has been set up and was accepted by the Ottawa Conference. Information has been compiled on the salaries and welfare of university librarians. Preliminary work on the evaluation of library education is in progress.[49]

By 1956, the CLA Committee working on salaries and personnel had split into two, one for public libraries and the other for university libraries. The report of the CLA Committee on University Libraries Salaries and Personnel, reported via *The Bulletin* in 1956, was the first to focus exclusively on university librarians.

Twenty-five libraries had responded in full to the gathering of salary schedules and information on working conditions. Of these, it was noted that only four had reached the public library standard for minimum annual salary of $3000 per year. More importantly, if some kind of academic status existed, it was usually assigned to the Chief and Assistant librarians; rarely were other professional librarians included.[50] Meanwhile, the recommendations for standards of employment were published in the May 1956 issue of the *Feliciter*. Of particular relevance, the Committee recommended that:

- "Librarians' salaries and work year should be commensurate with faculty salaries and work year for positions of similar academic and professional qualifications and responsibilities;"[51]
- "Because of their close association with and responsibilities for carrying out the educational programme of the university, professional librarians should be recognized as members of the academic community by receiving faculty status;"[52]
- Librarians should hold rank "commensurate with their academic and professional qualifications, the responsibilities of the position, and their length of service;"[53]
- Librarians "after one year of service in a permanent position, should have the same tenure as permanent members of the teaching staff;"[54] and
- "Sabbatical leaves should be granted to all professional librarians, on the same basis as to members of the teaching staff of equivalent rank in the same institution."[55]

There is no documented controversy from that time about such ambitions; everyone was in apparent agreement that some form of academic recognition and status for academic librarians was the goal. However, it would be another 10 years, a period which included the establishment of the CACUL in 1963 and its efforts on behalf of university libraries and librarians, to begin the process of transformation from position classification (and salaries) based on duties to a position classification scheme (and commensurate salaries) based on qualifications, ability, and experience, the essence of academic status.

Challenges Within

As the process of transformation began, there were four immediate challenges to be overcome internally within academic librarianship: standards for the library profession as a whole, what realistic standard to aim for within academic libraries, the issue of educational qualifications, and the translation of traditional grades of librarian work to that of faculty rank.

As noted above, the CLA had established standards for salaries in the public library sector, which became the measuring stick for salaries in university libraries. In 1958, the CLA Standards and Salaries Committee reported that academic library salaries were now "generally comparable with those paid in public libraries" but that they had "failed to increase at the same rate as those of their colleagues in the teaching faculties" and that they were "alarmingly low compared to teachers possessing similar academic qualifications."[56] Such a low standard represented a serious impediment to making a case to university administrators for improved academic library salaries. The Report continued:

> ... [t]he Committee feels that no significant gain can be made by academic librarians until there is a marked improvement in the salary standards of the library profession as a whole. Increased salaries in the teaching faculties have come about through the necessity of competition with other professions and industry. As long as fully qualified professional librarians continue to make themselves available at reduced rates, therefore, it is likely that academic administrations will accept them at their own valuation.[57]

The second challenge was to decide on a salary standard. In the past, standards for academic librarian salaries were set based on positions, as defined by duties and sorted by the size of the library as categorized in terms of such factors as available budget, volumes held in the collection, number of students, and numbers of professional and clerical staff. Salary standards for teaching faculty, as established by the CAUT, recommended absolute salaries (i.e., not a range) based on faculty rank, a criticism of the CAUT's standard being that it did not differentiate on the basis of size of institution or library. The second option considered was the Toronto Scale, used at the University of Toronto, which provided a salary range based on faculty rank. The third option was to set a standard based on an approximation of salaries paid across Canadian institutions.[58] The response from the membership was to adopt the CAUT standard as the goal,[59] a directive not followed when the following year's committee chose instead to revise salary standards for that year against the Toronto Scale.[60]

Thirdly, there was the issue of educational equivalencies, the report noting "the possession of bachelor's degrees and routine professional experience will not be readily accepted as sufficient qualification for positions of professorial rank. Advancement in academic libraries therefore will require higher academic qualifications or superior professional or scholarly achievement".[61] That said, the following year, Neil Harlow observed that, in some circumstances, faculty status equated to membership in particular faculties regardless of educational credentials, noting that, "in many professional schools in universities, degrees above a Master's level are still not common, although faculty in these fields are adjudged qualified for positions held," citing such examples as commerce, social work, law, home economics, physical education, and some areas of applied sciences.[62] Thus, in his opinion, "a shortage of highly qualified men and women with scholarly interests and attainments has been both cause and effect of existing conditions".[63]

The final challenge was how to establish reasonable equivalents between how libraries had classified their staff according to titles and duties and size of libraries and the equivalent faculty ranks. The 1958 report noted, "Exact equivalents cannot be made, since the number of grades and the structure of levels in existing hierarchies are different".[64] Noting that it was logical to equate the role of chief librarian to that of professor and that of the associate and assistant librarians (all administrative) to that of associate and assistant professor, the report concluded, "This leaves the great majority of library positions, covering several grades, below professorial rank".[65]

The CACUL, when it came into being in 1963, decided to pursue its own annual salary survey of Canadian academic libraries, timed so the information gathered would inform local budgeting and negotiations.[66] It also monitored the salaries of teaching faculty through the Dominion Bureau of Statistics,[67] and, by its second year, had established a committee "to study the question of positions and ranks within the academic library structure".[68] By the third year, a Committee on Academic Status was also hard at work on all these issues.[69]

Challenges Without

Any decision on the assignment of academic status to academic librarians rested ultimately with the academic administration. Thus, a major challenge was to convince university administrators that the work of the library, in terms of materials and services, was integral to the teaching and research function and, hence, that professional librarians should be considered academic staff.

When the Constitution of the CACUL passed and was approved by the CLA Council in 1963, the CACUL assumed the leadership role for Canadian academic libraries. One of the first responsibilities transferred to it was the work being done on defining and establishing university library standards and, in short order, it began the process of conducting an annual salary survey of Canadian academic libraries, copies of which were, over the years, circulated to the Association of Universities and Colleges of Canada (AUCC) representing university presidents.[70] The CACUL also established a relationship with the Canadian Universities Foundation (CUF)[71] and, hence, the National Council of Canadian Universities and Colleges (NCCUC), forerunner to the AUCC[72] and, ultimately, was designated as an advisory committee to the AUCC.[73] The CACUL also involved itself in various studies being done on Canadian universities and on the library resources available to support the growth of post-secondary education in the 1960s. It did this by taking action on Edwin Williams's report on *Resources of Canadian University Libraries for Research in the Humanities and Social Sciences* (ca.1962), by making submission to the (Vincent) Bladen Commission on *Financing Higher Education in Canada* (ca.1964), and by co-sponsoring, with the AUCC, Robert Downs's report on *Resources of Canadian Academic and Research Libraries* (ca.1967).[74]

The Downs Report, described by Gurdial Pannu in 1968 as a "work of enormous magnitude and undisputed excellence" and "the most comprehensive and detailed library survey done in Canada,"[75] is of particular relevance. In essence, the Downs Report distilled, for Canadian academic libraries, the impacts on libraries of the growth within universities, especially as it related to a shortage of resources, including librarians. Of note were the first three (of six) recommendations from Section 5 of the "Summary of Recommendations" which, as reprinted in the CACUL newsletter, read as follows:

> To help raise the standards for personnel to staff the university and college libraries of Canada, and to correct the gap between supply and demand, the following measures are recommended:
>
> 1) Recognize professional librarians as key members of the academic community, requiring high standards for their appointment and according them all the perquisites of faculty status.
> 2) The co-operation of the Canadian Association of University Teachers should be enlisted to aid in obtaining academic status for professional librarians.
> 3) Make a clear separation of clerical and professional duties in libraries to free the professional librarians to carry on higher-level tasks; in institutions where the classification does not now exist, create a category of library technical assistant or subprofessional librarian to carry on duties requiring specialized technical training.[76]

No one could say that university administrations were unaware of the case to be made for academic status. At the 1966 annual meeting of the CACUL, even before the Downs Report was published, the CACUL committee on Position Classification and Salary Scales tabled a draft report. In this report, the Committee noted that:

> . . . the A.U.C.C.'s reaction to the Bladen Commission's Report—a Commission which received tangible evidence that 'the library problem' had now reached critical proportions—may be read as evidence that university authorities are now prepared to spend money on library staff and library resources; are prepared to experiment on new library techniques; and may be prepared to modify organizational patterns within the university, itself a traditionalist and many chambered nautilus. Before doing so, however, they are looking to librarians for direct answers to some very searching questions.[77]

Direct Answers to Very Searching Questions

Such was the perspective with which the Committee on Position Classification and Salary Scales wrote its report. Noting that professional librarians found themselves in an "indefensible limbo between faculty and clerical ranks,"[78] its report advocated aiming for an ideal by differentiating the roles of librarians vis-à-vis non-librarian staff and articulating the comparability of academic librarians to faculty counterparts for the purpose of furthering the cause of faculty status. That said, the Committee eschewed the adoption of professorial titles preferring to develop general categorical titles corresponding to six grades, equating to the well-known professorial equivalents from Instructor to Dean. These titles were designed to be easily recognizable across institutions, allowing for more descriptive, local titles and position descriptions to be maintained within each category. It was envisaged that these proposed ranks provided an alternative in career growth for librarians, with merit increases provided along horizontal lines and the option to move through the ranks without ever having to seek administrative roles in order to advance, unless the personal choice was made to do so. However, as with titles, so the salary scales did not follow faculty equivalents. Noting the departure of their report from the practice of faculty status as applied in the United States (i.e., identical titles and pay scales as for faculty) the Committee believed that:

> . . . with very few exceptions, most Canadian libraries have not reached the size and degree of specialization which would sustain the argument for professorial ranks and pay scales. Nor . . . have Canadian university administrators had sufficient time to accommodate themselves to a principle which has been pressed with growing insistence in the U.S.A. since the early 1920's . . . . Hence our recommended [salary] schedule indicates a lag in related salary floors between librarians and teaching staff, a condition which we consider to be necessary during this transitional period.[79]

Although the Committee's report was received at the 1966 annual meeting, it was not approved. After another couple of failed attempts at being approved, it came forward again in 1969, completely revised in terms of grades of professional positions (down to three from the original six) still allowing for local customization if refinement was necessary. This version emphasized that the rank assigned was to be based on qualifications, experience, professional development, and ability. The minimum acceptable qualifications were to be whatever was recognized by the CLA; however, for higher ranks, higher qualifications were to be expected and encouraged after experience was factored in. The revised report noted that professional staff with advanced degrees had an advantage, but noted that a doctoral degree was not to be considered mandatory at any level. The general expectations of each grade were articulated with the repeated reminder that grades assigned were independent of titles and duties.⁸⁰ No salary scales were included in this revised version, which finally passed at the 1969 annual meeting.⁸¹ Still one might wonder if the idea of salaries that lagged behind those of faculty, as originally proposed, informed the fact that, today, many of the academic librarian scales in Canadian university libraries fall below those of their comparable faculty rank.

The CACUL Committee on Academic Status had been charged to work with the Committee on Position Classification and Salary Scales but to focus less on salaries and classifications and more on the other attributes of academic status, namely academic freedom and tenure, sabbaticals, research and travel grants, participation in governance, and the merits of working with faculty associations and the CAUT.⁸² It had been at work since 1966, having provided a progress report at the 1967 annual meeting of the CACUL.⁸³ At the 1968 meeting, the Committee on Academic Status circulated three papers for discussion, the first and most important of these being a draft document entitled, *Principles of Academic Status in Canadian University Libraries*.⁸⁴ The second document was a sample brief clarifying why librarians should have academic status and acknowledging that, despite some movement in this direction, missing still were the pieces of status, salary, research, tenure, sabbaticals, and academic freedom.⁸⁵ The third and final document provided the results of a survey of 25 Canadian university libraries demonstrating that, at the time, only one institution considered its librarians to have faculty status, while 14 provided some form of academic status, and another 10 provided no formal status at all.⁸⁶ Interestingly, a survey done a few years earlier by the University of Manitoba regarding the pervasiveness of academic status for librarians and reported on at the 1965 annual meeting of the CACUL found, "in general, that the old established libraries tended to lack a policy [with respect to academic status] and eschew change in this field; new libraries were looking for a policy, while small, remote colleges generally accorded faculty status to their librarians."⁸⁷

As noted, the *Principles* document proved to be the most important. This document defined academic status, as "the possession of some, but not all, of the usual faculty privileges, with definite classification as academic, but always without faculty rank." ⁸⁸ The document made explicit that an advanced professional degree from an accredited library school was the appropriate minimum academic qualification. It went on to delineate the obligations of the librarians holding academic status: to be governed in the same way as faculty within their own institution were governed; to accept the 11-month work year, given that librarianship was a service-oriented profession; and to be involved in continuing education, in research and publishing, and in university committee work. Library administrators also had obligations: to share governance, to encourage research in library science by allowing time to do so, to recognize and support professional activities with time and travel allowances, and to provide the same opportunities for sabbaticals or study leaves as provided for faculty. And finally, in the case of university administrations, librarians were to have academic freedom as faculty did, to be eligible for tenure on the same basis as faculty, to be represented by the faculty association in matters relating to salary, to have some form of faculty library committee as advisory on academic policy, to be judged using comparable criteria to those used by faculty, and they were to have a contract of employment similar to that for teaching faculty.[89]

The *Principles* document was debated at the 1968 annual meeting, revised and circulated for comment in January 1969,[90] revised and circulated for comment again in May 1969,[91] and then revised from the floor of the annual meeting in June 1969.[92] Changes in the final version were subtle, but important. Basic required qualifications referenced the expectations of the CLA, the organization working on professional credentials, although it was acknowledged that advanced degrees might be required, depending on the position. Obligations for librarians were altered to remove the requirement to accept the standards, customs, and regulation of faculty, instead advising librarians to choose to accept them whenever such acceptance was appropriate. As well, there was recognition that, while an 11-month work year may well be the case, "this period of employment carries with it a usually unsurmountable [*sic*] obstacle to research and productive scholarship."[93] And, finally, the revisions allowed that librarians themselves would decide whether faculty associations would represent them. The obligations of library administrations were altered to clarify that they should consider implementing a committee system in order to involve librarians in library governance. Library administrations were also obligated to advocate to university administration on behalf of librarians for the same privileges and benefits accorded faculty. Finally, university administrations were obliged to evaluate, promote, appoint, and grant tenure to librarians according to criteria accepted in academic librarianship and, in the case of appointment, using the same processes as used for faculty.[94] As with the *Position Classification* document, the *Principles* document was accepted as policy at the 1969 annual meeting.[95]

The Role of the CAUT

The hard work done, the CACUL Committee on Academic Status was reconstituted with direction "[t]o collect information on the status of librarians in Canadian College and University Libraries."[96] As reported at the 1971 annual meeting, nothing much happened that first year after the passage of the *Principles* document. As described above, there had been quite a push in the previous year to get the document revised and revised again, with final revisions being made on the floor of the CACUL's 1969 annual meeting; perhaps those most involved needed a bit of break. However, the plan was to conduct a survey of Canadian academic libraries to determine "how the existing situation in academic libraries compared with the *Statement of Principles on Academic Status*," with a view to disseminating the results so local librarians could compare situations.[97] As Donald Redmond,

President of the CACUL for 1969-1970, observed, "Implementation of [academic status] is for the largest part still wishful thinking. Particularly in AUCC it is painfully obvious that librarians are third-class citizens in our universities, ranking somewhere behind students (who complain that they are treated as second-class citizens) and above campus police." [98]

The proposed survey was completed in time for the 1971 annual meeting and the situation did indeed look bleak. Fifty-eight surveys were sent out to the libraries of the AUCC institutions and 48 were returned. It was noted that while the survey had been intended to get a sense of how the principles of academic status for librarians were being applied in institutions relative to the benefits accruing to faculty, little was known about faculty benefits in each institution, making the results more of a comparison between libraries than between librarians and faculty.[99]

Of the responses, the Committee was heartened to learn that the majority of institutions provided for board supported appointments although disappointed that the largest libraries did not make board supported appointments or did so only for senior staff. A majority of institutions provided about a month of vacation time and, while results showed that most librarians received fringe benefits similar to those provided to faculty members, the 12 dissenting responses to this question were noted by the Committee. Most respondents suggested that study leaves were supported, at least technically; however, the Committee's sense was that affirmative responses were only tentative, given that this benefit had not yet been tested in practice. There was widespread financial support for librarians to attend conferences with about half of the respondents funding to varying degrees attendance at learned conferences in particular, interpreted by the Committee as acknowledgment of the relationship of librarians to the wider academic community. In a majority of institutions, librarians were eligible for membership in the faculty associations but the Committee expressed concern for those librarians without such eligibility.[100]

It was a minority of institutions that provided librarians with tenure, sabbaticals, access to research grants, participation in university committees, direct representation on the academic senate, or a role within the governance structure of the faculties themselves. Only one library reported that librarians shared faculty titles, which the Committee did not find surprising, given that during the drafting of the *Principles* document, there was little-to-no support for faculty titles. Finally, on the question about the relationship between librarians' salaries and those of the teaching staff, responses indicated some relationship, but only three respondents specified a formal connection between the two with the Committee noting, "In most instances where specific salary relationships are given, [l]ibrarians' salaries are clearly well behind teaching faculty."[101]

What to do, what to do? At the 1971 annual meeting, it was recommended that, "in the matter of academic status, an approach be made to [the] AUCC and [the] CAUT with the intention of explaining [the] CACUL's objectives in this regard."¹⁰² It is unclear whether this recommendation was pursued immediately and it is especially unclear, when it came to the AUCC, what their response might have been.

On the other hand, as Calvin Evans described events, the CAUT made its own overtures to academic librarians by approving a recommendation of its Membership Committee encouraging local faculty associations to extend membership to those librarians wishing to join. In response, the CACUL membership, at their 1974 annual meeting, approved a motion to publicly endorse the CAUT recommendation and encourage librarians to pursue faculty association membership. That fall, representatives of the two organizations met to discuss the possibility of forming a joint task force on academic status for librarians. The CAUT was decidedly receptive to the invitation extended by the CACUL to collaborate on the further articulation of academic status and suggested the terms of reference be expanded to examine all aspects of academic status: appointments, renewal, dismissal, tenure, academic freedom, salaries and benefits, governance, and membership in faculty associations.¹⁰³ The outcome of this joint task force was the first draft of the *Guidelines on Academic Status for Professional University Librarians*, approved in principle by both bodies in 1975, revised jointly over the next two years, and approved by both organizations in 1977.¹⁰⁴

Evans, describing the formation of the joint task force, observed that the "CAUT was perhaps bolder in its approach than some librarians expected" and that "there were a few librarians who looked for nothing more than a motherhood statement."¹⁰⁵ In fact, the CAUT had its reasons for being so bold: the rise of the labour movement, the rise of collective bargaining, and their own librarian-members' demands for representation.¹⁰⁶

In the Context of the Labour Movement

We will never know to what extent academic status for librarians would have evolved and been accepted by university administrations if the labour movement and the concept of collective bargaining had not invaded the mindset of the Canadian public-sector, including universities, something almost unheard of prior to 1965. As described by Craig Heron in his book, *The Canadian Labour Movement: A Short History*, prior to the 1960s, employees in the public sector were, in most cases, denied the right to join unions or bargain collectively, but this was not seen as an issue. Public sector employees generally had better job security, higher salaries, and greater respectability than did most other workers and had organized themselves into departmental associations and, ultimately, federations. These federations would meet with management counterparts to discuss issues and make recommendations on working matters to government, recommendations frequently ignored. Heron noted, however, that by the 1960s, discontent with the way things were going was not readily curbed through consultative structures. Wages in the unionized private sector had begun to outstrip public-sector wages and the workplace was quickly becoming impersonal and bureaucratic with the imposition of capitalist principles to improve efficiencies. Organizational associations took on the characteristics of unions and started demanding collective bargaining rights and, by 1975, all provincial employees were granted some form of these rights.[107]

Professors, too, were caught up in the social and economic conditions of the times, seeing their relative prestige erode and respect for their judgment diminish in the context of rigid and bureaucratic management styles.[108] Instead of joining unions, however, many turned their local faculty associations into certified bargaining units and to the task of bargaining collective agreements, while others remained uncertified, by choice or by provincial legislation,[109] and chose (or not) to negotiate their own versions of what were essentially collective agreements. The movement spread rapidly across university campuses. In the face of declining economic status and recognition, collective bargaining strengthened salary negotiations, helped to secure shared power, and, in light of difficulty executing grievance procedures, allowed negotiation of detailed procedures grounded in law and with a final resolution of appeals.[110]

Librarians were thrown into this academic labour confusion, landing in, as characterized by Julie Schroeder, "the gap between faculty members and support staff."[111] According to Schroeder, it was up to the provincial labour relations boards to determine what were appropriate bargaining units for various groups of employees on university campuses, the determination of "appropriate" being based upon whether a community of interest existed among a given group of employees such as "to make it appropriate that they all have their terms and conditions of employment negotiated at one time by one bargaining agent."[112] Labour boards were concerned about fragmentation and appeared to favour larger, more inclusive units, but key among the considerations were not only the desires of the employees, management, and unions concerned but also agreement among the parties. Thus, the matter of whether the university already recognized the academic status of librarians influenced the assignment of librarians to the same bargaining unit as faculty. In some cases, such as at the University of Manitoba, inclusion of librarians into that faculty association for the purposes of collective bargaining was automatic because librarians were eligible to join the association; if the University had objected, the Manitoba Labour Relations Board would have had to rule. In other cases, such as that of St. Mary's University where librarians were not recognized as having academic status, the Nova Scotia Labour Relations Board excluded librarians from joining the same bargaining unit as faculty because the University objected to their inclusion (although it ultimately allowed the faculty association to be certified as the bargaining agent for librarians as a separate unit). As Schroeder pointed out, academic librarians could not assume they would be included in the faculty unit; it was up to them to convince labour boards of their community of interest.[113] Those librarians, early in the process of finding their community of interest, were left on their own, armed only perhaps with the *Principles* document and a belief that their work was best aligned with that of faculty. However, once defined, the *Guidelines* served as "formal notice to the university community that faculty and librarians did, indeed share a community of interest and would work together to defend it."[114]

Not Everyone Agreed

The idea of academic status had long been in the minds of academic librarians, but with the *Principles* document, the idea started to inform Canadian academic librarianship. The *Guidelines* gave the idea substance and meaning; collective bargaining made it a reality.

Writing in response to the 1968 draft of the *Principles* document, Don White noted that the only pieces, in his opinion, that made this document specific to academic librarians was reference to academic freedom and tenure, hence scholarship. He challenged the practicality of these principles, given the realities of academic librarianship, expressing his opinion thus:

> As our libraries increase in size and complexity, we must recognize that we are channeling our efforts more and more into dealing with administrative problems and less and less into actively engaging in scholarship . . . . Our present attitude of subtle ambivalence towards scholarship and administration is only one of the larger issues illustrating the gulf between our avowed aims and behaviour 'on the job.' As long as these issues go unresolved, one must question our faith in the inviolability of academic status. For most librarians in universities at present, academic status with tenure represents only a festoon for our façade of principles and a less-than-honest link with teachers and researchers.[115]

Five years later, before the *Guidelines* were drafted but as collective bargaining was forcing the issue, Elizabeth Ward, one of six librarians seeking their community of interest at St. Mary's University, advocated for a union that retained "the unique identity of librarians," even if such a union was part of the CAUT[116] and reminded librarians "of the necessity of promoting the form of academic status, not necessarily faculty status, that is best suited to the needs and aspirations of the library professional."[117] Ruth Hafter, University Librarian at St. Mary's University, concurred, noting, "academic status cannot be classed as a 'motherhood' issue because a number of prominent university librarians oppose it, a substantial proportion of University administrators ignore it, and many non-University librarians are both puzzled and suspicious of the concept."[118] Although she agreed that tenure (and, by extension, academic freedom), sabbaticals and study leaves, and committee work were beneficial to librarians (and the library), she disagreed that there was any common interest when it came to wages, evaluation of work, or grounds for promotion. She suggested that librarians would be better served by forming a provincial union inclusive of all librarians with a form of librarian status akin to academic status but focused on conditions of work and promotion specific to the profession.[119]

Donald Savage, then-Executive Director of the CAUT, agreed with these differences. He acknowledged both that the nature of librarian work was indeed different from faculty work, and that the professional service and administrative components did pose problems in achieving academic status. However, he did not see the issue as insurmountable. He felt it would require working together with library administrators to set workloads and schedules consistent with librarianship and librarian roles within the university and stated that "[a]cademic status does not require absolute identity with teaching faculty."[120]

Of course, part of the workload issue was the expectation that librarians have an 11-month work year which, as previously noted, the *Principles* document acknowledged as an obstacle to research and productive scholarship,[121] research and scholarship being among the criteria named in the *Guidelines* for evaluation purposes. John Wilkinson (final Chair of the CLA College and University Libraries Committee in 1963) noted, "Librarians should *not* be expected to fill their one-month's holiday with 'research and writing' (few faculty would); but they should be prepared to spend many an evening and weekend in productive study over and above their 'professional performance'."[122] Savage reiterated this statement when he said, "there must be real equivalence [with respect to scholarly activity]. Those librarians who opt to be *de facto* clerical staff working nine to five without other responsibilities and commitments will simply not achieve equal contractual terms with faculty."[123] However, he sympathized with librarians whose library administrators saw scholarship as something to be accomplished in addition to existing responsibilities, and advocated for the incorporation of release time into the librarians' schedules (in addition to sabbaticals), citing the situation at Laurentian University as a case in point.[124] As reported by Joan Mount in 1978, librarians at Laurentian University had been recognized, since 1976, as having faculty status with the same ranks, salary scales, and expectations as faculty. Although parallels in workload components had been negotiated, things came to a head when, during a promotion hearing, administrative responsibilities (deemed to be the parallel of graduate student supervision for the faculty) were not recognized and the lack of comparable scholarly output was. As Mount stated, "it was fruitless to argue that personnel resources in the library were stretched to the extent that librarians could not spare substantial amounts of time for research without jeopardizing either their traditional professional service or their family life."[125] This was an important observation in the context of librarianship being a feminized profession and women's domestic roles at the time vis-à-vis the family unit. Unfortunately, things have not improved much. In a study conducted in 2006, David Fox found that these year-round schedules continue to preclude "engagement in sustained, meaningful scholarship,"[126] noting that it was clear from written comments that, "it is precisely during the 'extended work-week'—during evenings and weekends—that many university librarians make time for their research."[127]

The experience of Laurentian University was also a good lesson in the definition of what constituted scholarship. As noted, Laurentian University librarians had faculty (not academic) status and, as such, when the time came to evaluate librarians for the purposes of promotion, the Promotions Committee took the stand that librarians were expected "to research and publish like the teaching faculty, specifically like those in the humanities stream."[128] Savage took a broader perspective on this particular matter, noting that, "it is important in considering both the weight and the definition of criteria that inappropriate faculty models not be adopted on the evaluation process."[129] He recognized that scholarly activities take many forms given the discipline and can differ from the traditional perspective of published research but he did insist that, whatever constituted scholarship for librarians, there must be real equivalence.[130] This was, in fact, how the situation at Laurentian was resolved. When the faculty association certified, some long standing issues with the concept of research in other non-traditional areas surfaced. The School of Nursing, for example, commented, "We tend to try and call everything research because we have come to value research. Rather, we should be valuing scholarly activity of which research is one."[131] As a result, a longer statement on scholarly activity was negotiated that was more beneficial and inclusive of the activities of all types of faculty[132] but, as David Fox found, it is still the more traditional forms of scholarship that are perceived as important for tenure and promotion.[133]

In an article written after the acceptance of both the *Positions Classification* and the *Principles* documents in 1969, Stephen Horn pointed out that the new classification structures, as they were described in the *Position Classifications* document, were in conflict with the *Principles* document, in that in the description of the different ranks, there remained an implicit hierarchy of authority.[134] Indeed, the *Principles* document was silent on the inclusion of librarians in any governance model but the *Guidelines* were not. The *Guidelines* made explicit the expectation that librarians would be eligible for participation in governance throughout the university, but especially in the libraries.[135] This caught the attention of Margaret Beckman, someone who had been active in the CACUL and on the Committee on Academic Status and who was now writing as the Chief Librarian at the University of Guelph. She argued that a library council—composed of professional librarians, accountable to the academic senate, responsible for the policies and procedures of the library, and proposed as a means to counter authoritarian and bureaucratic decision-making—was unworkable in a library situation. She proposed instead a consultative management model that sought the advice of librarians but left the decisions to the library director (the director being accountable to the president, or the board, or the senate but, nonetheless, the final authority in the library).[136] Savage replied to Beckman in a letter published the following September:

> [T]he crucial difference between Ms. Beckman and the CAUT/CACUL proposal seems to be whether or not a management team headed by the Chief Librarian develops these proposals and then consults the librarians thereby, in my opinion, ensuring that consultation will only result in marginal changes or whether the original team is composed both of management and of the librarians or their elected representatives. It seems generally agreed at the moment that evaluation schemes and similar devices are much more likely to succeed when self-created than where they are laid down from on high even if opinions are asked for first . . . . If German factory workers can sit on the boards of their companies, why cannot the elected representatives of the librarians sit on the management committee of the library?[137]

On the flip side, Savage admonished librarians that it was "unreasonable to demand academic status and then refuse the responsibilities of that status by failure to create . . . participatory governing structures within the library. Those who refuse to participate have no moral right to complain about tyranny in the library."[138] In 2008 and in the context of contemplating the formation of a local library council, this author undertook a quick and informal survey of Canadian university libraries to determine how prevalent such bodies were and to learn from other libraries about structures and pitfalls. It was interesting to find out that only about 50% of the libraries (13 of 25 responses) had something akin to a library or management council. Most of those reporting a library council or similar body included all academic librarians and most (but not all) of these bodies reported to the equivalent of an academic senate. There were mixed reviews about the effectiveness of these bodies but five respondents perceived their council to be ineffective or not as effective as it could be, the main reason being attributed to the relationship of the council to the university (or chief) librarian.[139]

William Watson, then-Chief Librarian at the University of Waterloo, was skeptical of the need for librarians to have academic status. In a presentation to the Ontario Association of College and University Libraries made after the acceptance of the *Principles* document in 1969, he asserted that "[a]cademic librarians would be well to pay less attention to status and its perquisites, and more to professional responsibilities."[140] He felt that the pay was sufficient for the qualifications of the day and the jobs plentiful (although it is worthwhile remembering that Watson's presentation was made at the close of the 1960s as growth was starting to level off and labour unrest on university campuses was starting to ramp up). He felt the work year for librarians was appropriate for the work associated with librarianship. He agreed with the perspective that tenure was protection for those delivering mediocre results. He felt that librarians already had access to study leaves and sabbaticals by making proposals to their library administrators, and that those benefits did not need to be codified. He believed librarians' inclusion in university governance was already possible. He identified the desire for academic status as being an issue of public esteem and concluded, as he had begun, that the professionalism to be strived for by librarians was one of focusing on meeting users' needs.[141] What Watson didn't quite understand, given, no doubt, that he was a library administrator and on the granting, rather than the receiving, end of requests, was that there was no due process at the time for accessing these benefits, such access being contingent on the benevolence of the library administrator.

Watson was correct in concluding that academic status was an issue of public esteem. As Savage noted, "academic status is not easily defined since it is a psychological and political matter as well as a question of contractual terms . . . . In North America, status is frequently measured by pay. If professional librarians were to be paid as support staff, they would be treated as support staff. If they were paid salaries similar to faculty, they would be treated equally as professionals."[142] Of course, elevating the status, the 'public esteem,' for librarianship, was indeed the objective from the beginning of the CLA in 1946. It was a strategy purposefully pursued to attract people into the profession generally and into academic librarianship specifically during a time of rapid growth and expansion when there were not enough librarians, something perhaps forgotten in the economic and social contractions of the 1970s.

The Current Status of Academic Status

Key points outlined in the *Guidelines* as they were originally published in 1979 included: types of appointments comparable to faculty; ranks and salary floors comparable to faculty; promotion through the ranks based on criteria determined by librarians but reflective of professional performance, professional and academic service and scholarly activities; due process when dealing with personnel issues; benefits and leaves comparable to those available to faculty; involvement in library and university governance; tenure; academic freedom; and collective bargaining done by faculty associations.[143] In 1986, the CAUT assumed responsibility for monitoring the state of academic status for librarians. The most recent of these biennial surveys was released in 2012 and, with 63 of 67 universities responding to the survey, it provides the best summary of academic status available. Although the responses might be informed by the wording and interpretation of the survey questions, taken at face value, it is clear from this 2012 survey that developing consistency in the definition of academic status for librarians continues to be a work in progress.

Today, librarians in approximately 85% of the Canadian universities that are members of the CAUT, have found their community of interest with their faculty colleagues, defined as being represented by their faculty associations and working under collective agreements that accord with some, if not all, of the *Guidelines*. In fewer than half is there total compliance with the *Guidelines* and even these have local interpretations.[144]

Thirty years ago, Savage noted: "The manner and extent to which [academic status], in all of its components, has been achieved by librarians at Canadian universities has been influenced by the method of governance and type of administration at each institution." [145] Indeed, regardless of institution, this influence means that the same terms and conditions of employment that faculty members might take for granted are things that librarians cannot assume and will need to read carefully in any collective agreement.

The CAUT Survey outlines some of the more blatant variations. Librarians are not always participants in university governance structures, either directly or through eligibility as members of the academic staff, nor, in some cases, are they necessarily expected to be involved. Librarians do not always hold the majority of seats on their appointment and review committees. Librarians may not always have the same number of career ranks to progress through as do faculty members. The salary floors of the librarian ranks may not always be on par with those of the faculty ranks. Engagement in scholarly activity and research may not always be an obligation, or even an expectation, of employment. Time to engage in scholarly activity and research, in terms of annual release time available or sabbatical leaves to be applied for, may not always be a valid expectation for a librarian to have. Yes, the majority of Canadian universities offer the majority of attributes considered by the *Guidelines* to constitute academic status for Canadian academic librarians but, according to the CAUT Survey, it is a rare institution that offers all of these without some sort of footnote qualification.[146]

Conclusion

It has been almost 35 years since the approval of the *Guidelines* by the CAUT and the CACUL. The librarian activists of that era did tremendous service getting academic librarians recognized for their contributions to the academic mission of universities. Since then, it has fallen to academic librarians within institutions to shape the local interpretation of academic status, a job, for the most part, well done. That said, there is a sense that the original goal of academic status is yet to be achieved and will remain so until there is commonality in both the expression and experience of academic status, both within institutions with respect to faculty colleagues and across institutions with respect to academic librarian colleagues. Only then will academic librarians, as a whole, have achieved true academic status.

Bibliography

"ACRL History." American Library Association, http://www.ala.org/acrl/aboutacrl/history/history.

Appelt, D. C. "From the President of CACUL: Executive Meeting [25 October 1966]." *CACUL Newsletter*, no. 7-8 (1967): 13-15.

"Association of College and Research Libraries Joint Statement on Faculty Status of College and University Libraries." American Library Association, http://www.ala.org/acrl/standards/jointstatementfaculty.

Association of College and Research Libraries, University Libraries Section, Committee on Academic Status. "Status of College and University Librarians." *College & Research Libraries* 20, no. 5 (September 1959): 399-400.

Beckman, Margaret. "Library Governance." *CAUT Bulletin* 24, no. 5 (March 1976): 22.

Bell, I. F. "President's Mid-Year Report." *CACUL Newsletter* 2, no. 5 (1970): 457-64.

Blackburn, Robert. "Report of the President." *CACUL Newsletter* no. 1 (1963): 3-4.

Bletcher, Hazel. "On the Formation of a Canadian Library Association: Paper Given before the Alberta Library Association." *Canadian Library Council Bulletin* 2, no. 2 (December 1945): 19.

CACUL Committee on Academic Status. "Principles of Academic Status in Canadian University Libraries: Draft Report [24 June 1968]." *CACUL Newsletter* 2, no. 1 (1969): 12-13.

———. "Principles of Academic Status in Canadian University Libraries: Revised Draft May 1969." *CACUL Newsletter* 2, no. 2 (1969): 93-94.

Canadian Association of College and University Libraries. "Annual General Meeting [Minutes, 10 June 1969]." *CACUL Newsletter* 2, no. 4 (1970): 397-402.

———. "Annual Meeting 1967 [Minutes, 17 June 1967]." *CACUL Newsletter*, no. 9 (1967): 16-20.

———. "Annual Meeting and Workshop - 1965." *CACUL Newsletter* no. 6 (1966): 18-21.

———. "Annual Meeting and Workshop, Halifax: Report from the Secretary [9 June 1964]." *CACUL Newsletter* no. 3 (1964): 14-16.

———. "CACUL Annual Meeting [Draft Minutes, 1971]." *CACUL Newsletter* 3, no. 1 (1971): 12-16.

———. "Committee on Academic Status: Terms of Reference." *CACUL Newsletter* no. 9 (1967): 30.

———. "General Meeting [Minutes, 26 June 1963]." *CACUL Newsletter* no. 2 (1964).

———. "Minutes of the CACUL Annual General Meeting at Hamilton, Ontario [24 June 1970]." *CACUL Newsletter* 2, no. 6 (1971): 588-92.

———. *Position Classification and Principles of Academic Status in Canadian University Libraries*. Ottawa, ON: Canadian Library Association, 1969.

Canadian Association of College and University Libraries, Academic Status of Librarians [Committee]. "Reports of Committees: Academic Status of Librarians." *CACUL Newsletter* no. 7-8 (1967): 5.

Canadian Association of College and University Libraries, and Canadian Association of University Teachers. *Guidelines on Academic Status for University Librarians*. Ottawa, ON: Canadian Library Association, 1979.

Canadian Association of College and University Libraries, Committee on Academic Status. "CACUL Committee on Academic Status: Report, June, 1968." *CACUL Newsletter* no. 10 (1968): 9-15.

Canadian Association of College and University Libraries, Salary and Budget Survey Committee. "Salary and Budget Survey." *CACUL Newsletter* no. 7-8 (1967): 9.

Canadian Association of College and University Libraries, Salary Survey Committee. "Report of the CACUL Salary Survey Committee." *CACUL Newsletter* no. 2 (1964): 9.

Canadian Association of College and University Libraries, Committee on Academic Status. "Committee on Academic Status Report." *CACUL Newsletter* 2, no. 6 (1971): 609-24.

Canadian Association of College and University Libraries, Position Classification & Salary Scales. "A Draft Report on Position Classifications and Salary Scales in Canadian Academic Libraries." Calgary, Alberta: CACUL, 1966.

Canadian Association of University Teachers. "Librarian Salary Survey and Academic Status Survey. Part 1: Salaries, Salary Scales and Academic Status." Ottawa, ON: Canadian Association of University Teachers, 2012.

Canadian Library Association. "Annual General Meeting, 1958: Standards and Salaries." *Canadian Library Association Bulletin* 15, no. 2 (September 1958): 66-75.

———. "Annual Meeting: Reports of Meetings, Colleges and University Librarians." *Canadian Library Association Bulletin* 6, no. 2 (1949): 101.

———. "Annual Reports of Officials, Projects, Sections, Committees for 1959-1960." *Feliciter* 5, no. 9 (Part 2) (May 1960): 1-50.

———. "Association Activities." *Canadian Library Association Bulletin* 11, no. 6 (1955): 273-78.

———. "The CLA-ACB Committees 1960-1967: College and University Libraries Committee." *Canadian Library: the Bulletin of the Canadian Library Association - le Bulletin de l'Association canadienne des Bibliotheques* 24, no. 6 (May 1968): 590-629.

———. "Committees: 1 September 1955 [to] 31 August 1960." *Canadian Library: the Bulletin of the Canadian Library Association - le Bulletin de l'Association canadienne des Bibliotheques* 17, no. 6 (May 1961 1961): 331-81.

———. "Conference Reports: Summary Reports of Sections, Research Libraries." *Canadian Library* 17, no. 3 (November 1960): 137-50.

———. "From Council to Association." *Canadian Library Association Bulletin* 3, no. 1 (October 1946).

———. "Library Associations of Canada, 1900-1946." *Canadian Library Association Bulletin* 11, no. 6 (1955): 270-72.

———. "Library Standards for Salaries." *Canadian Library Association Bulletin* 3, no. 1 (October 1946): 19-20.

Canadian Library Association, College and University Libraries Committee. Canadian Library Association Papers. Library and Archives Canada.

Canadian Library Association, Committee on Salaries. "Report of the Committee on Salaries, 1947-1948." *Canadian Library Association Bulletin* 5, no. 1 (July 1948): 46-49.

———. Canadian Library Association Papers. Library and Archives Canada.

Canadian Library Association, Committee on University Libraries Salaries and Personnel. "CLA-ABC Committee on University Libraries Salaries and Personnel: Summary of Replies to Questionnaires, 1955 and 1956." *Canadian Library Association Bulletin* 12, no. 6 (1956): 225-31.

Canadian Library Association, Committee on University Salaries and Personnel. "Salaries and Personnel (University Libraries)." *Feliciter* 1, no. 3 (May 1956): 27-42.

Canadian Library Association, Salaries and Personnel Committee. "Annual General Meeting: Summary Reports of Committees, Salaries and Personnel Committee." *Canadian Library Association Bulletin* 10, no. 7 (June 1954): xvi-xvii.

Canadian Library Association, Salaries Committee. "Annual General Meeting of the Corporation: Committee Proceedings, Salaries Committee." *Canadian Library Association Bulletin* 9, no. 2 (1952): 50-51.

Canadian Library Association, Standards and Salaries Committee (University and College Libraries). "Sub-Committee on Standards and Salaries (University and College Libraries)." *Feliciter* 4, no. 10 (June-July 1959): 57-59.

Canadian Library Association, Standards and Salaries Committee (University Libraries). "Report of the Standards and Salaries Committee (University Libraries)." *Feliciter* 3, no. 11-12 (July-August 1958): 1-4.

Commission of Inquiry. *Libraries in Canada: A Study of Library Conditions and Needs*. Chicago, IL: American Library Association, 1933.

Dominion Bureau of Statistics. "DBS Daily Bulletin: Thursday, December 3, 1964." *CACUL Newsletter* no. 3 (1964): 5.

Donnelly, F. Dolores. "The National Library in the Library Community: Current Developments and Trends." *Archivaria* 15 (Winter 1982-1983): 96-111.

Downs, Robert B. "Resources of Canadian Academic and Research Libraries: Summary of Recommendations." *CACUL Newsletter* no. 10 (1968): 40-47.

Evans, Calvin D. "Librarians and CAUT: Historical Overview and Future Directions." *CAUT Bulletin* 24, no. 5 (March 1976): 12-13.

Fowlie, Les. "The National Conference of Canadian Universities and Colleges and the Canadian Universities Foundation." *Canadian Library* 19, no. 5 (1963): 351-52.

Fox, David. "Finding Time for Scholarship: A Survey of Canadian Research University Librarians." *portal: Libraries & the Academy* 7, no. 4 (October 2007): 451-62.

———. "The Scholarship of Canadian Research Librarians." *Partnership: The Canadian Journal of Library & Information Practice & Research* 2, no. 2 (2007): 1-25.

Hafter, Ruth. "Academic Status - the Wrong Name, the Wrong Game." *APLA Bulletin* 39, no. 1 (Spring 1975): 9-12.

Heron, Craig. *The Canadian Labour Movement: A Short History*. 3rd ed. Toronto, ON: James Lorimer & Company Ltd., Publishers, 2012.

Horn, Steven. "The Professional Ladder." *Canadian Library Journal* 27, no. 3 (May-June 1970): 200-01.

Hulse, Elizabeth. *The Morton Years: The Canadian Library Association, 1946-1971*. Toronto, ON: Ex Libris Association, 1995.

Hunt, Edna. "Why Join the Research Libraries Section of CLA?" *Canadian Library Association Bulletin* 16, no. 3 (November 1959): 148-50.

Jacobs, Leona M. "Library Councils in Canadian Academic Libraries: A Summary of Responses." University of Lethbridge, 2008, http://www.uleth.ca/dspace/handle/10133/564.

Jenkins, Kathleen. "Review of the Association's Constitutional Structure, Traditions, Inter-Relations with Sections and Committees, with Critical Comment." *Canadian Library Association Bulletin* 7, no. 3 (November 1950): 91-96.

Kroll, Susan, ed. *Academic Status: Statements and Resources.* Chicago, IL: Association of College and Research Libraries, 1994.

Lewis, Doris E. "CACUL as of October 1964: Excerpts from CACUL President's Report to the Fall Meeting of the Canadian Library Association." *CACUL Newsletter* no. 3 (1964): 3-4.

———. "Report of the President." *CACUL Newsletter* no. 4 (1965): 3-4.

Lochhead, Douglas G. "The Research Libraries Section and the Canadian Library Inquiry." *Canadian Library: the Bulletin of the Canadian Library Association - le Bulletin de l'Association canadienne des Bibliotheques* 18, no. 6 (May 1962): 258-61.

McAnally, Arthur M. "Status of the University Librarian in the Academic Community." In *Faculty Status for Academic Librarians: A History and Policy Statements*, 1-30. Chicago: American Library Association, 1975.

Morton, Elizabeth Homer. Canadian Library Association Papers. Library and Archives Canada.

———. "These Years of the CLA-ACB: 1955-1960." *Canadian Library: the Bulletin of the Canadian Library Association - le Bulletin de l'Association canadienne des Bibliotheques* 17, no. 6 (May 1961): 294-395.

———. "Winnipeg Conference." *Canadian Library: the Bulletin of the Canadian Library Association - le Bulletin de l'Association canadienne des Bibliotheques* 20, no. 2 (September 1963): 49-58.

Mount, Joan. "Faculty Status at Laurentian-Two Years Later." *Canadian Library Journal* 35, no. 6 (December 1978): 427-31.

News-Herald (Vancouver). "The Canadian Library Council." *Canadian Library Council Bulletin* 1, no. 2 (December 1944): 17.

Pannu, Gurdial S. "The Downs' Survey: A Summary and a Review." *Canadian Library* 24, no. 6 (May 1968): 638-41.

Post-Secondary Learning Act, RSA 2003, c. P-19.5, http://www.qp.alberta.ca/574.cfm?page=p19p5.cfm&leg_type=Acts&isbncln=9780779737932.

Redmond, Donald. "Annual Report of the President to CACUL-ACBCU for 1969-1970." *CACUL Newsletter* 2, no. 6 (1971): 593-94.

Savage, Donald C. "73-74 Reports: Report from the Executive Secretary." *CAUT Bulletin* 22, no. 6 (1974): 24-27.

———. "A Historical Overview of Academic Status for Librarians." *Canadian Library Journal* 39, no. 5 (October 1982): 287-91.

———. "Letters: Library Governance." *CAUT Bulletin* 25, no. 1 (September 1976): 14.

Schmidt, C. James. Introduction to *Faculty Status for Academic Librarians: A History and Policy Statements*. Chicago, IL: American Library Association, 1975.

Schroeder, Julie. "The Bargaining Unit for the Academic Librarian." *Canadian Library Journal* 32, no. 6 (December 1975): 463-73.

Thomson, Ashley. "Five Years Later: Faculty Status at Laurentian." *Canadian Library Journal* 38, no. 4 (August 1981): 221-24.

Ward, Elizabeth. "The Community of Interest and Academic Status." *Canadian Library Journal* 31, no. 6 (December 1974): 540-43.

———. "Libraries and Unions: The Saint Mary's University Experience." *Canadian Library Journal* 31, no. 3 (June 1974): 238-40.

Watson, William. "Professional Status and Professional Responsibilities." *CACUL Newsletter* 2, no. 4 (1 June 1970): 416-27.

White, Don. "Academic Status: Right or Rite?" *Canadian Library Journal* 26, no. 4 (July-August 1969): 287-89.

Wilkinson, John. "Letters: Faculty Status." *Canadian Library Journal* 36, no. 1-2 (February/April 1979): 52.

Out of the "Library Ghetto:"
An Exploration of CAUT's Contributions to the Achievements of Canadian Academic Librarians

Jennifer Dekker

Introduction

It has been puzzling to Canadian academic librarians that professional library associations have not been effective advocates for the profession and especially for librarians as workers.[1] There has been a flurry of discontent regarding various attacks on the profession which range from the devaluation of the professional degree to the replacement of academic librarians by less qualified and less costly staffing arrangements. For those with longer memories, it seems clear that the gains librarians made in the 1970s and 1980s are being dialed back today. These attacks have been especially noticeable since about 2008—and yet, when one gauges reactions, professional library associations are practically nowhere to be found. In contrast to the silence of professional library associations, the Canadian Association of University Teachers (CAUT), an association not even focused on librarians, has displayed more dedication to and success in improving the working conditions of academic librarians today and in the past. Recently, CAUT was proactive when the academic freedom of librarians at McGill University was attacked and even threatened censure.[2] It created a campaign against the budget cuts to Library and Archives Canada as well as an umbrella campaign to counteract government interference in other cultural institutions.[3] In these few but powerful examples, academic librarians in Canada have learned that in terms of pushing their issues forward, library associations cannot and will not be successful, and in most cases they will not even try.[4] Academic librarians have increasingly realized that, in order to defend their interests, they must align with CAUT and local faculty associations rather than library associations. This paper traces the historical evolution of the relationship between Canadian academic librarians and CAUT and emphasizes how CAUT has worked with librarians to achieve real workplace improvements.

Methodology

The author searched Library and Archives Canada's online finding aids and requested all open records in the CAUT fonds relating to academic librarians—15 boxes of documents in total, though each box did not necessarily contain many files or documents about librarians, which in itself is a telling fact. The records consisted primarily of surveys, memoranda, personal letters, minutes of meetings, periodical articles and salary data. They were transcribed over the course of several months in 2012 and then verified against the originals. (Readers should note that not all of the records were clear and that, although the author has made historically verifiable assumptions based on the documentation, not every conclusion is supported strictly by archival evidence. When this was the case, secondary evidence was sought and is cited.)

Though the records are intermittent in terms of content and time periods, they are instrumental in shedding light on the role that CAUT played in the labour organization of academic librarians in universities across Canada. They also bring into closer focus the roles that professional library associations and in particular the Canadian Association of College and University Librarians (CACUL) played in the early days of librarians' labour efforts. The documentation partly explains why CAUT is and has been such a significant presence in the lives of Canadian academic librarians for the past 60 years.

The Historical Context of Canadian Post-Secondary Education

Several historians have written excellent works on the history of post-secondary education in Canada, including Robin S. Harris,[5] Paul Axelrod (focusing on Ontario),[6] Neil Tudiver[7] and Philip A. Massolin.[8] These authors unanimously write about the rapid growth of higher education in Canada in the postwar period. Participation rates peaked and universities expanded to accommodate the thousands of war veterans as well as the first wave of baby boomers. University enrollment doubled in the 10 years between 1945 and 1955, and doubled again by 1960.[9] It was a time of exceedingly rapid growth, including faculty employment. But this expansion presented its own set of issues which, when combined with unresolved factors predating the war, created tense conditions in Canadian higher education, particularly from the faculty point of view.

University Financing

University financing was a major point of discussion during this time. Harris provides a comprehensive chapter on this subject with a strong focus on how university funding became the domain of the provinces and how the religious affiliation or secularism of an institution became the primary qualifying criterion in whether a university would receive public monies.[10] Axelrod enhances this history by reporting the changes in higher education economics between the prewar era and the 1970s in Ontario. During this period, government control and oversight of higher education was somewhat formalized, but because universities insisted on retaining independence, government always had a rather haphazard and arm's length role. Before World War II in Ontario, only three non-denominational universities were provincially funded: the University of Toronto, the University of Western Ontario, and Queen's University. They were often funded at the whim of the Premier, who was usually also the Minster of Education. The postwar period saw McMaster University pull away from its Baptist roots and obtain some provincial funding, and public monies were likewise disbursed to several other technical colleges. But the process for requesting and granting funding remained informal and the provincial government had no regular method for determining the needs of the universities.[11]

University Governance

University governance and administration also became a point of contention as decision-making followed much the same random pattern as financing. Government contributed to institutions and programs which it believed the voting public supported but it had no mechanism for determining what the public really preferred. There was no evidence that factors such as demographic trends were taken into account, nor whether the Premier had consulted more extensively than an abstract and unspecified public opinion.[12] As a result, both professors and administrators became more and more disturbed with decision-making in universities. It became such a consternation in fact that in 1964, the National Conference of Canadian Universities and Colleges (NCCUC), known today as the Association of Universities and Colleges Canada (AUCC) and CAUT jointly financed a commission headed by British academic administrator, James Duff, and American political scientist, Robert Berdahl, to examine the state of university governance and recommend improvements. The report that resulted from this Canada-wide examination of university government noted that universities were generally governed by two separate bodies—a Board of Governors and a Senate—but that faculty representation in these bodies was all but non-existent. The Board's composition was usually a "mixed process of self-perpetuation and governmental selection" with the former (Board of Governors) dominating at private institutions and the latter at provincial universities."[13] The report noted that in most cases alumni composed a large minority of Board members and faculty members were regularly excluded. Academic senates, it concluded, were also far from representative of faculty members since most were heavily dominated by ex-officio members such as the President, Vice-Presidents, Deans, alumni, external community members, appointees from the provincial government, and occasionally a few Board members. The report went on to note that although senates were responsible for setting academic policy and developing academic programming, in reality, the Boards were making decisions regarding expansion and development and deferred to faculty only on narrow matters of curriculum.[14]

Academic Freedom

In 1958, seven years after the founding of CAUT, which had been primarily preoccupied with professors' financial concerns since its inception, professor Harry Crowe was dismissed by United College (then part of the University of Manitoba) for writing a letter criticizing the college's administration and voicing concerns about a possible Conservative party victory in upcoming provincial elections. Although he was hardly the first academic to be penalized by a university administration that did not recognize the right of professors to critique society, states or universities, his case catapulted the issue of academic freedom into the spotlight, further straining the relationships between faculty members and university administrations.[15]

The Perfect Storm

The combination of massive demographic changes in university enrollments, large but seemingly random increases in financing for post-secondary education, lack of appropriate governance in universities, and attacks on academic freedom were among the factors that led to a heightened level of dissatisfaction among professors working in Canada. These were exacerbated by the desperate state of faculty salaries which meant that, as early as 1946, Canadian scholars were leaving for the United States or the United Kingdom where they were paid an average of 20% more.[16] Those who stayed sought improvements to their working conditions, which led both to the creation of CAUT and contributed to the unionizing of professors, and eventually librarians.

The Founding of CAUT

CAUT was founded in 1951 at an opportune time: Canadian universities were tentatively exploring the world of collective bargaining and the academic labour movement was just dawning in Canada. Concern over factors already mentioned led 16 Canadian faculty associations to form a national association of university professors.[17] South of the border, John Dewey and Arthur O. Lovejoy had already formed the American Association of University Professors (AAUP) in response to breaches of academic freedom.[18] In the UK, the Association of University Teachers (AUT) was officially formed in 1919. An equivalent association was formed in Scotland in 1922 but later joined AUT.[19] Unlike AAUP, AUT was formed to assist in collective negotiations for the purposes of improving working conditions; in other words, it was a labour-focused organization. CAUT would eventually follow AUT's path and become involved in the unionization of faculty members rather than exist simply as an advocacy or professional group.

The Seeds of Labour Organization

There are many publications regarding the origins and reasons for faculty labour organization in Canada[20] but unionization and collective bargaining for professors and librarians were more widely studied in the United States. By the late 1970s, several major research projects and theses had been published or made available describing social and economic factors leading to faculty unionization as well as individual and group demographics that generally resulted in support for collective bargaining.[21] These studies reported pre-unionization circumstances in the US quite similar to those in Canada and were useful when examining librarians' predilection for organizing and unionizing.

In terms of timing, Canadian academics were nearly a decade behind their American counterparts. By 1973, when Canadian certification drives began in earnest, there were already 133 bargaining units affiliated with the National Education Association (NEA), the American Federation of Teachers (AFT) or AAUP in the US.[22] There were also 360 unionized faculty associations already certified there.[23] To be fair, French-language post-secondary institutions in Québec certified earlier than their counterparts in English Canada, with engineers leading the way at Sherbrooke in 1970, and the Chicoutimi and Trois Rivières campuses of the Université du Québec following soon after.[24] Librarians on the other hand, were comparatively late to the table, and did not join local faculty associations or CAUT until the late 1970s. This historical fact is not necessarily a result of conscious choice but was the consequence of a lack of awareness of librarians' roles in universities on the part of faculty members and faculty associations—a situation that CAUT worked hard to rectify.

Academic Librarian Salary Survey

CAUT became involved in the working lives of academic librarians in Canada when it launched a salary survey of professional librarians in 1959-1960. By 1957, CAUT realized that librarians working in universities were isolated and vulnerable and could not rely on professional associations to achieve improvements in working conditions, despite best efforts to raise awareness of problems such as low salaries. CAUT, on the other hand, was already familiar with universities' structures, administrations, and faculty associations and was better equipped to champion change. But what factors prompted CAUT to survey Canadian academic librarians in the first place? There are no documents that justify a sudden interest in librarians and the survey is the earliest piece of evidence related to librarians in CAUT's files. Since it is a question impossible to answer based on the available archival material, articles from the same time period concerning academic librarians were sought. The earliest appeared in the November 1956 issue of *Canadian Library Journal* (predating the CAUT survey by at least three years) and was titled "Salary Scale Recommended for College and University Libraries in Canada." The article recommended an annual increment of 6%.[25] A follow-up article appeared six months later with a much more proscriptive tone regarding salaries. It reported on a resolution passed at the Annual General Meeting of the CLA, where the previous year's salary recommendations were renounced as being inadequate since Canadian academic librarian salaries in 1957 had already exceeded the 6% increase. In a slightly more defensive tone, this article extolled the value of librarians in the university teaching context, stating that qualifications for librarians were equivalent to the members of the teaching faculty and that university librarianship demanded special training and ability. Finally, it recommended that, in principle, the professional salary standards for librarians be based upon salary standards for teaching members of the faculty, which was the very first reference to equity between Canadian academic librarians and university teaching faculty.[26] A third article appeared in June 1959. By this time, CLA was clearly mobilized around the issue of salaries for academic librarians. It released new data on academic librarian salaries and noted that, while increases in academic librarian pay had occurred over the past year, they had not kept pace with increases allocated to teaching faculty—the second time within less than three years that equity between academic librarians and teaching faculty was suggested.[27] CLA had embarked on a proactive if not hardline position regarding academic librarians. It was around the time that this article appeared that CAUT embarked on its survey.

Although librarians' salaries had previously been collected and compiled each year by the Dominion Bureau of Statistics as well as the Canadian Library Association, CAUT's survey included questions beyond the scopes of the official statistical agency of Canada or CLA.[28] Questions unique to higher education, such as how many librarians had teaching duties and whether librarians had academic status were included in CAUT's survey. It also requested details regarding librarians' ranks and whether librarians with advanced degrees were compensated financially for having achieved them. CAUT inquired about schedules of work, including whether librarians were employed for the academic year or on longer appointments and whether salary increases were expected in the coming year.[29] (The length of appointment was particularly contentious in several of the US studies of librarians' pre-unionization working conditions since librarians were often required to work a 12 month schedule, while faculty were often hired on 10 month contracts; in other words, librarians worked all year while professors did not.[30] This was an important point for librarians seeking tenure or faculty status because it meant librarians were disadvantaged compared to teaching faculty by not having a semester of no on-campus work obligations in which to perform their scholarly activities.)

The survey was sent to all CAUT member associations and 80% (24) replied though four of the returns were incomplete. Two hundred and forty six professional librarians were represented in the results. It is interesting to note that the questions not only focused narrowly on salary. It is evident that CAUT was also attempting to ascertain whether librarians should form part of CAUT's membership base, because at this point in time, they did not.

The salary survey uncovered the following facts regarding the salaries and working conditions of academic librarians:

- 15 librarians (6%) were assigned teaching as part of their workload;
- 4 associations reported that all librarians had academic status;
- 17 reported that the University Librarian had academic status or equivalent and, of these, 2 indicated that they also had the rank equivalent of Professor;
- 5 of the 17 above indicated that the deputy university librarian also had academic status but only 1 had an equivalent ranking to a professor, which was at the rank of Associate;
- 13 associations reported no special compensation for advanced degrees, but 8 indicated that librarians with advanced degrees were promoted more quickly and were more likely to receive additional compensation when deserved.
- Most librarians reported a 12 month work year. The average work week was 36.2 hours, with many reporting shorter hours in the summer term.
- 14 associations stated that they expected librarians salary increases the following year, while 5 reported that they did not expect any increases and 2 did not respond.[31]

Of the survey results, compiler Joseph P. Zweig of Sir George Williams College in Montreal (now part of Concordia University) concluded, "In most universities, the librarians find themselves in a minority group. They are not able to muster the numbers required to present their case. They are often forced to become dependent on a larger university group such as the local CAUT association to express their views, to speak for them, and to safeguard their welfare."[32] CAUT had quickly identified librarians' lack of institutional power, and though librarians in 2014 might bristle at the statement by Zweig, it was historically accurate.

That a national organization of faculty associations should suddenly perform a salary survey of librarians would surely have been encouraging, especially in the context of the recommendations made by CLA. Unfortunately CLA probably did not have the influence to convince universities to pay librarians more, nor the research capacity to put forward well-informed policy. But it seemed to have gotten things started, at least as far as CAUT was concerned. In terms of national support, at that point in time Canadian librarians had only recently managed to establish a national library association to represent their interests—they had relied on and been active in the American Library Association (ALA) since 1876, even providing a Canadian President in 1926-27.[33] But after attempts in 1900, 1925 and 1934, CLA finally emerged from the Canadian Library Council (a section of the ALA) in 1946. When CLA was created, there were major hopes for the association, but it was clear by the 1960s that its resources were stretched thin. One of the few professionals working at CLA commented, "We had no research facilities in the office . . . We had a fairly adequate clerical staff but a marked shortage of professional staff and an almost complete lack of research capacity."[34] This limitation most certainly would have had a serious impact on what could have been achieved for librarians working in any sector. Presumably CAUT, with a much stronger research orientation and recognition on university campuses could fill this gap.

Soon after CAUT published its salary survey, faculty associations across Canada began contacting CAUT directly to ask whether librarians were eligible for membership in local associations. CAUT replied with uncertainty. In a letter to the secretary of the Waterloo University College Faculty Association, CAUT's Executive Director responded, "Insofar as the Association is concerned, it seems to me that the Association should decide whether it wishes professorial status for librarians and should decide its position largely on the ground of the professional qualities of the librarians themselves . . . the matter probably has always been dealt with on a strictly ad hoc basis. Perhaps this is the right way to do it."[35]

Despite the initial optimistic entrée into librarian issues by way of the salary survey, CAUT was not convinced that librarians could or should be members of their local associations, or of CAUT itself. But in 1961 CAUT was still preoccupied with financial issues—gathering and circulating information on academic salaries as well as campaigning for secure funding for Canadian universities. Like CLA, CAUT's budget, staff and capacity were limited. And while librarians would eventually grow to represent an important constituency group, in 1961, this was not the case. As a result, CAUT was careful regarding how many resources it was willing to devote to this group of academic workers whose interests it was not sure it could represent.

The relationship between CAUT and professional librarians would soon begin to solidify however, due in large part to the 'Downs Report' of 1967. This report was co-sponsored by CACUL and AUCC and funded by the Canada

Council and the Council on Library Resources in Washington, D.C.[36] It was the product of a recommendation of a 1964 study, *Forecast of the Cost of Academic Library Services in Canada, 1965-1975: A Brief to the Bladen Commission on the Financing of Higher Education*.[37] The goal of the Downs Report, according to CACUL, was to assess present resources, needs, and to plan for meeting these needs in terms of book collections, buildings, and staff.[38] Although not the official title of the report, the Downs Report was named after Robert Bingham Downs, Dean of Libraries at the University of Illinois and a stalwart defender of professional and academic status for librarians. Consequently, in the section on personnel, Downs' report recommended "full recognition of professional librarians as key members of the academic community."[39] With respect to implementation, the report suggested that "the co-operation of the Canadian Association of University Teachers should be enlisted, if possible, in obtaining proper recognition of the academic character of professional librarianship, and thereby suitable status for librarians."[40] On its face, this seemed peculiar since one of the Steering Committee's co-sponsors, CACUL, had the working conditions and salaries of academic librarians as part of its own mandate.[41] Had CACUL been capable or likely to achieve the goal of professional status for librarians, the report surely would have recommended that librarians continue to work through CACUL. But the report did not make that statement. The implication was that, although librarians had a professional association that could have advocated for their professional needs, CAUT was seen as the organization most likely to further librarians' goals.

Downs' recommendation of working with CAUT did not come out of thin air. A beacon of the professionalization and status movement of academic librarians in the US, Downs had probably suggested CAUT because a decade earlier, AAUP had itself championed professional (i.e., faculty) status for academic librarians. In a book Downs edited called *The Status of American College and University Librarians* and specifically in one of the chapters he himself contributed, Downs reminded readers that in 1957 AAUP Council declared that librarians of professional status were engaged in teaching and research and were therefore eligible for membership in AAUP. He further noted that in 1958, 738 librarians were members of AAUP, making them the 20th most numerous of a possible 46 subject fields in universities.[42] Fitting librarians into the mould already occupied by professors was clearly part of the strategy because he went on to write that an overwhelming majority of university library administrators had concluded that close identification with the teaching faculty was most likely to accomplish the aims of librarians (professional/faculty status, with corresponding rights and responsibilities). He outlined several options, including:

1) faculty status where each librarian would be assigned a suitable rank in the faculty hierarchy,

2) inclusion of professional librarians in the academic classification with equivalent ranks or,
3) definition of librarians as academic without any attempt to integrate exactly library positions with faculty ranks.[43]

Downs understood that the best way to achieve any of those three outcomes would have been for librarians to work alongside CAUT rather than attempt to do so on their own or via a professional association. CAUT took its role seriously; in May of 1970, it released a report by Associate Executive Secretary, Edward J. Monahan, based on a study "L'Étude sur les Membres qui Constituent l'Association Locale des Professeurs—1969-1970." (Study of Members of Local Faculty Associations—1969-1970.[44]) The report was prompted by a request received from "'Libraries for Tomorrow,' a group formed to urge implementation of the major recommendations of the Downs Report including gaining academic status for professional librarians in colleges and universities."[45]

In order to begin the work recommended by the Downs Report, CAUT developed another survey; this time regarding librarians' faculty association membership (and more importantly their status within the university). It was the first national snapshot that Canadian academic librarians would have of their status from coast to coast. Other than communication with each other through informal networks or through the CAUT office (by mail), it is unlikely that librarians in different parts of the country were aware of working conditions of librarians elsewhere. Canada's geographical sprawl, the small number of universities in the 1960s and 1970s, and high costs of long distance communications and travel would have been significant impediments to librarians' forming any collective knowledge of their working conditions and status. There were groups established in Ontario (Institute of Professional Librarians of Ontario)[46] and in British Columbia (Council of Western Canadian University Librarians, or COWCAL)[47] but COWCAL in particular appeared to be short lived and neither evidenced serious attempts to share data about their members with groups in different provinces. Therefore CAUT's survey was critical in developing an understanding of the status of academic librarians in Canada at the close of the 1960s.

CAUT asked faculty associations to respond to questions regarding their membership composition including librarian members. (Readers should keep in mind that the survey had the purpose of determining the status of librarians but also the secondary function of assessing whether librarians should become CAUT members which would justify allocating future resources to librarians.) Of the 28 faculty association responses:

- 18 provided full and regular membership to librarians;
- 5 provided associate membership (librarians were non-voting members of the association);

- 2 faculty associations responded that librarians had the opportunity to run for election to full membership in the faculty association;
- 3 did not respond regarding the type of membership that librarians were extended.[48]

The following groupings indicate whether and what status was accorded librarians at responding institutions and whether they were eligible for membership in CAUT[49]:

Group 1 (6 responses): The University Librarian and librarians *with* teaching responsibilities were members of the faculty association: Acadia, Alberta, Dalhousie, McMaster (only on appointment to an academic department), Nova Scotia Tech, and Waterloo.

Group 2 (1 response): The University Librarian and librarians without teaching responsibilities were members of the faculty association: Simon Fraser University.

Group 3 (16 responses): The University Librarian and librarians *with or without* teaching responsibilities were members of the faculty association: Bishops, Brandon, University of British Columbia, Calgary, Lethbridge, Manitoba, McGill, Memorial, Moncton, Mount Allison, Regina (but the University Librarian was excluded), St. John's, Saskatchewan, Trent, Victoria and Windsor.

Group 4 (11 responses): No librarian members were members of the faculty association: Brock, Carleton, Laval, Montreal, New Brunswick, Queen's, Sir George Williams, Toronto, Western (librarians could be elected members at a special vote at the AGM. But even if elected, Western librarians were not CAUT eligible), Winnipeg and York.

Group 5 (4 responses): Librarians were non-voting members of the faculty association and were not CAUT eligible: Lakehead, Mount St. Vincent, Ottawa and St. Mary's.

Group 6 (4 responses): University librarians only were members of the faculty association: Mount St. Vincent, Notre Dame University of Nelson (B.C.), St. Francis Xavier and Waterloo Lutheran.[50]

As to the general membership of faculty associations at the time of the survey, it is worth noting that in 1969-1970, the following university employees were also commonly included as either regular or associate members: deans, department chairs, directors, registrars, emeritus professors, invited professors, rectors, vice-rectors, part-time professors, laboratory staff, bursars, extension supervisors, health services supervisors, physical plant supervisors, postdoctoral fellows, personal assistants and secretaries to the president (when appointed with academic status), psychological councillors, etc . . .[51]

Based on the survey's results, librarians still had a long way to go to achieving universal membership in faculty associations and in CAUT. Nonetheless, because of CAUT's strong presence in Canadian universities at the time, librarians must have seen CAUT as the best possible ally to achieve the benefits that associations regularly negotiated for their members. And though the Downs Report only briefly mentions the academic status of librarians, other documentation corroborates that status, and in particular faculty status, was quickly becoming a pressing issue for academic librarians.[52]

Slow but Steady

In a letter dated June 25, 1970, Edward Monahan of CAUT wrote to the Vice President of Memorial University of Newfoundland on the eligibility of librarians to be full members of their local faculty associations:

> ...I think it fair to judge that there is a correlation between eligibility for full membership in a faculty association and faculty status. With very few exceptions, persons who do not enjoy faculty status are ineligible for membership in the faculty association. I may say that I was a bit surprised to see how many (19) faculty associations now provide eligibility to professional librarians irrespective of whether they perform teaching duties. Only a few years ago, this number was much smaller.[53]

This letter provides anecdotal evidence that librarian faculty association participation had improved and that CAUT was supporting an activist political agenda with data gathered from surveys. Unfortunately, the records do not indicate why inclusion in faculty associations had increased, how much the situation had improved, and whether CAUT's interest in librarians had impacted participation.

CAUT continued to work on behalf of librarians and in 1974 released the results of another survey called "Terms and Conditions of Employment for Librarians" based on comparisons of librarians' and professors' working conditions. In 1974:

- None of the 48 universities in Canada responding to the survey offered librarians the same ranks as professors;
- 6 universities responded that librarians had equivalent ranks to professors but 37 said that they did not. Of this group, only 1 reported that librarians and professors also had the same salary and salary scales as professors, while 5 others did not;
- 2 universities had the same procedures for promotion and renewal for librarians and professors while 4 did not;

- 1 university responded that librarians had tenure on the same terms as professors, while librarians at 5 other institutions did not;
- 2 of 6 universities had the same grievance procedures for librarians as professors, while 4 did not.

Regarding collective bargaining:
- In 13 of 55 cases, the faculty association bargained on behalf of librarian members, and of these, only four had single salary scales for professors and librarians, while eight had separate scales for professors and librarians and one did not respond.[54]

The year after the release of this survey on equivalencies in working conditions between professors and librarians, CAUT turned a corner in its support of academic librarians. There was no longer any question of whether librarians deserved the attention and support of CAUT. CAUT and CACUL jointly worked on a draft document on academic status for librarians and CAUT sent it to all university presidents. Only one response was kept in the CAUT files. Written by Willard Allen, Associate Vice-President Academic at the University of Alberta (and a former President of CAUT, 1969-1970), the letter claimed that the draft document was both unworkable and inappropriate and must be substantially revised. He wrote:

> The library is an academic service for faculty and students. Its operations are service operations and not ends in themselves. This in no way denigrates the importance of its function or the value of librarians within the university. The faculty model assumes that each individual operates independently of others in selecting the area of his own research and within broad limits uses his own approach to his discipline in teaching. All professors have the same kinds of responsibilities . . . by contrast the library is a hierarchical administrative structure within which duties are allocated and responsibilities and experience are related in quite different ways from those found within a faculty structure.[55]

Despite Allen's opinion, CAUT pursued its agenda of academic status for librarians, which became the critical and unifying goal for academic librarians in Canada. CAUT's document enunciated its point of view: that librarians were partners with faculty members in contributing to the scholarly and intellectual functions of the university and thereby deserved academic status as well as corresponding rights and responsibilities. The document further recommended that procedures relating to terms and conditions of librarian appointments be analogous to those for faculty members, including entitlement to research and study leaves at levels of financial support comparable to faculty and eligibility for travel and research funding. With respect to governance, CAUT stated that librarians should be entitled to participate fully in the academic affairs of the university and be eligible for membership on the governing bodies of the university. Finally, CAUT recommended procedures for appointment, promotion, salary recommendations and economic benefits for librarians.[56]

The draft statement did more than just broadcast CAUT's position regarding academic librarians. It encapsulated librarians' self-perception and codified a set of principles that librarians have been trying to achieve ever since. It also gave academic librarians legitimacy inside the relatively exclusive, overwhelmingly male, and professor-dominated world of higher education. Finally, the document signaled CAUT's support of academic librarians in collective bargaining. Its completeness and its structure suggested that it was intended to help librarians negotiate provisions in their own collective agreements since it spelled out articles and clauses, which were easily recognizable as contract language.

CAUT anticipated presenting the guidelines at its first Council meeting in 1976. Donald Savage, then Executive Secretary of CAUT, sent a memo to the Presidents of all local and provincial associations informing them that:

> The CAUT Board and Council passed a resolution that Council approve the CAUT CACUL proposed guidelines on the academic status of professional librarians, that is to say the principle that CAUT should recommend terms and conditions of employment for librarians similar to those in the Policy Statement on Academic Appointment and Tenure and that CAUT should support governance procedures for librarians both inside and outside the Library parallel to those accorded to faculty members and that the Council authorize the board to approve the document after detailed examination."[57]

The following is an exact transcription of the implementing motions:

1) That individual faculty associations seek to bring about the necessary changes in librarians' working conditions to enable librarians to meet academic criteria;
2) That local faculty associations and CAUT protect librarians from being judged solely on the basis of such criteria until they have had sufficient opportunity to meet them; and
3) That the Council authorize the Board subject to ratification by Council to approve the document after detailed examination and that the Board consult CACUL and the Academic Freedom and Tenure Committee and other interested parties prior to its discussion of the detailed clauses.[58]

Furthermore, Savage pledged to distribute the policy to librarians for discussion at a CACUL meeting in Toronto in June of 1976 because he wanted librarians' endorsement of the guidelines, not just CAUT Council approval. However, Savage knew the challenge that lay ahead as he wrote, ". . . we are aware that a number of Chief Librarians will oppose the motion and the draft document and could possibly carry the day in CACUL. In that unhappy event, CAUT will proceed with its review of the proposed document and will still consider it at the October Board meeting."[59]

The Academic Status 'Manifesto'

In crafting and circulating the *Guidelines on Academic Status for Librarians* to university presidents, faculty associations and other professional associations, the CAUT-CACUL Committee launched librarians into a new struggle for increased decision-making in their workplaces, better working conditions and salaries, and equity with teaching faculty—most of which was to be negotiated at collective bargaining tables around the country. To varying degrees, both libraries and bargaining units that included librarians have been sites of negotiation ever since. The *Guidelines* not only asserted that librarians should have more power within their libraries or immediate workplaces but also equity with professors. Librarians therefore would have had to negotiate with their professor colleagues to be heard, included and valued equally (especially critical in collective bargaining) and furthermore, would have had to negotiate with those who held power in their libraries and workplaces. In the 1970s, rank and file librarians were mostly female, did not hold the same advanced educational credentials as professors, and were fighting the perception of being support staff; negotiating power relationships with professors or even being considered colleagues would have been a very difficult struggle. And yet, some achieved significant gains. Robert Haro wrote, "The demand of academic librarians for recognition and participation has resulted from the emergence of a creative restlessness sweeping over most of our college and university campuses; and it may be, in the future, characterized as the emergence of librarian militancy."[60] Tom Eadie also captured the spirit of the times when he wrote that librarians in the 1970s were accustomed to demanding a greater share of voice in decision-making: "[they] were of the generation of student activists, some of whom had challenged more senior administrations than those to be found in academic libraries."[61]

CAUT gave academic librarians license and encouragement to fight for their goals; objectives that librarians believed to be both attainable and deserved. CAUT validated and codified these in its *Guidelines* but it also achieved consensus from within the closed confines of the professoriate. The challenge did not end with the *Guidelines*, as CAUT continued to work alongside librarians in various support capacities. Evidence exists regarding several meetings organized and hosted by CAUT with packed agendas on how to move librarians forward. One of these took place in August, 1976 and included items such as how to encourage all faculty associations to admit librarians as full members, how librarians could enter into the organized labour movement as unionized workers, and whether it was better to create independent unions of their own or have librarians join existing faculty associations where possible. Other discussions centred around library and university governance and salary parity with faculty members. CAUT further agreed to compile the current terms and conditions for employment of university librarians, to conduct a survey regarding government in Canadian university libraries, and to collect comparative information on university library salaries across the country. In other words, CAUT provided much of the support that academic librarians needed in order to make strong arguments—whether among librarian colleagues, faculty colleagues, or at bargaining tables.[62]

As it became more heavily involved in collective bargaining on Canadian campuses, CAUT continued to observe, document and analyse the working conditions of librarians. In a proactive move, it offered CACUL members a workshop on collective bargaining during the annual meeting of CLA in 1978. This event was highly anticipated by both the organizers and CLA members; pre-registration indicated interest from over 100 participants.[63] The year being 1978, readers should not be surprised by this. As mentioned in the opening paragraphs of this chapter, the late 1970s were ripe for collective bargaining in universities. CAUT and CACUL were likely aware that librarians would need to develop some skill in bargaining since many would be negotiating alongside faculty members, or would have to make strong arguments for their proposals that professors would bring to the table. In both scenarios, librarians would have to convince their teaching colleagues as well as administrators that their demands were worth the time and effort spent in negotiations. The final few documents in CAUT's files include articles and news clippings about collective bargaining. These were very much focused on academic libraries, including two publications by the Association of Research Libraries (ARL): SPEC Kit no. 8 (June 1974)[64]—a collection of various documents pertaining to collective bargaining at ARL libraries—and "Review of Collective Bargaining Activities in Academic and Research Libraries."[65] Clearly, CAUT was monitoring collective bargaining activities in North American research libraries. Other documents were a "Memo of agreement between the Governing Council of the University of Toronto and the UTFA," [66] an article from *Feliciter* describing how librarians were eligible for membership in UTFA[67] and another published in *Athenaeum* (Acadia University's student newspaper) describing how female librarians' salaries averaged a full $6,000.00 below men's at Acadia and were "perhaps the most affected by gender disparity in wages." [68] The last document is an unidentified article published in the CAUT *Bulletin* (probably from 1976 or 1977), which describes librarians' status vis à vis collective bargaining in various Canadian academic libraries.

Into the 1980s

Accessible records from the 1980s show librarians galvanizing around collective bargaining and focusing on improving working conditions, especially in achieving a greater share of decision-making in their libraries. There is hardly anything publicly accessible in CAUT's files after 1981, but a published transcript of a talk given by CAUT's Executive Director, Donald Savage, to the CACUL Academic Status Committee in 1982 demonstrates that CAUT persisted in its support for librarians, especially regarding academic status. In his speech, Savage marked the passage of eight years since he and the former CAUT President and CACUL Committee on Academic Status Chair had proposed a joint task force on the subject.[69] It was out of that task force that the *Guidelines on Academic Status for Professional Librarians* emerged and dealt not only with the contributions that librarians made to their universities but also with the essential elements of "appointments, dismissal and suspension, grievances, salaries and other economic benefits, research and travel funds, leaves and university and library governance."[70] Savage described the efforts of academic librarians in much more political terms than had previous CAUT officers. He wrote:

> Ten years ago many chief librarians considered themselves to be the only members of the library staff who had or should have academic status. Many were men who treated their staff as female office help, a form of secretarial assistance, and hoped to maintain this situation by creating a library ghetto apart from the rest of the academic enterprise.[71]

Savage reinforced that every time a librarian joined a faculty association, was elected officer or served on a negotiating team, served on senate or one of its committees, or received working conditions similar to faculty, or rejected classification systems similar to support staff, she asserted her academic status.

Conclusion

This chapter opened with Canadian librarians' dissatisfaction with professional library associations. It attempted to trace the historical relationship between CAUT and Canadian academic librarians in order to explain why so many librarians turn to CAUT instead of library associations when there is an attack on the profession or its practitioners. In addition to documenting the collaboration between early librarian labour activists and CAUT, the records at Library and Archives Canada highlighted what is not being achieved today: nearly 40 years after CAUT published its guidelines on academic status, librarians still face arbitrary terminations and working conditions far less optimal than what was imagined many years ago.[72] What is the next chapter? After having benefited for so long from CAUT's leadership, librarians must mobilize alongside CAUT and take ownership of our struggle for meaningful academic freedom, tenure, status, equitable salaries, and collegial decision-making in the workplace.

Bibliography

American Association of University Professors. "History of the AAUP." http://www.aaup.org/about/history-aaup.

Arnold, Gordon. "The Emergence of Faculty Unions at Flagship Public Universities in Southern New England." *Labor Studies Journal* 22, no. 4 (1998): 62-87.

Association of Research Libraries. "Review of Collective Bargaining Activities in Academic and Research Libraries." *ARL Management Supplement* 1, no. 3 (1973).

Association of Universities and Colleges of Canada, Berdahl Robert Oliver, Canadian Association of University Teachers, Duff James. *University Government in Canada: Report of a Commission Sponsored by the Canadian Association of University Teachers and the Association of Universities and Colleges of Canada.* Toronto: University of Toronto Press, 1966.

Axelrod, Paul Douglas. *Scholars and Dollars: Politics, Economics and the Universities of Ontario, 1945-1980.* Toronto: University of Toronto Press, 1982.

Bélanger, Gérard. "La Syndicalisation des Professeurs d'Université." *Relations Industrielles/Industrial Relations* 29, no. 4 (1974): 857-864.

"The Birth of COWCUL." *Feliciter* 14 (December-February 1968), 25.

Bognanno, Mario F. and Edward L. Suntrup. "Occupational Inclusions in Faculty Bargaining Units." *Industrial Relations* 14, no. 3 (1975): 358-363.

Branscomb, Lewis Capers, Ed. *Case for Faculty Status for Academic Librarians* Chicago: American Library Association, 1970.

CACUL and Commission on the Cost of Higher Education. *Forecast of the Cost of Academic Library Services in Canada, 1965-1975; a Brief to the Bladen Commission on the Cost of Higher Education.* Waterloo, Ont: University Press, 1964.

Cameron, David M. 2002. "The Challenge of Change: Canadian Universities in the 21st Century." *Canadian Public Administration/Administration Publique du Canada* 45, no. 2 (2002): 145-174.

Canadian Association of Research Libraries. "CARL Historical Overview, 1976-2013." http://www.carl-abrc.ca/uploads/Publications/2013-08-07%20CARL%20History.pdf.

Canadian Association of University Teachers. 1951-2004. Fonds. Boxes MG28-I208, R7226-0-9-E. Library and Archives Canada.

Canadian Association of University Teachers. "Canada's Past Matters." http://www.canadaspastmatters.ca/.

———. "CAUT Withdraws Consideration of Censure of McGill University." Canadian Association of University Teachers. http://www.caut.ca/issues-and-campaigns/librarians-and-libraries/2012/11/26/caut-withdraws-consideration-of-censure-of-mcgill-university.

———. "Guidelines on Academic Status for University Librarians."

Chung, Joseph H. "Le Syndicalisme des Professeurs d'Université - Quelques Réflexions." *Relations Industrielles/Industrial Relations* 28, no. 2 (1973): 325-342.

Cruzat, Gwendolyn Marie Stiggins. "Collective Bargaining in Academic Librarianship." PhD diss., Wayne State University, 1976.

Dekker, Jennifer. "Librarians Silenced at CLA Conference." Bibliothécaires de l'APUO/APUO Librarians. http://apuobibliolib.wordpress.com/2012/06/01/librarians-silenced-at-cla-conference/.

———. "Who Speaks for Libraries and Librarians (2/2)." Progressive Librarians Guild Toronto Area Chapter. http://plggta.org/archives/154.

Downs, Robert Bingham. "The Current Status of University Library Staffs." In *The Status of American College and University Librarians*, edited by Robert Bingham Downs, 13-27. Chicago: American Library Association, 1958.

———. *The Status of American College and University Librarians*. Chicago: American Library Association, 1958.

———. "Status of Academic Librarians in Retrospect." *College & Research Libraries* 29 (1968): 253-258.

Downs, Robert Bingham, Association of Universities and Colleges of Canada, Berdahl Robert Oliver, Canadian Association of University Teachers, and James Duff. *Resources of Canadian Academic and Research Libraries*. Ottawa: Association of Universities and Colleges of Canada, 1967.

Driscoll, James Walter. "Determinants of Faculty Attitudes Towards Collective Bargaining for the Faculty at Cornell : Participation and Trust in the Decision-Making Process." PhD diss., Cornell University, 1975.

Duryea, E.D. and Robert S. Fisk. *Faculty Unions and Collective Bargaining*. San Francisco: Jossey-Bass, 1973.

Eadie, Tom. "Remembrances of Things Past." In *Critical Issues in Library Management: Organizing for Leadership and Decision-Making: Papers from the Thirty-Fifth Allerton Institute*, edited by Bryce L. Allen and Terry L. Weech, 73-85. Urbana-Champaign, Ill.: Graduate School of Library and Information Science, University of Illinois at Urbana-Champaign, 1995.

"Equal Pay for Work of Equal Value." *Athenaeum* 40, no. 20 (1978).

Garbarino, Joseph W. "Faculty Unionism: From Theory to Practice." *Industrial Relations: A Journal of Economy and Society* 11, no. 1 (1972): 1-17.

Haro, Robert P. "Collective Action and Professional Negotiation: Factors and Trends in Academic Libraries." *ALA Bulletin*, July-August (1969): 993-996.

Harris Robin Sutton. *A History of Higher Education in Canada, 1663-1960.* Toronto: University of Toronto Press, 1976.

Harry Crowe Foundation. "Harry Sherman Crowe (1922-1981)." https://www.crowefoundation.ca/about/harry-crowe.asp.

Horn, Michiel. *Academic Freedom in Canada: A History.* Toronto: University of Toronto Press, 1999.

Hulse, Elizabeth. *The Morton Years: The Canadian Library Association, 1946-1971.* Toronto: Ex Libris Association, 1995.

Kemerer, Frank R. and J. Victor Baldridge. *Unions on Campus.* Jossey-Bass Series in Higher Education. 1st ed. San Francisco: Jossey-Bass, 1975.

Knox, John William. "Trade Unionism in Canadian Universities: An Empirical Study of Unionised and Nonunionised Academic Staff at Canadian Universities." PhD diss., University of Bradford (United Kingdom), 1987.

Ladd, Everett Carll and Seymour Martin Lipset. *The Divided Academy: Professors and Politics.* New York: McGraw-Hill, 1975.

Linnell, Greg. "The Institute of Professional Librarians of Ontario: On the History and Historiography of a Professional Association." *The Canadian Journal of Information and Library Science/La Revue Canadienne des Sciences de l'Information et de Bibliothéconomie* 30, no. 3/4 (2008): 175-199.

Lockhart, Andrew. "The Canadian Library Association's Failure to Advocate for Librarians and Libraries." Progressive Librarians Guild London Chapter. http://plglondon.wordpress.com/2012/01/27/the-canadian-library-associations-failure-to-advocate-for-librarians-and-libraries/.

Lozier, G. Gregory, Kenneth P. Mortimer, and Pennsylvania State University. *Anatomy of a Collective Bargaining Election in Pennsylvania's State-Owned Colleges.* University Park, Pa: Center for the Study of Higher Education, Pennsylvania State University, 1974.

Marshall, John. "Search for Status." *Library Journal* 91 (1966): 5556-5563.

Massolin, Philip A. "Modernization and Reaction: Postwar Evolutions and the Critique of Higher Learning in English." *Journal of Canadian Studies* 36, no 2 (2001): 130.

MUFA Librarians. "Statement of the MUFA Librarians regarding the Firing of Donna Millard and Barbara McDonald April 27, 2000. http://www.mcmaster.ca/mufa/LibrarianDismissal2009.pdf.

Muller, Robert Hans. "Faculty Rank for Library Staff Members in Medium-Sized Universities and Colleges." *Bulletin of the American Association of University Professors* 39 (1953): 421-431.

Murray, James Gibson. "Power and Politics in Academe: Faculty Unionism in Ontario." Educat.D diss., University of Toronto, 1985.

Penner, Roland. "Faculty Collective Bargaining in Canada: Background, Development and Impact." *Interchange* 9, no. 3 (1978): 71-86.

Riley, Jack. Collective Bargaining in Illinois State Universities: A Study of Faculty Attitudes." PhD diss., University of Illinois at Urbana-Champaign, 1976.

Roll, Susan K. "Library & Librarian Crisis at St. Paul University." http://apuobibliolib.wordpress.com/2013/05/25/library-librarian-crisis-at-st-paul-university/.

"Salary Scale Recommended for College and University Libraries in Canada." *Feliciter* 2 (1956): 23.

Samek, Toni. "Library Workplace Speech, a Modern Irony! The Push for Library Workplace Speech." Concerned Librarians of British Columbia. http://concernedlibrarians.blogspot.ca/2009/02/library-workplace-speech.html.

Savage, Donald C. "A Historical Overview of Academic Status for Librarians." *Canadian Library Journal*, October 1982: 287-291.

Shera, Jesse H. "The Case for Faculty Status of Academic Librarians." *Educational Studies* 1, no. 2 (1970): 100.

Sloniowski, Lisa. "Who Speaks for Libraries and Librarians (1/2)." Progressive Librarians Guild Toronto Area Chapter. http://plggta.org/archives/113.

Smart, John C. "Professors and Unions: A Study of Collective Bargaining in the Academic Profession. Presented at the Annual Meeting of the American Educational Research Association." San Francisco: American Educational Research Association, April 23, 1976.

Stewart, Penni. "Academic Librarians are Under Attack." *CAUT Bulletin* 56, no. 10 (2009): May 23.

Sub-Committee on Standards and Salaries (University and College Libraries), CLA. "Report on the Standards and Salaries Committee (University Libraries)." *Feliciter* 4, no. 10 (1957): 57.

Systems and Procedures Exchange Center and Academic Collective Bargaining Information Service. *SPEC Kit on Collective Bargaining*. Washington, D.C.: Systems and Procedures Exchange Center, 1974.

Thomas, Bruce. "Status, and all That." *Library Journal* 89 (1966): 2275-2280.

Thompson Mark. *The Development of Collective Bargaining in Canadian Universities*. IIR reprint series: Proceedings of the 29th Annual Meeting of the Industrial Relations Research Association, December 1975. Vancouver: Institute of Industrial Relations, University of British Columbia, [1975].

Tudiver, Neil. *Universities for Sale: Resisting Corporate Control Over Canadian Higher Education*. A CAUT Series Title. Toronto: J. Lorimer; Canadian Association of University Teachers, 1999.

Turk, James. "History of CAUT." Canadian Association of University Teachers. http://www.caut.ca/pages.asp?page=1021.

"U of T Faculty, Librarians Vote. Librarians at the University are Eligible for Membership in the Faculty Association." *Feliciter* 23, no. 1(1977).

"University and College Libraries. Sub-Committee on Standards and Salaries. [Salaries of Librarians in Academic Institutions]." *Feliciter* 4 (1959): 57-59.

University of Toronto and UTFA. "Memo of Agreement between the Governing Council of the University of Toronto and the UTFA (1976)."

Part Two
Case Histories

A "Honey" of a Union Deal:
Gender and Status in the Labour Action of Carleton University Librarians, 1973 – 1975

Martha Attridge Bufton[1]

When the small group of Carleton University librarians began to think about becoming part of a formal bargaining unit in 1974, they knew that one option was to join a union that would include all non-managerial library employees.[2] Retired librarian, Susan Jackson, still believes that this was not a viable choice for anyone at that time, except perhaps the university librarian, Geoffrey Briggs, because "his idea was that he would have a honey union of all the library staff that he would, of course, then have some nice influence on."[3] If Jackson and her colleagues were going to unionize, their goal would be to gain more authority over the terms and conditions of work for themselves, not for the chief librarian. Plus, as former librarian, Valerie Swinton, recalls, they considered themselves to be professionals and wanted to be recognized for the "degreed" nature of their work rather than to be mistaken for employees who had "high level clerical" jobs, not substantively different from other library staff.[4] After much soul searching, the decision was made: "we discussed CUPE[5], we discussed CUASA[6], we discussed this PIPSC[7] kind of organization and decided that, really, our interests were more allied to the academic group" that belonged to the Carleton University Academic Staff Association (CUASA).[8] By the early summer of 1975, Carleton librarians had struck their own "honey" union deal. In February of that year, CUASA council members admitted librarians into the association and the following June, the Ontario Labour Relations Board (OLRB) recognized CUASA as the sole bargaining agent for Carleton academic staff and the first certified faculty association in Ontario. This was a significant change for the librarians—most of whom were women.

They had gained the legal right to bargain terms and conditions of work without joining a trade union and a forum within which to legitimately negotiate their status as academic and professional staff.

This chapter explores how and why this process of unionization unfolded as it did at Carleton University. While this collective action had its roots in the professional culture nurtured by Carleton's first university librarian, Hilda Gifford, the librarians were driven largely by a desire for equity in the workplace, something that connected them to other librarians and other workers in this era. Between 1973 and 1975, they formalized their collective efforts and successfully argued that they shared a "community of interest" with Carleton professors. Central to this success was the absence of any reference to the inequalities and lack of occupational status that resulted from the feminized nature of their work. As such, both gender and status played significant and complicated roles in the labour activism of these Canadian academic librarians.

Hilda Gifford and Early Recognition for Librarianship

Carleton University president, W.E. Beckel, wrote to retired chief librarian, Hilda Gifford, on September 10, 1982 and his message was short but sweet: members of Senate had voted to award her an honorary Doctor of Literature *honoris causa* to recognize her contribution in creating a "sophisticated" library that met the needs of a 20th century university.[9] This honour suggests that, by the second half of the 20th century, university librarianship was recognized as both academic and professional in nature. As Gifford explained (in 1959) librarians in previous centuries had acted as the gatekeepers of libraries that were designed and organized to preserve book collections that remained locked away on shelves, closed to most readers and not widely circulated, if at all.[10] She believed that this work was a "far cry" from that of the modern librarian, who was expected to develop and administer library holdings that were held on shelves kept open to readers and integral to the teaching and research of faculty and students. As contemporary librarians, Gifford and her colleagues had a duty to bring "readers and books together in the closest possible relationship."[11]

Hilda Gifford arrived at Carleton College in August, 1948,[12] with the credentials, aspirations and challenges of her generation of academic librarians. In the 1930s, she had received the standard professional training of a baccalaureate and a one-year bachelor of library science from McGill University, and was hired as the chief librarian at Carleton College. At this time, women dominated the occupation but female library heads were in the minority; they were typically found managing small libraries.[13] While she seemed to fit this occupational stereotype, in fact Gifford was an exception to the rule. Carleton was always destined to be a university and Gifford was hired by senior college administrators to ensure that the library buildings, collections and staff became the "heart of the academic community."[14] Over the next 20 years, Gifford applied professional standards to the creation of a central university library that would meet the needs of both students and faculty. The building design, based on the principle of "open shelves," would encourage independent study by making the collection accessible to readers and she was guided, in the selection of materials, by policies and procedures she developed in collaboration with faculty members[15] as well as library colleagues at other institutions, both in Canada and internationally—"whimsy was not in her book."[16] Gifford also believed that a team of trained professional staff should manage an academic library and that this group should constitute at least 30% of the total staff.[17] By 1951, the college library staff included four professional librarians and she continued to hire "buckets" of "baby librarians" even through the labour shortage of the early 1960s.[18] As a result, in 1965 she led a team of 15.5 full-time professional librarians.[19]

Consistent with the historically gendered nature of librarianship, most of the new librarian hires in the 1960s and early 1970s were women.[20] Salaries appeared comparable to those at other Canadian universities: in 1967, the national median salary for non-managerial professional librarians was $6,102 and at Carleton, it was $6,800.[21] However, this relative position masked the longstanding "double ghetto" faced by Canadian librarians.[22] Traditionally, salaries were lower than for both male-dominated occupations and some other female-dominated occupations such as teaching.[23] Within the field, women generally made less money than men and were less likely to be promoted into senior managerial positions, particularly in large libraries.[24]

Low salaries do not appear to have been a particularly contentious issue at Carleton at this time but inadequate compensation had certainly featured in discussions amongst librarians since the turn of the century.[25] So too had the division of labour between professional and non-professional library staff. For example, W.E. Henry, chief librarian at the University of Washington, summed up his frustrations on this issue in 1922: the role of library work in education was misunderstood because most library users defined librarianship narrowly in terms of the service offered at the "lending desk"—everyone was a librarian.[26] Like many of his contemporaries, Henry blamed the lack of occupational status on the predominance of women in the field. Educational reforms during the 1920s, in both Canada and the United States, were introduced to further professionalize the field and encourage more men to consider library work, but almost 50 years later, female library workers continued to outnumber their male counterparts and librarians were still sensitive to the encroachment on their occupational boundaries[27] by employees without specialist credentials. At Carleton, professional librarians had exclusive rights to managerial jobs, such as departmental head positions and specific functions, such as reference work.[28] However, there were library assistants in both the acquisitions and cataloguing sections "doing work at a high enough level that . . . they felt that they were doing librarians' work"—a belief that might have stemmed not only from the nature of the assistants' own work, but their observation that librarians were filing cards in the card catalogue.[29]

Cumulatively, these issues led to a national discussion on occupational status amongst Canadian academic librarians, one of which Gifford was undoubtedly aware, given that Carleton submitted data to the 1967 Downs study on resources in Canadian university and college libraries.[30] In its report, the committee explicitly warned university administrators that they could have difficulty recruiting professional librarians if librarians were not "recognized as an integral part of the academic ranks."[31] Descriptions of the status of librarianship at participating institutions were included in the national study and Carleton's entry clearly demonstrates that its librarians did not have full academic standing. "Librarians have faculty status socially and in academic processions, but are regarded as a professional group, eligible for study leaves, faculty club and retirement benefits. The chief librarian serves on faculty committees . . . ."[32]

Although the Carleton librarians did not have official faculty status in the mid-1960s, Gifford actively promoted a sense of collegiality to reinforce their collective identity as a team of academic librarians.[33] Some of her efforts were informal, such as the ritual of the morning break, when new librarians, like Susan Jackson, played hostess. "When I started at the library, in 1965, during the HGG era (Miss Gifford's memo signature) the junior librarians made tea for everyone."[34]

These attempts to "socialize" the largely female staff also included events held outside of the library. Librarians do not seem to have attended Gifford's famous Scottish country dancing parties but were invited to her home on other occasions. However, their gendered role at these gatherings was similar to that at the morning breaks and reflective of prevalent cultural ideas regarding the sexual division of labour that could result in even professional women playing roles at work that resembled the domestic responsibilities traditionally assigned to women, such as server or mother.[35] As Jackson wryly notes, it was a "different time."[36] "[Miss Gifford] often sponsored get-togethers at her house . . . she used to have her young librarians, her young ladies, . . . come and serve at her tea parties and her evening parties. We got to pass around the canapés."[37]

Some of Gifford's efforts, however, were more formal and, in contrast to the stereotypically feminine nature of their roles at social activities, more gender neutral. By example, she encouraged her colleagues to join professional organizations and she also explicitly suggested that the librarians engage with the campus community to "have a presence, so that we would be seen as part of the picture."[38] Gifford also advocated for institutional acknowledgement of the contribution that librarians made to the university. In particular, she insisted that the librarians be invited to the general faculty board meeting, hosted each fall by President A.D. Dunton, and that their names be listed in the university calendar, alongside those of professors.[39] These forms of recognition were significant enough that, when they were neglected, at least some librarians were openly unhappy. "And then one year we didn't get an invitation and it was a big hoo-hah. Where are our invitations? And . . . one year they dropped the librarians out of the calendar. And so that caused a big hoo-hah as well."[40]

Hilda Gifford was not a supporter of unions. In fact, she "had no interest in unionizing, she thought it was a terribly bad idea."[41] Yet, as the chief librarian, she helped nurture a culture that, to some degree, facilitated unionization at Carleton because it not only contributed to an on-going consciousness of librarianship as both professional and academic work, but also reinforced, to some degree, the gendered nature of the work. She designed and developed a library based on occupational standards that was staffed and managed by trained librarians and she also promoted the recognition of their contribution to the educational work of the university. Moreover, through her own activities, Gifford demonstrated that, by participating in professional associations, librarians had the opportunity to regulate their working conditions. However, she also hired a generation of librarians whom she socialized to be "young ladies" and whose work was not fully recognized as either academic or professional in nature. When the Carleton librarians began to organize in the mid-1970s, the contested nature of their status as academic staff might have seemed new to some organizers but, in fact, it was not.

From Association to Unionization in the 1970s

Hilda Gifford resigned from her position as chief librarian in 1968 to become the university's collections librarian and, over the next five years, challenges to the *status quo* were the order of the day as Canadians across the country were caught up in Trudeaumania, public sector labour action, and the Canadian Royal Commission on the Status of Women.[42] On the Carleton campus, both faculty and support staff members questioned their workplace status.[43] In the late 1960s, Carleton professors started pushing for binding negotiations with senior administrators, rather than merely consultations on terms and conditions of work and by 1973, library support staff had tried but failed to unionize. Carleton's professional librarians appear to have been more focused on day-to-day responsibilities than in gaining new rights and privileges. Nonetheless, they were aware, to some extent, of the debates happening amongst other librarians, both provincially and nationally. Most specifically, Canadian librarians were discussing women in librarianship, professionalization versus unionization and academic status.[44]

The professional librarians at Carleton began to join these broader conversations more actively in the early to mid-1970s and, as was true for previous generations, pay was a catalyst for action. Serials librarian, Valerie Swinton, succinctly expressed her concerns in early 1974, in a letter to Professor R.J. Crowther, the director of the Canadian Association of University Teachers (CAUT) office in Halifax. For several years, the professional librarians had been dissatisfied with their salary increases and had come to realize that there were no formal policies and procedures to define their work and thus their occupational status.[45] As a result, the "position of librarians is undefined in a number of areas . . . . [L]ibrarians are considered neither academic nor non-academic staff."[46] Over the next 18 months, this discontent led to more formal labour activism and, by June 1975, the majority of librarians had become members of a legal bargaining unit when the OLRB certified CUASA. Throughout this transition, the librarians were driven by a moral agenda: to participate in employment-related decision-making. As Swinton looks back on this period, she thinks that,

> the motivation to it was more to have greater say in making decisions for the library.... [S]ome librarians felt that... "Wouldn't it be nice if we could all sit together and talk this out and have our ideas heard as well?" Because we were a small group of professional librarians and just felt we weren't ever consulted about things.[47]

Ultimately, the journey to unionization was a quest for equity through the recognition of their status as professional, academic staff.

Between January and October 1974, the professional staff committee members pursued two key goals: to develop work standards and to identify a group with which they might align in order to "effectively represent our interests."[48] They made some early, though limited, progress in their efforts to identify appropriate terms and conditions of work. The formation of the committee coincided with the efforts of the IPLO to develop professional employment and work standards. By comparing current practices at Carleton to the IPLO standards, committee members confirmed that, in key areas, such as appointments and promotions, there were no stated and accepted standards in practice at the university.[49] For example, when Swinton became the head of the serials department, she did not compete formally with other candidates for the job.

> In those days, the way you got the job was the chief librarian chose you. ... He took me for lunch at the Faculty Club and said, "I'd like to offer you this position, I think you can do it." And I was flabbergasted because ... how old was I when I came to Carleton? I think I was 27 or 28 by that time. And I'd only had a couple of years' experience and I didn't know anything about serials other than what I'd learned in library school.[50]

The majority of professional librarians were in favour of basing their own work standards on the IPLO guidelines but the committee's attempts in July to pursue the issue of work standards with Geoffrey Briggs seem to have been unproductive.[51]

The committee was even less successful in identifying a larger group with which to form a strategic alliance. Their options included membership in the Professional Institute of the Public Service of Canada (PIPSC), the Carleton University Support Staff Association and CUPE. They began by contacting CUASA representatives in April 1974 but, although CUASA members might have seemed to be natural partners, these initial attempts to meet with faculty members were unsuccessful.[52] Fortunately, other Ontario academic librarians were more receptive to collaboration so, in September, Swinton and Elspeth Ross traveled to York University in Toronto where university and college librarians were meeting to informally discuss the issues of librarian membership in faculty associations and collective bargaining.[53]

Although described as "essentially a forum for exchange of information," there was some urgency to the discussions. Both CAUT and the Ontario Confederation of University Faculty Associations (OCUFA) were actively debating the question of collective bargaining for faculty and alternatives to trade unionism. OCUFA had already proposed a system of province-wide negotiations but only librarians at seven of the 15 Ontario universities were full members of faculty associations; if the OCUFA model was introduced, clearly some librarians, including those at Carleton, would be excluded from bargaining.[54] In addition, then CUASA president, Jill Vickers, had reported that individual OCUFA representatives had responded coolly to the idea of academic status for librarians.[55]

The "York" meeting triggered the next phase of collective action for Carleton librarians as they renewed their efforts to partner with CUASA, after Swinton and Ross returned to Ottawa. In early October, Swinton and colleague, Martin Foss, contacted Vickers, who responded almost immediately with the news that not only had the issue of librarian membership been raised at a CUASA council meeting in late September but that CUASA was "seriously" considering applying for certification to the OLRB.[56] As such, she believed that the association could potentially offer professional librarians some substantive benefits to membership—something Vickers thought would otherwise have been impossible because the association lacked "the power to negotiate salary increases and fringe benefits for our own members," let alone those in another occupational group.[57]

While Vickers recognized that other Carleton professors did not necessarily understand librarianship or the librarians' need for benefits such as study leave, she encouraged her CUASA colleagues to "explore librarians' membership"[58] and a committee was struck to address this issue within weeks of her initial contact with the librarians. Although they had established a tentative—and seemingly positive—relationship with the CUASA president, the librarians decided to formalize their relationships with each other as well as other organizations by creating the Association of Professional Librarians of Carleton University (APLCU).[59] The APLCU was "really the precursor to moving towards unionization"[60] and, over the next three months, the new association met virtually every week and two members—Swinton and Neal Brearley—were assigned to the CUASA subcommittee tasked with exploring the membership of librarians in CUASA.

The APLCU's agenda was contingent on the CUASA council decision to move forward with collective bargaining. Faculty members had been on high alert since the Carleton general faculty board meeting the first week of October. Generally, it was understood that the Canadian economy was currently in a downturn and in addition, "there was a great deal of buzz because it was very clear that the . . . provincial funding was not going to be good."[61] At the October 6 meeting, President Oliver was famously understood to announce that salary increases were impossible without unionization.[62] Moreover, many present believed that he also suggested that the only way to solve the university's current financial crisis might be to lay off faculty members, a message that Geoffrey Briggs apparently repeated in a subsequent meeting with library staff in which he observed, "that the funds were really bad, it was highly unlikely that anybody was going to get any more money, that people might be let go, and the only way to save yourself was to bring political pressure to bear."[63]

At a meeting in late November, 80 to 90 CUASA members voted to "endorse collective bargaining in principle" and this support was sufficient for the CUASA council to launch an official certification drive.[64]

The librarians realized that they were being called upon "sooner than we would like to make a decision about faculty association membership and collective bargaining"[65] and they began to gather the information and support they needed to move forward as a group. In addition to promoting two CUASA educational sessions, to be held in January 1975, members of the APLCU arranged a series of noontime information sessions for librarians on collective bargaining, featuring representatives from key interest groups that could provide an alternative to CUASA, including CAUT and CUPE. At this time, organizers from both CAUT and CUPE were vying to represent faculty members as well as librarians in labour negotiations. Frances Montgomery still has the impression that the lunch hour sessions simply confirmed what the librarians already believed: they were more naturally aligned with professors than with non-academic staff.[66] On February 3, the CUASA sub-committee on librarian membership supported both academic status for librarians and their membership in the association. Eleven days later, the CUASA council voted to amend its constitution to define members as "all academic staff," including librarians, and at a special APLCU general meeting on February 24, the majority of librarians voted for collective bargaining and chose CUASA as their preferred bargaining agent.[67]

The CUASA council promptly applied for certification to the OLRB.[68] On April 4, the Board gave conditional approval to the application and all but five of the librarian positions were included in the overall bargaining unit.[69] However, the OLRB had a number of outstanding issues to resolve before it issued the final certificate to CUASA and made the unprecedented decision to require a representation vote, even though more than the required number of faculty members had already signed cards indicating their support for CUASA as the bargaining agent. This support for CUASA remained and by the time the vote was held on April 14, 27 librarians had voluntarily chosen to join the faculty association and were amongst the 79.8% of CUASA members who voted in favour of CUASA as the designated bargaining agent.[70] On June 18, the Board certified CUASA as the legal and sole bargaining agent for academic staff at Carleton and while union membership did not make academic status for librarians inevitable, they were now in the legal position to negotiate this standing.

Overcoming Resistance

When Valerie Swinton reflects on the process of unionization, she realizes that it was not as peaceful as it seemed at the time. "I think I was a real Pollyanna .... I kind of was skipping around in my little pink dress and not paying attention to the mood of the day and what was going on. Clearly, there was some opposition in the library and on the campus, among the campus administrators."[71]

Certainly, there were individual managers or administrators on campus who disapproved of CUASA's certification drive and Jackson still thinks that Geoffrey Briggs seemed "very unhappy" when the librarians opted to join.[72] However, Swinton's experience was not so surprising, given that the official reactions were generally understated during the certification drive. Although senior administrators privately considered the "case for excluding library staff" from the faculty bargaining unit[73], they are remembered as not "so much actively stating it [opposition] as sort of more in sorrow .... 'Do you really know what you're doing' kind of tones"[74] and President Oliver openly expressed relief when unionization was accomplished "without the spirit of acrimony."[75] Moreover, the librarians seem to have enjoyed a significant degree of solidarity, unlike both Carleton faculty and support staff, who were experiencing divisive differences in opinion on the appropriateness of unionization within their respective groups. Some faculty members, however, still questioned whether a community of interest existed between themselves and their professional colleagues in the library and to gain sufficient support for their inclusion in CUASA, the librarians had to convince the association's council members that the two groups had substantive shared interests. To do so, they argued that librarianship was educational in nature and that they needed to belong to a large, powerful group in order to gain occupational status. They also suppressed any reference to the gendered occupational inequalities i.e., collective bargaining was never an issue of the status of women, despite the fact that a key ally, CUASA President, Jill Vickers, believed that female librarians and faculty had a common cause because, as women, they had experienced "some really nasty stuff."[76]

Former chief librarian, Geoffrey Briggs, still has very decided views on unionization at Carleton. He explains "the advent of unions"—both CUASA and the Carleton University Support Staff Association—in terms of situational and economic factors.[77] In Briggs' opinion, unions resulted from "Carleton's financial position and the way it was handled by [President] Michael Oliver, the growing acceptance of unionization in North American universities, and in the case of the Library the realisation that forming a union with the faculty offered the opportunity of a more formal career structure and improved salaries."[78] Briggs does not remember having any real objection to unionization and certainly there is no evidence that he tried to obstruct the activities of either the Professional Staff Committee or the APLCU.[79] However, he seems to have questioned the premise of academic status and the right of librarians to participate in management decisions, which he still considers as an intrusion into the "sphere" of the university librarian.[80] It is unclear whether he articulated his views in this way during the certification campaign although Jackson's lingering impression is that he would have been more comfortable negotiating with a single bargaining unit, such as those being formed at Canadian public libraries. Plus, she wonders at the timing of the February 1975 promotion of a senior librarian into a managerial position that soon after was excluded from the bargaining unit.[81]

Perhaps unexpectedly, Valerie Swinton and the other APLCU council members seemed to have had continuing support from the majority of librarians. Early American library union organizers faced stiff resistance from librarians and historically Canadian librarians were consistently more interested in professionalization than unionization.[82] Public library librarians only began to unionize extensively in the late 1960s, later than their American counterparts, with those in academic libraries trailing them.[83] Certainly there were librarians at Carleton who openly opposed collective bargaining and seem to have been concerned about the "lack of harmony, and conflict with Mr. Briggs."[84] Such protest was minimal, however, and at the time that CUASA applied for certification, the APLCU represented more than 50% of the professional staff.

If librarians did not experience significant dissent from within their ranks or opposition from university administrators, they certainly knew that resistance could come from Carleton professors, given that, generally, Canadian faculty members were not convinced that librarianship was scholarly in nature.[85] To overcome this opposition, the APLCU representatives on the CUASA sub-committee had to convince the CUASA council that they shared a community of interest with librarians. The librarians' official position on faculty status and membership in CUASA was contained in a submission made to the association's membership sub-committee, a group that included two faculty members and the two librarians. Unlike other currently available documents on academic status that could be long and detailed,[86] Swinton's and Brearley's statement was brief and focused on three key points: the educational nature of their work; the shared interests of librarians and faculty; and the need for a powerful ally.[87] They argued that librarianship could not be thought of simply as the provision of an "add on" service or routine, clerical work. Instead, librarians were integral to teaching and research at the university and were entitled to five sets of rights and responsibilities: participation in university and library governance; economic benefits; conditions of employment; academic freedom; study leave and access to research funds.[88]

CUASA members at large may not have acknowledged the shared occupational interests between themselves and the librarians but there were members of the CUASA council who did and were influential allies prior to the final membership vote. Professor Andrew Brook was one of the two faculty representatives on the membership sub-committee. He understood the librarians' perception that "they weren't getting a very good deal out of the university;" it made sense that they needed greater input into their terms and conditions of work because "the librarians had no governance documents at all. I mean their careers were run at the whim and fancy of the university librarian."[89]

Arguably, however, the most powerful supporter was CUASA's president, Jill Vickers, who, according to Swinton, "encouraged us, included us and persuaded the faculty association that it was a good fit for us to be part of their organization."[90] Vickers arrived at Carleton in 1969, not only philosophically committed to associations but also sensitive to the issues being raised at "the height of the women's movement."[91] Some of her own experiences as a young, female faculty member were decidedly unpleasant and her concerns about campus-wide "nasty" problems, such as sexual harassment, a lack of daycare and maternity leave aligned her with the librarians—"because the librarians were mostly women."[92]

Gendered inequalities were fundamental yet difficult to articulate in the context of unionization. Brearley and Swinton made no reference to occupational inequities or the status of women, even though some Carleton librarians, such as Swinton, did frame workplace issues in terms of inequality, at least off the record: "Oh, we all read Germaine Greer and all the seminal feminist stuff. And we ... were talking about things like 99% of the employees in libraries are female but 90%, 99% of the leaders in libraries are male and how fair is that?"[93] Jill Vickers is still not surprised that gender was omitted from the unionization campaign. Although women from academic units across campus were motivated to get heavily involved in the association as a result of "the gender agenda," they also realized that it had to remain a "sub-agendum," as it would not have been a mobilizer for most faculty members, the majority of whom were men.[94]

Instead of raising issues of daycare and lower starting salaries for women, CUASA organizers ran a successful certification campaign on the premise that professors needed "contractual rules of the game" to protect themselves, given that jobs were being threatened by a president "who was clearly going to close departments" in a period of financial stringency.[95] Even engineering and economics professors, who were very outspoken in their opposition to unionization, were mobilized by the idea of "rule of law."[96] By avoiding these gender issues in their position statement, therefore, Swinton and Brearley were simply being consistent with the strategic approach of the broader unionization campaign. They were also acknowledging the unspoken understanding that when some professors questioned the community of interest with librarians, they were really asking "how can women's work be the equivalent of men's work?"

At the beginning of February, the CUASA sub-committee formally approved Swinton's and Brearley's submission and submitted its final report to the CUASA council within weeks.[97] In their review, committee members stated that they found no "base-level disagreements" between the ambitions of the professors and librarians—in fact, "these desires seem consistent with—indeed, complementary to—the aims of CUASA."[98] On the strength of these findings and with little to no fanfare, the CUASA council voted to admit librarians into the association less than six weeks after the committee had begun its work.

Conclusion

The minutes of the APLCU meeting on Friday, July 11, 1975 show that "J. King and F. Montgomery are to prepare the press release to publicize our unionized status."[99] The OLRB had made its final ruling in mid-June and by the time the press release went out, association members were already in discussions with Jill Vickers and other CUASA representatives on initial bargaining positions.[100] Formal talks with the University's negotiating team began mid-July and over the next four months, the librarians "got busy" writing their own bargaining positions on key terms and conditions of work, such as salaries, appointments, promotions, and rankings.[101] Their goal was "to create language that would provide a reasonably equitable and transparent set of processes under which peoples' working lives would be regulated . . . . What we discovered was that there was no transparency . . . . It was total murk."[102]

If resistance seemed insignificant prior to certification, the librarians definitely faced opposition during the first round of collective bargaining. CUASA negotiators had difficulty reaching agreement with "the university on the librarians," and the issue of salary levels was a key sticking point.[103] Eventually, however, they reached a settlement that legally encoded their status as academic staff and provided "radical" improvements to their working conditions and the contractual language to align themselves with faculty, while separating them from other library staff.[104] However, the designation of librarians as academic staff did not necessarily confer full faculty status, particularly if that standing was measured by participation in university governance as efforts to have librarians elected to the University's Senate were rebuffed.[105]

A 1975 study of public library formation in the United States concluded that unionization was intended "to enhance the 'professional' status of the job in order to achieve status equivalent with expectations . . . . [T]here is no apparent rejection of administrative authority or attempt to displace the administrative hierarchy."[106] This analysis seems to be compatible with the experiences of librarians at Carleton University. As professionals, they were dissatisfied with their currently low occupational status, as reflected by inequitable working conditions as well as a lack of recognition for their expertise and contributions to university teaching and research. They did not want to change the structure of institutional governance; they hoped to participate more fully in both academic and library decision-making. Moreover, they did not hesitate to engage in labour activism, which is consistent with the further finding that female employees were not "a crucial obstacle to unionization."[107]

Sex, however, is not gender. Although the librarians did not openly acknowledge the feminization of their occupation and the double ghetto reality of low wages and the overabundance of male leaders, their status was clearly influenced by traditional sex roles. These cultural roles undoubtedly underpinned the resistance of some male faculty members to the idea that they shared a community of interest with librarians—no matter how politely this opposition was expressed—as well as the decision to avoid any reference to gendered inequities in the campaign to gain membership in CUASA. Professionalization facilitated the ability to regulate occupational boundaries, to some degree, but failed to break through these cultural barriers. Unionization too did not immediately result in an "eruptive" break in these attitudes—according to Jill Vickers, female professors were still expected to be able to type in the late 1970s and academia has persisted in being a "chilly climate" for women—but, over time, collective bargaining did produce improvements in working conditions.[108] The United Nations declared 1975 International Women's Year as part of its strategy to put an "end to discrimination and . . . increase . . . support for women's full and equal participation."[109] It is fitting that both female librarians and professors at Carleton succeeded in their collective efforts that year to introduce more equitable labour practices into their workplace—these women really did strike a "honey" of a deal.

Bibliography

Armstrong, Pat and Hugh Armstrong. *The Double Ghetto. Canadian Women and Their Segregated Work*. Don Mills, Ontario: Oxford University Press, 1978.

Association of Professional Librarians of Carleton University. (1974). Minutes. December 4.

Association of Professional Librarians of Carleton University. (1975). Minutes. March 14. April 15. April 25. July 11.

Association of Professional Librarians of Carleton University. Collective Bargaining Committee. *Report*. February 1975.

Beckel, W.E. Letter to Hilda G. Gifford. September 10, 1982.

Bishop, Olga B. *The Use of Professional Staff in Libraries: A Review 1923 –1971, CLA Occasional Paper No. 81*. Ottawa: Canadian Library Association, 1973.

Board of Governors, Ottawa Association for the Advancement of Learning (Carleton College) (June 2, 1958). http://www6.carleton.ca/records/ccms/wp-content/ccms-files/OAAL-INC-Carleton-College-BOG-Minutes-1948-06-0238S.pdf.

Brearley, Neil and Valerie McDougall. *Librarians and CUASA: A Statement to the Sub-Committee Exploring the Membership of Librarians in CUASA*. 1975.

Briggs, Geoffrey. E-mail to the author. November 1, 2011.

Brook, Andrew. Interview with the author. April 17, 2011.

Brook, J.A., B. Wand, V. McDougall, and N. Brearley. *CUASA Report of the Sub-Committee on Membership of Librarians* (n.d.).

Bruce, Lorne. "Professionalization, Gender and Librarianship in Ontario, 1920 – 1975." *Library and Information History* 28, no. 2 (2012), 117-134.

Bureau of Public Personnel Administration. *Proposed Classification and Compensation Plans for Library Positions. Report of the Bureau of Public Personnel Administration to the Committee on the Classification of Library Personnel of the American Library Association*. Washington, D.C.: Bureau of Public Personnel Administration, 1927.

Canadian Association of College and University Libraries. *Guide to Canadian University Library Standards. Report of the University Library Standards Committee of the Canadian Association of College and University Libraries 1961–1964*. 1965.

Canadian Library Association. *Salary Scales Recommended for Public Libraries, College and University Libraries in Canada*. Victoria: Canadian Library Association, 1957.

Case for Excluding Library Staff from Bargaining Unit, March 3, 1975, Office of the President Fonds, Acc. # 1997-21, PRES-232-12, Collective Bargaining—CUASA Correspondence, Part I. Carleton University Corporate Archives, Ottawa, Ontario. 1975.

Cheda, Sherrill. "That Special Little Mechanism." *Canadian Library Journal* 31, no. 5 (1974), 422–432.

Cheda, Sherrill, Linda Fischer, Mary Ann Wasylycia-Coe, and Phyllis Yaffe. "Salary Differentials of Female and Male Librarians in Canada." *Emergency Librarian* 5, no. 3 (Jan./Feb. 1978), 3–13.

The Chilly Collective, eds. *Breaking Anonymity. The Chilly Climate for Women Faculty*. Waterloo, Ontario: Wilfrid Laurier University Press, 1995.

"Council Summary". *CUASA News* 5, no. 1 (October 1974).

Downs, Robert B. *Resources of Canadian Academic Research Libraries*. Ottawa: Association of Universities and Colleges of Canada, 1967.

Dunham, Mabel. *Library Work as a Profession for Canadian Women*. Presidential address. Ontario Library Association Fonds F1195, MU 2246, B287359. Archives of Ontario, Toronto, Ontario. 1920.

Editorial. *American Library Journal* 1, no. 1 (1876), 12.

Euler, Hon. W.D. Minister of Trade and Commerce. *Survey of Canadian Libraries. Being Part III of the Biennial Survey of Education in Canada, 1936–1938*. Ottawa: J.O. Patenaude, I.S.O. (1939).

Evans, Cal. *Report on York Meeting* (n.d.). In the author's possession.

Evans, Calvin D. "Librarians and CAUT: Historical Overview and Future Directions." *CAUT Bulletin, Special Report*, (March 1976), 12–13.

Evans, Calvin D. and Tom Eadie. "AALO. Elaboration of the Fourteen Points in Answering the Question "What is it we want as University Librarians?" in the author's possession, (n.d.).

Farr, David. Unpublished tribute to Hilda Gifford. University Communications, A294 2004-17 Hilda Gifford File. Carleton University Library Archives, Ottawa, Ontario. 2004.

Foss, Martin. Memorandum to Geoffrey Briggs. July 15, 1974. In the author's possession.

Garrison, Dee. *Apostles of Culture: The Public Librarian and American Society, 1876–1920*. New York: Free Press, 1979.

Gifford, Hilda. "Function and the Library Building." *Royal Architectural Institute of Canada Journal* 36, no. 4 (1959), 104–105.

Guyton, Theodore. L. *Unionization: The Viewpoint of Librarians*. Chicago: American Library Association, 1975.

Henry, W.E. "Recruiting for College and University Libraries." *Bulletin of the American Library Association, Papers and Proceedings of the Forty-Fourth Annual Meeting of the American Library Association* 16, no. 4 (July 1922), 124–125.

Howe, C.D. Minister of Trade and Commerce. *Libraries in Canada, 1944 –1946. Being Part III of the Biennial Survey of Education in Canada, 1944 –1946*. Ottawa: Edmond Cloutier, Printer to the King's Most Excellent Majesty, Controller of Stationary. (1946).

Howe, Hon. C.D. Minister of Trade and Commerce. *Survey of Libraries 1948 –1950. Part III of the biennial survey of Education in Canada, 1948 –1950*. Ottawa: Edmond Cloutier, Queen's Printer and Controller of the Stationary, 1952.

Hubbard, Katherine. E-mail from Development and Alumni, McGill University to the author. April 25, 2012.

Hughesman, Jack. *Union Representative Looks at Librarians*. Canadian Library Association Conference 1973 Proceedings. 1973.

Jackson, Susan. E-mail to the author. November 15, 2012.

Jackson, Susan. Interview with the author. April 8, 2011.

Jackson, Susan and Montgomery, Frances. Interview with the author. April 24, 2012.

Jones, Ben. Honorary Degree Citation for Hilda Gifford. Public Relations and Information Services fonds, University Communications, ACC 1996—17 PINFO-28 Convocation Fall 1982. Carleton University Library Archives, Ottawa, Ontario. 1982.

Linnell, Greg. "The Institute of Professional Librarians in Ontario: On the History and Historiography of a Professional Association. 2008. http://eprints.rclis.org/12214/, accessed July 1, 2012.

McEown, Don. Interview with the author. March 14, 2011.

McDougall, Valerie. Letter to Professor R.H. Crowther, Canadian Association of University Teachers. May 9, 1974. In the author's possession.

Milner, Nina. "*Lady Librarian*": *The Feminization of Librarianship in Canada, 1880 – 1920*." Master's thesis, University of Ottawa, 1992.

Montgomery, Frances. Interview with the author. June 11, 2011.

Mudge, Charlotte R. "Collective Bargaining of Librarians in Canada: Issues and Concerns." *Argus* 11, no. 3/4 (1982), 91–96.

Nelson, William H. *The Search for Faculty Power. The History of the University of Toronto Faculty Association 1942 – 1992*. Toronto: The University of Toronto Faculty Association and Canadian Scholars' Press, 1993.

Oliver, Michael K. "Forum". *This Week Times Two. Special Edition*. Ottawa, Carleton University (April 10, 1975).

Professional Staff Committee. Carleton University Library. *York University Meeting of University and College Librarians in Ontario*. Ottawa, September, 1974. In the author's possession.

Public Relations and Information Services fonds, Hilda Gifford File, University Communications, ACC 1996-17 Fall Convocation, November 7, 1982. Carleton University Library Archives, Ottawa, Ontario. 1982.

Rastin, Sandra. "Organizing Tactics in a Faculty Unionization Drive in a Canadian University." *Labor Studies Journal* 25, no. 2 (2000), 99–119.

Sangster, Joan. *Transforming Labour. Women and Work in Postwar Canada*, Toronto, Buffalo, London: University of Toronto Press, 2010.

Shanley, Catherine. "The Library Employees' Union of Greater New York, 1917 –1929." *Libraries and Culture* 30, no. 3 (1995), 235–264.

Shearer, Kenneth D. and Ray L. Carpenter. "Public Library Support and Salaries in the Seventies." *Library Journal* 101, no. 6 (1976), 777–783.

Spencer Garry, Lorraine and Carl G. Garry, eds. *Canadian Libraries in Their Changing Environment*, Toronto: York University, The Centre for Continuing Education, 1977.

Swinton, Valerie. Interview with the author. May 30, 2011.

Systems and Procedures Exchange Centre. Association of Research Libraries. *Paraprofessionals in ARL Libraries*. SPEC Flyer, 21. 1975.

United Nations. "WomenWatch. Information and Resources on Gender Equality and Empowerment of Women. History of International Women's Day." 2013. http://www.un.org/womenwatch/feature/iwd/history.html.

Van de Graaff, John H., Burton R. Clark, Dorotea Furth, Dietrich Goldschmidt, and Wheeler, Donald F. *Academic Power. Patterns of Authority in Seven National Systems of Higher Education*. New York: Praeger Publishers, 1978.

Vickers, Jill. Interview with the author. May 4, 2011.

Vickers, Jill. Letter to Martin Foss and Valerie McDougall. October 10, 1974. In the author's possession.

Vickers, Jill McCalla, and June Adam. *But Can You Type? Canadian Universities and the Status of Women*. Toronto: Clarke, Irwin & Company, 1977.

Academic Librarianship:
The Quest for Rights and Recognition at the University of Toronto[1]

Harriet M. Sonne de Torrens[2]

Introduction

The dedication of librarians at the University of Toronto Libraries (UTL) was matched by a determination to obtain professional and academic rights,[3] a quest that can be traced back to the early twentieth century when librarianship shifted from a male, to a chiefly female, profession. The 1960s and 1970s proved to be a pivotal period for academic librarians at the University of Toronto (U of T). What transpired during these two decades at U of T was, to some degree, conditioned by external developments in the profession, the rise of feminism and the growth of publically funded graduate programs in Ontario's post-secondary institutions, as well as internal developments, such as the rapid expansion of the UTL system and the librarians' growing awareness that they were professional academics.[4] In this historical narrative, the pivotal event, known as the *Reference Revolution* of 1974, marked a turning point and signalled not just the end of an era for the Chief Librarian, Robert H. Blackburn, but a new epoch for librarians at U of T[5] because shortly thereafter, in 1974-1975, they joined the University of Toronto Faculty Association (UTFA).[6] The courageous actions of a few benefited many. In a more or less chronological sequence, this chapter is an examination of the key events that preceded the *Reference Revolution* and the consequences of this pivotal moment in the history of librarianship at U of T. In reality, however, many of the issues in this chronological overview did not occur in sequential isolation but retained close connections to the past, often overlapping each other and taking on different guises through this 20 year period.

The labour history of academic librarians at U of T has remained a relatively silent partner in the published histories of the UTL, U of T and the affiliated colleges.[7] In some respects, this is surprising, given that U of T is one of the largest and oldest post-secondary institutions in Canada (established in 1849) with a library collection that today rivals the major Ivy League collections in North America.[8] In addition, the UTL system has consistently employed the largest number of librarians compared to other post-secondary institutions in Canada. The labour history of academic librarianship at U of T is far from straightforward and may well have discouraged those considering such an undertaking. Today, the UTL system consists of 43 libraries at a tri-campus University (St. George, Mississauga and Scarborough), all with individual histories and unique relationships with the central UTL system. From another perspective, however, history's silence is not surprising, given the gender biases associated with a profession that has employed primarily women.[9] Though history has been silent, U of T librarians have not—nor have the faculty who fought on their behalf.

In the reconstruction of this historical overview, a range of sources, such as oral memories, interviews, newsletters and archival documents have been assembled to provide readers with the fullest possible view of the milieu in which change became inevitable.[10] A comprehensive analysis of academic librarianship at U of T in its full complexity and scope, however, is beyond the confines of this chapter. But it is hoped that this contribution will offer an introduction to the primary sources and key events, encouraging others to pursue further studies on this subject.

Gender discrimination in the librarian profession at U of T has deep roots in the labour history of women, as well as in the historical development of the educational programs for the profession.[11] Except for senior administrators, librarians employed in the U of T libraries have been predominantly women since the early twentieth century.[12] Even in recent times (1991 to 2009), 74% of librarians holding full-time positions were female and 84% of part-time librarian positions (from 1992 to 2009) were female.[13] But this was not always the case. In the nineteenth century, academic librarianship was a male dominated profession connected with senior faculty members at U of T, beginning with John McCaul, Vice-President of King's College, who was confirmed as the first librarian, part-time, in 1843. This reflected similar trends in the United States and a long-standing historical tradition in European countries.[14] In 1849, with the new University Act, the President of U of T was the Librarian and had full custody of the library.[15] In this initial phase, the responsibilities of librarianship were assigned to the senior faculty and administrators of the institution, who were recognized as scholar-librarians, because the library was recognized as a pivotal player in the growth and development of the institution.[16] This would change with the introduction of women into the profession.

The shift from a chiefly male, to a predominantly female profession began in the late 1800s when women were "given permission"[17] to work as apprentices under the Librarian, Hugh H. Hornby (1892-1923), shortly after his presidential address before the Ontario Library Association in 1903, when he advocated for more "special training" for cataloguers.[18] Additional, skilled personnel were required to attend to the daily cataloguing and maintenance of growing collections.[19] Grace Hunter, president of the Women's Literary Society and later a member of her father's law firm, worked under the Librarian in the summer of 1898.[20] Mabel Chown (BA, 1900) was also an "unpaid assistant" who later became the first President of the University Women's Club of Toronto.[21] Thus commenced the marginalization of women, a labour trend that would continue through until the mid-1970s and early 1980s.

The formal education for librarians at U of T started when the Ontario Department of Education, in Toronto, began offering courses in the history of librarianship and cataloguing. The success of this early initiative led the apprentice of Hugh H. Hornby, Winifred Barnstead, to become the Director of the University's first Library School in 1928,[22] which, at that time, came under the auspices of the Ontario College of Education.[23] The U of T Library School, one of only a few in Canada, would remain under the Department of Education until the Master's Program was established as the minimum requirement for professional librarians in 1969-1970, at which time, the Library School at U of T came under the responsibility of the University proper. With the establishment of formal educational programs, there was a rapid feminization of the profession.[24]

Internal gender policies encouraged attitudes which restricted female faculty and librarians from seeking long-term careers at the University well into the 1950s and, in the case of librarians, added to the derogatory stereotypes that developed about librarians being prim and bespeckled spinsters.[25] In the World War II period, the President's Reports of 1939-1940 and 1948-1949 described the profession of librarianship as one of the "feminine professions,"[26] rather than one of the "masculine professions." Librarianship was understood to be one of the "four classic female professions—education, library science, social work and public health,"[27] which were devoted to service and the moral betterment of society. The conceptual theories of what constituted the gendered professions restricted theoretical and academic knowledge to the masculine professions and skills to the feminine professions.[28] Further de-professionalization of librarianship occurred in 1931, when the U of T's Board of Governors approved a policy that stated, "it was undesirable to employ married women in the University unless the Board members are satisfied in individual cases that such persons require to earn money in the support of their families."[29] From today's perspective, one can understand how such a policy would have had a negative impact on women working as professors or academic librarians, either from the perspective of not marrying or refusing to submit the financial evidence regarding the need to continue to work. There was resistance, but no effective change to the policy. In 1931, Mabel Chown, library apprentice of Hugh H. Hornby, sent a letter to President Robert Falconer, objecting to the University's decision to approve a policy of not hiring married women in 1931.[30]

In 1936, U of T offered an accredited undergraduate degree program in library science. The instructors in the new program included Bertha Bassam, Florence Murray, and Robert H. Blackburn, who was appointed Chief Librarian, in 1954.[31] In 1959, the Canadian Library Association issued its "Professional Qualifications for Librarians in Canada," which required a Bachelor of Library Science Degree (BLS), in Canada or a Master of Library Science Degree (MLS), in the United States. By the 1960s and 1970s, the collective memory of what constituted a "feminine" versus "masculine" profession may have faded, but the student enrolment remained predominately female, averaging more than 80%. For example, in 1964-1965, there were 21 male students out of an enrolment of 115 and, in 1971-1972, there were 36 male students out of an enrollment of 312. In 1979, in the U of T Library Studies Program, 81 students were women and only 15 were men.[32]

By the 1960s and 1970s, the gender biases associated with the "feminine profession" had infiltrated the administrative structure of the library system and had resulted in salary and promotion inequities which were not to be addressed until Carol Moore became the Chief Librarian (1986-2011)[33] and UTFA became involved in negotiating salary parity for the librarians in the mid-1980s.[34] Unlike the public library system, the discrimination against librarians has historically been more serious in university settings.[35] From 1843 to 1982, the University Librarians, Acting Chief Librarians and senior administrators were nearly always men.[36] It was precisely these unspoken biases and escalating inequities that would erupt in the 1970s.[37] The first woman director of the UTL system was Marilyn Sharrow (July 1982 - June 1985), followed by Carol Moore (July 1986 - June 2011), who was one of the librarians involved in the *Reference Revolution* in 1974.

Graduate Studies and Academic Librarianship

The growth of provincially-funded graduate studies in the 1960s had a major impact on changes in the formal education of librarians and consequently, began to define academic librarianship at the U of T.[38] In 1964, the province-wide shortage of librarians prompted the formation of the *Ontario University Presidents' Research Committee* to form a subcommittee to review the educational qualifications for academic librarians and the future needs of post-secondary institutions, given the increasing student enrolment and numerous new graduate programs.[39] The subcommittee's brief, dated February 5, 1964, *The Supply of Librarians: A Report to the Presidents of the Provincially Assisted Universities of Ontario from the Presidents' Research Committee* stated, "For the expansion programme of the universities of Ontario, an adequate supply of librarians is second only in importance to an adequate supply of teaching staff."[40] The committee calculated that an additional 400 librarians would be needed for the Ontario universities to address the new graduate programs. In addition, it was recognized that major revisions to the education of librarians needed to be made if librarians were to meet the new demands and responsibilities determined by the growth of specialized graduate programs.

There was a general acknowledgement that the current library school programs would be unable to provide the training needed with the advancement of higher education and this was a particular concern for U of T, whose plans for expansion included a new research library. The committee recommended that an urgent request be made to the provincial government for special support to accelerate the training of librarians and that the university presidents authorize a study of the education of librarians, which would include graduate work and research in the field of library science. Furthermore, it was recognized that diploma courses for library assistants were needed in institutes of technology.[41]

In the *Graduate Studies in the University of Toronto: Report of the President's Committee on the School of Graduate Studies 1964-1965*, the U of T committee asserted the importance of the "University of Toronto Library for advanced study and research in a number of fields"[42] and acknowledged that the days of faculty assisting in the development of collections was no longer a viable or practical option.[43] This shift, from faculty involvement to librarians assuming full responsibility for the collections and resources, accentuated the need for higher degrees. Simultaneously, it fueled the large scale plans for expanding the U of T library system. The book budget had more than doubled with the rise of graduate programs from $272,000, in 1961-1962, to $734,000, in 1964-1965.[44]

In the process of reviewing faculty needs, the U of T Presidential Committee on the School of Graduate Studies acknowledged that there were serious internal administrative problems in the existing library system as well as a need to recognize librarians as professionals. "There has been and there may yet be a most serious library staffing problem" and the "annual turnover of staff in the library is so high that it seems to us extraordinary that the system has worked as well as it has."[45] The *Annual Reports* by the Chief Librarian, from 1965 to 1972, confirm that the turnover of both librarians and support staff were high. After the unionization of the support staff in 1969, the turnover for this group declined, whereas the turnover for librarians ranged anywhere from 9.8% to 16% in any single year.[46] In the *Report of the President's Committee on the School of Graduate Studies 1964-1965*, it was noted that the low salaries of librarians and equating librarians with non-academic staff were destructive to the overall health of the library system. They recommended that professionally-trained librarians be remunerated appropriately to reflect their responsibilities and education:

> The Committee therefore takes the most serious view of the salary question for the library staff [librarians]. The present system of relating such salaries to the non-academic salary scales prevailing throughout the University is destructive of all efforts to improve the quality of service in the

University of Toronto library. It is our most urgent recommendation that this practice cease at once. We propose that this University recognize the reality of this aspect of the complex overall library problem by establishing in its pay scales a category entirely separate from that of other non-academic staff, for professional librarians. If this is not done, the personnel problem will quickly begin to dictate the level of library services in an ever more discouraging manner.[47]

The same report noted that "the University will never, in the final analysis, be more distinguished than its library resources permit"[48] and that "the present system of relying for the most part upon professorial selection [in collection development] is faulty."[49] As an interim step, the committee urged that trained bibliographers be appointed in the library to work with the departments requiring collection development. Moreover, there was a growing recognition that the U of T library required research scholars to actively work on the research collections: "It may well be that in some more exotic areas the bibliographer and the scholar will be one and the same person."[50] These suggestions, though not overly promoted, proved to be a major shift in emphasis that differentiated the needs of librarianship in academia from those working in other areas of librarianship. Gradually, the additional acquisition of graduate degrees in specialized areas with language skills and a professional MLS degree proved to be a winning combination for many, who have built the invaluable collections in the U of T libraries.

A key figure in the changes initiated at U of T was Brian Land, Director of the University of Toronto Library School (1964-1973), and long-time participant in the provincial organization, called the *Institute of Professional Librarians of Ontario* (IPLO, 1954-1975).[51] The active work of the IPLO had raised the standards and minimum requirements for librarians in Ontario. Many U of T librarians in the 1960s and early 1970s were committed and active members of the IPLO, a unique period in the provincial history of librarianship before collective agreements became the norm at libraries, schools and in post-secondary institutions.[52] In 1964, Brian Land began to implement changes in the institution's programming, which would result in a series of major turning points for the profession:

- In 1965, the historical relationship between the U of T Library School and the provincial Department of Education ceased and the U of T Senate established and assumed full responsibility for the school;[53]
- The accreditation of a new graduate program, the Master of Library Science (MLS), at U of T, by the American Library Association, resulted in the first master's degree being awarded in 1970; and
- The introduction of a doctoral program in library science, in 1970, with the first degrees awarded in 1974.[54]

During this period, many U of T librarians returned to school to obtain the MLS, in addition to their earlier Bachelor degrees or other degrees they had acquired, recognizing the need to upgrade their qualifications to meet the new standards.[55] The MLS reinforced the professional status of librarians, similar to what was happening in teaching, nursing and other professions, in this period. Furthermore, the Association of College and Research Libraries' (ACRL) push for new policies concerning appointments, promotion and tenure for academic librarians in 1973-1974, and its "Model Statement of Criteria and Procedures for Appointment, Promotion in Academic Rank and Tenure for College and University Librarians" reinforced efforts to assert the academic status of librarianship in Canada and was referred to in the report that the U of T librarians prepared for the Chief Librarian after the *Reference Revolution*, in 1974.

Organizing Librarians and LAUT

The concerns expressed in the *Graduate Studies in the University of Toronto: Report of the President's Committee on the School of Graduate Studies 1964-1965* for the proper remuneration of librarians and the need for internal reform in the UTL system were quickly forgotten by administrators once plans for a new research library were initiated in the late 1960s. As a result, internal unrest escalated. Support staff in the library unionized and were certified by CUPE Local 1230, in June 1969. Six months later, the Librarians' Association of the University of Toronto (LAUT) was formed to provide a voice for the librarians. This was the first organized attempt by librarians to address their professional concerns. Cloaked in secrecy, personal invitations were extended by Richard Landon[56] and Jack Cain to like-minded librarians to meet at Hart House and in private homes, after work hours, over a period of many months to discuss the problems in the library and the need for a professional association.[57] The covert actions were essential, as there was concern that an open call would evoke the wrath of the administration (as indeed happened, once LAUT was publically announced[58]) and dissuade the contributions of interested librarians. The clandestine meetings were called to discuss the formation of LAUT, an entity which they hoped would address professional issues, as well as the broader, mounting internal library issues. The first public meeting was held on September 18, 1969. The archival correspondence between Robert H. Blackburn and James Feeley, one of the founding members of LAUT, shows that LAUT was under pressure to acquire "pre-approval" before holding its meetings as its existence made the Chief Librarian uneasy. The pressure for the Chief Librarian's pre-approval to hold meetings and conduct surveys continued, as can be seen in the April 1974 survey, undertaken by LAUT. The opening statement says ". . . the study is being done, with the approval of the Chief Librarian, in order to assist the recently formed Joint Business Affairs/Internal Affairs Task Force on Employment Conditions of Non-Academic Female Staff." Ultimately, the close ties with administration weakened LAUT's ability to address some of the more serious issues facing the library and librarians.

The first executive of LAUT consisted of James Feeley (President), Richard Landon (Vice-President), Gail Wilson (Treasurer), and Barbara Cunningham (Secretary).[59] In this initial phase, gender biases prevailed even among those who were leading LAUT; it would not be until the mid-1970s when women would begin to assume leadership roles in LAUT. Three committees were struck: the *Ad Hoc* Membership Qualifications Committee; the Information Committee, otherwise known as "the People Committee"; and a LAUT Committee to address the issues raised by the Commission on University Governance (CUG). The purpose of LAUT was "to promote the welfare of the libraries, librarians and other library staff of the University of Toronto."[60] LAUT was not dedicated primarily to librarians' issues. A group of members drafted the *Statement on Aims and Objectives of Proposed Association*, dividing their professional interests into two inter-related, broad categories pertaining to the librarians' roles in the library and in the academic community. These broad categories included discussions of professional autonomy, involvement in the internal decision-making processes, improved communication in the library system, formation of a fair dispute policy, greater mobility in the UTL system, opportunities for professional development, recognition of librarians as academics in the U of T community with academic status, and the importance of librarian representation in University decision-making bodies. These concerns would remain unresolved and would eventually lead to the *Reference Revolution*.

LAUT was officially recognized by the U of T Board of Governors, in February 1971, as representing the librarians' interests.[61] From 1969 to 1977, LAUT pursued a number of projects: a submission to CUG, the formulation of a grievance policy under the People Committee in 1970[62] and a survey on the status of librarians at the University. LAUT remained active until UTFA became the official bargaining representative for librarians, after which LAUT continued to exist—initially, as a parallel collaborator and later, as a social entity—but was no longer recognized by the administration as a viable representative for negotiating librarians' issues.

The issue of whether U of T librarians should unionize or acquire faculty status was raised by LAUT in 1973-1974. Reference librarians, Pat Fysh and Jane Clark, prepared a report entitled, *Unionization and Faculty Status*, each complete with a bibliography of current scholarship on the subjects, listing the pros and cons of each option. This report was made available via the Faculty of Library Science. Given the current climate of the period and the growing discontent among faculty,[63] it is interesting to read that the section on unionization concluded with, ". . . [i]t is possible that, within the next few years a large portion of the people employed at this University, faculty included, will be operating under some form of collective bargaining,"[64] which is exactly what transpired in many Canadian post-secondary institutions.⁶⁵ The section entitled *Faculty Status* credited the work of the ACRL, *Standards* (1971),⁶⁶ *Model Statement of Criteria and Procedures for Appointment, Promotion in Academic Rank, and Tenure for College and University Librarians* (1973) as the starting point. At this stage, there was no clear consensus among the librarians on which way the majority should vote, nor was there a shared consensus on how "academic status" should be defined: "Whether we in this institution take it to mean the identification of librarians with the faculty, or only the recognition of librarianship as a worthwhile profession in itself, or something in between, is up to us to decide."⁶⁷

LAUT retained a role in the community, parallel to that played by UTFA in the 1980s, as UTFA, in this early period, had not yet formed a standing committee for librarians. For example, in response to the U of T's new Employment Equity Policy, in 1986, LAUT undertook a survey of the status of U of T librarians resulting in the report, *Professional Opportunities Committee Report* (1987). It was noted that female librarians did not progress through the ranks at the same rate, in proportion to their numbers, as did male librarians. Nor did the women receive the same remuneration or take the same number of research leaves as did their male colleagues.

Librarians and University Governance

For the first time in the 120-year history of the U of T, under the leadership of President Claude Bissell (1958-1971), no mention of the library or the Chief Librarian was made in the *University of Toronto Act*, revised in 1971. Nor did the membership in the constituency for Governing Council mention the Chief Librarian or librarians. These revisions were to effectively sever the library, as an academic unit, and librarians as participants in institutional governance and simultaneously declared librarians as non-academics and "not" major stakeholders in the University—unlike students, faculty and administrative staff. This was a complete reversal of the role librarians had historically played in the early growth and history of the University, when senior faculty had the responsibility of the libraries and during the time of the bi-cameral system.⁶⁸ In the initial phase, the responsibilities of librarianship were assigned to the senior faculty and administrators of the institution because it was recognized as having a pivotal role in the growth and development of the institution.⁶⁹ This changed with the introduction of women into the profession.

Later, Robert H. Blackburn would lament that the new Act turned over the governance of the University to a highly political board with the loss of a forum for senior academics.⁷⁰ Subsequent publications on the University's decision to adopt the unicameral system of governance have been relatively quiet about the ramifications of these decisions to exclude the library and librarians. This raises numerous questions. Did librarians even voice their concerns? Did anyone speak up on behalf of the library and librarians? Librarians were not silent, as the existing publications would lead us to believe. In fact, several statements were presented but they were not seriously considered by the community.

In October 1969, the report by CUG,[71] *Toward Community in University Government* (1970), made 107 recommendations for revising the tenure process, search committees, appointments, training and staff development, supporting the unicameral system, and the establishment of the Governing Council consisting of 66 people (20 elected faculty members, 20 elected students, 20 lay members and six others) which would replace the bi-cameral system of the Senate and the Board and revise the existing *University of Toronto Act*.[72]

One of the more retrograde and short-sighted recommendations by the CUG was the inclusion of academic librarians in the "support staff" category, with no reference to their academic backgrounds, scholarship, education or work with faculty in the community, a negative recommendation that would begin to ferment and disillusion the community.[73] This was the exact opposite of what was transpiring at other post-secondary institutions in Canada and the US. The relegation of U of T librarians to the administrative staff disregarded their long-standing, academic contributions to the University and their professional status, forcing them to compete for the seats on Governing Council with administrative staff. To date, this situation remains unchanged. Given that librarians are a minority in comparison with the growing number of administrative staff, the chances of them acquiring enough votes to secure a seat has proved to be very slim, over the years. Most importantly, librarians considered themselves to be academic professionals, not support staff. Effectively, librarians were not recognized as participants in the governance of the institution.

After the release of the 107 recommendations, a University-Wide Committee (UWC)[74] met with faculty, students, librarians, and others interested in governance issues, from October 1969 to June 1970. Major stake-holders were asked to write and submit briefs to the Chairman, Martin L. Friedland, for consideration.[75] The library was given two seats on the UWC, which required an election to be held by LAUT to select two from the nominated LAUT members.[76] Marion Brown and Wasyl Veryha were elected to the committee. The unicameral system was recommended and the new *University of Toronto Act* came into force on July 1, 1972, followed by the MacDonald review in 1977.

From October 1969 to June 1970, before the *University of Toronto Act* (1971) was approved, several briefs were submitted advocating for the participation of the library and librarians in the governance process by the Chief Librarian, LAUT, and individuals from the federated colleges. For the most part, faculty were silent about the role of the library and librarians. One of the few exceptions was the brief submitted by Dr. J.K.W. Ferguson, Director, Connaught Medical Research Laboratories, dated April 27, 1970, in which he wrote that the Librarian, Editor of Publications and Diet Counsellor should be added to the academic staff in the constituency of the unicameral system.[77] In May 1969, the Association of the

Teaching Staff (later renamed "UTFA"), under president Prof. Frederick E. Winter, from the Fine Arts Department, submitted a brief supporting the unicameral system because "the existing system of university government is outmoded, unresponsive to change and wasteful of the time of Faculty Councils, Senate and Board of Governors."[78] They strenuously objected to student parity with regard to governance and policies for faculty, and it seemed to them "unrealistic that the alumni of the University *qua alumni* should be represented on the governing body . . ."[79] The comments made about the library were equally pointed, with several recommendations concerning internal administrative problems. The public airing of many issues should have prompted internal action in the library. However, it did not. The same issues emerged as concerns in the 1974 *Reference Revolution*, but with a different set of recommendations. At this time, the Association of Teaching Staff was ". . . convinced that the present 'chain of command' in the UTL is such as to insulate the professional librarians from Faculty, needs and views."[80] They supported the need for a Library Council, suggesting that it include students, with the Chief Librarian reporting to the Library Council. Essentially, the faculty association wanted to revert the authority of the library system back to users, to the faculty and students, a somewhat out-dated and impractical proposal, given that that had been rejected with the establishment of graduate programs in the 1960s. It was recognized, at that time, that faculty had neither the time, skills, nor scope of knowledge to manage a modern, complex library system.

The Chief Librarian wrote several statements on different issues to CUG, but with little overall success. The first was submitted on April 16, 1969, when Robert H. Blackburn wrote to Mr. Robin Ross, the Secretary of the CUG requesting a minor change in the *University of Toronto Act*, with regard to the membership of the University Councils. In his first brief, he advocated for the inclusion of senior library staff. He requested that the "Chief Librarian or his delegate" be made an *ex-officio* member of the Council of each faculty, school, University College and other constituent colleges, "since the library must serve the programme of each of these units it is most useful to have a seat on the Council."[81] The second brief, which advocated for librarians collectively, was sent on January 12, 1970 and attempted to "correct a serious oversight in the CUG proposal regarding academic staff members who do not teach in classrooms."[82] Robert H. Blackburn notes that the report ". . . defines the academic community, however, simply as teaching staff and students, and states that nobody else can be considered to have a similar stake in the University as an academic institution."[83] He went on to defend librarians, editors at the press, and scientists doing research at the Connaught Laboratories as stake-holders:

> . . . 170 librarians form approximately one-quarter of the staff employed in our various libraries. This number does not include the librarians who have been appointed to full-time teaching in the School of Library Science and in some divisions of the University. Recognition of these peo-

ple as academic staff is justified by the academic qualifications . . . Several of our people have three or more degrees and several are working toward higher degrees in order to improve their qualifications . . . some carry part-time teaching appointments in addition to their work in the library . . . the Chief Librarian is included among the Deans and Directors . . . librarians sit on various faculty and college committees . . . librarians are eligible for research grants from the University's Research Board on the same basis as teaching staff . . . the strongest claim, however, relates to their duties. Librarians deal in the selection, interpretation and dissemination of knowledge in all fields and many languages . . . for librarians now to be classified as support staff with no academic stake in the university, worthy, to participate only in those decisions that affect their well-being (p.15-1) and not those which affect the academic welfare of the University, could have serious consequences. This proposal in the *Report* has been a blow to the morale of the librarians now on staff . . .[84]

On Feb. 3, 1970 Robert H. Blackburn, clearly frustrated by what was transpiring, wrote a letter to the editor of the *Bulletin* concerning the CUG forum, suggesting that the CUG obtain professional expertise for ". . . when the Provincial Government receives the report of the University-Wide Committee, it is likely to pay more attention if some acknowledged experts in organizational theory and practice have been consulted officially, and have said that the new scheme could actually work."[85]

Shortly thereafter, on February 10, 1970, LAUT submitted three briefs. The first, written by Richard Landon[86] and Michael Rosenstock,[87] took issue with librarians being equated with support staff:

> . . . [LAUT contends] that the term "support staff" has little meaning when applied to librarians. While, in some areas, librarians 'support' teaching staff and students by providing services of a unique type, in others teaching staff and students play a supporting role by helping to strengthen resources which librarians create and administer . . . that the excessively narrow definition of the term 'academic' does not do justice to the complexities of a modern university . . . librarians should have full voting membership on the Governing Council as a distinct component of the academic community . . . only by participating fully in the decision-making process at its highest level can librarians make their distinctive academic contribution to the life of the university . . .[88]

The second brief was written by Miss Sheila Laidlaw, Librarian in the Circulation Department and one of the librarians who would later participate in the *Reference Revolution*.[89] The third brief submitted was from Mrs. E.M. Smith, Victoria College Library, who re-affirmed the central role of an academic library and librarians to build, sustain and maintain these collections: ". . . if librarians are to shape library policy effectively, to build up collections which will serve their purpose as an integral part of the learning process ... librarians [must have] representation on all academic and governing councils and committees of the University."[90]

There was a complete disconnect between the recommendations of the 1960s concerning librarians and the libraries and the actions of those in administration in the 1970s. With regard to the silence of faculty and administrators, many held traditional biases about the role of librarians as professional academics and were out-of-touch with what had transpired in the profession and what was happening at other Canadian and American universities. In fairness to those who supported the concerns of the librarians but left no documented record of this support, it should be noted that during this period many faculty found themselves engaged in underlying power struggles brought about by the new proposed governance structure; faculty became pre-occupied with territorial disputes that had impacts on the new policies for tenure, evaluations and representation in the governance process. The shifts of power in the recommendations for the new governance structure by the Commission served to de-stabilize, rather than calm, the community.

In 1977, at the time of the five year review, which had culminated in the John B. MacDonald report, *A Review of the Unicameral Experiment*, UTFA, LAUT and Robert H. Blackburn once again submitted briefs calling for the recognition of librarians as academics and, hence, deserving of a designated seat on Council. Both UTFA and LAUT requested that librarians be recognized as a separate electoral constituent now that they were members of UTFA. The MacDonald report responded by suggesting that change of status was not a good reason for creating an additional seat and a special constituency. "In view of their new identification with the teaching staff (through membership on the University of Toronto Faculty Association) it is logical that their eligibility be moved to the teaching staff constituency."[91]

The debate that followed in UTFA questioned whether librarians were eligible for seats under the definition for the teaching staff in the *University of Toronto Act* (1971). UTFA legal counsel argued that there was no reason why the Act could not be interpreted to include librarians.[92] The resistance to change came from faculty members within UTFA, as "it was seen by many faculty members as an invasion of their preserve."[93] Even today, when the issue is raised, there is considerable discomfort among faculty to discuss the inclusion of librarians in this designation. It is time to recognize the roles of academic librarians in building a great research institute and to be more inclusive in definitions pertaining to academic staff while simultaneously recognizing professional differences between the professorial, teaching, and librarian streams.

The "Reference Revolution" of 1974

From 1971 to 1974, the Chief Librarian was engaged in the planning and construction of the Robarts Research Library, which began by opening the Rare Book Wing in 1972 and the Research Library in 1973. During this period, unresolved managerial issues, rapid growth of the libraries, increased workloads and higher user expectations resulted in escalating problems in the workplace for staff and librarians.

The *Reference Revolution*, in 1974, that resulted in Library reforms and professional changes for librarians at U of T, was ultimately triggered by the Chief Librarian's refusal to address salary inequities related to gender. On February 18, 1974, the Chief Librarian received a memo from 15 members of the Reference Department,[94] which consisted of Government Documents, Maps, Periodicals and Reference spread over three-floors of "Fort Book," the popular name given to the Robarts Research Library in those days. Robert H. Blackburn noted that it was an ultimatum. "It [the memo] contained a number of sweeping recommendations and unless I agreed by 1 pm the next day to implement all of them, I was to resign."[95] The actual memo stated that, in the interests of the University and the library, if he did not implement the recommendations listed in the memo, by May 1st, 1974 that he would "have no alternative but to resign the position as Chief Librarian." The librarians asked for a prompt and positive response or ". . . we plan to take the following steps. First at 1:00 p.m. on Tuesday, February 19, we will close public services in the Reference Department for two hours as a demonstration of our genuine concern and discontent. Second, we will take our case to the Governing Council as provided for in the University of Toronto Act. Third, we will contact all local news media in order to publicize the discrimination and inefficiency of the University of Toronto Library system."[96] The women who signed this memo recall feelings of deep anger and a sense of injustice over what transpired; even today, emotions are intense when recounting what transpired. The following day, February 19, 1974, Robert H. Blackburn met with those who had signed the memo. He declared that "they refused to discuss or even clarify their message, but agreed to compose a written *Reference Brief* in response to my questions."[97]

Ten days later, on March 4, 1974, 14 reference librarians submitted a signed brief entitled, *Submission by Members of the Reference Department, University of Toronto Library, in Response to Questions Raised by the Chief Librarian at the Meeting Held on February 19, 1974* (*Reference Brief*), to the Chief Librarian, who then submitted a copy to President John Evans (1972-1978).[98] On the same day, Robert H. Blackburn sent a memo to all departments saying "he had already asked the President to consider establishing a presidential advisory committee on the library and its place in the University" among other suggestions, in an effort to diffuse the situation.[99]

The actions of this small group of librarians (86% women)[100] were viewed, at the time, as rebellious, showing disregard for the library's established managerial hierarchy. In many respects, the documented arguments supporting the role of librarians in the governance structure of the institution by the Chief Librarian, Robert H. Blackburn, in the early 1970s, appear out-of-sync with the reality of work-place problems in the library. Looking back, it is apparent that the traditional, *military*-authoritarian managerial style sustained and endorsed by the Chief Librarian—himself a military man—was incompatible with the times, especially with the views and expectations of a newer generation of academic librarians. Moreover, the gender biases of the past remained deeply rooted in the hierarchical, managerial style employed in the library system. Given the disillusionment amongst staff, the tenor of the times, the absence of affirmative action, and the stalwart determination by administrators to adhere, no matter what, to out-moded attitudes, change was inevitable.[101]

The *Reference Revolution* was the result of the administrators' failure to recognize the importance of key issues and to not respond: to the concerns which had been raised on numerous occasions in the past. This was a serious misjudgement. In turn, the courage of these few individuals in the Reference Department empowered others, for the problems had become epidemic. Shortly after the submission of the reference librarians' *Reference Brief*,[102] many others joined in by sending their own letters to the Chief Librarian. These included librarians from the Rare Book Library, the Circulation Department, the Book Selectors, the Sigmund Samuel Library, Technical Services, and the Science and Medicine librarians.[103]

The term *Reference Revolution*, coined by contemporaries at the time, speaks to the milieu in which change was idealized as "revolutionary" and was associated with strong social values that sought equality and high standards as advocated in the feminist movement and growing mobilization of faculty at Canadian universities. The complaints leading up to the *Reference Revolution* had long been festering and the lack of responsiveness was notable, especially as compared to what was taking place at other post-secondary institutions in North America.

In Robert H. Blackburn's summary of the successful achievements of U of T's librarians since 1954, he failed to notice the norm outside the University community and see how internal achievements paled against developments in comparable institutions:

> Actually our librarians had come a long way since 1954 when they were first designated as a separate group apart from clerical ranks . . . [T]heir pension and other benefits were the same as for all members of the University staff . . . [T]hey were eligible for study leave and for grants from the University's Research Board. They were eligible to apply to me for travel assistance to attend professional and academic meetings . . . Some of them served as lecturers at the Library School or in other faculties, and were permitted to count their teaching time as part of their regular library duties.[104]

But the academic status and professional autonomy of academic librarians had been widely accepted and supported since the 1950s at many American universities[105] and was officially supported by the ACRL,[106] and by the Association of American Colleges and Universities (see their 1972 *Joint Statement on Faculty*

Status of College and University Librarians). In Canada, once provincial legislation permitted the unionization of public servants in the 1960s, faculty associations across the country certified and negotiated academic status and professional autonomy for faculty and librarians alike.[107] Robert H. Blackburn's perceptions were out-of-date.

The stressful move into the Robarts Research Library, in 1973, added to the internal strife. The absence of up-to-date policies and procedures required for managing a complex library system and the shortage of professional staff, given that nearly 33 librarian positions had been lost between the years 1969 to 1973, accentuated the internal pressures.[108] Community expectations had increased with the construction of the Robarts Research Library. For example, on May 24, 1973, a memo from 31 members of the Circulation and Reference Departments was sent to the Associate Librarian, Director of Reader Services, objecting to the new assigned hours of service from 10 pm to midnight through the week and on Sundays until 10 pm, with the expectation that librarians would resume their usual duties the following day.[109] There had been no previous discussion with those working in public service. This was the time of the *emergency librarian*, who was required to be in the building for all opening hours.[110] As the librarians pointed out "... we do not feel that the problems of maintenance and security are the responsibilities of professional librarians. These problems should be handled through the employment of security guards." Given the shortage of staff, they felt that "night duties cut heavily into the daytime work of librarians in public service" and that "the efficiency of the departments concerned will suffer at the very time when we are already working at the limit of our personal capacities."[111]

But, the tipping point—the single event that was to trigger the *Reference Revolution*—was the unfair treatment of Anne Woodsworth, the Head of the Reference Department from November 22, 1971 - February 1974, which catapulted her staff into action. Anne Woodsworth had been Robert H. Blackburn's protégé from 1970-1971, prior to assuming the Head of the Reference Department. In a memo from Robert H. Blackburn to senior staff, dated November 11, 1971, he noted that "... she has been my Assistant for Research and Administration. During that time she has planned and executed several research projects within the Library as well as for the Ontario Council of University Librarians on my behalf. Along with her regular duties as Department Head, she will continue to be responsible for such *ad hoc* research for me, utilizing the personnel and other resources of the Reference Department."[112] In 1973, she discovered that her salary, as a female administrator, was lower than her male counterparts, even though she had, in some cases, higher qualifications and more advanced degrees.[113] Her supervisor, H.C. Sholler advised her to consult with the Chief Librarian. Robert H. Blackburn refused to adjust her salary; even after Human Resources had been asked to intervene and negotiate a settlement, he again refused. At this point, Anne Woodsworth handed in her resignation. She informed her staff shortly thereafter. At the time, the Chief Librarian had said that he would not accept her resignation, as she was fired (a resignation would have prompted a University enquiry). Before leaving the University, Jean Yolton, a fellow librarian, the wife of the Acting President of York University, and the person who would later be appointed to replace her, told her that her career was essentially over.[114] However, shortly thereafter, Anne Woodsworth was head-hunted and she accepted the position of Director of the York University Library (1978-1983) and went on to be a leader in the profession. For the Chief Librarian, the ramifications of this event—his resistance to supporting affirmative action amongst his staff—would prove to be greater than he anticipated.

Anne Woodsworth's resignation caused an uproar in the Reference Department. Essentially, her colleagues viewed her treatment as unjust and yet another example of gender discriminatory practices and salary inequities. On February 25, 1974, members of the Reference Department wrote to Robert H. Blackburn asking that Anne Woodsworth be re-instated. On February 26, 1974, Robert H. Blackburn responded, not to the writers of the letter, but instead to their supervisor, the Acting Head of Reference Department, Jean Yolton, saying that he had ". . . the hope of re-establishing normal lines of communication." By not responding directly to those who wrote the letter, the Chief Librarian reaffirmed his deeply held, top-down style of management, and deepened the discontent amongst his colleagues. The letter did not mention the reasons behind Anne Woodsworth's resignation nor mention her re-instatement, saying only that ". . . members of the Reference Department are not the only ones who regret the loss of Mrs. Anne Woodsworth."[115] He did, however, point out that the previous Assistant Head of Reference, Carol Weiss [Moore], had not been selected to be Acting Head of Reference because of her ". . . own involvement in the present unrest in the department . . ." with the sole purpose of pointing out the consequences of speaking up.[116]

The *Reference Brief* led to reforms, initiating a series of internal and external reviews of the library. Many of the basic recommendations would be integrated into the first *Policy for Librarians* (1978). But the path for change was slow. The *Reference Brief* began by stating that "leadership and traditions have remained relatively unchanged for twenty years with the result that the administration has grown increasingly hierarchical, rigid and insensitive." It was not until the librarians became members of UTFA that their high turnover rate began to decline.

The *Reference Brief* addressed a range of issues and concerns about the library's administration and, in particular, policies for librarians about promotions, grievance and dispute settlements, professional autonomy and development. It recommended that the position of Chief Librarian be a five-year, contractual appointment, following the example of other senior faculty appointments at the University. All appointments, from department heads up, whether acting or not, should be made by search committee representatives. Objections were presented by both the Chief Librarian and the Associate Librarian, David Esplin, who argued before Governing Council that it would be difficult to recruit senior administrators under that policy, an argument still heard today. However, the history of lengthy appointment terms had resulted in slow responses to change in the library, a lesson learned that no one wanted to repeat.[117]

On March 8, 1974, President John Evans began to organize the Presidential Working Group on the Library and asked Prof. Peter Meincke to chair the committee.[118] This committee's final report, *Report of the President's Working Group on the Library* (known also as the *Meincke Report*), was completed June 12, 1974, followed by a response from President John Evans on June 28, 1974 for a combined report of 53 pages.[119]

The *Meincke Report* affirmed what the *Reference Brief* and the librarians had been saying for years, i.e., that the rapid growth in the library staff, the complexity of the library system, the move to a new environment, and the unionization of the support staff were all contributing factors to the current discontent. Most importantly, however, the recent changes to the governance structure at the University, the "revolutionary change in the style and practice of management" in the broader profession of librarianship, the "prevailing concern about the status of women," and the complete absence of women in senior management in the library were all identified as factors which resulted in the *Reference Revolution*.[120] The top-down managerial style of the library's administration did not lend itself to a collegial decision-making process that is understood as a part of professional autonomy and shared governance.

In response to the suggestions included in the *Meincke Report*, President John Evans supported the following initiatives:

1) A review of the library was to be undertaken by completing the Association of Research Libraries (ARL) management review program known as the Management Review and Analysis Programme (MRAP) of the ARL,[121]
2) Recognition of the need to establish, as practice, the formation of regular search committees in the hiring, promotion and review process and to formalize performance evaluations,
3) Recognition of the need for the Library Council to include members from the community,
4) The establishment of several new committees to examine policies and procedures in the Library.

In a confidential 14-page letter, the Chief Librarian stated his views and objections to the many changes being proposed, including the "open-door" policy of the Vice-Provost, which he regarded as undermining normal communication channels, and the formation of search committees, which he viewed as irrelevant.[122] The results of the *Reference Revolution* were to have far reaching ramifications, beyond the initial demise of authority at the senior management level in the UTL system.

Librarians and UTFA

Membership in UTFA proved to be the right choice for most, but not all. Prof. Jean Edward Smith, UTFA Chair of Salary and Benefits Committee, noted in a letter to Miss C.M. Blackstock of the Book Selection Department, on November 3, 1976, that 130 out of 194 eligible librarians at the University had joined UTFA. The next major challenge was the formulation, for the first time, of a *Policy for Librarians*.[123] On June 28, 1977, President John Evans consulted with UTFA President, Prof. J.M. Daniels, and they agreed to form a Working Group, to be approved by Governing Council, to formulate policies for librarians. The Working Group,[124] chaired by Prof. Roger Savory, was mandated to review appropriate rank structure for librarians, policies and procedures relating to permanent status, and methods of selecting and reviewing administrators at the level of department head and above. The final policies were to be presented to the Principals, Deans and Directors, the Academic Affairs Committee, and the Governing Council, for review. The "Report of the Working Group to Recommend Policies for Librarians" was completed on October 31, 1977.[125] Under the terms of the Memorandum of Agreement (MoA) with UTFA, the report would become part of the MoA upon ratification by both parties. For the most part, the librarians' policies were initially modeled on the *Haist Rules*,[126] but were gradually modified and became known as the *Savory Rules*, after Prof. Roger Savory. In a vote organized by UTFA, 84% of the librarians endorsed the policy in November 1977. In a press release to members of UTFA, Carol Moore, a member of UTFA's negotiating team in 1976, said "the results of the referendum indicated the depth of concern felt by librarians and the urgent need to establish effective procedures." [127] At this time, Prof. Jean Edward Smith noted that it was a victory for traditional processes at U of T. The tide would change and so would his view.

On November 24, 1977, UTFA members received a memo from Prof. Jean Edward Smith, now President of UTFA, that read, "Deans and Directors have accepted the principle of permanent status for librarians."[128] This was a major accomplishment, as permanent status is the equivalent of tenure. It recognized librarians as academics. The following issues, outlined in the *Draft for Discussion*, prepared by the Deans and Directors, were reviewed and comments from the Working Group were returned to the Deans and Directors on December 2, 1977.[129] Of special note was the request for a clause for dismissal, which would prove to be the amendment on which there would be no agreement and which resulted in UTFA's *"Unsigned Policy for Librarians"*:

1) The "concept of a University library" versus "the autonomy of local library units" was a concern for the Principals at Scarborough and Erindale Colleges. In response, for the sake of equity across the three campuses, the Working Group firmly adhered to the Chief Librarian's veto on appointments and promotions.
2) The Deans and Directors noted that the appointment of librarians to the academic staff, in Governing Council (as they were now members of UTFA) conflicted with the *University of Toronto Act*, which defines "academic" as "teaching staff." "Retaining this wording may require an amendment to the Act."[130] To date, this suggested revision has not been addressed nor have librarians been embraced in the Act's definition of teaching staff.
3) The Deans and Directors asked about the extent to which research is integral to the normal duties of librarians. In response, the Working Group stated that they were "at a loss to understand why the concept of scholarly research should be considered not to be part of the duties of a professional librarian . . . [I]n fact, the concept is recognised in the current University of Toronto Staff Manual [used before membership in UTFA] . . . for purposes such as advanced study of real benefit to the Library or scholarly research leading to publication." In addition, the following points were made:

- They supported research and study leaves but requested clarification between the two and noted that library service must be maintained. This distinction was never addressed in the policy.
- They requested a clause of dismissal for fiscal reasons (section 47). This proved to be the biggest hurdle. The threat to permanent status or tenure was part of the contemporaneous discourse and very much concerned the faculty at UTFA.[131] As a way of proceeding and agreeing to most of the policy, Prof. Jean Edward Smith added the following clause: "The principle of permanent status shall not preclude dismissal for reasons of fiscal stringency. The procedures and policies relating thereto *shall be negotiated* with the University of Toronto Faculty Association.[132]

On March 8, 1978, Prof. Jean Edward Smith distributed a copy of the *Report by the Working Group on Librarians*, for consideration, to the UTFA Executive. This was followed by a letter, on March 21, 1978, from Prof. Roger M. Savory, Chair of the Working Group on Librarians, to Prof. Michael Bliss, requesting support for the changes. On April 27, 1978, the Academic Affairs Committee met to discuss the Report of the Working Group to formulate the *Policies for Librarians*. The Academic Affairs Committee approved a clause on the policy for dismissals that ensured the approval of the policy, except for this section, and enabled negotiations to continue on this one section. The ruling by the Academic Affairs Committee was subsequently overruled by the Governing Council's Executive. On May 15, 1978, the President of UTFA wrote to members on the seriousness of what had transpired:

> I am writing to inform you of a matter of the utmost seriousness and importance. Namely, the recent decision by the Governing Council's Executive to reverse a unanimous finding of the Academic Affairs Committee and to refuse to negotiate the procedures pertaining to the dismissal of permanent academic staff for financial reasons . . . Academic Affairs twice has endorsed this concept by unanimous votes, each time stressing the essential nature of negotiations with faculty and librarians on an issue so crucial.[133]

What happened? Briefly, Governing Council objected to the term "negotiated" and instead inserted "consult with faculty . . ." The Working Group, on May 25, in order to keep the discussions and progress moving, accepted a compromise offered by the Academic Affairs Committee, which read, "The Governing Council defers until a later date the determination of how procedures governing the dismissal of permanent status librarians for fiscal reasons will be developed." This solution was rejected by Governing Council. As a consequence, on June 8, 1978, Prof. Roger Savory, wrote to the UTFA faculty and librarians saying that the blame for the present serious crisis "must rest fairly and squarely on the Governing Council's Executive . . . we strongly urge you to make representations to the Governing Council, and particularly to any members of the Governing Council."[134] Further correspondence was sent from Prof. Jean Edward Smith to President John Evans, but to no avail. Governing Council, on June 15, 1978, by-passed consultation with UTFA and the recommendation of the Academic Affairs Committee, and instead approved this clause: "The Governing Council will consult fully with the University of Toronto Faculty Association in the development of procedures related thereto."[135]

At this point, the *Policies for Librarians* had been approved, except for section 47 (financial exigency clause). On March 20, 1980, a revised statement was inserted into the MoA: "A working group on librarians met during 1977-78. A policy for librarians was approved by the Governing Council in June, 1978. This policy will become subject to this agreement upon the approval by the Association and thereafter not be changed by the University during the period of this agreement."[136] The *Policy for Librarians* was essentially approved by Governing Council but not by UTFA. The amended clause pertaining to the dismissal of librarians and the consultative reference to faculty members was a very real threat to the academic status of faculty, hence, under no terms could UTFA agree to this amendment, which subsequently resulted in the unsigned policies for librarians.

Conclusion

This chapter concludes with events from the late 1970s, however, the work of colleagues did not. Membership in UTFA was just the beginning. Colleagues had acquired academic status for librarians, with regular monetary improvements, as well as formalized research leaves (equivalent to faculty sabbaticals), and annual research days. Because UTFA is not unionized,[137] provincial labour laws that would impose deadlines and structure on the negotiation process do not apply; as such the process is a lengthy one. In the 1960s and 1970s, librarians struggled to define and assert their concerns about what constituted the "library" and what pertained to the professional status of librarians. Membership in UTFA and a broader community awareness about the profession, has helped to focus these concerns on professional issues today.

What is the status of librarians at U of T today? It has been more than 35 years since the *Policies for Librarians* (1978) and the MoA (1978) were written. Only Article VI of the MoA, pertaining to remuneration, workload and research leaves have been updated over these years. Essentially, faculty and librarians have had what are called "the frozen policies." At the writing of this chapter, representatives of UTFA and Governing Council in the Special Joint Advisory Committee (SJAC) are in negotiations to modernize the MoA. "At stake is the institutional capacity of UTFA as the only democratically accountable collective body solely representative of faculty and librarians at the University" and of particular concern is the ". . . process of good faith bargaining and dispute resolution featuring interest arbitration (rather than strikes) as a means to reach timely conclusions in negotiations"[138] Since UTFA remains uncertified, this is a pivotal moment in the labour history of faculty and librarians at U of T.

Bibliography

American Library Association. *Academic Status: Statements and Resources.* Chicago: Association of College and Research Libraries, 1988.

Arbuckle, Jennifer. "A Professional Librarian Views Library Unions." *IPLO Quarterly* 15 (January 1974): 109-116.

Association of American University Professors, "Statement on Faculty Status of College and University Librarians." *College and Research Libraries News* 35 (Feb. 1974): 26.

———. "Standards for Faculty Status for College and University Librarians; Revision." *College & Research Libraries News* 32 (Feb. 1971): 36-37.

Auerbach, W. "Discrimination Against Women in the Academic Library." *University of Wisconsin Library News* (Feb. 1972): 1-11.

Bassam, B. *The Faculty of Library Science, University of Toronto and Its Predecessors 1911-1972.* Toronto: University of Toronto Press, 1978.

Biggs, Mary. "Sources of Tension and Conflict between Librarians and Faculty." *The Journal of Higher Education* vol. 52, no. 2 (Mar. - Apr. 1981): 182-201.

Bissell, Claude. *Halfway up Parnassus: A Personal Account of the University of Toronto 1932-1971.* Toronto: University of Toronto Press, 1974.

Robert H. Blackburn, R.H. *Evolution of the Heart: A History of the University of Toronto Library Up to 1981.* Toronto: University of Toronto Press, 1989.

Boaz, Martha. "Labor Unions and Libraries." *California Librarian* 33 (April/July 1971): 104-108.

Burgh, Anne E. and Benjamin R. Beede, "American Librarianship," in *The Role of Women in Librarianship 1876-1976: The Entry, Advancement, and Struggle for Equalization in One Profession,* eds. Kathleen Weibel and Kathleen M. Heim. Phoenix, AZ: The Oryx Press, 1979.

Burke, Sara Z. *Seeking the Highest Good: Social Service and Gender at the University of Toronto 1888-1937.* Toronto: University of Toronto Press, 1996.

Cinman, Israel. "CAUT Enters New Era: Structure Aimed at Strengthening CAUT's Role in Collective Bargaining and Lobbying Governments." *CAUT Newsletter* (1974).

Clark, Jane and Pat Fysh. *Unionization and Faculty Status. University of Toronto.* [n.d. 1974].

Commission on the Government of the University of Toronto, University of Toronto. *Toward Community in University Government.* Toronto: University of Toronto Press, 1970.

Cooper, Michael D. "A Statistical Portrait of Librarians: What the Numbers Say." *American Libraries* 7, no. 6 (Jun. 1976): 327-330.

Curtis, Joanna B. "Professionals Form a Union" *IPLO Quarterly* 15 (January 1974): 89-100.

Dewey, Melvil. "The Profession." *American Library Journal* I (1876): 5-6.

Downs, Robert Bingham. "Status of Academic Librarians in Retrospect." *College and Research Libraries* 29 (1968): 253.

Epstein, C.F. *Woman's Place: Options and Limits in Professional Careers.* Berkeley: University of California Press, 1970.

Ford, A. *A Path Not Strewn with Roses.* Toronto: University of Toronto Press, 1985.

Friedland, Martin L. *The University of Toronto: A History.* Toronto: University of Toronto Press, 2002, revised edition, 2013.

Globe and Mail. "Women still outnumber men in the library science programs." Proquest. *The Globe and Mail (1936-Current).* May 31, 1979, http://search.proquest.com/docview/1239261631?accountid=14771

Harris, Roma .M. *Librarianship: The Erosion of a Woman's Profession.* Norwood, N.J.: Ablex Publishing Corporation.

———. "Keeping Silent About Women." In *Librarianship: The Erosion of a Woman's Profession,* edited by R.M. Harris, 12-14. Norwood, N.J.: Ablex Publishing Corporation, 1992.

Horn, Michiel. *Academic Freedom in Canada: A History.* Toronto: University of Toronto Press, 1999.

Houser, L. *The Institute of Professional Librarians of Ontario: An Analysis, 1954-1975.* Toronto: Institute of Professional Librarians, 1975.

Hyman, R. and G. Schlachter, "Academic Status: Who Wants It?" *College and Research Libraries: News* (Sept. 1972): 209-210.

Irvine, B.J. *Sex Segregation in Librarianship.* Westport, Connecticut: Greenwood Press, 1985.

Kiefer, N. *The Impact of the Second World War on Female Students at the University of Toronto 1939-1949.* Toronto: University of Toronto, 1984.

Librarians Association of University of Toronto (LAUT). *Report.* 1969-1971. UTARMS B72-1105.

———. *Professional Opportunities Committee Report.* Toronto, 1987.

Macdonald, J.B. *The Governing Council System of the University of Toronto 1972-1977: A Review of the Unicameral Experiment.* Toronto: [University of Toronto Press], 1977.

Massman, Virgil F. *Faculty Status for Librarians.* Metuchen, N.J.: Scarecrow Press, 1972.

McReynolds, Rosalee. "A Heritage Dismissed." *Library Journal* 110, no. 18 (1985): 25-31.

Mleyner, Darryl. "Professional Unions." *California Librarian* 31 (April 1970): 110-118.

Nelson, W.H. *The Search for Faculty Power: The History of the University of Toronto Faculty Association 1942-1992.* Toronto: Canadian Scholars Press, 1993, reprinted 2006.

Ontario University Presidents' Research Committee. *The Supply of Librarians: A Report to the Presidents of the Provincially Assisted Universities of Ontario from the Presidents' Research Committee.* [n.d. 1964].

Passet, Joanne E. "Men in a Feminized Profession: The Male Librarian 1887-1921." *Libraries & Culture* vol. 28:4 (Fall, 1993): 385-402.

Prentice, Alison. "Bluestockings, Feminists, or Women Workers? A Preliminary Look at Women's Early Employment at the University of Toronto." *Journal of the Canadian Historical Association/Revue de la Société historique du Canada* 2, no. 1 (1991): 231-262.

President's Committee on the School of Graduate Studies, University of Toronto. *Graduate Studies in the University of Toronto: Report of the President's Commission on the School of Graduate Studies 1964-1965.* Toronto: University of Toronto Press, 1965.

Schiller, A.R. *Characteristics of Professional Personnel in College and University of Libraries.* Springfield: Illinois State Library, 1969.

Strachan, John. *General Regulations for the Management of the King's College Library.*

University of Toronto Faculty Association. "Librarians Endorse Savory Report." Press Release. November 23, 1977.

———. Letter to UTFA Members. November 24, 1977.

University of Toronto Libraries. *Annual Report of Chief Librarian.* 1970-1971, 1971-1972, 1974-1975. UTARMS P78-0537.

University of Toronto Library. *MRAP Newsletter* 7. October 4, 1974.

———. *MRAP Newsletter.* October 4, 1974.

University of Toronto. *A Brief Sketch of Its History and Its Organization.* Toronto: University of Toronto Press, 1947.

———. *Facts & Figures.* Toronto: University of Toronto Press, 1993-2011.

———. President's Committee on the School of Graduate Studies. *Graduate Studies in the University of Toronto: Report of the President's Committee on the School of Graduate Studies 1964-1965.* Toronto: University of Toronto Press, 1965.

Wallace, Stewart W. *A History of the University of Toronto 1827-1927.* Toronto: University of Toronto Press, 1927.

Weibel, K., K.M. Heim and D.J. Ellsworth. *The Role of Women in Librarianship 1876-1976: The Entry, Advancement and Struggle for Equalization in One Profession.* Phoenix, Arizona: The Oryx Press, 1979.

Working Group on the Library. *Report of the President's Working Group on the Library* (known also as the *Meincke Report*). June 12, 1974.

Wright, E.O., J. Baxtor and G.E. Birkelund, "The Gender Gap in Workplace Authority: A Cross-National Study." *American Sociological Review*, 60 (1995): 407-435.

Ontario College Librarians' Campaign for Parity—Networking for Social Change

Robin Inskip and David L. Jones

This chapter covers the 17 year campaign of Ontario Colleges of Applied Arts and Technology (CAAT) librarians to achieve equal working conditions and pay for work of equal value when compared to the Ontario community college teachers and counsellors. In the early 1970s, the authors of this chapter were recent graduates and in their first professional positions (Inskip Seneca College; Jones Humber College). Documentation of the early part of the campaign has been published.[1] Other documentation is in the submission from the CAAT Academic Bargaining Team.[2] The post-1980 analysis of the CAAT Academic Librarians' equality campaign draws from the experiences and writings of CAAT academic librarians, who continued the push for parity for another decade.[3]

This chapter makes use of the theories of the diffusion and adoption of innovations and of social ecology in a rapidly evolving environment which included changes both to the governance of Ontario community colleges and to women's rights in social, legal, economic and employment sectors. It will briefly introduce the concepts of 1) innovation as it is referred to in this chapter, 2) the impact of rapid environmental change on organizations and 3) social ecology's academic and practice-based approaches for organizations to cope with rapid change. An innovation is a new idea, product, or behaviour; while it may be familiar to some, it still needs wider distribution and a process to share information about it. Rogers' *Diffusion of Innovations* explains how new ideas spread via communication channels over time to members of a social system composed of individuals, organizations, or agencies that share a common culture and are potential adopters of an innovation.⁴ Such innovations are initially perceived as uncertain and even risky. To overcome this uncertainty, most people seek out others like themselves, who have already adopted the innovative idea. Thus the diffusion process consists of a few individuals who first adopt an innovation, then spread the word among their circles of acquaintances—a process which typically takes months or years.

In a more popular vein, in 2000, Malcolm Gladwell wrote *The Tipping Point*, which made the *New York Times* and *Wall Street Journal* best-seller lists. The premise in *The Tipping Point* is that small changes can have big effects, such as when a few people start behaving differently. The new behaviour can ripple outward until a critical mass or "tipping point" is reached. Gladwell's thesis is that ideas, products, messages and behaviours "spread just like viruses do."⁵ Gladwell conceded in 2013 that *The Tipping Point's* methods may not be needed for diffusing simple ideas, such as a new song or fashion. He also admitted that "the more I've thought about this since writing *The Tipping Point*, the more it strikes me that the argument I was making was really specific to a certain kind of idea—to complex, relatively new, and sophisticated ideas."⁶ Gladwell's nuance follows Rogers' definition of complexity as "the degree to which an innovation is perceived as relatively difficult to understand and use."⁷ Complexity is therefore negatively correlated with the rate of adoption. Thus, excessive complexity of an innovation is an important obstacle in its adoption.⁸

Complex problems are social ecology's strength; its primary purpose is creating communication channels to facilitate shared meaning and potential joint actions for complex, sophisticated and relatively new ideas or problems. Organizations need innovations and new channels of communication to deal with complexity in turbulent environments.⁹ Trist and Emery expanded the important work on structural and communication changes in work processes originally developed by Britain's Tavistock Institute, and cast their focus on the complex environments and mega-problems impacting both individuals and multiple organizations.¹⁰ As Barbara Gray, the principal scholar advancing social ecology theory, states:

> Under turbulent conditions, organizations become highly interdependent with others in unexpected but consequential ways. Turbulence occurs when organizations, acting independently in diverse directions, create unanticipated consequences for themselves and others. Turbulence cannot be managed individually because disruptions and their causes cannot be adequately anticipated or averted by unilateral action. In the face of turbulence, the ability of any single organization to plan accurately for its future is limited by the unpredictable consequences of actions taken by seemingly unrelated organizations.¹¹

Social ecology's main means of dealing with turbulence is collaboration. Gray further elaborates that "Collaborative alliances have been identified as a logical and necessary response to turbulent environments," and goes on to say:

Collaboration offers an antidote to turbulence by building a collective capacity to respond to turbulent environments. Through collaborative efforts, the stakeholders gain appreciation of their interdependence, pool their insights into the problem, increase variety in their repertoire of responses to the problem and achieve increased reciprocity, efficiency and stability. In most cases, creative solutions are needed that exceed the limited perspective of each individual stakeholder.[12]

Background for the 17 Year College Librarians' Campaign

The Ontario community college system which includes 22 non-degree post-secondary institutions was created in the late 1960s by the Ontario Ministry of Colleges and Universities as an alternative stream to traditional universities.[13] The Colleges of Applied Arts and Technology (CAAT) absorbed the existing Trades and Technology Institutes and created over a dozen new regional colleges. The colleges were handed a new governance structure (consisting of the Council of Regents), which operated as an autonomous "super" board that reported to the Ministry of Colleges and Universities in Ontario. This governance was legislated—not chosen—a fact that has sometimes led to conflict.[14] Other issues complicating development were the jurisdictional scuffles between the CAAT Boards of Governors (responsible for the management of each individual college) and the Council of Regents (on the management side) and the Ontario Federation of Community College Faculty Associations and the Civil Service Association of Ontario (CSAO) (on the academic employees' side). Discord ultimately prevented a successful negotiation of a first, system-wide contract until 1971, despite the colleges having been established in 1967.

These failed negotiations resulted in an arbitration award, which produced a Memorandum of Agreement in April 1972 for the 1971-73 contract period, which was very unfavourable to librarians. While this first contract provided teachers and counsellors with five classifications and a wide salary range ($6,200 - $16,000) without the requirement to supervise employees, librarians received a classification of only 2 ranges (Librarian I $7,700 - $10,000; Librarian II $9,500 - $12,200) with a supervisory requirement for the Librarian II classification. Furthermore, the teachers' contract was for a 10 month year, while librarians' contracts were for 11 months.[15]

While the colleges struggled with their new organization and management, women's equality became a major social force in the 1970s. Feminist campaigns challenged women's traditional roles and stereotypes, including those emanating from the workplace.[16] These campaigns were important because librarians were believed to be part of a disadvantaged "woman's" profession. Stromberg describes the complex problems of predominantly female professions thus:

... nursing, teaching and librarianship emerged in their modern forms in the nineteenth century, in a patriarchal society with a powerful sex role ideology that viewed women as especially sensitive, moral, and self-sacrificing by nature—an ideology that, when the need for women's labor arose, could be adapted to support their work in the serving professions ... these professions emerged as organization-based rather than entrepreneurial, occupations whose female workers were generally directed by men. The largely female image and labor force of these professions made the workers vulnerable to low wages, poor working conditions and discrimination. These professions shared many contemporary problems as well. These include sometimes poor working conditions, short career ladders, and modest earnings potential; considerable intra-occupational sex segregation by which the minority of men tend to rise to the top of the field; and difficulties in achieving consensus about how to secure their futures at a time of considerable internal and external technological, economic, and organizational change.[17]

The feminist challenge to women's traditional roles gained official prominence in Canada with the ground-breaking federal Royal Commission on the Status of Women in 1970. Three of its recommendations were vital to the struggle for equality of Ontario's college librarians:

- Recommendation 5, which suggested that the federal government ratify the International Labour Organization's (ILO) Convention 100 with respect to Equal Pay.[18] As of June 1971, 71 countries had already ratified the Convention but Canada had not.[19]
- Recommendation 8, which stated that the federal *Female Employee Equal Pay Act*, the federal *Fair Wages and Hours of Work* regulations and equal pay legislation of provinces and territories require that (a) the concept of skill, effort and responsibility be used as objective factors in determining what is equal work, with the understanding that pay rates thus established will be subject to such factors as seniority provisions; (b) an employee who feels aggrieved as a result of an alleged violation of the relevant legislation, or a party acting on her behalf, be able to refer the grievance to the agency designated for that purpose by the government administering the legislation; (c) the onus of investigating violations of the legislation which will be free to investigate, whether or not there are complaints have been laid; (d) to the extent possible, the anonymity of the complainant be maintained. (e) provision be made for authority to render a decision on whether or not the terms of the legislation have been violated, to specify action to be taken and to prosecute if the orders are not followed.[20]
- And finally, Recommendation 11 was also relevant, which stated, "We recommend that the pay rates for nurses, dietitians, home economists, li-

brarians and social workers employed by the federal government be set by comparing these professions with other professions in terms of the value of the work and the skill and training involved."[21]

Despite the Royal Commission, provinces had the jurisdictional responsibility for ensuring that labour laws and regulations secured women's employment equity. In the case of Ontario college librarians, a 1973 Green Paper on the Status of Women called *Equal Opportunity for Women in Ontario* was the first official provincial statement about the major problem of women's disadvantages in work. It proposed that the Ontario government re-examine the appropriate sections of the Employment Standards Act to broaden the concept of equal pay; however, the paper also expressed concern that the legislation of the time was ill equipped to deal with the more sophisticated forms of income discrimination based on sex.[22] The Ontario Government subsequently established the Ontario Status of Women Council to support research, hold public hearings, and make recommendations to improve women's employment conditions and opportunities.[23] Both federal and provincial initiatives were important first instruments of social change, which compelled the authors to focus on achieving the recommendations for equal pay for work of equal value in female-dominated professions and in particular for librarians in Ontario colleges. Therefore, they created a network called CLAC (CAAT Librarian Action Committee) whose function was to research and communicate these innovative ideas. Ontario college librarians' equality with teachers and counsellors was CLAC's theme for change.

First Action Steps

Disparities between the classification schemes and salary ranges of counsellors, teachers and librarians in the original 1972 arbitration award stimulated responses from the nascent CLAC. The award had included discriminatory terms and conditions for librarians to which CLAC promptly and officially responded.[24] Through this process, members of CLAC discovered that, although librarians had been mentioned as part of the bargaining group, no actual librarian from either side had been consulted in the negotiation process. In the 14 page memorandum presented to the arbitration board and copied to the CSAO, CLAC argued that librarians had not been properly represented at the proceedings. Data were therefore provided regarding librarians' pedagogic roles within the colleges, along with their salaries, vacations, classification structures, academic status, and academic qualifications *vis à vis* other academic staff. CLAC's appeal was unsuccessful in changing the 1972 award; however, its failure made clear the need for a long term, multi-faceted information and lobbying campaign to make the injustices known to the power brokers within the union, the college management and the provincial government. With the first agreement expiring in August 1973, CLAC had time to develop a stronger strategy and position itself for the next round of negotiations. To acquire evidence, the authors conducted a survey in 1973 on behalf of CLAC to expand on the nation-wide survey of community college librarians conducted by Qureshi in 1971 and to document the facts about librarians' qualifications, classifications and salaries across Ontario.[25]

Inskip, who had just joined Seneca College Library, was introduced to Ontario CAAT librarians' contractual issues and became an active participant in CLAC in November 1972. She brought with her experience and active membership both in feminist organizations and in government policy development networks. CLAC members felt that it was essential to establish effective communication among the unionized college librarians and to be a compelling voice for the CAAT librarians. CLAC recognized that the librarians represented a tiny minority within the CAAT academic unit—approximately 37 librarians out of a provincial total of over 5,000 academic members. CLAC members also realized they suffered from the "female image"[26] often applied to librarians, nurses and social workers (See Recommendation 11 of the *Royal Commission on the Status of Women*, above). CLAC members were early adopters of the innovative issue of discrimination against female-dominated professions and started communicating this message immediately.

Working toward the 1973 Provincial Contract Negotiations

The authors became the key network leaders in CLAC which worked to develop collaborative networks and to communicate the innovative idea that librarians deserved equal pay for work of equal value in Ontario community colleges. Although CLAC members were based primarily in the geographic area of Toronto, they established ties with colleagues across the province. In late 1972, the authors became Executive members of their respective union chapter locals (Jones as Branch Secretary at Humber College and Inskip as Campus Steward at Seneca College), thereby integrating fully into the CAAT's academic unit's decision-making structure.

Participation at the provincial level on the CAAT Academic Bargaining Team resulted in increased support from CSAO. Although formal representation was impossible, the January 1973 Academic (Provincial) Divisional Meeting passed a motion to include a representative of the counsellors and the librarians as a Resource Person at the Divisional level. There was also a provision in the CSAO Bylaws which stated that the Branch (College) Executive Committee should have representation from all occupational groups. This was interpreted to apply to librarians and counsellors in the various colleges. Jones became the librarian resource person at the CAAT Divisional level and Inskip as Alternate Representative from Seneca College to the CAAT Divisional level, which was composed primarily of Presidents of the 22 college union branches.

This integration allowed librarians to develop rapport with teaching colleagues and to persuade them of both the contributions and needs of CAAT librarians. In addition, valuable information was gleaned about the complex issues that faced the academic staff at this early stage in the development of union-management relations. Support for the librarians' cause was built through active participation in the CAAT Academic Division and in intra-union relations and provincial concerns. For example, the CAAT Academic Division was a driving force in the stormy transition of CSAO (considered by some a "sweetheart union"[27]) to the Ontario Public Service Employees Union (OPSEU) with a new focus on social concerns.[28] Through supporting this difficult integration on behalf of all members of the CAAT Division, the authors succeeded in building trusting relations. In turn, the CAAT Academic provincial executive granted them complete freedom to speak for college librarians' inequities in public forums and in the press. As well, the authors were given informal responsibilities to speak on CAAT Academic issues at CSAO and later at OPSEU annual conventions.

But the support of OPSEU was insufficient to effect the desired changes because management needed to be educated as well. Local managers of librarians were generally the college Chief Librarians, who identified with their unionized colleagues' issues. Library administrators also had to contend with the low salaries, unfair classification structures as well as limited opportunities for advancement due to the small size of most college library staffs. CLAC's first strategy to address these problems was practical. Through the CAAT Academic Bargaining Team's negotiations, it focused on salary range adjustments to parallel that of the CAAT Associate Master (Teacher) and Counsellor IV levels. This short-range adjustment would raise the salary ceilings to levels equal to those of Ontario academic librarians in universities. CLAC's long-range goal, however, was to restructure the librarians' classification to be either fully parallel with CAAT counsellors and teachers or to be completely integrated into the same structure.

CLAC Enters the Provincial Scene: Government, NGOs and Media

The CSAO and the CAAT Academic Division supported the demand for parity in salary. Librarians were clearly a female-dominated profession with higher educational qualifications than their predominantly male counterparts.[29] They reflected a situation identified in both the 1970 *Royal Commission on the Status of Women in Canada* and the 1973 Ontario Government's Green Paper, *Equal Opportunity for Women in Ontario: a Plan for Action (*see earlier references in this chapter). At the same time, there developed new opportunities to communicate more widely on how the innovative theme of equal pay for work of equal value was both essential and in line with other NGOs (such as the National Action Committee on the Status of Women). The media were sympathetic. CLAC used these opportunities to prepare the ground for the next round of the CAAT Academic Bargaining Team's provincial negotiations.

For example, after Robert J. Welch, Provincial Secretary for Social Development tabled the Green Paper, *Equal Opportunity for Women in Ontario: A Plan for Action* in 1973, CLAC responded in the form of a two-page letter summarizing their issues, namely the unequal salary scales and academic/professional qualifications of predominately female librarians vis à vis counsellors and teachers in the overall Academic Unit and requested a forum in which to formally present the CLAC case. The letter was signed by 15 CAAT librarians and copied to other stakeholders. [30] Following four months of silence, CLAC re-sent its letter with a covering note. This second communication stimulated brief replies. Mr. Welch redirected the letter to Mr. Jack McNie, Ontario Minister of Colleges and Universities. CLAC followed up by sending a letter to Mr. McNie. Mr. James Auld, the new Minister of Colleges and Universities, responded on March 1, 1974. The Minister's letter ignored all of CLAC's points except the issue of salary, for which Mr. Auld directed librarians back to the CAAT Academic Bargaining Team and its negotiations with the provincial Council of Regents. Indeed, Mr. Auld's letter ignored CLAC's key problem: librarians' classifications were a provincial management right and not within the scope of the CAAT Academic Division negotiations with the provincial Council of Regents. Consistent, indeed persistent, communication proved key to CLAC's eventual success. A follow up was directed to Mr. Norman Sisco, Chairman of the Council of Regents (March 21, 1974) and copied to eight other officials.[31] Mr. Sisco's April 11, 1973 reply mentioned a "Classification Sub-committee," a management only group, where he said the librarians' classification was "presently under examination." Mr. Sisco also reminded CLAC that ". . . librarians are the employees of their respective colleges and not the Council of Regents, or the Ministry of Colleges and Universities . . ."[32] Librarians were on familiar, yet unpleasant grounds: no government or educational organization took responsibility for CAAT librarians' equality and discrimination issues. A parallel channel of communications and a course of action were then pursued. The Ontario Status of Women Council, chaired by Laura Sabia, who was an innovator and early adopter for the innovation of equal pay for work of equal value, was approached. [33] CLAC submitted a Brief, "The CAAT Librarian: Role versus Image," and made a formal presentation to the Council of May 6, 1974. The Council accepted the arguments and at its next meeting (June 13, 1974) made the following recommendation:

> Since professional librarians in the C.A.A.T.s have academic qualifications equivalent to those of teaching staff and counsellors in the Colleges, and since the library is an integral part of the learning process of the Colleges, the Ontario Status of Women Council recommended that classification of staff in C.A.A.T.s should be by professional and academic qualifications, experience and responsibility and should combine teaching staff, counsellors and professional librarians; salaries and fringe benefits should be equal for all categories within that classification.[34]

The Ontario Status of Women Council's recommendation for CAAT librarians' equality was forwarded to Mr. Auld, Minister of Colleges and Universities by both CLAC and the Council. In addition, the CAAT librarians' situation was raised in the Ontario Legislature by Margaret Campbell, MPP, during debates of the estimates for the Ministry of Colleges and Universities on May 30, 1974 and June 19, 1974.[35]

Communicating with Library and General Media: The CLAC Network-Building Function

As early adopters of the innovation of equal pay for work of equal value in 1973, CLAC members worked to diffuse the idea of parity for Ontario community college librarians by meeting with the media and college and government decision-makers. CLAC moved beyond the direct environment of the CAAT Academic Unit's governance by distributing copies of correspondence, press releases and presentations to all target organizations in an effort to increase influence. CLAC issued a press release about its campaign in November 1973 to major library journals across North America. The release was picked up by American Library Association's Social Responsibilities Round Table *Bulletin*, *Wilson Library Bulletin*, *Library Journal* and the Canadian Library Association's *Feliciter*. The library media continued its coverage in May-June 1974 after CLAC sent out a press release on the Ontario Status of Women Council's endorsement of the CAAT librarians' equality issues. *Feliciter, Quill & Quire* and *Library Journal* picked up the news of the Status of Women's endorsement. CLAC continued its network-building and communications functions and sent copies of all news stories regarding the endorsement by the Status of Women Council to decision-makers in government, the Council of Regents, colleagues in the CAAT Academic Division and the CSAO. This provided the platform to communicate the CAAT librarians' equal pay for work of equal value innovation to general media, including newspapers and TV stations in Ontario. Here was an Ontario-based, well-documented case of gender bias and discrimination to complement other media stories emerging from the Status of Women Council's review of Ontario workplaces. In addition, CLAC also understood that general newspaper and TV coverage would signal credibility and importance to key decision-makers: the Ontario Ministry of Colleges and Universities; the Council of Regents; and the Committee of Presidents of the CAAT; as well as the CAAT Academic Bargaining Division and the CSAO. By the mid-1970s, the National Action Committee on the Status of Women and its affiliate feminist organizations had raised the public profile of many women's issues.[36] In May 1974, CLAC issued a press release to all mainstream media in Toronto and across Ontario. This timing coincided with heightened public awareness of the present and future roles of librarians and libraries because there was considerable publicity about the Special Libraries Association Annual Conference in Toronto that June. The results of CLAC's press release were gratifying. Not only was coverage received in the library press but also in the two major Canadian newspapers (*Globe & Mail* and *Toronto Star*). The authors were interviewed on Global Television News (a national television station) and subsequently wrote an article updating the Council's endorsement and the resulting publicity, which was published in the *IPLO Quarterly* in January 1975.[37] CLAC continued its activism in network-building and communications, ensuring that all key provincial targets, both on the management side and on the union side, received copies of the Council's endorsement and of the major newspapers and TV stations news coverage of CAAT librarians' parity issues relating to gender discrimination.[38] CLAC members relentlessly called, met, photocopied and mailed their innovative messaging to key stakeholders. A comprehensive list of key people and organizations was developed and cover letters were specifically written to each. Informal progress reports were submitted to members of the National Action Committee on the Status of Women and to other federal and provincial feminist organizations. CLAC's job was to keep the CAAT librarians' issue top of mind for decision-makers.[39]

1973–1975: Contract Negotiations

Meanwhile negotiations for the 1973-75 contract dragged on. Major jurisdictional issues between CSAO and the Ontario government focused on the scope of negotiations and the independence of the arbitration board. The initial arbitration, under Judge J.C. Anderson, was picketed on March 6, 1974 by librarians, teachers and counsellors. They felt that the Anderson Arbitration Board was biased because the government appointed two of the three arbitration board members, thereby stacking the board against employees, something it was able to do under the Crown Employees Collective Bargaining Act (CECBA). After talks failed and 88.7% of members from across Ontario rejected management's position, Judge Anderson agreed to step down and an *ad hoc* board was set up under Justice Willard Z. Estey.[40] The CAAT Academic Division Bargaining Team submitted its brief to the Estey board in December 1974. The brief included extensive research and documentation supporting the case for parity between librarians and teachers and counsellors. Justice Estey released the final award on June 20, 1975. CAAT librarians received only a small across-the-board salary adjustment of $650.00 and the award addressed none of the CAAT academic librarians' issues with respect to parity.[41] Furthermore the minimal across-the-board increases for librarians actually *widened* the gap between the salary ceiling available to librarians and that available to teachers and counsellors because the dollar value of the percentage increments to the teacher and counsellors far exceeded that for librarians. In the following negotiations (1975-1977), the Academic Bargaining Team (which included a librarian) maintained its support of librarians. Indeed the CAAT Academic Division executive voted to support the CAAT Bargaining Team's position by volunteering to forgo 0.25% of the across-the-board increase in their salary demands for all academic staff in order to fund the reclassification of positions and salary rectification of librarians. Management refused to consider the Bargaining Team's proposal. The CAAT Academic Division's innovative bargaining proposal, however, demonstrated the union's commitment to the equal and important contribution of college librarians and acknowledged the results of CLAC's dedication to its cause.

Changes in the 1980s

The social, legal and political environments for discrimination against particular occupations changed considerably in the 1980s.[42] A 1984 report by another Royal Commission, this time on Equality in Employment (Chaired by Justice Abella), was published. It defined systemic discrimination as follows:

> Systemic discrimination "means practices or attitudes that have, whether by design or impact, the effect of limiting an individual's or a group's right to the opportunities generally available because of attributed rather than actual characteristics . . . . It is not a question of whether this discrimination is motivated by an intentional desire to obstruct someone's potential, or whether it is the accidental bi-product of innocently motivated practices or systems. If the barrier is affecting some groups in a disproportionately negative way, it is a signal that the practices that lead to this adverse impact may be discriminatory.[43]

Further to the Commission, section 15 of the *Canadian Charter of Rights and Freedoms* provides a legal basis on which to challenge laws that discriminated on the basis of race, national or ethnic origin, colour, religion, sex, age or mental or physical disability.[44] Consequently, the National Action Committee on the Status of Women, its 700 affiliate organizations and Ontario's Equal Pay Coalition (a group of trade unions, church and community groups) eventually lobbied the Ontario provincial government to pass its first Pay Equity Act in 1987. The Act mandated employers to proactively prepare pay equity plans by identifying wage gaps between men's and women's work using the criteria of skill, effort, responsibility and working conditions.[45]

1980–1989: Innovation and Action Sustained

Inskip and Jones left the colleges in 1979 and 1980 respectively, however the CAAT Academic Bargaining Team pushed librarians' demands at the bargaining table well into the 1980s. CAAT librarians active in the CLAC campaign included Lynne Bentley and Cheryl Salkey of Humber College. Bentley's presentation to the Community and Technical Colleges Libraries (CTCL) section of the Canadian Association of College and University Libraries (CACUL) at the June 1989 Canadian Library Association (CLA) Conference provides the basis for the case history from 1980–1989.[46] In essence, the CAAT Academic Bargaining Team continued to push for librarians' academic equivalency and parity, while provincial management and the Council of Regents continued to see librarians as a separate profession with market equivalents outside the colleges, which resulted in no major progress for librarians.

There were also larger contentious issues affecting the entire CAAT Academic Bargaining Unit, most notably working conditions and academic freedom. These led to a landmark three-week strike of all CAAT academic staff in 1984. Librarians took an active role in the strike and drew attention to their solidarity with teaching and counselling colleagues. In the process of the strike, librarians educated their colleagues on the issues and discrimination facing librarians. This strike was ended by provincial back-to-work legislation but resulted in major gains in long-standing teacher workload issues. Once again, there were only incremental advances for librarians: three additional steps were added to each librarian classification level. Parity was denied. The maximum Librarian II salary still remained about $6000 below that of the teacher/counsellor grid.

The strike however, had set the stage for the 1987 round of negotiations. This featured a major push for equality to comply with the ground-breaking 1987 Ontario Pay Equity Act, which recognized the depressed salaries and working conditions of female-dominated professions. The CAAT Academic Bargaining Team focused on librarians' equivalency with counsellors, perceived as a closer parallel to librarians than teachers. CAAT counsellors, however, already enjoyed full status with the teachers. Again the normal provincial negotiation process failed to resolve the librarians' issues and concluded on March 3, 1988, settling all issues except those of librarians. The 1988 settlement, however directed a special interest arbitration board to deal with the issues of librarians' salaries and vacations to determine the value of the job of librarian compared to the value of the job of teacher and counsellor based on factors of skill, effort, responsibility and working conditions (based on the Ontario Pay Equity Act). OPSEU (the successor union to CSAO) dedicated special resources to the arbitration and established a Librarians' Arbitration Working Group, including three CAAT librarians to research and document the librarians' case. OPSEU worked closely with the librarians through this joint committee, even producing a video to illustrate the actual roles of librarians and to counter any traditional or discriminatory notions of librarians or biases against them among members of arbitration board.

Final Settlement

The arbitration concluded with an award on January 13, 1989—on the first of four days scheduled for hearings. It provided librarians with the long-sought parity with teachers and counsellors. The award included:

1) Full pay equity between librarians, teachers and counsellors; the separate salary grid for librarians was abandoned, and librarians were integrated into the salary grid.

2) The troublesome bifurcated classification system was eliminated and replaced with a single classification. This change redressed a long standing inequity for those librarians who were forced to remain at the Librarian 1 classification because they did not supervise other librarians.
3) Librarians were awarded 42 vacation days per year to make their vacation allocation equal to teachers and counsellors. Prior to this award, librarians' vacation days were capped at 32 days after 10 years of service.[47]

Conclusion

Over many years, CLAC networked to communicate the educational contribution of college librarians equal to their teaching and counselling colleagues. CLAC also demonstrated successfully how and why management systemically discriminated against the CAAT librarians very early in the days of equal pay for work of equal value. Seventeen years of CLAC's efforts for CAAT academic librarians resulted in their eventual integration and parity with CAAT teachers and counsellors in 1989. The authors assumed and maintained union responsibilities at the local and provincial levels in the CAAT Academic Division. This integration provided access and influence in provincial bargaining and earned the trust and support of colleagues. Simultaneously, CLAC identified and communicated strategically within a province-wide network of key decision-makers in government, NGOs and the media. CLAC's persistent communication of (1) its innovative message: equal pay for work of equal value, and (2) how decision-makers systemically discriminated against CAAT librarians was key to its eventual success. In the days before email or Twitter, ideas, arguments and facts were communicated to multiple networks through more traditional means. The work of CAAT librarians mirrored both the nation-wide social marketing of the National Action Committee on the Status of Women and the province-wide efforts of the Coalition for Equal Pay, that worked with federal and provincial legislators in the development of the 1985 *Canadian Charter of Rights and Freedoms* and in the 1987 *Ontario Pay Equity Act*. CLAC's work was part of the fabric of the major social change in evaluating the true value of performed work.

Bibliography

Abella, Rosalie Silberman. *Equality in Employment: A Royal Commission Report.* Ottawa: Minister of Supply and Services Canada, 1984. http://worthwhile.typepad.com/files/abella1984-part1-eng.pdf.

Bentley, Lynne. Unpublished transcript of presentation to the CTCL Section, CACUL at the CLA Annual Conference, Edmonton, 1989.

Canada. *Constitution Act (1982), Part 1, Canadian Charter of Rights and Freedoms.* Section 15. 1982. http://laws-lois.justice.gc.ca/eng/const/page-15.html.

Canada. Royal Commission on the Status of Women in Canada. *Report of the Royal Commission on the Status of Women in Canada.* 1970. http://epe.lac-bac.gc.ca/100/200/301/pco-bcp/commissions-ef/bird1970-eng/bird1970-eng.htm.

CAAT Academic Bargaining Team. *Submission to the Estey Arbitration between The Civil Service Association of Ontario (CSAO) Academic Bargaining Unit and The Council of Regents for the Colleges of Applied Arts and Technology.* 1974. http://hdl.handle.net/10402/era.31760.

Chisholm, Rupert F. *Developing Network Organizations: Learning from Practice and Theory.* Addison-Wesley Series on Organizational Development. Don Mills, Ontario: Addison-Wesley, 1988.

Cornish, Mary and Fay Faraday. "Litigating Pay and Employment Equity: Strategic Uses and Limits—the Canadian Experience." Paper presented to the International Pay and Employment Equity for Women conference held by the New Zealand Advisory Council on the Employment of Women. Wellington, New Zealand June 28-29, 2004.

Dennison, John D. and Paul Gallagher. *Canada's Community Colleges: A Critical Analysis.* Vancouver: University of British Columbia Press, 1986.

Emery, Fred and Eric Trist. "The Causal Texture of Organizational Environments." Paper presented to the 1963 International Psychology Congress, Washington D.C. Reprinted in *Human Relations*, vol. 18 (1965): 21-32.

———. *Towards a Social Ecology.* New York: Plenum, 1972.

Emery, Merrelyn and Ronald E. Purser. *The Search Conference: A Powerful Method for Planning Organizational Change and Community Action.* San Francisco; Jossey-Bass. 1996.

Fisher, Roger, William Ury and Bruce Patton. *Getting to Yes: Negotiating Agreement Without Giving In.* (3rd ed.). New York: Penguin, 2011.

Fleming, William Gerald. *Ontario's Educative Society, Vol. 4, Post-secondary and Adult Education.* Toronto: University of Toronto Press, 1971.

Gladwell, Malcolm. *The Tipping Point: How Little Things Can Make a Big Difference.* Boston: Little Brown, 2000.

Graham, Astley W. and Charles J. Fombrun. "Collective Strategy: Social Ecology of Organizational Environments." *Academy of Management Review* 8, no. 4 (1983): 576-87.

Gray Barbara. *Collaborating; Finding Common Ground for Multiparty Problems.* San Francisco: Jossey Boss. 1989.

———. "Creating Collaborative Advantage." London: SAGE Publications, 1996. 57-80. http://dx.doi.org/10.4135/9781446221600.

Gray, Barbara and Donna J. Wood. "Collaborative Alliances: Moving from Practice to Theory." Introduction to the first special issue on Collaborative Alliances of the *Journal of Applied Behavioral Science* 27, no. 1 (1991): 3-22.

Harris, Roma Maria. *Librarianship: The Erosion of a Woman's Profession.* Norwood, NJ: Ablex Publishing Corporation. 1992.

Husham, Chris. *Creating Collaborative Advantage.* Thousand Oaks, CA: Sage. 1996.

Inskip, Robin. "Building Consensus and Power in the Library Community; the Marketing of School Library Services by a Provincial Library Association." *Emergency Librarian* 11, no. 4, (1984) 9-13.

———. *The Marigold System: A Case Study of Community Networks and Community Development.* Halifax: Dalhousie University School of Library and Information Studies Occasional Paper, 1987.

———. "Planning and Facilitating Interorganizational Collaboration," (Unpublished doctoral dissertation) University of Toronto, Toronto, 1992.

Inskip, Robin and David L. Jones. "Community College Librarians—A Dispatch from the Front." *IPLO Quarterly* 16, no. 3 (1975): 146-149.

Jones, David L. and Robin Inskip. *Ontario Community College Librarians' Equality Campaign (1973 - 1975).* Brampton: Information and Research Services, 1975. http://hdl.handle.net/10402/era.31759.

Landsberg, Michele. *Writing the Revolution.* Toronto: Second Story Press, 2011.

———."Charting Equality: Feminist Activism and the Charter of Rights," in *Writing the Revolution.* 251-287. Toronto: Second Story Press, 2011.

Oliver, Christine. "Strategic Responses to Institutional Processes." *Academy of Management Review* 16 (1973): 145-79.

Ontario. Provincial Secretariat for Social Development. *Equal Opportunity for Women in Ontario: A Plan for Action, June 1973.* [Toronto], Provincial Secretariat for Social Development. 1973.

Overlaet, Robrecht and Sara Aerts. *Cultural Aspects of the Search Conference Method.* Katholieke Universiteit Leuven, 1999. https://lirias.kuleuven.be/bitstream/123456789/223280/1/OR_9930.pdf.

Pasmore, William A. and Gurudev S. Khalsa. "The Contributions of Eric Trist to the Social Engagement of Social Science." *Academy of Management Review* 18, no. 3 (1993): 546-569.

Pennsylvania State University. "Barbara Gray." http://php.smeal.psu.edu/smeal/dirbio/displayBio.php?t_user_id=b9g.

Qureshi, M.J. "Academic Status, Salaries and Fringe Benefits in Community College Libraries in Canada," *Canadian Library Journal* 28, no. 1 (1971): 41-45.

Ramirez, Rafael, John W. Selsky and Kees van der Heijden. *Business Planning for Turbulent Times; New Methods for Applying Scenarios.* 2nd ed. Washington: Earthscan, 2010.

Rogers, Everett M. *Diffusion of Innovations.* 5th ed. New York: Free Press, 2003.

Sacks, Danielle. "Fifty Percent of 'The Tipping Point' is Wrong. Jonah Berger Shows You Which Half." *Fast Company* (March 18, 2013). http://www.fastcompany.com/3006693/fifty-percent-of-the-tipping-point-is-wrong-jonah-berger-shows-you-which-half.

Sahin, Ismali. "Detailed Review of Rogers' Diffusion of Innovations Theory and Educational Technology-Related Studies Based on Rogers' Theory." *The Turkish Online Journal of Educational Technology—TOGET*, 5, no. 2 (2006). http://www.tojet.net/articles/v5i2/523.pdf.

Skolnik, M.L. "The Evolution of Relations between Management and Faculty in Ontario Colleges of Applied Arts and Technology." *Canadian Journal of Higher Education* 18, no. 3 (1988): 83-112.

Stromberg, Ann H. "Women in Female-dominated Professions." In A.H. Stromberg and S. Harkess (Eds.), *Women Working: Theories and Facts in Perspective.* 2nd ed. Mountain View, CA: Mayfield Publishing Company. 1988.

Teamsters. *Definitions of Common Labor Terms.* http://www.teamster.org/content/definitions-common-labor-terms#s.

Trist, Eric L. "A Concept of Organization Ecology." *Australian Journal of Management* 2 (1977): 162-75.

———. "Referent Organizations and the Development of Inter-organizational Domains." *Human Relations* 36, no. 3 (1983): 247-68.

Trist, Eric L., Fred Emery and Hugh Murray (Eds). *The Social Engagement of Social Science: A Tavistock Anthology.* Philadelphia: University of Pennsylvania Press. 1990-1997. (vol. 1 The Social Psychological Perspective; vol. 2 The Socio-technical Perspective; vol. 3 The Socio-ecological Perspective).

van der Heijden, Kees. *Scenarios: The Art of Strategic Conversation.* 2nd ed. Wiley, 2005.

Wamsley, Gary L. and Mayer N. Zald. "The Environments of Public Managers: Managing in Turbulence," in *Handbook of Organizational Management.* William B. Eddy (Ed.). New York: Marcel Dekker, 1983.

Wildavsky, Aaron B. *Speaking Truth to Power: The Art and Craft of Policy Analysis.* Boston: Little Brown. 1979.

Part Three

Current Issues and Experiences

Librarians as Teachers, Researchers and Community Members

Meg Raven, Francesca Holyoke, and Karen Jensen

Introduction

In the 2012 Canadian Association of University Teachers (CAUT) Librarian Salary Survey, 92% of academic librarians working at Canadian universities reported that they have academic status similar to that of teaching faculty. Like teaching faculty, academic librarians' workload responsibilities are usually defined in collective agreements. Most are familiar with the workload triad assigned to teaching faculty: teaching, scholarly activities/research and service to the community. Librarians with academic status typically find their workload responsibilities defined in terms of professional practice (or librarian duties), scholarly activities and service to the community. The CAUT Survey also reported on terms of employment for librarians at Canadian universities. Ninety-three percent of academic librarians responding to the survey reported workload language that includes professional practice; 79% had a responsibility to participate in scholarly activity; and 89% included service as a component of their workload. Only six Canadian universities[1] (9%) identified *teaching* as a specific workload responsibility for librarians, which suggests that defining teaching as a formal librarian responsibility is not a priority for most academic staff associations.

The literature suggests,[2] and most librarians would likely agree, that the majority of librarians' working lives are dedicated to fulfilling the responsibilities of professional practice, with little time available for scholarship or service. In this chapter, we explore the areas of teaching, research and service as separate, yet integral, components of our work that are essential for advancing and protecting our profession. While we see multiple advantages to dedicating quality time to all areas of our workload, the reality is that these activities often compete for the same parcel of time. With ever-increasing workload demands, it is essential that collective agreements and faculty handbooks are documents that ensure equity and balance. In the following sections, we introduce some of the rewards and challenges of academic librarianship, and suggest ways to balance professional practice, teaching, scholarly activities and service.

Librarians as Teachers

The debate as to whether librarians are teachers has raged in the professional literature for years. Loesch[3] and Simmons[4] provide some of the best evidence that librarians' abilities to transform questions into teaching opportunities make them first and foremost teachers. Julien and Genuis report, in their survey of Canadian librarians, that 79% of respondents "identified instructional work as being integral to their professional identity."[5] And Kemp neatly summarizes the benefits of librarians teaching as including "closer interaction with students over an extended period of time, a deeper understanding of faculty workloads, student needs and administrative requirements, a new way of collection development, enhancement of faculty status, increased intellectual stimulation and sharper self-assessment of performance."[6] For now, the debate seems to have cooled with one hoping most academic librarians gravitate toward supporting teaching as a component of librarianship. This seems to be the case, as evidenced by contemporary research having to look back farther and farther to find arguments that oppose teaching as a function of librarianship: Johnson[7]; Wilson[8]; Borchuck and Bergup[9]; Shera.[10] While the specifics of this debate continue to be interesting, our focus, in this section, is the advantages to academic librarianship of including teaching *as a named component of our workload.*

The data gathered in the 2012 CAUT Librarian Salary Survey of 62 Canadian universities confirms that academic librarians are involved in substantial and varied teaching.

Types of teaching done by academic librarians at Canadian universities:	
Workshops	95%
Integrated instruction in non-library courses	77%
Library courses (non-credit)	42%
Library credit courses	27%
Non-library credit courses	34%

Table 1 (CAUT, 2012)

Survey respondents, who took time to elaborate on their answers, explained that in cases where librarians do not provide any kind of workshop-based teaching, it was because of small staff complements and no ability to dedicate time to such work. Those universities with librarians teaching outside the library (34%) provided the explanation that some librarians had an MLIS, plus another advanced degree, and held part-time teaching appointments in subject departments like Biology or English. While 27% of libraries reported offering library-based credit courses, what the data do not indicate is whether these courses are of equal weight to traditional discipline-based credit courses. Anecdotal information suggests many of these courses are often not of equal weight or credit hours.

Respondents also indicated that their teaching audience reached beyond students with some indicating considerable time dedicated to providing instruction to faculty in areas such as copyright.

How Teaching is Operationalized for the Academic Librarian

The CAUT survey data and the literature[11] suggest that librarians tend to label a lot of different activities as teaching: the one-shot classes, various workshops, team-taught courses, integrated course content, the full stand-alone library-based credit course, in-service training, work with faculty, and the teachable moments at the reference desk. It is often only when one begins to teach full-fledged credit courses that the extent of the difference between these practices begins to emerge and we see that a lot of what librarians do is not teaching, but is rather instruction. This distinction is further compounded because even if librarians do not differentiate between teaching and instruction, professors and administrators do. To them, teaching means credit courses, not the litany of activities described above.

Both teaching and instruction have important places in the work portfolios of academic librarians. Students need to be instructed on how to use scholarly sources, such as databases and specialized research tools. At these times, we provide information and explanations to build a skill. Students practice and master this skill. However, students also need the opportunity to be taught to critique, for example, the power relationships that exist between information producer and information consumer. In this case, teaching becomes two directional and highly interactive; it involves real learning and includes the study, critique and evaluation of an idea.[12] Both of these activities are fundamental to librarians' work, as one activity often informs the other. As such, we should not seek to replace either activity, but instead seek to value the depth and variety of teaching and instruction we are able to offer. We should recognize, however, that the variety itself may make it harder for external constituents to understand what we do.

There are some good pedagogical and administrative reasons for teasing apart our teaching and instructional activities. Recognizing that teaching requires additional pedagogical inputs encourages librarians to invest time in developing their skills in this area. From an administrative point of view, it will be easier for faculty colleagues to understand the distinctions between teaching and instructional activities when we stop trying to "disguise" all librarianship "as teaching."[13] As emphasized above, the instructional work we do is very valuable; we should stop apologising for it or trying to disguise it as teaching. By categorizing these two activities in ways that correspond to work done by other academic staff, we provide better guidelines for the evaluation of our work, for example, during reappointment, promotion and tenure processes. However, what is more important than distinguishing between librarians' teaching and instructional practices, is how we manage this type of work in our contracts and collective agreements. In collective agreements, we tend to assign teaching to the professional practice category of our workload. Teaching is not named, as are research and service, nor is it drawn out as a specific responsibility, as it is for faculty. By bundling teaching together with professional practice it becomes invisible, uncompensated work.

The Workload Issue

The fact that the teaching done by librarians receives little formal attention has serious repercussions. A 2009 Discussion Paper, authored by the CAUT Librarians' Committee, on the *Expanding Role of Teaching by Librarians in Post-Secondary Institutions* outlines the changes to teaching carried out by academic librarians and its subsequent impact to librarians' workloads. Widespread university curriculum changes, aggressive student recruitment, and the mainstreaming of technology have had the effect of changing bibliographic or library instruction programs into information literacy programs.[14]

The Discussion Paper calls for greater analysis of the impact of teaching on workloads, as librarians report that instruction is often viewed as a duty that must be accomplished in addition to more regular responsibilities.[15] Others report exhaustion from their roles as teachers.[16] Related to this is the workplace stress that can result from a lack of support from library administrators or colleagues who do not understand the value of teaching, or begrudge the time teaching takes away from traditional library practice. If some librarians are investing more time in teaching, will there be workload implications for all? The flip side of this argument is the concern that librarians who are not teaching may become vulnerable and viewed as less valuable to the library.[17]

Teaching as a Librarian Workload Criterion

If there is evidence to suggest that academic librarians have a long history of teaching and instructing, then why have we so systematically omitted teaching as a distinct activity from workload language and instead let it be subsumed by professional practice? As discussed in the following sections, a similar fate has not befallen scholarship and service. These two activities, regardless of how much time librarians actually have to dedicate to them, have long merited discrete places in the contract language of academic librarianship.

A common argument made to justify not including distinct teaching responsibilities in workload language is that few librarians have had formal teacher training[18] and are therefore unprepared to teach. While it can be argued that the majority of teaching faculty also have limited teacher training, most enter their chosen professions expecting that they will teach because normal contracts specify workloads that include teaching, research and service. Academic librarians may not have the same expectation, even with expanding teaching requirements, due to this lack of contract articulation. Related to this is the fact that not all librarians may elect, or may be able to teach[19] and that this may somehow disadvantage those members if teaching is specified as a workload criterion. As a transitional solution, academic staff associations involved in contract negotiations could propose teaching language modeled around administrative service. After all, not all librarians begin their careers with administrative responsibilities, but instead grow into these roles. A workload clause which asserts that responsibilities "may include teaching" would help integrate a workplace practice into contract language. Another avenue worth considering is a specific librarian teaching stream that could be modeled on the "alternative teaching" or "excellence in teaching" language that is available at some universities to faculty heavily involved in teaching.

There are also the matters of equity and compensation. Most faculty routinely have one semester free of teaching so that they may focus on scholarly activities. Such is not the case for librarians, who are tied to the library over the calendar year rather than the academic year. Would regularized, contract-mandated teaching exacerbate this inequity? On one hand, identifying teaching as a workload responsibility may lead to greater equity with teaching faculty, but on the other, an increased teaching workload may, in fact, prevent librarians from taking on more research. Equitable compensation must also be considered when librarians assume a formal responsibility for teaching. When teaching is incorporated into professional practice, librarians may not be adequately compensated for their work. At Mount Saint Vincent University, in Halifax, Nova Scotia, librarians began to teach a main-streamed credit course as part of their workload in 2009. Because this teaching was collapsed into professional practice, there was no increased compensation at that time, nor was there any success in bargaining for increased compensation when the contract was renewed. This suggests that university administrations have a vested interested in keeping teaching language out of librarian workload articles.

If collective agreements are not accurately describing the full slate of workload responsibilities of academic librarians, it is worth investigating whether professional job postings better reflect workload responsibilities. It is easy to believe that contract language could lag behind current workload practices, but job postings for librarians should accurately describe the responsibilities of a position. A review of academic librarian jobs posted to the Canadian Librarian Association (www.cla.ca/careers) and American Library Association (joblist.ala.org) web sites between October 2012 and September 2013 revealed that teaching is almost exclusively mentioned in the context that incumbents support the teaching of other constituents. American advertisements frequently required "teaching experience" for "instructional responsibilities," while Canadian jobs exclusively sought candidates with instructional experience alone. These types of job postings further confirm that the language used when advertising a position frequently does not accurately represent actual workload responsibilities.

Librarians must consider seriously if academic librarianship is a service profession or an academic discipline. If it is an academic discipline, then we must embrace the academic model of teaching, research and service, and strive to write contract language that blends all three of these workload components *with* our professional practice, not *into* our professional practice. By unbundling teaching from professional practice, we can begin to recognize it as more than just another professional activity. Teaching then becomes a distinct category of work, no longer invisible in collective agreements and hiring advertisements.

Accurately naming our work is a necessary step not only to advance the goal of greater parity with faculty colleagues, but by naming teaching as a workload criterion, academic librarians also will be better able to: hire with teaching in mind, establish criteria for the evaluation and review of teaching, participate in professional teaching opportunities, serve as full members of university curriculum committees, and participate fully in all areas of campus life.

Librarians as Researchers

There is an underlying assumption that, while teaching as an integral part of an academic librarian's responsibilities has yet to be clearly articulated, space for the librarian as researcher has been accommodated in workload under scholarly activity. In the Canadian context, where nearly all academic librarians are part of faculty associations or unions, the national body, CAUT, provides model clauses for contract or collective agreement language. These clauses point to an aspirational reach:

> CAUT – Model Clause on Scholarly Activities of Academic Librarians
>
> 1) The University recognizes the importance to its academic mission of librarians' continuing development as members of the academic staff, and acknowledges that their pursuit of research, study, educational and other scholarly activities brings benefits to and enhances the reputation of the University, the profession and the individual librarian.
> 2) Librarians shall have academic freedom as provided elsewhere in this agreement to pursue research, study, educational and other scholarly activities.

3) The pursuit of research, study, educational and other scholarly activities shall constitute a normal component of a librarian's workload.
4) A librarian shall have the right to devote up to 40% of normal workload to the pursuit of research, study, educational and other scholarly activities.
5) The scheduled duties of librarians shall be arranged so that there is regular and sufficient uninterrupted time for the pursuit of research, study, educational and other scholarly activities.
6) Librarians shall be entitled to sabbatical leave as provided elsewhere in this agreement in order to pursue research, study, educational and other scholarly activities.
7) Research, study, educational and other scholarly activities performed by a librarian shall be considered in the librarian's performance appraisal, promotion, or tenure evaluation.
8) These provisions shall apply equally to librarians appointed on a part-time or limited-term contract basis.[20]

The Model Clause serves two purposes. The first is the inclusive understanding of "research, study, educational and other scholarly activities," which "brings benefits to and enhances the reputation of the University, the profession and the individual librarian."[21] This understanding permits setting aside the discourse on research as a type of scholarly activity: here the assumption will be that scholarly activity and research are synonymous.

The second aspect is distributed across clauses which suggest that such activities "shall constitute a normal component of a librarian's workload," that "up to 40% of normal workload" should be devoted to these pursuits and that librarians' scheduled duties "shall be arranged so that there is regular and sufficient uninterrupted time" for such work.[22]

In January 2013, the American Association of University Professors (AAUP) and the Association of College and Research Libraries (ACRL) revised their joint Statement on the Faculty Status of College and University Librarians that provides some support to librarians being involved in research. However, in trying to cover the gamut of faculty status with reference to librarians' roles in university governance and the development of curriculum, the role of research in librarians' work is dispensed with in two sentences: "They are involved in the research function and conduct research in their own professional interests and in the discharge of their duties. Their scholarly research contributes to the advancement of knowledge valuable to their discipline and institution."[23]

In addition to the recognition of librarians' research by associations, organizations or unions, there has also been much written about librarians conducting research. Watson-Boone, Lowry, Koufogiannkis and Crumley and Kennedy and Brancolini[24] are among those providing an introduction to the themes of this now voluminous body of work.

Are Librarians Conducting Research, and if so, How?

The cottage industry of new research-oriented library journals, the plethora of blogs and their postings earnestly discussing such, and workshops[25] to help develop and carry out such endeavours all suggest that research for librarians is well-established. Indeed, in the 2012 CAUT Librarian Salary Survey, 79% of those responding indicated they had a responsibility to participate in scholarly activity. What is not clear from the data is whether those responding consider scholarly activity/research a normal part of their workload. The question arises because the same literature, blogs and workshops reconfirm that it remains a challenge to carve out time for scholarly activities.[26]

And yet, if numbers from the Hildreth and Aytac[27] survey hold true for Canadian academic librarians – that of a sample of articles published in 23 library and information science journals, nearly half (47.1%) were practitioner-only in authorship rather than academic – then clearly this is beginning to form a significant workload component.

The 2012 CAUT Librarian Salary Survey reveals that only one Canadian university, Laurentian, reported that its librarians could devote 40% of their time to research. This is accomplished through contract language, which makes no distinction in such provisions among the professoriate, instructors, librarians or archivists.[28] For the rest, it is a patchwork of support through sabbaticals (71%) and research days (48%). Where sabbaticals are good for longer term research undertakings and research days are perhaps an attempt to provide uninterrupted time, neither of these supports suggest that research or scholarly activity is part of the normal workload.

There has yet to be a definitive survey querying how librarians are carrying out such volumes of practitioner-related research. However Fox[29] and Catano, et. al.[30] identify that most librarians, like most faculty, work many more hours than the standard 36.25 to 40 hour week. It is reasonable to surmise that again, like faculty, much of the research done by librarians is carried out as an extra or overload activity.

How Others Perceive Librarians' Scholarly Activity

If due to less-than-robust contract language, rank and file librarians are more likely to see scholarly activity as something to be undertaken above and beyond their normal workload, what is the perception of faculty colleagues, library educators and administrators? In exploring faculty colleague perceptions' of librarian work, much of the literature has focused on how to build partnerships for either instructional/information literacy purposes or for collections development. More recent writings subsume collaboration with librarians as members of research teams in the new guise of the embedded librarian.[31] Christiansen, Stombler and

Thaxton instead looked at "neglected faculty-librarians relations" as a subject of study and found an "asymmetrical disconnection between librarians and faculty." Where "Librarians are aware of faculty and the work they do, and are continually striving to increase the contact with them . . . By contrast, faculty do not have a solid understanding of librarians' work and are not seeking similar contact."[32] The authors go on to provide two theoretical frameworks which provide an organizational explanation and a status-difference explanation, both of which rest on the assertion that "[i]n the view of librarians, this disconnect interferes with their ability to meet their work goals, the highest of which is serving students."[33] The fact that librarians' research was not considered, by either the authors or the faculty they interviewed, is disheartening.

Wyss's 2010 article about library school faculty perceptions' of librarians found that these faculty members believe that, not only may the MLS degree be insufficient to prepare librarians for faculty status, but also that librarians are further disadvantaged in producing research because of their schedules. While library school faculty believe that sabbatical and research leaves will facilitate research and improve their graduates' publication rates, the general conclusion Wyss came to is that, although upon finishing their degrees new librarians may be "prepared to assume professional duties in an academic setting, they may be less well prepared to perform activities such as research and publication."[34]

If faculty colleagues are generally unaware of librarians' work and the fact that it might include research, and if library educators believe their former students may be unprepared for research, what is it that administrators understand about librarians' research?

A fair proxy for the administrators' views of research and scholarly activities are those of the Canadian Association of Research Libraries (CARL).[35] With regard to research, these are elucidated in a series of CARL documents, among them "Librarians as Researchers and Writers," "Research Competencies for CARL Librarians" and "Core Competencies for 21st Century CARL Librarians." These all place an emphasis on applied, directed research closely linked to job tasks or responsibilities. Much of this research is useful, and professional practice must be informed by such scholarly activity. However, when the profiled research opportunities cover "user expectations & customer service" or "intellectual freedom and copyright" without reference to fair dealing, it becomes clear that research is intended to be limited in scope and chiefly related to what helps to make either the library or the librarian more productive.

Where the CARL documents provide one view, a recent study by Berg and Jacobs examines the perspectives of Canadian academic librarians as to the impediments they face when conducting research. Berg's and Jacobs' conclusions note the disconnections between the perceptions of librarians and their administrators. They acknowledge that, for librarians, "time is perhaps the most cited issue in the professional literature in relation to librarians and scholarship."[36] Library administrators seem to be of the view that librarians are unprepared to carry out research, which is perhaps what has given rise to the CARL initiatives.

Should the librarian require help to get started with research, rather than promoting mentoring among faculty/librarian colleagues,[37] or encouraging librarians to take advantage of their collective agreement provisions, CARL promotes a Librarians' Research Institute (LRI), now in its second year (2013). The preparatory material for the 2012 version indicated "course projects should be anchored to real work-place issues or research issues" and when formulating research questions, consideration should be given to "institutional mandate or strategic plan, individual job area or position" and lastly "individual interest." The LRI is still in its early iterations. If it successfully moves away from an emphasis on research originating from these most recent suggestions "toward the creation of a sharing, reflective research community,"[38] it may well help in encouraging academic librarians to incorporate research more explicitly into their workloads.

In the United States, Kennedy and Brancolini have been successful in obtaining grant funding to develop the "Institute for Research Design in Librarianship," as proposed in their 2012 article.

Why Librarians must take on Responsibility for their Research

Academic librarians who truly wish to pursue research must take on that responsibility: if they do not, their research will be defined for them by others. In "The Scholarship of Canadian Research University Librarians," Fox suggests that librarians are intrinsically motivated to pursue research because "Despite the fact that scholarship activity is often a requirement for tenure and promotion in universities, it appears that librarians' primary purpose for engaging in scholarship is to learn and grow as professionals."[39] In the absence of self-directed research, others will operationalize that activity as a very limited, closely job-related function. This seems to be the emphasis reflected in the CARL documents with echoes from both the US and the UK.[40] Notable among these sponsored initiatives is an emphasis on applied research or research to establish value, much like in a product, market-driven, highly corporatized environment.

Among the new models emerging from such think-tanks is that of the "embedded" librarian. This certainly has some appeal and may well provide an enriched working environment. But it may also, as other embedded professionals have learned, constrict what can be questioned and then disseminated: this may be a very appealing model and may well be the kind of research a librarian wishes to pursue. However, this approach does subsume the librarian's own research interest to the group with which he or she is embedded. This should not be the only or preferred avenue for librarians' research.

With all of these approaches to research comes a loss of the academic freedom to choose what it is one will investigate.

There is much in the Jacobs, Berg and Cornwall 2010 article, "Something to Talk About: Re-Thinking Conversations on Research Culture in Canadian Academic Libraries," that advocates for more collegial, bottom-up efforts to developing librarians' scholarly activities. This theme is revisited in Jacobs' and Berg's 2013 article. In addition to providing research help, there must also be advocacy for academic librarians to make use of their contract provisions. Rather than implying that it is the increased presence of faculty unions that has raised expectations about librarian scholarship, is it not just as likely that good contract language and the protections of tenure and academic freedom have, in fact, helped to create the very climate wherein such aspirations might be nurtured?

Librarians as Community Members

In addition to teaching and research, service plays an important role in academic librarianship. For librarians, service is meant to be defined in a consistent manner with campus definitions for the teaching faculty. In the United States, ACRL's Guideline for the Appointment, Promotion and Tenure of Academic Librarians includes, as possible evidence for promotion, "contributions to the educational mission of the institution . . . organization of workshops, institutes or similar meetings; public appearances in the interest of librarianship or information transfer . . . contributions to the advancement of the profession: for example, active participation in professional and learned societies as a member . . . service as a member of a team of experts, or other means of disseminating professional expertise."[41] It is this idea of professional expertise that stems from librarians' professional practice that sometimes leads to our service being called "service to the profession" rather than academic service, the term used by teaching faculty. However, for librarians with academic status, service also encompasses service to the community (the university and the wider community), analogous to the types of service performed by teaching faculty and including contributions to both library and university governance. These contributions, along with service to the academic staff association, are essential in protecting and advancing academic librarianship.

Walter's 2013 editorial, "The 'Multihued Palette' of Academic Librarianship," shows that the debate continues over whether librarians merit faculty status. He writes that assertions such as "libraries are in a time of dramatic and continuing change" and "there is a difference between the work and role of the teaching faculty and the work and role of librarians" do not, in and of themselves, justify removing faculty status from academic librarians. These assertions "appear to assume a unified model of faculty work that simply does not exist anymore (if it ever did)."[42]

It is the diversity of faculty work across an academic institution and the diversity of academic institutions themselves – their missions, values, history and aspirations – that shape retention, tenure and promotion procedures, which include definitions of academic duties, and, in the case of service, the communities being served. Many institutions, conscious of the variation across academic disciplines, adopt general policies, leaving discipline-specific clarifications of tenure criteria to departmental documents that remain out of collective agreements and faculty handbooks. California State University is an example of an institution that allows for discipline-specific clarifications of tenure criteria. The academic senate responded to claims that service was being de-emphasized for teaching faculty by issuing the report *Faculty Service in The California State University (CSU): an Integral Component in the Retention, Tenure, and Promotion of Faculty*.[43] It includes comments, submitted by campus academic senate chairs and their academic administration, that provide practical ways to address the sense that service is not given enough weight in retention, tenure and promotion decisions. Suggested remedies take two paths: attention to the orientation of faculty serving on university and college level retention, tenure and promotion committees in order to reduce the potential for uneven implementation of policy; and encouraging academic departments to introduce additional emphasis on service into their criteria documents.

Benefiel, Miller, Mosley, and Arant-Kaspar found that the standard measure of librarian service to the profession appears to be participation in professional societies at the committee level or above. However, they conclude that "service as a component of tenure criteria for librarians (and indeed for academics generally) is not well defined, either in the literature or in tenure and promotion documents."[44] Since 2001, service definitions are more prevalent. Librarians form a distinct minority group within the academy, and consequently, their retention, tenure and promotion criteria are often specified in collective agreements with definitions. Concordia University's definition for librarians is slightly different from that of the teaching faculty. Found in article 17.01, section c) of the collective agreement, it is brief, but clear:

> Service to the University and the community, which in general includes:
> - participation on University-wide bodies;
> - administrative work not included under Article 17.01 a); [i.e., professional librarian activities]
> - committee membership at all levels of the University, including those mandated by this Agreement;
> - the taking of an active part in scientific, cultural, educational, professional, governmental and social bodies, together with activities involving expertise or popularization which are relevant to and compatible with the librarian member's professional role;
> - service to the Association;
> - outside professional activities.[45]

Note that participation on library committees, with the exception of those mandated by the agreement, is included under professional librarian activities, not service. In addition, teaching credit courses at other institutions falls under the service category as outside professional activities.[46] Service to the academic staff association or union regularly counts as service in Canadian retention, tenure and promotion documents.

As with teaching faculty, time available for all aspects of librarians' academic work is an issue. There have been attempts to quantify how librarians divide their time between professional practice, research and service. These attempts have been stymied by not really knowing the length of an average librarian workweek. Fox[47] notes that data from a variety of American and international sources suggest that the time commitment of the average professor is in the range of 49 to 56 hours per week on all activities related to university employment. His 2006 survey of librarians employed by Canadian Association of Research Libraries (CARL) institutions showed a comparable average of 47.4 hours with a standard deviation of 8.5 hours. Fox estimates that this is on a par with the time commitment of the average university professor because the large standard deviation shows that the results were widely distributed. Almost one-third of the full-time librarians reported working 50 or more hours per week on all activities combined. This leads to questions about the costs of the time it takes for librarians to pursue their own research or engage in peer reviewing others' scholarship.[48] It is perhaps this question of time that is a factor in ALA-accredited library school faculty members being noncommittal about the concept of granting librarians faculty status equivalent to that of the teaching faculty or of having faculty-status librarians being covered by the same tenure policy as teaching faculty.[49] Interestingly, the survey results show that library school faculty members do believe "that faculty status academic librarians should be eligible for the same sabbatical and research leaves as teaching faculty, that they should be involved in library governance, and that involvement in university governance improves the perception among the teaching faculty of academic librarians."[50] Wyss sees the support for librarian involvement in library governance as being "in recognition of the fact that academic librarianship has become so complex that no library director/dean could have sufficient expertise in all areas of librarianship to exercise sound judgment throughout that broad range."[51]

Henry and Neville[52] suggest that size and reputation of an institution may influence the research productivity of librarians. Fleming-May and Douglass[53] note that research productivity tends to be a top concern of teaching faculty, especially at research universities. A McGill Association of University Teachers internal report on librarian academic status, tenure and academic freedom supports this argument. The report notes that librarians are motivated to participate in both teaching and research because they recognize that McGill University is one of the most important centers of teaching activities and research in Canada. The report also notes that McGill librarians relish the opportunities they have for teaching and research. Some of the opportunities in question relate to service duties, again depending on exactly how "service" is defined. There is no denying that many opportunities for teaching and research begin as service, and there is discussion in the literature of the interrelation of academic duties and the difficulties in separating and weighting them for the purposes of retention, tenure and promotion.

Artificial Separation of Academic Duties

Academic duties are sometimes artificially separated and categorized, while they are, in fact, blended. Fox reports that librarians who participated in a survey "observed that it is sometimes difficult to separate time spent on scholarship from time spent on other professional responsibilities."[54] Brown[55] writes that it is important to separate out when an activity stops being study to keep abreast of one's field (professional practice) and crosses the line to research. Brown's research topics are well-integrated into her position, explaining why her daily time logs over seven years show a combined allocation of research and service ranging from 17 to 26%, lower than stipulated in the library faculty workload policy. Her logs reveal that time spent on research had not reduced the time spent on position responsibilities, but had instead taken time from service. Parker-Gibson writes that a corollary to providing release time for research is "helping new librarians manage their service commitments so that they are not overburdened too quickly in their formative professional years."[56] Similarly, D. Lee warns new librarians to choose service activities carefully: "While most candidates will excel at one or two areas and be satisfactory in the third, stellar activity at the service level will seldom compensate for substandard performance in the other two areas, especially in research."[57]

Massé and Hogan's edited volume, *Over Ten Million Served*, supports the argument that academic duties should not be separated.[58] Christensen writes that being protected from service "implies both that service is something negative, even dangerous, to be sheltered from (at least while one is developing one's scholarly profile) and that once one is tenured, one suddenly no longer needs or deserves protection."[59] She suggests that this practice at research universities creates the myth that every other institutional or professional demand distracts from the real work of research. V. Lee notes that "[t]o give service value, it needs to be in the reward structure, and faculty must have the kinds of teaching workloads that allow service to inform teaching and research, as well as all three informing each other, rather than 'wasteful, dangerous splits'."[60] Van Slyck encourages "new faculty to find the kind of service that will do 'double-duty,' that is, contribute broadly and deeply to their professional growth—and to their resumes."[61]

The advice to delay service until after tenure is common. In March 2012, proposed changes to the process for granting tenure at McGill University were debated in the academic senate. It was proposed that superior performance be required in the categories of research and teaching and "reasonable" for the category of other contributions, rather than "superior" in any two of these three categories and "reasonable" in the third. One argument against the change was that a signal to assistant professors that one aspect was less important than the others would lead to a devaluation of service. The proposed changes also send a mixed message to graduate students, as there had been an initiative to recognize service on students' transcripts and now service was being de-emphasized on the faculty side. A final concern was that the proposed changes "would fundamentally alter the character of McGill."[62] The Provost asked senators to consider whether the proposed changes fit with McGill being a research-intensive and student-centred university. One professor said that it is very hard for junior faculty to excel in all three areas and that teaching and research were essential aspects, while there would be time for service throughout a tenured professor's career. Although this discussion was about tenure requirements for teaching faculty, librarians need to understand the larger community and the general debate on the value of service.

What are the Problems with Service?

Due to the combination of time constraints, retention, promotion and tenure requirements, and preparation for the profession, librarians probably still find service easier and tend to gravitate towards it, as D. Lee noted in 2007. However, teaching faculty may not be that different. Christensen[63] writes that many teaching faculty genuinely enjoy their service commitments, and Chancy[64] considers outreach work very satisfying, even though it goes, for the most part, undocumented. Both authors, however, discuss the problems associated with too much service.

> Junior colleagues of color are by and far disadvantaged by a notion in our field [i.e., literature] that suggests that service to the institution will win one special graces, when it often results in women finding themselves underpublishing and untenured at the end of their tenure-track years and frustrated by the lack of progress with institutional change after their many years of service on committees meant to address such change.[65]

According to Christensen, "program administration can be a particularly egregious example of the double standard evident so often in the service arena . . . [S]ome institutions ultimately punish those who perform such work by not renewing, tenuring, or promoting them, since they have not also published sufficient 'traditional' scholarship."[66]

How will Service be Affected by Librarians Devoting more Time to Teaching and Research?

The changing requirements for librarian teaching and research will most likely affect service patterns. Schrader, Shiri and Williamson[67] note that "the University Library at the University of Saskatchewan presents itself at the forefront of research leadership in academic librarianship in Canada, with arguably the most demanding standards of research expectations for librarians in the country."[68]

The University Library Standards for Promotion and Tenure, in discussing scholarly work, indicate that "[p]ublication in *reputable* [italics added] peer-reviewed outlets is the primary evidence in this category" and go on to quantify the output: "the appropriate vehicles for dissemination of scholarly work will include *one or more* [italics added] of the following peer reviewed outlets."[69] Fleming-May and Douglass recommend that librarians not only "increase scholarly output in reputable journals (high impact, high usage, reputable among leaders in the field) and high impact conferences," but also that this increase be especially in journals and conferences in non-library and information science disciplines.[70] One benefit of this push to publish outside of library journals is that there should no longer be concerns about the value of participating in subject-oriented associations outside of librarianship.[71]

Since there is a finite amount of time and the number of academic librarians hired is unlikely to increase, how will these tenure requirements be met? In conjunction with a practical plan to improve the quantity and quality of librarians' research at the University of Saskatchewan, there appears to be a de-emphasis on service in the library standards. The sections entitled "Contributions to the Administrative or Extension Responsibilities of the Library, University or Both" and "Public Service and Contributions to Academic and Professional Bodies" both indicate that candidates for tenure as Librarian I or II need not meet any requirements in this category unless such duties are specified on appointment. Public service is normally defined as extending the librarian's expertise to the community outside of the university library, and it is "accorded recognition insofar as the activities entail application of expertise associated with the candidate's position in the University Library."[72] Service to academic, professional or scientific organizations might include: service on the committees or executives of academic or professional organizations; service on selection committees for provincial, national or international granting organizations; or service on the editorial board for academic, professional or scientific journals.

The University of Saskatchewan appears to be shifting some activities that used to be accepted as librarian scholarly activities to the service category. Service is now being defined more narrowly. Teaching faculty members describe the tendency to mislabel some intellectual work that is closely aligned with scholarly activities as service and then undervalue this work.[73] Narrow definitions of service may actually hinder efforts to advance and protect the librarian profession. One of the privileges of being an academic, with academic freedom, is the ability to perform a different kind of service, not necessarily the sort designed to please university administrators. Krebs writes that her own service work in academe arose from more than the desire to "do good" that motivates all service work. Krebs espouses a progressive model of service, "one in which we are willing to force change, even incremental change—to disrupt without destroying."[74] Her approach is to be slightly annoying, to make something lasting out of her national service work. As an example, she developed a real plan, "a bullet-pointed series of recommendations for English department chairs, the adoption of only one or two of which by most chairs could really change the profession over a few years."[75] Certainly, a blunt, bulleted list is sometimes the best way to make an impact.

With more demanding requirements for teaching, and research and research dissemination, it is likely that some forms of service traditionally performed by academic librarians will decline. But perhaps the need to share professional expertise at all levels of the academic institution and the need for informal mentorship and faculty association work will rise now that retention, tenure and promotion requirements are being laid out in ever-increasing detail. The work of ensuring that the spirit and the letter of collective agreements and faculty handbooks are respected will still have to be done. As librarians gain understanding of their minority status within the academy, they may take more active roles in university and library governance. Such active roles are central to promoting the value of libraries and librarians.

Conclusion

It has been posited that in addition to professional practice, teaching, research/scholarly activity and service are all vital components of the academic librarian workload. The challenges lie in managing both time and expectations, creating meaningful contract language, and finding ways to work within the scope of such language.

Suggestions for managing these challenges include the reassignment of non-professional duties so that librarians may focus time and attention on the more professional aspects of their positions. Academic librarians should acknowledge that staffing levels are a management responsibility: librarians should not defer teaching, scholarship or service due to inadequate staffing. Administrators must be encouraged to support academic librarians in the fulfillment of all of their workload responsibilities, and librarians need to better manage these parts of workload through thoughtful contract language and work with their Faculty Associations and bargaining committees. At the local and national levels, librarians need to continue to survey the profession on teaching, research and service practices so as to establish benchmarks and gauge progress.

Librarians should work to form collegial partnerships within and beyond the library. Through these relationships will come a better understanding of what it is that librarians do, how all academic work is inter-related and how well-rounded academic librarianship is important to the overall health of the academy. Part of this external work could include lobbying for curricular changes in MLIS programs so that students better understand the range of work that comprises academic librarianship. Graduates hoping to work in an academic setting should understand that such work encompasses teaching, scholarship and service. They should be prepared to teach credit courses as part of their regular workload; they should be prepared to fully participate in a spectrum of scholarly activities; and they should expect to be involved in service with the wider academic community.

As a complement to professional practice, teaching, scholarship and service each contribute to reinvigorating the role of librarians and libraries on campuses. Academic librarians who are fully engaged in all aspects of their workload are more likely to be recognized as full partners in the academy and will find themselves drawn into broader strategic discussions and decision-making on campus.

Bibliography

AAUP and ACRL. *Statement on Faculty Status of College and University Librarians.* http://www.aaup.org.proxy.bib.uottawa.ca/file/faculty-status-of-librarians.pdf.

Balcziunas, Adam and Larissa Gordon. "Walking a Mile in their Shoes." *College & Research Libraries News* 73, no. 4 (2012): 192-195.

Benefiel, Candace R., Jeannie P. Miller, Pixey Anne Mosley and Wendi Arant-Kaspar. "Service to the Profession: Definitions, Scope, and Value." *Reference Librarian* 35 (2001): 361-372.

Berg, Selinda Adelle, and Heidi L.M. Jacobs. "Academic Librarians and Research: A Study of Canadian Library Administrator Perspectives." *College & Research Libraries* 74, no. 6 (2013): 560-572.

Borchuck, Fred P. and Bernice Bergup. *Opportunities and Problems of College Librarians Involved in Classroom Teaching Roles.*: ERIC Document No. ED134216. 1976.

Brown, Jeanne M. "Time and the Academic Librarian." *portal: Libraries and the Academy* 1, no. 1 (2001): 59-70.

CAUT. *Librarian Salary Survey.* Ottawa: Canadian Association of University Teachers, 2012.

———. *Model Clause on the Scholarly Activity of Academic Librarians.* Ottawa: Canadian Association of University Teachers, 2003.

CARL. "Librarians' Research Institute." Canadian Association of Research Libraries, http://www.carl-abrc.ca/en/research-libraries/librarians-research-institute/2013-librarians-research-institute.html.

CARL Library Education Working Group. 2008. *Librarians as Researchers and Writers: Research Priorities for Canada's Research Libraries.* Ottawa: Canadian Association of Research Libraries.

CARL Library Education Working Group and 8Rs Research Team. 2007. *Research Competencies for CARL Librarians.* Ottawa: Canadian Association of Research Libraries.

CARL Library Education Working Group and Building Capacity Subcommittee. 2010. *Core Competencies for 21st Century CARL Librarians.* Ottawa: Canadian Association of Research Libraries.

Catano, Vic, Lori Francis, Ted Haines, Haresh Kirpalani, Harry Shannon, Bernadette Stringer and Laura Lozanzki. "Occupational Stress in Canadian Universities: A National Survey." *International Journal of Stress Management* 17, no. 3 (2010): 232-258.

Chancy, Myriam J.A. "Outreach: Considering Community Service and the Role of Women of Color Faculty in Diversifying University Membership." In *Over Ten Million Served*, edited by Michelle A. Massé and Katie J. Hogan, 139-152. Albany, NY: State University of New York Press, 2010.

Christensen, Kirsten M. "The Value of Desire: On Claiming Professional Service." In *Over Ten Million Served*, edited by Michelle A. Massé and Katie J. Hogan, 123-138. Albany, NY: State University of New York Press, 2010.

Christiansen, Lars, Mindy Stombler, and Lyn Thaxton. "A Report on Librarian-Faculty Relations from a Sociological Perspective." *Journal of Academic Librarianship* 32, no. 2 (2004): 116-121.

Coker, Catherine. Wyoma van Duinkerken, and Stephen Bales. "Seeking Full Citizenship: A Defense of Tenure Faculty Status for Librarians." *College & Research Libraries* 71, no. 5 (2010): 406-420.

Concordia University and Concordia University Faculty Association. *Tentative Collective Agreement for 2012-2015* http://www.cufa.net/collective_agreement/2012-2015.html.

Devlin, Keith. *Devlin's Angle* (blog) http://devlinsangle.blogspot.ca/http://devlinsangle.blogspot.ca/2012/03/difference-between-teaching-and_01.html.

Fleming-May, Rachel A. and Kimberly Douglass. "Framing Librarianship in the Academy: An Analysis using Bolman and Deal's Model of Organizations." *College & Research Libraries* 75, no. 3 (2014): 389-415.

Fox, David. "Finding Time for Scholarship: A Survey of Canadian Research University Librarians." *portal: Libraries and the Academy* 7 (2007): 451-462.

———. "The Scholarship of Canadian Research University Librarians." *Partnership: The Canadian Journal of Library and Information Practice and Research* 2, no. 2 (2007).

Gerrard, Angie and Jessica Knoch. "Trial by Fire: New Librarians as Team Teachers." *Academic Exchange Quarterly* 8, no. 4 (2004): 12-15.

Henry, Deborah B. and Tina M. Neville. "Research, Publication, and Service Patterns of Florida Academic Librarians." *Journal of Academic Librarianship* 30 (2004): 435-451.

Hildreth, Charles R. and Selenay Aytac. "Recent Library Practitioner Research: A Methodological Analysis and Critique." *Journal of Education for Library and Information Science* 48, no. 3 (2007): 236-258.

Hill, Janet Swan. "Wearing Our Own Clothes: Librarians as Faculty." *Journal of Academic Librarianship* 20 (1994): 71-76.

Jacobs, Heidi L.M. and Selinda Adelle Berg. "By Librarians, for Librarians: Building a Strengths-Based Institute to Develop Librarians' Research Culture in Canadian Academic Libraries." *Journal of Academic Librarianship* 39 (2013): 227-231.

Jacobs, Heidi L.M., Selinda Adelle Berg, and Dayna Cornwall. "Something to Talk About: Re-Thinking Conversations on Research Culture in Canadian Academic Libraries." *Partnership: The Canadian Journal of Library and Information Practice and Research* 5, no. 2 (2010): 1-11.

Johnson, R.N. "Faculty Status for Academic Librarians: What do Nonteaching Faculty Teach?" *Tennessee Librarian: Quarterly Journal of the Tennessee Library Association* 49 (1997): 8-9.

Julien, Heidi. "A Longitudinal Analysis of Information Literacy Instruction in Canadian Academic Libraries." *Canadian Journal of Information & Library Sciences* 29, no. 3 (2005): 289-313.

Julien, Heidi and Shelagh K. Genuis. "Librarians' Experiences of the Teaching Role: A National Survey of Librarians." *Library & Information Science Research* 33, no. 2 (2011): 103-111.

Kemp, Jane. "Isn't Being a Librarian Enough? Librarians as Classroom Teachers." *College & Undergraduate Libraries* 13, no. 3 (2006): 3-23.

Kennedy, Marie. R. and Kristine. R. Brancolini. "Academic Librarian Research: A Survey of Attitudes, Involvement and Perceived Capabilities." *College & Research Libraries* 73, no. 5 (2012): 431-448.

Kesselman, Martin A. and Sarah Barbara Watstein. "Creating Opportunities: Embedded Librarians." *Journal of Library Administration* 49, no. 4 (2009): 383-400.

Koufogiannakis, Denise and Ellen Crumley. "Research in Librarianship: Issues to Consider." *Library Hi Tech* 24, no. 3 (2006): 324-340.

Krebs, Paula M. "Not in Service." In *Over Ten Million Served*, edited by M.A. Massé and K.J. Hogan, 163-170. Albany, NY: State University of New York Press, 2010.

Laurentian University Faculty Association and the Board of Governors of Laurentian University. "Collective Agreement, 1 July 2011 - 30 June 2014", http://www.laurentian.ca/webfm_send/71.

Lee, Deborah. "On the Tenure Track: Strategies for Success." *C&RL News* 68 (2007): 626-661.

Lee, Valerie. "'Pearl was Shittin' Worms and I was Supposed to Play Rang-Around-the-Rosie?' An African American Woman's Response to the Politics of Labor." In *Over Ten Million Served*, edited by Michelle A. Massé and Katie J. Hogan, 261-274. Albany, NY: State University of New York Press, 2010.

Loesch, Martha Fallahay . "Librarian as Professor: A Dynamic New Role Model." *Education Libraries* 33, no. 1 (2010): 31-37.

Lowry, Charles B. "Research and Scholarship Defined for Portal: Libraries and the Academy." *portal: Libraries and the Academy* 4, no. 4 (2004): 449-453.

Massé, Michelle A. and Katie J. Hogan, eds. *Over Ten Million Served: Gendered Service in Language and Literature Workplaces*. Albany, NY: State University of New York Press, 2010.

McGill University Senate. "Minutes", http://www.mggill.ca/senate/sites/mcgill.ca.senate/files/minutes_march_21_2012.pdf.

Neville, Tina M. and Deborah B. Henry. "Support for Research and Service in Florida Academic Libraries." *Journal of Academic Librarianship* 33, no. 1 (2007): 76-93.

Newhouse, R. "Professional at 28." *Library Journal* 131, no. 7 (2006): 34-36.

Parker-Gibson, Necia. "Library Mentoring and Management for Scholarship." *Library Philosophy and Practice* (2007): 1-8.

Rapple, Brendan A. "The Librarian as Teacher in the Networked Environment." *College Teaching* 45, no. 3 (1997): 114.

Schrader, Alvin M., Ali Shiri and Vicki Williamson. "Assessment of the Research Learning Needs of University of Saskatchewan Librarians: A Case Study." *College & Research Libraries* 73 (2012): 147-163.

Shera, J.H. "Library-Instructional Integration on the College Level." In *ACRL Monographs, no. 13: Report of the 40th Conference of Eastern College Librarians*, edited by H.G. Bousfield. Vol. 13, 7-8, 13. Chicago: Association of College and Reference Librarians, 1955.

Simmons, Howard L. "Librarian as Teacher: A Personal View." *College & Undergraduate Libraries* 6, no. 2 (2000): 41-44.

University of Saskatchewan. "University Library Standards for Promotion and Tenure", http://library.usask.ca.proxy.bib.uottawa.ca/employment/files/Library%20Standards%20-%20July%201%202011.pdf.

van Slyck, Phyllis. "Welcome to the Land of Super-Service: A Survivor's Guide . . . and Some Questions." In *Over Ten Million Served*, edited by Michelle A. Massé and Katie J. Hogan, 195-207. Albany, NY: State University of New York Press, 2010.

Walter, Scott. "The 'Multihued Palette' of Academic Librarianship." *College & Research Libraries* 74 (2013): 223-226.

Watson-Boone, Rebecca. "Academic Librarians as Practitioners-Researchers." *Journal of Academic Librarianship* 26, no. 2 (2000): 85-93.

Weiss, Stephen C. "The Origin of Library Instruction in the United States, 1820-1900." *Research Strategies* 19, no. 3 (2003): 233-243.

Wilson, Pauline. "Librarians as Teachers: The Study of an Organization Fiction." *Library Quarterly* 49 (1979): 146-162.

Wyss, Paul Alan. "Library School Faculty Member Perceptions regarding Faculty Status for Academic Librarians." *College & Research Libraries* 71 (2010): 375-388.

Highs and Lows:
An Examination of Academic Librarians' Collective Agreements

Marni R. Harrington and Natasha Gerolami

In September 2011, members of the librarian and archivists bargaining unit from the University of Western Ontario's Faculty Association went on an 18-day legal strike. Key bargaining issues often include compensation and benefits, and this negotiation was no different. Members were seeking a contract that was fair and equitable, and addressed the pay gap between Western Librarians and Archivists and colleagues at comparable Canadian universities. Other issues included concerns about the documented scope of service and scholarly activities, and annual reporting and reviewing protocols. Another goal was to negotiate an agreement with expiry dates corresponding to the faculty for amalgamation of the agreements in the future, and to further protect the status of the librarians and archivists. In Western's case, work stoppage was used to effectively emphasize the importance of workers' rights in the expired agreement that were not being suitably addressed by the employer.

The strike at Western is just one example of the contentious issues and ongoing struggles that academic librarians have endured; it also highlights the difficulty in documenting librarians' labour in Canadian collective agreements to the satisfaction of its members. The following chapter focuses specifically on the collective agreements themselves. Unionism in Canada today is mainly directed by contracts between bargaining units and employers. In Canadian academic settings, the negotiated contract is the collective agreement. Within this framework, the collective agreement acts as a protective document and the grievance process is used to redress violations of a worker's rights, as stipulated in the agreement. Furthermore, collective agreement provisions can be used to gain control over the trajectory of library work. In this study, we use collective agreements as evidence of the gains that librarians have made through negotiations and as a basis to analyse the clauses that may undermine librarians' autonomy or decision-making ability.

The work for this chapter is based on an analysis of a subset of collective agreements for professional librarians in Canadian universities, with a focus on how academic librarian labour is described and codified. Specifically, it is the documents that are discussed, not the enactment of the collective agreements, although it is understood that what is written and what is practiced may not be equivalent. Through a mixed-method approach, using both quantitative and qualitative analyses, the collective agreements are compared and contrasted for similarities and gaps. A limited amount of university metadata external to the collective agreements were also collected for comparison purposes (e.g., student population). The data are used to address generally, what provisions are documented in academic librarians' collective agreements to protect academic freedom, professional practice, autonomy, and decision-making power in relation to the distribution of work and appropriate workload balance. Relationships between provisions that protect status, autonomy and decision-making are hypothesized to be associated with greater benefits for librarians, such as salary.

Literature Review

The Labour Movement and Libraries

Recent labour literature discusses the "crisis" in the labour movement, which arises as austerity measures make it an increasingly difficult environment in which to fight for workers' rights. For example, in the recent strike action by librarians and archivists at Western, it was tough for the membership to request a wage increase, particularly in a city like London, Ontario with a disproportionately high unemployment rate. In this environment, union leaders are pressured to give in to concessions, and workers regularly give up past gains.[1] Capitalist restructuring has succeeded as members of the public are starting to believe that workers must make these concessions in order for the economy to remain relevant and competitive. Furthermore, current library literature documents the political climate in which library unions must operate. There is a direct attack on labour in Canada and the United States, with changes to legislation and the introduction or proposed introduction of "right-to-work" legislation, which erodes labour power and unity amongst workers. To protest these legislative changes and restructuring, librarians are joining other workers' movements, taking to the streets, the legislatures, and city halls across the United States and Canada; librarians are protesting changes that erode collective bargaining, workers' rights, and budget stability, which result in negative effects on libraries, library workers, and library services.[2]

Despite these crises, or perhaps because of them, the library literature continues to focus on the role and benefits of unions and unionization. Handbooks and guides for academic library practice outline the history, law, rationale and support of unionization.[3] Library scholars document their local work environment along with the benefits of unionization[4] and librarians have become active members in large academic unions.[5]

National library and teaching organizations also support library unionization. For example, the American Library Association states,

> The ALA supports library employees in seeking equitable compensation and recognizes the principle of collective bargaining as an important element of successful labor-management relations. We affirm the right of employees to organize and bargain collectively with their employers, without fear of reprisal. These are basic workers' rights that we defend for thousands of academic, public and school library professionals.[6]

More explicitly for academic libraries, the Association for College and Research Libraries (ACRL) and the Canadian Association of University Teachers (CAUT) provide standards and guidelines to assist with collective bargaining, and have also set standards for working conditions and other miscellaneous provisions for academic librarians' collective agreements.[7]

Unions in Canadian Academic Libraries

It is no surprise that academic librarians are affiliated with unions in Canada. Statistics Canada (2012) recently reported that 72% of workers in the education sector work in a unionized environment. Further, a current survey of Canadian libraries reported that close to 2,000 full-time professional librarians work in academic libraries.[8] Additionally, in 2007, David Fox reported that 63% of academic librarians working in Canadian Association of Research Libraries (CARL) universities were considered "faculty," suggesting a union or faculty association affiliation.[9] These figures highlight the prominent role that unions have with Canadian academic librarians.

Some Highs and Lows

One of the assumed benefits of unionization that is well documented in the academic library literature is better wages. As academic librarians gain faculty or academic status, they may also gain more responsibility, which may then be linked to higher compensation. To investigate this claim, Rachel Applegate conducted one of the few large-scale studies investigating unions in public and private academic libraries in the United States.[10] She examined the relationship between unionization and salary, along with many other variables. Her findings indicate that unionized librarians at public institutions are somewhat better off than their non-unionized counter-parts. Interestingly, she noted that the group that earns a higher wage operates in worse working conditions in terms of resources available for students. Applegate suggests that the costs of higher wages for librarians, often associated with union affiliation, draws money from the budget and negatively affects library staffing and resource allocation. The end result would be fewer professional librarians, and less money for collections and other library resources.

Deborah Lee also conducted a large-scale study of academic libraries in the United States, using 10-years of Association of Research Libraries (ARL) data to investigate the impact of tenure on starting salaries.[11] She hypothesized that there would be a wage differential due to tenure; specifically, she hypothesized that tenure-granting institutions would have lower starting wages for academic librarians, on the assumption that academic librarians would trade-off wages for job security. However, she found that tenure opportunities did not affect starting salaries for academic librarians.

Faculty status, tenure and requirements for research and scholarly output are all themes that are provided for in collective agreements. However, these themes are frequently discussed independently of unionization or more specifically, the documented provisions in collective agreements. For example, there is a large body of literature outlining the requirements, merits and drawbacks of a faculty model of tenure and research for librarians.[12] Bill Crowley examined Canadian academic librarians' actual status in universities and found that librarians lack the equivalent status of faculty; Stephanie Horowitz's citation analysis research found that librarians with faculty status are likely to have a slightly greater professional impact than those without faculty status.[13] It is noted that these works do not consider the collective agreement provisions from which the status elements originate.

Past research in Canada and the United States has highlighted academic librarians' dissatisfaction with issues, such as workload and the ability to participate in collegial decision-making processes.[14] Concerns about librarian status also persist (e.g., professional identity and the relationship between librarians and teaching faculty). More than 100 peer-reviewed papers have been written on the classification of academic librarians, with the dominant view that academic librarians should be classified and compensated as faculty.[15] For academic librarians who have academic status, concerns remain that teaching faculty do not adequately recognize their work and contributions to teaching and learning in universities. Librarians are often included with faculty in the same bargaining unit because they are a community with similar interests. However, teaching faculty far outnumber librarians in amalgamated bargaining units, leading to concerns that librarian issues go unnoticed and librarians go largely unrepresented.[16] Librarians at McMaster, for example, created a separate bargaining unit from faculty in 2010, hoping that they would be more adequately represented. At McGill University, there has been a long history of librarians struggling for academic freedom where it has been the norm for faculty.

Despite the amount written about academic librarian unions, there are only a few studies that examine the provisions in academic librarians' collective agreements. Almost 20 years ago, Gloria Leckie and Jim Brett examined 32 Canadian collective agreements that govern academic librarians.[17] They documented the key provisions that provide librarians with academic or faculty status, and compared the provisions to the CAUT guidelines. The authors noted discrepancies between the guidelines and the provisions librarians have negotiated. They also discussed the variety of academic status models in universities across Canada. Roma Harris and Juris Dilevko reviewed Canadian public and academic librarian collective agreements, and found a number of provisions in public library agreements that deal with the impact of technological change on library work.[18] These included provisions addressing de-professionalization and changes to workload. However, they found that similar provisions for academic librarians were almost completely absent from their collective agreements. Other authors highlight parallels between the values of the profession and collective agreement provisions. For example, Deanna Wood found that librarians' commitment to information access and opposition to censorship are reflected in collective agreement provisions that address academic freedom.[19]

Faculty status, tenure, research, workload, and academic freedom are hallmarks of academic faculty provisions that are not always codified in collective agreements for academic librarians. In this chapter, we look at what is codified, and discuss the specific provisions that are available or absent in the collective agreements sampled. The literature is sparse on collective agreements for academic library workers and about librarian engagement with these documents. In this chapter, we start the discussion.

Method

To explore Canadian university librarian collective agreements, a purposive sample of agreements was collected. A proportional number of medical-doctoral, comprehensive and primarily undergraduate universities were chosen, and the sample included at least one collective agreement from each Canadian province. At the time of the review, all 24 collective agreements examined were current. There are currently 98 Canadian universities listed in the Association of Universities and Colleges in Canada, 82 of which belong to the Canadian Association of University Teachers.[20] This study investigates 24 institutions, representing 29% of the CAUT member universities (see Table 1).

The demographic information collected includes student population, number of professional librarians, and institutional memberships in CARL and ARL. These data are used to further categorize institutional expectations from the library. For example, student population numbers, which indicate a larger university and would place more of a demand on the library system, should be related to the number of librarians. Student population was drawn from Association of Universities and Colleges of Canada's (AUCC) 2011 enrolment statistics and included undergraduate and graduate full- and part-time students. Populations ranged from 2,300 to 55,050 students, with a mean of 19,031.

For institutional comparisons, predetermined thematic elements were identified in each of the 24 agreements. We developed these themes from our exposure to the agreements through experiential negotiation processes, previous research projects, and issues gleaned from a review of the literature. Findings from the thematic data are explored qualitatively. However, some characteristics within the themes are quantifiable. These data, along with supplementary information about the 24 universities and libraries, were also collected to categorize the institutions and explore relationships between themes.

Results and Discussion

We begin this section with demographic information for the collective agreements sampled, and the results of salary correlates. Rights and responsibilities of academic library workers are investigated by analyzing provisions around hours of work, responsibilities of labour, research and teaching. And finally, we analyse autonomy of work and academic freedom for further similarities, gaps, and omissions within the documents sampled.

Demographics

The predominant collective agreement model in Canada is one that incorporates both teaching faculty and librarians. Table 1 outlines the 24 universities sampled with their location, type of institution and whether the collective agreement includes faculty. Notably, 20 (83%) of the librarian groups are part of the faculty agreement, and the remaining 4 (17%) have a discrete "librarian" agreement.

The number of librarians within each bargaining unit from the sample were collected from the individual faculty associations and by consulting the Directory of Libraries in Canada.[21] The number of librarians in this sample ranged from 1 to 76, with a mean of 29. Understandably, a correlation between student population and number of librarians was found, $r = .82$, $t(22) = 6.80$, $p < .001$, indicating that, as expected, larger universities have more librarians.

University	Location	Institution Type	Joint Collective Agreement
Dalhousie University	East	Medical-doctoral	y
McMaster University	Ontario	Medical-doctoral	n
Huntington University	Ontario	Medical-doctoral	y
University of Western Ontario	Ontario	Medical-doctoral	n
University of Saskatchewan	Central	Medical-doctoral	y
University of Manitoba	Central	Medical-doctoral	y
University of Calgary	West	Medical-doctoral	y
University of Alberta	West	Medical-doctoral	n
University of New Brunswick	East	Comprehensive	y
Memorial University of Newfoundland	East	Comprehensive	y
Concordia University	East	Comprehensive	y
York University	Ontario	Comprehensive	y
University of Windsor	Ontario	Comprehensive	y
University of Guelph	Ontario	Comprehensive	y
Ryerson	Ontario	Comprehensive	n
Wilfred Laurier University	Ontario	Comprehensive	y
University of Prince Edward Island	East	Mostly undergraduate	y
Mount Allison	East	Mostly undergraduate	y
Acadia University	East	Mostly undergraduate	y
Cape Breton University	East	Mostly undergraduate	y
Laurentian University	Ontario	Mostly undergraduate	y
Lakehead University	Ontario	Mostly undergraduate	y
Brandon University	Central	Mostly undergraduate	y
University of Lethbridge	West	Mostly undergraduate	y

Table 1. Canadian University Collective Agreements Sampled

Relationships Between Salary and Various Provisions

The entry-level salary floor documented in the collective agreements is used for this analysis. It is understood that the actual starting salaries may be higher than what is documented in the agreements, however, this study is about collective agreements in their written forms. Future work will address mobilization of the agreements by librarians and administrators. The range of salary floors is $46,000 to $63,659, with a mean of $54,642. As shown in Table 2, almost one-third (7 out of 24) of the agreements sampled have the same salary floor for entry-level librarian and faculty/lecturer positions. It was hypothesized that librarians' floor salaries would differ based on the type of institution (medical-doctoral, comprehensive, mostly undergraduate), however, no significant differences were found, $F(2,21) = 0.75$, $p > .4$. Similarly, there was not a significant relationship between student population and salaries, suggesting that entry-level salaries of librarians at schools with more students are not different than their smaller counterparts.

A correlation was also expected between salary and the responsibilities or autonomy granted to librarians, i.e., that salary floors would be higher for: librarians on tenure track/continuing appointment; librarians who do not have a specified number of hours in a workweek; and librarians who work in research libraries. *T*-tests were conducted to investigate whether salary floors are influenced by these variables for the universities sampled; there were no significant differences found.

Salary range	Frequency and % of total	CARL Members	ARL Members
< $50,000	4 (17%)	3	2
$50,001 to $55,000	9 (37.5%)	4	2
$55,001 to $60,000	9 (37.5%)	5	2
> $60,001	2 (8%)	2	2

Table 2: 2012-13 Floor salaries for entry-level positions and membership to research library associations

Phi-correlations were conducted to investigate relationships between variables. Results indicate no significant relationships between any two binary variables investigated, including whether hours of work are stated, tenure, and membership to research library associations. Although differences were expected between and within many of the quantifiable variables, none were found. For example, it was hypothesized that there would be significant relationships between documented entry-level salaries and other elements like predetermined hours of work, workload, and tenure opportunities. It was thought that a higher salary, more autonomy to control workload and hours of work, and job security in the form of tenure, would be apparent. For the universities sampled, this is not the case.

Rights and Responsibilities for Academic Librarians

Workload has been one of the least satisfying aspects of work for academic librarians.[22] Requirements for work may be located in a variety of places in collective agreements, including clauses on workload, duties, and rights and responsibilities. In some instances, there are workload and responsibilities clauses specific to librarians, and in other agreements, librarians' workload duties are combined with teaching faculty. Articles on "rights and responsibilities" outline the academic and professional responsibilities of librarians, such as maintaining scholarly competence, fulfilling professional responsibilities, and dealing ethically with students. Collective agreements may include, in these sections, lists of activities that constitute professional practice or research/scholarly work. Workload clauses typically outline the elements of work required to fulfill a member's responsibilities, usually in some combination of duties to the profession, including teaching, service and research. Expected hours of work are often included in the workload articles.

Hours of Work

Close to half of the collective agreements sampled (42%) articulate librarians' duties by stating a specific number of hours of work to be performed each week. The range is from 32.5 to 36.25 hours. The University of Guelph notes that librarians have a fixed number of hours that they must work but the exact number is not documented in the collective agreement. Of the 10 collective agreements with a fixed number of hours, the majority have predetermined weekly hours (7/10), with 35 hours as the most frequent number of hours to be worked per week.

A specified set of work hours may be advantageous for librarians because they may be compensated for additional work. For example, five collective agreements stipulate that librarians working more than the set number of hours in a week will get "equivalent time off" in another week. The use of a predefined work week, however, does not fit with the faculty model, which gives faculty the autonomy, freedom and responsibility to make professional decisions to manage their own work. Librarian autonomy is threatened in some of the collective agreements because librarians do not have control of their work. For example, at York University, librarians must make a written request to the University Librarian in order to have "a flexible distribution of the thirty-five (35) hours per week" (Article 18.17).

The CAUT guidelines state, "Academic staff associations must negotiate workload provisions in collective agreements or terms of employment that enable librarians to determine and arrange their own workload."[23] Analysis of the collective agreements suggests that many librarians do not have the autonomy or flexibility to determine the number of hours worked, or the scheduling of work hours. There are, therefore, many associations that have been unsuccessful in meeting the standard set out in CAUT's guidelines.

Responsibilities of Labour

Librarian labour is categorized in a variety of ways, and the precise language describing the work also varies. The majority of the collective agreements (21/24) divide librarians' duties into three basic categories: professional practice, research/scholarly/academic activity, and service to the university and/or community. What constitutes professional practice, research, and service duties varies widely. Some collective agreements provide long lists, which explain the various responsibilities and tasks that make up professional practice, research, and service.

Professional practice is variously defined in the collective agreement but reference to such things as public service, information literacy, collection development, and maintenance of information systems are typical. Brandon University's collective agreement goes one step further to include full job descriptions for the various positions in the library (Reference Librarian, Cataloguer, etc.). Some collective agreements, such as those at the University of Saskatchewan and Huntington University, provide minimal or no details about librarians' responsibilities.

Though all of the collective agreements include professional practice, research, and service, there is variation in the requirements for librarians across the country. For example, three collective agreements (12%) indicate the amount of time to be spent on each responsibility. The workload of an academic member (including teaching faculty and librarians) at Laurentian University is outlined as:

> (40%) teaching/professional librarianship/archives management, including the supervision of graduate and undergraduate students; forty percent (40%) scholarly activity, including commitments to external granting agencies; and (20%) university governance, administrative duties, and other contributions to the university (Article 5.40.2).

Alternatively, librarians at McMaster University dedicate 75% of their time to "job responsibilities" and 25% to "professional service and professional activity" (Article 25.03). The librarians and archivists at the University of Western Ontario allocate 80% of their time to professional practice, 10% to academic activity, and 10% to service.

The remaining collective agreements do not provide explicit guidelines. For example, in five collective agreements, librarians are asked to carry out "an appropriate combination" of professional practice, research, and service without specifying what that appropriate combination entails. The collective agreements at Memorial University and the University of Prince Edward Island indicate that, of the three responsibilities, the principle duty is to professional practice.

Research/Scholarly Activity

The requirement of librarians to research, publish and engage in other forms of scholarly activity varies tremendously from one collective agreement to another. As noted above, varying degrees of time are dedicated or required by librarians to engage in research/scholarly activity. Yet, there are further issues that arise in the collective agreements. In some instances, librarians' collective agreements have very narrow definitions of research/scholarly activity. The requirement to conduct research, for example, may be left to the discretion of the University Librarian, or is deemed optional. There are collective agreements that have very broad definitions of research and scholarly activity to permit for publications, research to improve professional practice, and professional development as scholarship. In some instances, research has been limited to work that advances the library or librarianship. At the University of Western Ontario, research is defined in a very narrow fashion as: "a) the creation of new knowledge, including understanding or concepts; b) the creative application of existing knowledge; c) the organization and synthesis of existing knowledge; that is relevant to librarianship or archival practice" (Responsibilities of Members, Article 3).

Most of the collective agreements examined have very broad language that leaves it open for librarians to contribute in general to the creation of knowledge as their expertise, education and work experience permits. Guelph University's collective agreement gives librarians the flexibility to pursue research, professional development, and creative activities, which are not defined in a narrow sense. Scholarship can be specific to the profession, as in Article 25.10 (d) where a librarian may be involved in "the pursuit of knowledge through formal study and/or pursuit of further academic credentials related to the academic and professional responsibilities of Librarians." It can also be as broad as Article 25.10 (a) "the creation of new knowledge, understandings or concepts."

Librarians who have not traditionally been involved in research have other activities that they may include in the research/scholarly activity component of their dossier, while also granting librarians the opportunity to be more involved in research similar to the traditional faculty model. This is an important distinction for librarians who have expertise in librarianship along with advanced degrees in other disciplines, and may seek a broader understanding of research. Acadia University's collective agreement, for example, states that librarians' research is required to be "related to librarianship, archival studies, or another discipline related to their work" (Article 17.03). A generous interpretation of this collective agreement, then, would permit a music librarian to publish a musical score, for example, and have it considered as a publication for his or her evaluation. Unfortunately, what is written in a collective agreement and what happens in practice can be two very different things.

Interestingly, the collective agreement language that is perhaps the most unhelpful for librarians is the use of "may" when describing workload and duties. For example, at the University of Windsor, librarians' workload "*shall* include library service" but it "*may* include research and academic activity" (Article 5.55, *emphasis added*). Similarly, at the University of Alberta, librarians "may participate in professional and scholarly research and may request that individual research projects be included in the specific responsibilities assigned" (Article 7.03). This language does not guarantee that the librarian will be allowed to participate in research and scholarly work. The requirement to make "requests" to have research projects included in assigned responsibilities leaves the librarian at the mercy of administrators. In contrast, the language in Lakehead University's collective agreement is stronger because it makes research a right while also giving librarians the flexibility to choose to focus their expertise elsewhere: "Although not required to do so, a librarian member has the right to be involved in research" (Article 16.11.01).

Lakehead University, unfortunately, also requires that librarians ask for release time from their other duties to pursue research. In other collective agreements, such as Dalhousie University's, mention of librarians and research/scholarly activity remains absent altogether.

The collective agreements sampled demonstrate varying degrees of commitment to librarians' research/scholarly activity. Another way to examine this commitment to research/scholarly activity is through library memberships in organizations such as CARL or ARL. Membership may be seen as library administrations' commitment to "strengthening and promoting research libraries." Of the 24 universities, 14 (58%) libraries were CARL members and 8 (33%) belonged to ARL. The libraries that belonged to ARL are all members of CARL. The hypothesis was that libraries belonging to these organizations would value the research/scholarly activity role and expertise that professional librarians have and that this would be reflected in higher salaries. Analyses, however, do not indicate a significant relationship between salary and institutional membership to either CARL or ARL (see Table 3). Although interesting, but not statistically relevant, two libraries which are members of both CARL and ARL document the highest floor salaries for entry-level library positions.

Independent Variable	Yes/No	$t(22)$	p
Hours of work stated	10/14	-0.86	> .4
Tenure for librarians	22/2	-1.4	> .2
CARL member	14/10	-0.6	> .5
ARL member	8/16	-0.67	> .5

Table 3: Results of t-tests using salary floor as a dependent variable

It is well documented that there may be hurdles in finding time to fit research/scholarly activity into the day-to-day responsibilities of a librarian.[24] Many collective agreements acknowledge this by guaranteeing days for research/scholarly activity. There is a range of research/scholarly activity days stated, including York University's 22 days, Mount Allison's 20 days, and the University of Manitoba's 12 days.

Teaching Responsibilities

There are a number of librarian tasks that clearly involve teaching, such as course-related instruction, and information literacy workshops. The role of teaching is generally acknowledged in statements on professional practice. In some instances, a clear provision for teaching is given, and occasionally, librarians are assigned teaching loads similar to teaching faculty. For example, at Huntington

University librarians may teach up to 9 credits. At Concordia University, "[t]he maximum number of sections of library related courses that can be assigned to probationary and tenured members is two (2) per academic year unless the librarian member agrees to teach more" (Article 17.04(d)). At the University of Windsor, a "credit course(s) may be assigned as part of a librarian's workload assignment only if requested by the librarian and with the agreement of the University Librarian/Law Librarian and the Dean of the Faculty wherein the credit course(s) is listed" (Article 5.55).

The huge variety and extremes in workload distribution and details in collective agreements raises many questions. Do librarians benefit, in terms of clarity of expectations, and better understand their roles if their duties are defined in detail? Or do the long lists outlining professional practice make it more difficult for librarians to control their work and stifle their ability to respond to changes in the profession? How do collective agreement provisions about job descriptions, hours of work, and division of tasks impact librarians' autonomy in the workplace?

Autonomy

Numerous clauses in collective agreements ensure that faculty have both autonomy and decision-making power in the workplace. Autonomy is gained when librarians are able to participate on library councils, appointment committees, or are elected to Senate. Participation gives them some control over their working environment. When these avenues of participation are absent, control diminishes. Research suggests that librarians have been unsatisfied with the decision-making power that they have.[25] In the collective agreements analyzed, librarians frequently have provisions that protect their rights to participate on governing bodies.

In the workload Article for librarians at Cape Breton University, the autonomy and professional judgment of librarians is acknowledged through the following statement,

> In particular, Librarians, as information professionals in a university setting, face a unique challenge in increasing the access of patrons to changing sources of information. It is the responsibility of each Librarian to self-identify their professional, personal skills and knowledge needed for current and anticipated responsibilities; to continuously assess their skills, aptitudes and knowledge; and to identify personal learning strategies that anticipates and complements the evolving information needs of CBU and our community (Article 28.4).

An example of overt restrictions on managing workload is seen in the librarians' collective agreement at McMaster University: "Union stewards and other Union representatives will not leave their duties without first obtaining the permission of their supervisor, or designate" (5.03 a). In contrast, autonomy is supported when librarians are given explicit permission to work for the union in other collective agreements.

Academic Freedom: A Right or Responsibility?

Librarians are granted academic freedom in all 24 collective agreements sampled. The academic freedom clauses in collective agreements where librarians and faculty were in the same bargaining unit provided academic freedom to "members," "members of the bargaining unit," "employees" and "academic staff," which thereby granted academic freedom to all teaching faculty and professional librarians. In a couple of instances, librarians were specifically mentioned. Ryerson's collective agreement refers to "Faculty Members *and* Professional Librarians." Lakehead University's collective agreement is the only agreement in which there is a different clause for faculty members than for librarians:

> Faculty members have the right to examine, question, teach, learn, investigate, speculate, comment, publish, and criticize, without deference to prescribed doctrines. Academic freedom makes possible commitment that may result in strong statements of beliefs and positions, and protects against any University penalty for exercising that freedom. Academic freedom carries with it the duty to use that freedom in a manner consistent with the scholarly obligation to base research and teaching on an honest search for knowledge (Article 15.01.01).

> Librarian members have the right and responsibility to make knowledge, ideas, and information freely available, no matter how controversial, without deference to prescribed doctrine or institutional censorship. Academic freedom also ensures the member's right to disseminate the results of his/her research and to express his/her professional opinion freely and publicly, without University penalty for exercising that freedom. Members recognize that academic freedom involves a duty to use that freedom in a responsible way (Article 15.01.02).

The rights granted to academic staff in academic freedom clauses are regularly joined to duties and responsibilities. For example, Acadia University's academic freedom clause notes that "Academic freedom carries with it the duty to use that freedom in a manner consistent with the scholarly obligation to base research and teaching on an honest search for knowledge" (Article 5.40). In some instances, the collective agreement refers to the "*responsible search for knowledge*" or mentions that the search should be for "*truth*" as well as "*knowledge.*" Despite minimal variations, these duties are outlined in almost all the collective agreements analysed.

In some instances, additional duties and responsibilities are placed on librarians in the academic freedom and work responsibilities clauses that do not exist for teaching faculty. At Lakehead University, for example, "[f]aculty members have the right to examine, question, teach, learn, investigate, speculate, comment, publish, and criticize, without deference to prescribed doctrines" (Article 15.01.01). Librarians, according to the academic freedom clause, "have the right and *respon-*

sibility to make knowledge, ideas, and information freely available, no matter how controversial, without deference to prescribed doctrine or institutional censorship" (Article 15.01.02, emphasis added). Wilfred Laurier University's collective agreement states: "[t]he censorship of information is inimical to the free pursuit of knowledge. The collection, organization, and dissemination of knowledge will be done freely and without bias in support of the research, teaching, and study needs of the university community. The Parties agree that no censorship based on moral, religious, or political values shall be exercised or allowed against any material which a Member desires to be placed in the library collections of the University" (Article 7.3). A similar clause exists in the Ryerson University collective agreement. Expectations such as these place responsibility on librarians to ensure that censorship does not occur in the library.

Librarians and teaching faculty have the right to their opinions and to disseminate them in the pursuit of knowledge. However, such rights come with corollary duties. If a member has the right to academic freedom, then everyone in the university community has a corollary duty: the requirement to not restrict their ability to disseminate their knowledge or opinions. An additional responsibility is placed upon librarians in the above noted collective agreements that require them not only to respect another's right to academic freedom but to actively disseminate other people's ideas; this is a responsibility not requires of faculty. These provisions are consistent with values and codes of ethics promoted by a number of national library associations,[26] but could the *requirement* to disseminate information also be a violation of librarians' academic freedom?

Conclusions and Future Work

It is unrealistic to expect that a one-size-fits-all approach to collective agreements would be achievable or even beneficial, for academic librarians. However, an in-depth analysis of a subset of academic librarian agreements shows a troubling lack of consistency across many important provisions. The quantitative and qualitative results do not provide a definitive picture of what effective provisions look like; rather disparities in provisions across universities highlight the realistic challenges librarians face when working under a collective agreement. Workload, duties, responsibilities and job descriptions are themes that vary widely and are not well documented.

Most Canadian academic librarians in this analysis work a prescribed number of hours per week, and must make formal requests for their research and scholarly pursuits. It is also notable that clauses that specify the nature of librarians' research tend to lessen autonomy rather than increase it. Interestingly, no correlation was found between salary and any quantifiable variables relating to workload, status or research responsibilities.

Although the descriptions of librarians' rights and responsibilities are examined for suitability of representation in the collective agreements, they are material items that can be mobilized (or ignored) by stakeholders to meet their interests. Further research is necessary to develop a complete picture of how academic librarians use their collective agreements, and the decision-making authority that librarians have in their workplaces. Interviews with academic librarians would provide a more robust picture of the degree of autonomy that librarians actually have, regardless of documented provisions. This approach echoes Applegate's when she states that "[c]learly, union contracts constrain managerial decision making. How this works out in the details of reality needs exploration."[27] She suggests that case studies and interviews might fill the gap. Talking to librarians could also further highlight undocumented details about salaries, responsibilities, research and teaching, working hours, experiences with autonomy and academic freedom.

It is understood that this research does not capture all that happens in the day-to-day practice of academic librarians. Rather, discussions are based on what is documented in the articles of collective agreements. Building on the results of the current analysis, Canadian academic librarians working in unionized environments should be interviewed about how to mobilize and increase their autonomy in their day-to-day work. Further research, along with the current findings, will better inform advocates of the needs and priorities of librarians in Canadian university libraries. By giving a voice to academic librarians and their workplace challenges, these results could be the basis for transforming institutional processes and reworking collective agreements to further empower librarians.

Bibliography

American Library Association. *Code of Ethics of the American Library Association*. (1939). Last modified January 22, 2008. http://www.ala.org/advocacy/proethics/codeofethics/codeethics.

———. (2011). *ALA Statement in Support of Worker's Rights to Collectively Bargain*. http://www.weac.org/blue/Legislative/ALA-letter.pdf.

Applegate, Rachel. "Who Benefits? Unionization and Academic Libraries and Librarians." *Library Quarterly* 79, no. 4 (2009): 443-463.

Association of College and Research Libraries, *Joint Statement on Faculty Status of College and University Librarians.* (1972). Last modified October 2012. http://www.ala.org/acrl/ standards /jointstatementfaculty.

Association of Universities and Colleges in Canada. *Enrolment by University.* (2011), http://www.aucc.ca/canadian-universities/facts-and-stats/enrolment-by-university/.

———. *Listing of Universities in Canada.* (2013), http://www.aucc.ca/canadian-universities/our-universities/.

Bernstein, Alan. "Academic Librarians and Faculty Status: Mountain, Molehill or Mesa." *Georgia Library Quarterly* 46, no. 2 (2009): 12–15.

Brundin, Michael R., and Alvin M. Schrader. *National Statistical Profile of Canadian Libraries.* Last modified November 2012, http://www.cla.ca/AM/Template.cfm?Section=Advocacy&Template=/CM/ContentDisplay.cfm&ContentID=13785.

Camfield, David. *Canadian Labour in Crisis: Reinventing the Workers' Movement.* Halifax: Fernwood Publishing, 2011.

Camp, John A., David G. Anderson and Anne Page Mosby. "In the Same Boat Together: Creating an Environment for Research and Publication." In *Building on the First Century: Proceedings of the Fifth National Conference of the Association of College & Research Libraries*, 9–11. Chicago: Association of College and Research Libraries, 1989.

Canadian Association of University Teachers. *Academic Status and Governance for Librarians at Canadian Universities and Colleges.* (1993). Last modified September 2010. http://www.caut.ca/about-us/caut-policy/lists/general-caut-policies/policy-statement-on-academic-status-and-governance-for-librarians-at-canadian-universities-and-colleges.

———. *Member Associations.* (2013). http://www.caut.ca/about-us/member-associations.

Canadian Library Association. *Canadian Library Association Code of Ethics.* Last modified June 1976. http://www.cla.ca/AM/Template.cfm?Section=Position_Statements& Template=/CM/ContentDisplay.cfm&ContentID=3035.

Cirasella, Jill and Maura A. Smale. "Peers Don't Let Peers Perish: Encouraging Research and Scholarship Among Junior Library Faculty." *Collaborative Librarianship* 3, no. 2 (2011): 98–109.

Crowley, Bill. "The Dilemma of the Librarian in Canadian Higher Education." *Canadian Journal of Information and Library Science* 22, no. 1 (1996): 1-18.

Dickter, Laurence. "Empowering Library Workers through Collective Bargaining." *Public Libraries* 41, no. 3 (2002): 141-2. *Directory of Libraries in Canada.* Toronto: Greyhouse House Publishing, 2012.

Fox, David. "A Demographic and Career Profile of Canadian Research University Librarians." *The Journal of Academic Librarianship* 33, no. 5 (2007): 540-550.

Gillum, Shalu. "The True Benefits of Faculty Status for Academic Librarians." *Reference Librarian* 51 (2010): 321-8.

Harris, Roma and Juris Dilevko. "Bargaining Technological Change in Canadian Libraries." *Canadian Journal of Information and Library Science* 22, no. 3 (1997): 20-36.

Horowitz, Stephanie A. "Faculty Status and the Publication Impact of ARL Librarians." *A Master's Paper for the M.S. in L.S. degree, University of North Carolina.* (2007): 21-22, http://ils.unc.edu/MSpapers/3331.pdf

Jacobs, Heidi L.M., Selinda Berg and Dayna Cornwall. "Something to Talk About: Re-thinking Conversations on Research Culture in Canadian Academic Libraries," *Partnership: The Canadian Journal of Library and Information Practice and Research* 5, no. 2 (2010), https://journal.lib.uoguelph.ca/index.php/perj/article/view/1247#. UmguPXAQaSo.

Latham, Joyce and Wyatte Ditzler. "Collective Effort: The American Union and the American Public Library." *Library Trends* 59, no. 1-2 (2010): 237-55.

Leckie, Gloria and Jim Brett. "Academic Status for Canadian University Librarians: an Examination of Key Terms and Conditions." *Canadian Journal of Information and Library Science* 20, no. 1 (1995): 1-28.

———. "Job Satisfaction of Canadian University Librarians: A National Survey." *College and Research Libraries* 58, no. 1 (1997): 31-47.

Lee, Deborah. "Faculty Status, Tenure, and Compensating Wage Differentials Among Members of the Association of Research Libraries." *Advances in Library Administration and Organization* 26 (2008): 151-208.

Maragou Hovekamp, Tina. "Unions in Academic Libraries." In *The Successful Academic Librarian*, edited by Gwen Meyer Gregory, 111-24. Medford, NJ: Information Today Inc., 2005.

McCook, Kathleen Peña. "Collective Bargaining is a Human Right: Union Review for 2011." *Progressive Librarian* 38/39 (2012): 69-90.

Meyer Gregory, Gwen and Mary Beth Chambers. "Faculty Status, Promotion, and Tenure-What are You Getting Into?" In *The Successful Academic Librarian*, edited by Gwen Meyer Gregory, 57-66. Medford, NJ: Information Today Inc., 2005.

Milton, Suzanne. "Librarians: Key Players in Faculty Unions." *American Libraries* 21, no. 3 (2005): 5-7.

Statistics Canada. *Union Membership and Coverage by Selected Characteristics*. Last modified October 26, 2011. http://www.statcan.gc.ca/pub/75-001-x/2011004/tables-tableaux/11579/tbl01-eng.htm.

Wood, Deanna. "Librarians and Unions: Defining and Protecting Professional Values." *Education Libraries* 23, no. 1 (1999): 12.

Librarians as Faculty Association Participants: An Autoethnography

Justine Wheeler, Carla Graebner, Michael Skelton, and Margaret (Peggy) Patterson

Background

Librarians have fought and continue to fight for academic status; however once achieved, we have found the label of "academic" to not always be comfortable. Within our community of librarians, questions have been raised regarding our taking on any status beyond that of professional librarian.[1] In spite of this, the reality is that most Canadian university librarians do have academic or faculty status, and are required, through collective agreements or employment contracts, to perform as academics.[2]

In the Canadian context, understanding the definition of "academic status" and what it means can be obscured by terminology. The terms "faculty status," "academic status" and "tenure" are used interchangeably in the colloquial sense when, in fact, they have different but often overlapping meanings. In Canada, most librarians working in universities have academic status which, according to the Canadian Association of University Teachers' policy statement includes: 1) time and provisions for scholarship; 2) procedures and conditions of appointment analogous to faculty, and 3) the right to full participation in university affairs, including governance.[3]

In contrast, the majority of most American librarians have faculty status, which denotes that they have identical rights, responsibilities and status as do teaching and research faculty.[4] This includes tenure. By comparison, academic status for Canadian librarians usually means holding the equivalent employment status to tenure through the conditions of continuing employment. Complicating matters further, as Leona Jacobs states in her chapter in this volume, most research and discussion on status comes from literature authored by our American colleagues and focuses on faculty status.

Nonetheless, we share many similarities with our American counterparts. Indeed, when we compared the Association of College and Research Libraries' standards for faculty status to the actual working conditions of Canadian academic librarians, with the exception of holding tenure, many Canadian academic librarians would meet the criteria outlined for American librarians.[5]

Regardless of the terminology used or whether librarians have tenure, what can be said is that academic librarians in Canada and in the US have much in common with faculty members within the universities in which they work.

Another area that needs further clarification, with respect to the academic status of librarians, is that of membership in associations or unions for faculty or academic staff. For the purposes of this chapter, we will use the term "faculty association" to refer to both faculty and academic associations, and to both faculty and academic unions and to refer to the body that represents the interests of its faculty and librarian members in collective bargaining and advocacy.

The Board of Directors of faculty associations represents librarians, and other academics, on matters that significantly affect our working lives and identities, including: workload, the right (and even the scholarship imperative) to take leaves, and the nature and means of assigning and assessing our activities, duties and responsibilities. We need this faculty collective to understand and to advocate for the specific needs and rights of academic librarians, especially as we undergo the collective changes that are occurring across many of our campuses, in post-secondary research, and in learning policies and practices.

It should be noted that there are differences between the mandates and bargaining rights of faculty associations and unions, and these differences can vary by province. In broad generalities, unions have the right to strike, while associations do not. The role of unions is also often prescribed by provincial legislation. However, regardless of the type of bargaining unit that exists, academic librarians in these units are treated consistently with other faculty members in their educational setting.

Finally, for the purposes of this chapter, a *Board of Directors* refers to the elected members of the faculty association whose duty it is to represent and advocate for all faculty members and librarians on issues pertaining to the negotiated collective agreements at their institutions. The Board of Directors usually includes members of the Executive (President, Treasurer, Grievance Officer, etc.). Of course, the structure of boards can vary significantly, as can the delineation of specific roles and responsibilities.

Researcher–Participants

As for the imperative of this issue for the authors, although much has been written in the library literature regarding the need for librarians to participate in academic governance, the literature fails to provide data on academic governance participation rates. Notably, one national Canadian study has looked at job satisfaction of university librarians. Perhaps tellingly, in that study, out of 25 variables describing aspects of practice of university librarians, participation in university decision-making ranked as the least satisfying aspect of practice for survey respondents.[6]

And what of those academic librarians who chose to actively participate in faculty associations? The finding above corresponds with the anecdotal experience of the authors, and it further prompts the question of an investigation into the question of membership and appropriate—or even effective—governance. The authors of this chapter are three librarians and one professor, all of whom have been active in their faculty associations. We are all Canadian-based but located across the country in the provinces of British Columbia, Alberta and Ontario. Three of us are women, and two of us have held the position of President of a faculty association. We all have multiple years of experience on our respective boards of directors, and we share many common experiences from this work.

Nevertheless, we also discovered many differences in our working lives. Only one of the librarians was required to do scholarship. The same librarian was also the only librarian whose university grants tenure to librarians. In the case of the other two librarians, permanent continuing positions are granted to librarians at their universities. One of the librarians had spent a career working part-time; the others work full-time. Finally, two of us are near the end of our careers, while the others are mid-career. Despite some differences, we came together with our varied backgrounds, experiences and locales around our common belief in the importance of the work of faculty associations and the desire to delve more deeply into the meaning of our shared experiences working for faculty associations.

Autoethnography

We decided that the most suitable method for us to use to engage in creating collaborative meaning from our experiences was to conduct an autoethnographic study. *Autoethnography* is a form of interpretive inquiry that is embedded in both the practices and philosophies of narrative inquiry and of ethnography. It explicitly acknowledges and embraces the researcher as participant, and as such, autoethnography is a first person narrative in which the researchers are part of the phenomenon being studied.[7] However, autoethnography is not simply about storytelling. Instead, participants are asked to find and to explore the deep meaning in their stories and experiences through an analysis of their dialogues and their openness to shared discovery. In other words, participants seek a deeper understanding of their culture through the sharing and reflecting on their stories and the association of their stories with others within that culture.[8]

Autoethnography deliberately avoids definition in favour of evocation. As Carolyn Ellis said ". . . autoethnography seeks validity through verisimilitude: it evokes in readers a feeling that the experience described is lifelike, believable and possible."[9] As such, this method for journeying into the co-creation of shared meaning proved to be appropriate for our exploratory study.

Theoretical Framework

While autoethnography helped us focus on dialogue and personal stories in order to evoke disclosure it was our theoretical framework of liminality that allowed us to construct deep meaning from our conversations.[10] Liminality is the process by which an individual undergoes a process of transformation. In his work, "The Rites of Passage," Arthur van Gennep describes a series of transition rites accompanying various changes in life, relative to social status or milestones.[11] These changes were identified as: separation, transition (or margin) and reaggregation (or incorporation). In his subsequent analysis of Gennep's work, anthropologist Victor Turner notes that of these three phases, margin is pivotal and is better described using the term "limin." According to Turner, ". . . limin—the Latin word for threshold—, signifying the great importance of real or symbolic thresholds at this middle period of the rites, though being cunicular, 'being in a tunnel,' would better describe the quality of this phase in many cases, its hidden nature, its sometimes mysterious darkness."[12] In its simplest form, liminality is the space between here and there.

Liminality has been used in previous studies to explain the nature of libraries.[13] However, except for Rachel Singer Gordon's now defunct blog, "The Liminal Librarian" (which had a different focus than this study), liminality has not been used to describe the experience of academic librarians. For us, liminality resonated as an appropriate lens through which to view our work because, as Pamela Bettis, Michael Mills, Janice Miller Williams and Robert Nolan showed in their 2005 study,[14] and further endorsed in a related study[15] liminality can be used both as a theoretical framework and as an explanation for making sense of interactions. It therefore provides a useful framework for grounding our collective experiences. Furthermore, it helped us to understand our experiences, while also providing an explanation of them.

Design of Study

Between January and June of 2013, the three librarians met on four occasions via conference calls. Each meeting was approximately one to two hours in length. The meetings were recorded and after each meeting, we separately reviewed the recordings. Dialogue was unstructured in order to allow space for participants to explore various paths to meaning.[16] We discussed our backgrounds, what drew us to participate in faculty associations and our experiences within them. During our third meeting, we delved deeper into the themes that most spoke to each of us, all the while "exploring patterns, linkages and images that described our individual and collective experiences of transitioning."[17] Our co-author, who is not a librarian, had previously published an autoethnography, and she guided and advised us through the process.

Balancing what we believe to be important gains in understanding an experience that still remains significantly under-documented, let alone studied, in professional and research literature, the limitations presented by an auto-ethnographic approach encompass many of the criticisms common to all interpretive research. These criticisms include the small participant sample; not meeting standard social science standards; and a questioning of the reliability, validity and generalizability of the study and its findings. These criticisms have been addressed in many articles and in many different ways. For us, the most compelling refutation of potential criticism comes from Carolyn Ellis, Tony Adams and Arthur Bochner who eloquently state: "questions of reliability refer to the author's credibility; while validity means seeking versimitude; and finally, generalizability is constantly being tested by the readers."[18] In other words, it is the reader who is constantly testing the credibility, validity and generalizability of the study through comparing the study to their lived experiences and reflecting on their response to the text.

Emergent Themes and Discussion

As librarians seeking to discover and explore our academic identities, we found our stories by exploring: 1) what conditions led each of us to participate in faculty associations; 2) what our experiences were as members and leaders within faculty associations; and 3) what we perceived as the impact our participation had on library and faculty colleagues.

Through this autoethnographic process, the following five themes emerged: 1) identity; 2) social justice; 3) bridging; 4) professional confidence; and 5) perceptions of other librarians.

Theme One: Identity—Proud but Invisible

As libraries change, so too do the identities of librarians. We discussed how apparently self-destructive the profession of librarianship can be. We are gatekeepers, who hold the keys to the information kingdom, yet we are active participants in crafting our own demise through increased development of access and direct discovery to both open source and fee-based electronic scholarly content. While we may see our mediation role as being increasingly important, it seems, paradoxically, to our faculty colleagues and our patrons to be increasingly irrelevant, leaving librarians increasingly challenged to articulate just what it is we do and should do.

Do you remember Erica Olsen's clarion call to librarians? It was called "Why You Should Fall to Your Knees and Worship a Librarian."[19] There were t-shirts and posters and we all loved her for articulating so clearly what we believed to be true. Certainly, all of the participants in this research felt a great deal of pride, connection and meaningfulness from their work.

People become librarians because they know too much. Their knowledge extends beyond mere categories. They cannot be confined to disciplines. Librarians are all-knowing and all-seeing. They bring order to chaos. They bring wisdom and culture to the masses. They preserve every aspect of human knowledge. Librarians rule. And they will kick the crap out of anyone who says otherwise.[20]

This sentiment, while empowering, also reflects an underlying anxiety felt by librarians that they have been marginalized in the academy. Indeed, while university libraries are often seen as the metaphorical hearts of academic institutions, the same can't necessarily be said of librarians—that role falls to research faculty. It is the research faculty who attract students to their programmes, apply for funding in the form of grants and government support—not the librarians.

> *It's the idea of visibility. We are giving ourselves a voice we didn't have before. By participating in the faculty association, we move from a degree of marginalization to having a voice and being heard. But then the danger is that with faculty associations, university administration will try and marginalize you again because faculty associations themselves are often marginalized.*

There was a sense among the participants that librarians form part of the opaque infrastructure of universities. Yet the reality is that librarians' expertise in collection development, instruction, research support, and scholarship, are fundamental to the success of academic institutions.

Theme Two: Social Justice

Librarianship is more than just a job. The profession also includes people who are deeply committed to social justice. As Bharat Mehra, Kevin Rioux and Kendra Albright state, "traditions of fairness, open inquiry, service and humanism have long characterized the library and information science (LIS) professions."[21]

In this regard, perhaps most revealing was our discussion on what drew us to the work of faculty associations. Often it was formative experiences that compounded a societal service ethos with social justice aims within the workplace: one of us described the unfairness she saw at work when she was a non-unionized worker. Another described their grandfather's work in the union as one of their earliest memories.

> *I think it was a reawakening. When I was in my 20s, I was really into social justice and justice issues but then I graduated and then got busy with a job and my family. So when this negative thing happened, I was really open to unions*

already and had a good perspective. I have found my last four years with the Association really rewarding.

When asked: "Why did you volunteer to be part of the Executive?" the common answer again centered on the issue of social justice. As librarians, we saw the need to defend ourselves and our colleagues, who we perceived not to be in a position to defend themselves.

I saw a pattern emerge that the faculty association tended to overlook this group (librarians and archivists) and asked they be mindful going forward not to forget about them . . .

We became active in faculty associations because we have a natural tendency toward social justice or because we, or someone we know, benefited from the intervention of their association. We found an impetus or catalyst was involved; something that rankled or hurt—or, a desire to give back. In short, as one of participants stated, it was *time to stick one's neck out of the tortoise shell* and go from the invisible middle toward taking our place as an academic member. Thus, we began taking the first steps in "our rite of passage" from being uncertain and unsure to moving towards professional confidence.

Theme Three: Bridging

Because some of our colleagues within the academy really don't understand what we do as professionals, they view librarians as being almost invisible. This allows us to work in the background, and can fly under the radar to accomplish a great many things without a lot of fanfare.

As we sought deeper meaning from our stories, we became aware of a recurring theme in our stories in which we served as information conduits and sounding boards. Perhaps, as academic librarians, we are uniquely suited to view issues from a variety of perspectives. Certainly, we felt that this liminality allows us to occupy an understated central or neutral role. Viewed as being neutral by our faculty colleagues, many of them tend to seek us out to "talk"; to express themselves in a non-threatening environment where they can bounce ideas around and possibly develop a different point of view.

Librarians don't have a lot of baggage. I felt like Switzerland—I'm seen without an agenda. As a result, I could suggest solutions that didn't seem to occur to others.

We were the central road—we could see both sides of the issues.

We felt that, where many of our colleagues in the academy tend to see matters only in black or white, from our perspectives as librarians who are involved in their faculty associations, we often view issues in various shades of grey, and often, in colour. That is not to say that we are totally indifferent. When the need arises, we can and frequently have stood up and taken sides. We have helped to summarize the discussions around us and have been able to put forward a strong voice of reason. Helping individuals to formulate different perspectives has been one of the most rewarding aspects of our position on faculty association boards.

> *As individuals who work alongside the professoriate, we have the opportunity to lend our voices to the conversation and to supply our organizational expertise to the questions at hand.*

Interestingly, even after two of us left senior roles on executive committees, we found that many faculty and librarians still sought us out to discuss issues, knowing that we would listen and reflect honestly on their concerns. As such, we assumed the role of "bridgers" within our academic community. From our accumulated experience, we attempt to bring others along on the journey, point out pitfalls and hurdles, advise on alternate courses of action, and generally encourage members to use and understand the faculty association of which they are members. Indeed, we have acted as cheerleaders and as informal advocates, encouraging our colleagues to seek the advice of their faculty association officers when they encounter decisions by the administration that they think breaches the collective agreement. In this way, we distinguish ourselves from our place of work—the identity of librarian as agent is differentiated from the library as a neutral place. We become visible.

Theme Four: Professional Confidence

While we all have different reasons for actively participating in our faculty associations, our experiences are remarkably similar. In a way, we can each identify with what Joseph Campbell described as the "Hero's Journey" in *The Hero with a Thousand Faces*.[22] This underlying theme, echoed in Victor Turner's descriptions of liminality, requires the protagonist to leave the familiar and engage with extraordinary circumstances and events, moving through a series of cycles, both threatening and uplifting, until he/she returns home armed with new gifts, insights and abilities. In our own journey, we moved away from the familiarity and insularity of our libraries into greater contact with research and teaching faculty—and with university administration.

> *The first year, I didn't know what people were talking about; issues were from faculties I wasn't familiar with. I felt lost, a little bored because it was beyond me and I noticed, too, that* defacto *I was representing the library. Sometimes when I raised concerns, I felt like it was "wee little me" or "little librarian," representing a small group. I never felt condescended to but I was never sure if they understood where I was coming from.*

The wish to contribute and to provide useful context in our interactions with our fellow executive members was tempered somewhat, not only by a feeling of newness, but perhaps more by a need to be accepted and valued as equals. We didn't want to mess this up. We felt as if we carried the reputation of our profession on our shoulders and that no slippage was allowed. Gradually, this specter faded and we felt we belonged as peers. And, with time, our expertise and confidence related to non-library academic matters grew. The journey, however, is never linear, never straightforward, and is affected by circumstances as much as by intent.

> *There were many times when I felt like an outsider. At first, I didn't know what to expect, what issues would be discussed, what decisions had to be made. Equally, I'm not sure what the "old guard" on the Executive expected of me.*

But belonging was not without challenges. According to Statistics Canada 25% of volunteers put in 77% of the volunteer hours.[23] Over-reliance on a core group of people often leads to the sense that faculty associations are somewhat "cliquish." They often rely on a familiar group of old hands, with whom they are comfortable. We found that librarian ways were new to them and while they didn't look down on us, they really didn't fully understand our challenges. Once we found our "voices," we took the opportunity to inform our faculty colleagues. After some time, we felt comfortable voicing our concerns from our librarian perspective. It has been a progressive exercise. For two of us, stepping up to be the President of the faculty association was, in large measure, a test of the waters. It was an opportunity to see if faculty members would accept a librarian as their leader of the Association.

> *I feel more secure in my own skin in dealing with issues related to the association and faculties. And people seek you out to ask questions and I feel more confident in answering them—the whole idea that we are collegial, we will share our material, and treat others in a respectful manner.*

Participation in our respective faculty associations was good for us personally, and we believe important to how academic librarians are perceived by colleagues and administration. We stepped into a realm which had been largely unknown to us. Our success was due, in part, to our willingness to take risks and to gamble that we had much to contribute and these contributions would be valued both by our librarian colleagues and by our academic peers. The payoff was greater recognition of and support for librarians, a better understanding of our rights, honed negotiating skills, a greater understanding that faculty are neither homogenous nor monolithic, and an understanding that we are, in fact, colleagues.

> *And as a group, we no longer accept statements by administration at face value. We are simultaneously sought out for our opinions by colleagues but avoided by management.*

Theme Five: Perceptions of Other Librarians

> *[Because of] our status as academic staff, [it] is good for my colleagues to see me participating in the faculty association.*

During our involvement with our faculty associations, our librarian colleagues suddenly took new interest in the Association's activities. A certain degree of pride was noted, especially when colleagues would introduce us to visitors to the library. The introduction usually went, "here is _____ s/he is "the President of our Faculty Association."

> *My full time professional colleagues in the library were quite proud of the fact that a librarian, and a part-time librarian at that, was elected as President of the Association.*

Each faculty association provides information and support to its members and librarians are a microcosm within the association. Research shows that in the context of information-seeking, individuals turn to their peers before seeking out other resources.[24] As reference librarians, we know this and now we know this as active participants in faculty associations. Our colleagues seek us out for information that they might not have otherwise pursued or perhaps even known existed. We have garnered a wealth of information and now it is incumbent upon us to share it.

> *[My experience] makes me want to inform colleagues about the Faculty Association and what their rights/obligations are. [It] doesn't have to be all service all the time.*

> *We're looked at differently, not only by colleagues within the library, but also from colleagues outside of the library. The whole thing has been an affirmation that librarians are part of the academy and we are viewed as having additional value.*

Our collective experience as leaders in our faculty associations has helped us as mentors in the encouragement, recruitment, and promotion of younger librarian colleagues. We are in positions to recommend members for special committees and functions. We need to encourage colleagues to step up and take on roles in their faculty associations and not to fear speaking up, particularly because, while the participants of this study may have had positive experiences and impacts in their workplaces, institutional support for faculty associations still varies.

> *At the end of a 40-year career, I have been prodding my younger colleagues to get involved in the faculty association. I have spent the last year actively mentoring them and encouraging them to gain a better understanding of what their role is in the academy and the association.*

It's a heady feeling, as a professional librarian, to be sought out by academic colleagues because of the skills one has. Librarians are recognized for their ability to assess and analyze, for their nuanced and diplomatic approaches and for their ability to unpack difficult situations and provide alternative solutions. At least, this has been our experience. And it has only been enhanced by our involvement with our respective faculty associations. The opportunity to develop these skills, in the context of negotiating with administrators regarding salary, tenure and promotion, and contract language, is not something we would have encountered in our regularly assigned duties.

Conclusion

Using autoethnography as a method allowed us to "pull out" our experiences and examine them for meaning. Using liminality as our theoretical framework provided us with an explanation for how we were feeling, which hasn't previously existed in the library literature. We were able to view our experiences, as academic librarians, as experiencing liminality on more than one level. We construct our identity in a library environment undergoing transition as we concurrently try to move through uncertainty.

We participated in this study because we were motivated by our positive experiences as active members within our faculty associations. We wanted to share these experiences with academic librarian colleagues in the hopes of encouraging their involvement at their respective institutions. Although we suspect our experiences may not be unique—there is very little literature available on the participation of librarians in faculty associations—we wanted to provide a foundation for further research. Indeed, because of the lack of research in this area, we felt we had to perform an exploratory study in order to ground our future research, and offer paths of exploration for other researchers. We thus based our study wholly upon our own experiences and perceptions, analyzed through the autoethnographic exercise and examined within the framework of liminality. Further, we deliberately made use of first person narrative so that the reader could see himself or herself as the protagonist in our story and—we hope—experience verisimilitude.

As our conversations continued, we found that our stories were remarkably alike and common themes around identity, social justice and personal development emerged. As we each embarked on our own "Hero's Journey,"[25] we discovered that the only people holding us back were ourselves. We were already strong, engaged and active before taking on these roles—we couldn't have taken them on otherwise. What the journey uncovered was a new self-awareness and an affirmation of our strengths as individuals and as librarians.

Bibliography

ACRL. *Standards for Faculty Status for Academic Librarians.* http://www.ala.org/acrl/standards/standardsfaculty.

Bettis, Pamela J., Michael Mills, Janice Miller Williams and Robert Nolan. "Faculty in a Liminal Landscape: A Case Study of a College Reorganization." *Journal of Leadership & Organizational Studies* 11, no. 3 (2005): 47-61.

Bolin, Mary K. "Librarian Status at US Research Universities: Extending the Typology." *Journal of Academic Librarianship* 34, no. 5 (2008): 416-424. doi: 10.1016/j.acalib.2008.06.005.

Bosetti, Lynn, Colleen Kawalilak and Peggy Patterson. "Betwixt and Between: Academic Women in Transition." *The Canadian Journal of Higher Education* 38, no. 2 (2008): 95-115.

Campbell, Joseph. *The Hero with a Thousand Faces.* New York: Pantheon Books, 1949.

CAUT. *Academic Status and Governance for Librarians at Canadian Universities and Colleges.* http://www.caut.ca/about-us/caut-policy/lists/general-caut-policies/policy-statement-on-academic-status-and-governance-for-librarians-at-canadian-universities-and-colleges.

Cronin, Blaise. "The Mother of All Myths." *Library Journal* 126, no. 3 (2001): 144.

Dressman, Mark. "Congruence, Resistance, Liminality: Reading and Ideology in Three School Libraries." *Curriculum Inquiry* 27, no. 3 (1997): 267-315.

Ellis, Carolyn. "Heartful Autoethnography." *Qualitative Health Research* 9, no. 5 (1999): 653-667. doi: 10.1177/104973299129122153.

Ellis, Carolyn, Tony E. Adams and Adam P. Bochner. "Autoethnography: An Overview." *Forum Qualitative Sozialforschung/Forum: Qualitative Social Research* 12, no. 1 (2011): 40 paragraphs. Art. 10, http://www.qualitative-research.net/index.php/fqs/article/view/1589.

Firment, Erica. *Librarian Avengers* (blog). http://librarianavengers.org/.

Fox, David. "A Demographic and Career Profile of Canadian Research University Librarians." *Journal of Academic Librarianship* 33, no. 5 (2007): 540-550. doi: 10.1016/j.acalib.2007.05.006.

Hellsten, Laurie-Ann M., Stephanie L. Martin, Laureen J. McIntyre and Audrey L. Kinzel. "Women on the Academic Tenure Track: An Autoethnographic Inquiry." *International Journal for Cross-Disciplinary Subjects in Education* 2, no. 1 (2011): 271-275.

Kuhlthau, Carol C. "Inside the Search Process: Information Seeking from the User's Perspective." *Journal of the American Society for Information Science* 42, no. 5 (1991): 361-371.

Leckie, Gloria J. and Jim Brett. "Job Satisfaction of Canadian University Librarians: A National Study." *College & Research Libraries* 58, no. 1 (1997): 31-47.

Mehra, Bharat, Kevin S. Rioux and Kendra S. Albright. "Social Justice in Library and Information Sciences." In M.J. Bates, & M.N. Mack (Eds.), *Encyclopedia of Library and Information Sciences* (3rd ed., pp. 4820-4836) Taylor & Francis. doi:10.1081/E-ELIS3-120044526.

Plum, Terry. "Academic Libraries and the Rituals of Knowledge." *RQ*, 33 no 4 (1994): 496.

Singer Gordon, Rachel. *The Liminal Librarian* (blog). http://www.lisjobs.com/blog/.

Turner, Victor W. "Passages, Margins and Poverty: Religious Symbols of Communitas." In P. Bohannan, & M. Glazer (Eds.), *High points in anthropology* (2nd ed., pp. 503). New York: Knopf, 1988.

van Gennep, Arthur. *Rites de passage*. Chicago: University of Chicago Press, 1960. Translated by M.B. Vizedom and G.L. Caffe as *Rites of Passage*.

Vézina, Mireille and Susan Crompton. "Volunteering in Canada." *Canadian Social Trends, 93*. Ottawa: Statistics Canada, 2012. (11-008-XWE) http://www.statcan.gc.ca/pub/11-008-x/2012001/article/11638-eng.pdf.

The Quiet Librarian:
Workplace Complaints and Collegiality

G. Douglas Vaisey

In most workplaces, employees have the right to complain. Whether workplace conditions are hazardous or discrimination is occurring or wages do not match the regulated minima, every employee has the right to speak up. These situations deal with conditions to which workplace legislation applies. But in unionized environments, where more specific terms and conditions of employment are set out (hours of work, procedures for promotion, vacation entitlement, etc.), the complaint process is back-stopped by an even stronger provision—that of the grievance. A grievance is defined as "a formal allegation that there has been a violation of the legal terms and conditions of employment in a workplace."[1] The grievance process requires the employer and the union to meet, address, and (where possible) resolve employment issues.

The complaint and grievance process therefore provides an opportunity to clarify the terminology set out in a collective agreement or handbook, to address alleged inappropriate application of workplace rules or regulations, or to bring to the fore issues that may not be well addressed in the language governing the work environment.

The range of issues is broad. An example of the breadth of scope can be found in the Windsor University Faculty Association *Handbook for Grievance Officers*.[2] It can be as specific as the failure to pay a bonus or provide parking. It can be as general as a difference of opinion over academic freedom or the criteria for promotion.

What makes the complaint and grievance process essential to unionized workplace relations—whether for the individual and management or for the union and the university administration—is that it provides a mechanism to enforce the legal terms and conditions of employment. It is one way to address labour law or human rights matters where collective agreements are silent. As well, it deals with conflicting interpretations of particular wording in collective agreements. Words or conditions agreed to at the bargaining table may seem fine at the close of negotiations, but may fail in practice. There may be vocabulary that is ambiguous or leads to unintended consequences. Where either the employee or the employer has misread a policy, differed on the meaning of a clause, or failed to follow government regulations, a grievance (in particular) provides the opportunity to formally wrestle with and resolve problems. The resulting precedents establish a history of practice and set the direction for future similar issues.

Not every complaint results in a formal grievance. Many unions have grievance committees whose role it is to receive complaints, investigate their details, and determine whether to pursue matters further. Criteria include whether there is wording in the collective agreement, whether grievance (as opposed to informal resolution) is the most appropriate course of action, and whether there are reasonable grounds to anticipate success. The impact on all of the other members of the union needs to be weighed, since the union represents the entire membership. The filing of a grievance is therefore a matter of seriousness and not a tool to 'get back at' the employer for a perceived slight.

More importantly, a grievance forces the dispute into the framework negotiated between the parties. Most provincial legislation stipulates that a collective agreement contains provision for the final and binding solution of alleged violations, including by arbitration.

It is a form of due process that ensures the rights of the members of the bargaining unit and buffers against "creative solutions" that could undermine the rights of individual members or indeed the spirit of the collective agreement itself. In many arbitration decisions, adjudicators have emphasized that the grievance arbitration process is intended to be remedial and restorative rather than punitive.[3] In essence, a grievance attempts to *resolve* real and often-unintended problems arising in a workplace governed by a collective agreement; it is not intended to *punish* an employer nor to seek vindication for personal or professional injury.[4]

In an academic setting, it is easy to make the assumption that, if a person has a problem, he or she will complain, and that in unionized settings, grievances will be filed. There is little research into librarians' complaint behaviour, and the absence of investigation might lead to the erroneous conclusion that librarians have few reasons to complain and therefore few grievances. We will begin from the statement that "all grievances are complaints, but not all complaints are grievances."[5]

The literature on academic librarians, and indeed on librarians in general, has largely focused on job satisfaction, with an emphasis on career choice (did I pick the right career? would I make the same decision now?),[6] monetary rewards,[7] and general working conditions.[8] In a 2008 article on librarian careers, the comforting statistic is that 70% of librarians are either very satisfied or satisfied with their jobs.[9] What this very positive outlook masks is the reverse, that 30% of librarians are less than satisfied with their jobs. This chapter examines that less-than-positive side and asks the following questions:

- Do librarians have complaints?
- What are the natures of these complaints?
- Do librarians act on these complaints?
- If not, why not?

This investigation arose from preparation of a presentation for the October 2011 Canadian Association of University Teachers' Librarians' Conference.[10] A 20 question survey was conducted between September 27 and October 20, 2011, through a listserv accessible to Canadian academic librarians. There were 215 respondents, although some did not answer every question.

Job Satisfaction

On the issue of job satisfaction, 42% claimed "high" levels of satisfaction, while 47.2% asserted "medium" job satisfaction. This places our sample at a higher rate of job satisfaction than reported by Albanese in *Library Journal* and might lead us to the conclusion that all is well. When comparisons were done across institutions by size, there was no significant variation in job satisfaction. When examined by length of employment, job satisfaction was generally higher amongst men employed for five to ten years or for 20 or more years.

The survey *assumed* the existence of problems and focused on complaints and grievances. In spite of the apparent general satisfaction with work, two responses were revealing. When asked, "Have you ever filed a grievance?" 76.1% answered "No." But when asked, "Have you ever been *tempted* to file a grievance but did not?" 60% replied "Yes." We have a majority of individuals who have been tempted to complain formally, but who have not done so.

The survey defined size of institution as: small (5000 students or less), medium (between 5000 and 14,999 students), large (15,000 students or more) and very large (30,000 students or more), reflecting Canadian university sizes. There was a greater tendency to turn to the grievance process in small institutions than in very large ones.

Issues Giving Rise to Grievances

For the one in four librarians who formally complained through the individual grievance process, the issues, from most to least common, were:

- collegiality and respect,
- promotion,
- salary or remuneration,
- failure to follow procedures in the collective agreement,
- "poisoned workplace" conditions.

Where group grievances were filed, once again, "collegiality and respect" was at the forefront. (More detailed discussion of this issue follows later.) "Poisoned workplace" included such issues as favouritism and bullying. As evidenced in Keashley and Neuman's 2010 article, bullying in higher education has recently received increased attention; while their focus was on faculty members, the principles can be extrapolated to librarians.

When rated by institution size, the tendency for respondents to have no grievances decreased the larger the institution. Where grievances *were filed*, the category "other" represented the highest percentage response across institutions, incorporating an array of issues from "failure to follow the collective agreement" through to "poisoned workplace." Also included were issues such as annual and performance reviews where subjectivity is often a factor.

Among the 11 categories specifically itemized in the survey, "collegiality and respect" was the primary issue in small and medium-sized institutions (representing over 20% of grievances) and a significant issue in large to very large institutions (at 12.9% and 18.2%, respectively). When other issues were considered, sabbaticals resonated in small institutions, salary and tenure[11] in medium-sized ones, working conditions (physical environment) and workload in large institutions, and academic freedom and promotion in the very largest.

In some responses, a single grievance might encompass multiple issues (e.g., sabbatical, workload, and salary). One common thread was for "collegiality and respect" to be paired with other matters, often academic freedom and workload. The issue of workload, separate from "collegiality," was often combined with leaves, sabbaticals, and "other" causes, such as performance evaluations.

Issues Giving Rise to Complaint

With few grievances actually being filed, it seemed appropriate to inquire whether librarians *intended* to complain but chose not to do so. Three of every five respondents indicated having an unfiled complaint. The main issues were:

- collegiality and respect (58%),
- workload (35.3%),
- other (20%),
- academic freedom (16%), and
- physical working conditions (13.4%).

The "other" category, following after workload, included harassment or bullying, performance evaluation, privacy/confidentiality, merit pay, equitable access to library positions, and hiring non-librarians to do librarian work. At least three of these issues could be categorized under "collegiality and respect."

Three complaints stood out: collegiality and respect—increasingly significant the larger the size of the institution; workload—of concern in all institutions, but particularly prevalent in large ones; and the category "other" in small institutions. Although their issues were weighty (academic freedom, promotion, salary, and workload), librarians in the largest institutions showed surprising reluctance to grieve.

The reluctance to file a grievance was most pronounced among early-career librarians (65.8% of whom had a complaint but did not lodge it). The leading overall complaint continued to be "collegiality and respect," an issue for 29.2% of early-career, 35.1% of mid-career, and 23.5% of late-career respondents. The next most prominent complaint regardless of career stage, was workload. Interestingly, items most directly affecting career progress (promotion, tenure and sabbatical) represented less of an issue.

Collegiality and Respect

The presentation of the survey results in October 2011 gave rise to the question, "Did anyone define 'collegiality and respect'?" and so a follow-up survey was conducted in January-February 2012. There were only 92 responses (43% of respondents had not participated in the previous survey). McKinzie (2000) and Freedman (2012) focus on the centrality of this notion in the academic sphere, but remarked on a lack of definitions. Respondents to the follow-up were given a choice of 20 possible interpretations of "collegiality," in an effort to isolate the key elements of the concept. The majority agreed that the following were central to the notion of collegiality:

- respectful interpersonal relations (74.3%),
- cooperative workplace relationships (69.3%),
- equitable treatment by colleagues (67.3%),
- equitable treatment of colleagues (63.4%),
- consultation in decision-making (54.5%),
- consultation in planning (54.5%).

In the first question, respondents were allowed to pick as many definitions as they wished. When asked which *single* description addressed most closely the meaning of "collegiality," respondents identified "respectful interpersonal relations" and "cooperative workplace relationships."

Why Librarians Don't Complain

If collegiality and respect are so high on the list of issues giving rise to possible (but often unfiled) grievances, why don't librarians complain? The primary reason cited was fear:

- fear of reprisal (59.6%),
- fear of isolation (22%),
- fear of the impact on colleagues (18.3%), and
- fear of losing benefits previously granted (5.5%).

In institutions with 30,000 or more students, the fear of reprisal was remarkably high at 63.3%. Fear of isolation and insecurity about the grounds for complaint were cited more often by respondents in medium and large institutions, while fear of impact on colleagues struck home with librarians in medium-sized institutions.

Fear or insecurity is not unique to academic librarians. Part-time instructors or contract faculty, whose employment relies on periodic renewal, are equally vulnerable. No less so are untenured appointees and faculty members pending tenure and promotion. The threat that a faculty member or librarian is "not the right fit" for an organization (couched as, "worth of the candidate on a long-term basis" or ability to "contribute to the goals and stature of the university") leaves many feeling too vulnerable to complain.

With unionization in colleges and universities, many librarians gained access to tenure or permanency of employment. Tenure offers protection against arbitrary dismissal of an employee who is critical of the administration; the administration must show just cause or rely on layoff provisions in the collective agreement or the like to dismiss a librarian who enjoys a continuing appointment. The language of permanency protects academic freedom, outlines identifiable processes and criteria for promotion, sabbatical, or renewal, and offers protection during downsizing or budgetary retrenchment. But tenure is no panacea. It does not protect against marginalization. Nor does it deter managers from practicing favouritism. Tenure, likewise, does not diminish petty fault-finding, which can be a subtle and wearing form of harassment.

Fear in the library workplace would seem to fly in the face of all who express such high levels of job satisfaction. Some, who added comments to the survey, remarked that they, like junior and untenured faculty, were afraid to lose any chance at permanency of employment. One colleague noted that faculty members grieve against an often unseen Dean, whose office may be somewhat remote, whereas the University Librarian may have an office just down the hall. Recurring encounters with library administrators, against whom grievances are filed, are therefore very likely, as is the potential for interpersonal irritation. Other responses noted that complainants have been marginalized, taken off high-profile projects (in spite of their expertise), or re-assigned to positions of lesser authority during inter-departmental reorganization.

In the same survey, respondents were asked why they had never and would never consider filing a grievance. Although a large percentage (44.8%) suggested either a well-run workplace or a workplace where issues are resolved with managers, an equally significant percentage (36.8%) indicated that they were keeping their heads down (either to enjoy what work one can or to wait out retirement).

The well-run, problem-solving workplace was more representative of the small- to medium-sized university, while the "keep my head down" response was significant in institutions with 15,000 or more students. In these larger institutions, there was also a significant response to the "I have seen others punished" option.

Seeking Assistance or Advice

Let us examine where librarians turn when seeking assistance with a complaint. When asked, "where do you turn first", the answer was:

- the collective agreement (78.3%),
- faculty/librarian union reps (67%),
- close friends in the library (57%), and
- old hands in the library (43.1%).

But the first place we often turn may not be the source of best advice. When asked whence came the *best guidance*, respondents indicated:

- the grievance officer (60.7%),
- faculty/librarian union reps (57.6%),
- the collective agreement (37.3%), and
- other (55.6%)—professional officers, legal counsel, and folks with long experience.

And when asked about *second-best advice*, respondents indicated close friends in the library (34.4%), the collective agreement (33.7%), old hands in the library (30.4%) and faculty/librarian union reps (25.9%).

We can see that optimal advice is provided by union elements (the collective agreement, union representatives, or grievance officers). Most librarians who answered the survey had read sections of their collective agreement or handbook, with almost half focusing on "those sections that affect me." But some indicated that they did not proceed further out of uncertainty—questioning the validity of their case, the reception accorded by union officials, the fear of lost confidentiality. Unlike everything else librarians do in their professional problem-solving (confirm, verify and consult), in complaint handling, evidence suggests we stop short of the next step.

The collective agreement or negotiated handbook exists to set out the protocols and procedures that govern the workplace. In many instances, these clauses cover the large issues: appointment, promotion, permanency of employment, vacations, etc. Not every regulation that governs day-to-day management can be itemized in a collective agreement and, in some ways, libraries may create internal practice that, on close examination, runs counter to the spirit and intent of such agreements. The complexity of the negotiation process (especially where librarians are part of a larger faculty unit) means that many small matters never reach the bargaining table. The complaint and grievance process is one of few means through which workplace issues—not well covered in a collective agreement, not expressed in precise language, or open to subjective interpretation—can be resolved. Precedents flowing from grievance and arbitration decisions often clarify and define terms of workplace operation and supplement the wording found in collective agreements.

The Way Ahead

What can we learn from this? First, we need to recognize that 45% of librarians in the survey felt that their workplaces were either well-run or conducive to problem-solving. That said, in spite of positive reports of job satisfaction, there is also an undercurrent of unhappiness that has as its focus collegiality and respect. Respondents felt that clarifying and codifying the issue of "respectful interpersonal relations" might restore a more satisfying, less frustrating work environment. Where managers are more equitable and transparent (especially where workload, career progress and performance reviews are concerned) and consistent in the application of policies, criteria or guidelines, complaints appear to be fewer. One view is that this change might happen if 360-degree evaluations (ongoing performance review of library administrators) were implemented and if penalties were applied to administrators who bully, harass, or practice favouritism.

In the surveys, some respondents felt that colleagues ought to recognize that they too can be harassers and bullies, to the extent that it can upset the respectful equilibrium. The need for fairness, balance, and ethical behaviour applies to peer processes (for instance, where input into promotion, sabbatical or tenure applications is required) and to decision-making (notably where it impacts on another's workload or job assignment). As pointed out by Keashley and Neuman, and applicable to academic librarians, collegiality and autonomy are critical for academic freedom and the work of an academic, but some may feel that they could be invoked to prevent action that would address problematic behaviours. This in turn, can create a climate of non-congeniality, hostility and incivility, increasing the likelihood of bullying and mobbing.[12]

On the other hand, there is a need in consensus-driven organizations to recognize that there will be differing opinions, sometimes expressed strongly. Collegiality and respect is not to be confused with congeniality. Colleagues should not interpret the stridency and force of expression (especially where the opinion runs against the grain of consensus) as a lack of collegial attitude. There will be issues—from budget allocation to work assignment to policy initiatives—that give rise to opposing visions. The expression of a contrary viewpoint should not be an excuse to marginalize a colleague.

Much of the solution lies in better contract language. The overall objective is to create conditions for a safe, healthy, and well-regulated workplace. Several respondents to the survey called for improved wording in clauses dealing with harassment and bullying. This, of course, requires the acceptance at the bargaining table that workplace harassment and bullying occurs and, in worse case scenarios, can have serious consequences. In the same vein, getting administrations to agree to language on the evaluation of administrators and on consequences for their behaviours will be a challenge, but could lead to the collaborative workplace that so many highly-functioning libraries enjoy. Here, however, there is a caveat. Although the unionized workplace establishes formal relationships and problem-solving mechanisms between employer and employee, it is not as well set up to deal with member-to-member conflicts, which are all too common and often undermine general collegiality.[13]

Librarian surveys indicate that respondents like their work. They feel they have chosen well in their careers. But where fear inhibits the willingness to speak out, to complain, and, in serious situations to grieve, we are failing each other as academic professionals. If a small sample (as reported here for Canadian universities) indicates problems, what might a more methodical North America-wide survey tell us?

Bibliography

Albanese, Andrew Richard. "Take This Job and Love It." *Library Journal* 133, no. 2 (2008): 36-39.

Berry, John N. "Great Work, Genuine Problems." *Library Journal* 132, no. 6 (2007): 26-29.

Canadian Association of University Teachers (CAUT). Grievance Handling Workshop, n.d.). Participants' Manual.

Freedman, Shin. "Collegiality Matters: Massachusetts Public Higher Education Librarians' Perspective." *Journal of Academic Librarianship* 38, no. 2 (2012): 108-114.

Garcha, Rajinder and John C. Phillips. "US Academic Librarians: Their Involvement in Union Activities." *Library Review* 50, no. 3 (2001): 122-127.

Guyton, Theodore L. *Unionization: The Viewpoint of Librarians.* Chicago: American Library Association, 1975.

Hovekamp, Tina Maragou. "Organizational Commitment of Professional Employees in Union and Nonunion Research Libraries." *College and Research Libraries* 55, no. 4 (1994): 297-307.

Kathman, Jane McGurn and Michael D. Kathman. "Conflict Management in the Academic Library." *Journal of Academic Librarianship* 16, no. 3 (1990): 145-149.

Keashly, Loraleigh and Joel H. Neuman. "Faculty Experiences with Bullying in Higher Education: Causes, Consequences and Management." *Administrative Theory and Praxis* 32, no. 1 (2010): 48-70, http://www.ccas.net/files/ADVANCE/Keashly_Bullying.pdf.

Kreitz, Patricia A. and Annegret Ogden. "Job Responsibilities and Job Satisfaction at the University of California Libraries." *College and Research Libraries* 51, no. 4 (1990): 297-320.

Lanigan v. Eastern School District, 2013 PESC 12, http://www.canlii.ca/

Leckie, Gloria J. and Becky Rogers. "Reactions of Academic Librarians to Job Loss Through Downsizing: An Exploratory Study." *College and Research Libraries* 56, no. 2 (1995): 144-155.

Leysen, Joan M. and Jeanne M. K. Boydston. "Job Satisfaction among Academic Cataloguer Librarians." *College and Research Libraries* 70, no. 3 (2009): 273-293.

McKinzie, Steve. "Twenty-Five Years of Collegial Management: The Dickinson College Model of Revolving Leadership and Holistic Librarianship." *Library Philosophy and Practice* 2, no. 2 (2000): Spring. 9 pages, http://digitalcom mons.unl.edu/libphilprac/.

Parmer, Coleen and Dennis East. "Job Satisfaction among Support Staff in Twelve Ohio Academic Libraries." *College and Research Libraries* 54, no. 1 (1993): 43-57.

Pettas, William A. and Steven L. Gilliland. "Conflict in the Large Academic Library: Friend or Foe?" *Journal of Academic Librarianship* 18, no. 1 (1992): 24-29.

Rockman, Ilene F. "Job Satisfaction among Faculty and Librarians: A Study of Gender, Autonomy, and Decision Making Opportunities." *Journal of Library Administration* 5, no. 3 (1984): 43-56.

Voelck, Julie. "Job Satisfaction among Support Staff in Michigan Academic Libraries." *College and Research Libraries* 56, no. 2 (1995): 157-170.

Wakimoto, Diana K. "Benefits of Unionization Still Unclear for US Academic Libraries and Librarians." *Evidence-Based Library and Information Practice* 5, no. 1 (2010): 144-146.

Windsor University Faculty Association. (1988). *Faculty Association Handbook for Grievance Officers,* http://www.wufa.ca.

Academic Librarians at the Table—Bargaining for Parity

Mary Kandiuk

Introduction

While the trade union status and structures of representation for academic librarians vary across Canada, the Canadian Association of University Teachers (CAUT) *Librarian Salary and Academic Status Survey 2012* reveals that a large proportion of academic librarians employed at Canadian universities are members of certified trade unions that include faculty members and that serve as the exclusive agent for every librarian and faculty member in the bargaining unit. A collective agreement—a legally enforceable, binding contract negotiated between employers and unions—provides the "framework for working conditions" and outlines the terms and conditions of employment for the represented members.[1] The means for arriving at the collective agreement is collective bargaining, a process which has been described as a prescribed ritual.[2] Bargaining is oftentimes a puzzling exercise. The union comes to the table with many demands (some of them extreme) and little in the way of leverage (except job action, i.e., a strike, which is an option of last resort). Sometimes employers look for major concessions, but sometimes not; they hold most of the cards. So what is their incentive to give the union anything? Usually they have a legal obligation to bargain in good faith, which means they are obliged to try to reach an agreement. Bargaining resembles a kind of dance—Roger Fisher and William Ury call it a "minuet"[3] which involves short steps—but you can dance for a very long time. Countless hours are spent preparing bargaining proposals, and discussing and negotiating these proposals both with the employer and amongst one's own team, only to toss many of them aside and negotiate much of the agreement in a very short period of time, often in the final hours. You "get" things on occasion for reasons that can seem arbitrary and are often a function of timing and the right conditions, or the result of what the CAUT Bargaining Manual describes as "creative compromise."[4] Understanding and learning how to both navigate and manipulate the collective bargaining process can be very rewarding for those who find themselves a minority group in a larger union, like academic librarians. What follows is an attempt to demystify and guide academic librarians through the process offering personal insights as well as the experiences of other academic librarians who have also been "at the table."

Background to Unionization for Academic Librarians

Much has been written about the "historical marginalization of librarianship" due to the fact that, as Roma Harris writes, it is a "woman's profession" and the "undervaluing of library work [is] a product of its gendered nature."[5] Describing the status of academic librarians in the US in the early 20th century, Orvin Lee Shiflett writes, "[a]cademic librarians not at the higher administrative levels came to be viewed as workers by library directors, who saw their own role of administration as keeping the employees to the tasks at hand."[6] Dee Garrison writes, "[i]n librarianship, as in teaching and social work, the presence of women made more likely the development of an authoritative administrative structure with a stress on rules and generally established principles to control the activities of employees."[7] The trajectory of collective bargaining for academic librarians can be seen as a desire for change that stemmed partly from "the attempts of its members to mimic the higher status male professions."[8] As pointed out by Rachel A. Fleming-May and Kimberley Douglas, "as early as the 1911 Annual Meeting of the American Library Association, W.E. Henry presented the 'revolutionary' idea that 'the librarian or head of the staff should have the rank and pay of a professor,' and assistant librarians should be afforded academic rank." Furthermore, "the rationale Henry presented in support of this edict, that 'librarianship is a learned profession' whose members should be 'respected as educators by the faculty, not merely for the satisfaction of the staff but for the good of the library,' is essentially the same as that presented today."[9]

In addition to the issue of gender, underpinning unionization and collective bargaining for academic librarians is "class conflict." Michael F. Winter, who has written extensively on the sociology of librarianship writes, "[most] of us immediately recognize the organizational activities of unions as part of class conflict in industrial society, but we are slower to see this as an essential factor in the development of a profession."[10] Winter continues,

> The attempt to procure professional status is a keenly competitive process, elitist in form, which has for its major goal the appropriation of social rewards through restriction of access to privileged kinds of work ..

.. Despite the mystification of the class conflict dimension of the professionalization process, it is clear upon examination that it is exclusivist as well as elitist in nature. Viewed positively, the defense of occupational interests is an attempt to protect one's field of work. But viewed negatively, it is also an attempt to exclude allegedly "unqualified" others from the rewards of practice.[11]

It has been noted that "academics are generally not ideologically committed to the labor movement but rather are pragmatically concerned to improve their own terms of employment and professional standing"[12] and this holds true of academic librarians. Collective agreements define "the status of librarians as professionals by differentiating their function and responsibilities from those of paraprofessionals."[13] However, through collective agreements and the process of collective bargaining which secures those agreements, academic librarians seek to exclude those perceived to be unqualified from encroaching on their work (i.e., paraprofessionals) while simultaneously seeking to encroach on the territory previously perceived to be the territory of their faculty member colleagues. Meanwhile many faculty members seek to exclude librarians, whom they do not perceive as their equals, from the rewards of practice which include status and associated privileges and entitlements such as competitive salaries.

Unionization and the associated process of collective bargaining have provided academic librarians over the last few decades with some increased measure of control over their work, social and political status, and, not to be discounted, tangible material rewards. This is increasingly important where, as pointed out by Stephen Aby, "the trend in higher education over the last couple of decades has undermined the practice of shared governance."[14] "Universities are becoming increasingly corporatized and entrepreneurial, both in their values and in their management. Where once decisions were made by faculty and administrators together in a climate of collegial decision-making, now they are increasingly made by administrators exercising their management rights in a corporate model of governance."[15] Ernst Benjamin calls unionization the "antidote to corporatization."[16] As pointed out by Tina Hovekamp, [u]nionization provides a venue to secure the employees' role in college governance" and "collective bargaining guarantees the employees representation in the shaping of their working conditions."[17] Lothar Spang and William P. Kane write,

> [a]cademic librarians traditionally have had their interests represented through one or more means from among four choices acting singly in negotiating their own interests with administrators; relying on the judgement and goodwill of supervisors to promote librarian interests; participating in collaborative ventures with their fellow librarians to enhance professional interests; and/or; if available, joining a union, most often a large teacher collective for formal negotiations.[18]

Of these four options, being a member of a union is arguably the most advantageous choice with non-unionized academic librarians enviously eyeing the rights and privileges of unionized academic librarians. As CAUT points out an "association's strength is based on collective organization" and "unionization marks a significant shift in the balance of power" and "removes the employer's unilateral right to determine the terms and conditions of employment."[19] According to Rajinder Garcha and John C. Phillips, the "evidence is overwhelming that unionized librarians earn higher salaries than non-unionized librarians" (although this has been disputed by some studies)[20] and that rights of increasing concern to academic librarians, such as "academic and intellectual freedom must be secured contractually."[21]

The Movement by Academic Librarians to Unionize at York University

On October 28, 1970, Ontario university presidents received a circular from John B. Macdonald, Executive Director, regarding a survey undertaken by Dr. W.G. Tamblyn, President of Lakehead University, of the status of librarians in Ontario universities. "Included are the responses of 12 university presidents outlining current practice in their institutions. Nine of the Presidents mention 'pressure' or 'rumblings' at their respective universities. One states 'within recent months, I have heard half a dozen of our colleagues mention the fact that questions concerning the contractual arrangements with professional librarians are becoming a pressing matter within their respective institutions."[22] Librarians across the province were beginning to organize and, as will be revealed in this chapter, being "organized" is critical to achieving improvements for librarians at the bargaining table.

From 1962-1976, the York University Faculty Association (YUFA) was a voluntary association that promoted the interests of tenure-track/tenured teaching staff at York. In 1975, librarians joined faculty members in a move to form a trade union. The initiative on the part of librarians was spearheaded by a small group of politically astute and active librarians who saw clearly the advantages of aligning themselves with faculty, particularly from a labour perspective. This was part of a broader movement, as outlined by Martha Bufton in another chapter in this collection. As writes Jennifer Dekker:

> [l]ibrarians are present in the first collective agreement (1976-1978) ratified by YUFA after it became certified as a labour union. The background to this achievement for York librarians dates back to 1969–1970, when a group of librarians appealed to York administration to review the status, salaries and professional opportunities available to them at York University. A Committee called the Presidential Committee on Professional Librarians was formed and met regularly throughout 1975

and 1976. This committee, in addition to addressing the professional concerns of librarians, acknowledged that gender issues had contributed to the inequities experienced by the librarians. The following is from the minutes of the meeting of August 27, 1975: 'Librarianship is a sex-stereotyped profession and has been paid and evaluated in the past on that basis; in addition, men are, within the (York) system, very quickly promoted through the ranks to middle and upper management, so that women constitute almost the entire membership of the lowest professional ranks'.[23]

The Report of the Presidential Committee on Professional Librarians, also known as the Stewart Commission, stated that: "[p]hilosophically and logically, the committee agreed that 100% parity in salary scale between Librarians and Faculty (particularly if this report is accepted) was justified."[24] In 1985, Betty Joe Irvine described librarianship as suffering from "intraoccupational sex segregation" where "men dominate the pinnacle of a profession's institution and women its base."[25] Academic librarians have used collective bargaining to combat occupational segregation where, as Sarah Pritchard describes, "inequities [are] evident within the profession and when the profession is compared to others."[26] It is a common theme in the literature of the female-intensive fields that there exists "the need to adopt the values and definitions of the higher prestige male professions in order to advance their own status."[27] On August 29, 1973, Acting-Director of Libraries, Bill Newman, in a letter to the Secretary of Senate, asks that "the Senate Library Committee recognize that librarians should have academic status appropriate to being 'contributors to the academic enterprise'."[28] A chronology of events leading up to unionization states that on July 1, 1974, "York librarians become eligible for membership in YUFA, York University Faculty Association, following a unanimous vote by the membership at the March general meeting to accept them, and after appropriate constitutional changes."[29] It was an historic moment, securing York librarians a leadership position with respect to academic librarians and faculty association participation in Canada, a role that was to be assumed on numerous occasions in later years. Described by one librarian as entering "uncharted territory," the move to unionize was prescient on the part of academic librarians at York but not necessarily welcomed by all at the time. There was reluctance by some York academic librarians to abandon the emphasis on performing duties in the library to meet the demands and expectations associated with adopting continuing appointment procedures, such as research and scholarship. However, what cannot be denied is that in future years it is as members of YUFA and through collective bargaining that York librarians were able to achieve many significant gains in pursuit of parity with teaching faculty. This included the negotiation of salaries from amongst the lowest to the highest in the country (and on a par with faculty in Faculty of Arts) and breaking ground with the successful negotiation of annual research leaves (on top of sabbatical leaves) to support research and scholarship.

For academic librarians who are members of certified trade unions, the usual and logical union for them to belong to is the same union as faculty members. This is the situation at York and many other Canadian universities. Academic librarians are seen as sharing a community of interest with their faculty colleagues. "Community of interest" is used by labour boards to determine appropriate bargaining units in organized workplaces. Underpinning that determination is whether "employees in the unit share enough employment interests in common that the single bargaining agent can effectively represent all the interests of the collectivity. It does not mean an identity of interests, but a broad similarity of employment interests and an absence of seriously conflicting interests."[30] This is a double-edged sword with both advantages and disadvantages. As a group, librarians are usually too few in number to wield much clout on their own, as is demonstrated by some troubling developments in Ontario that are described by several authors in this collection.

> In most provinces, and in the federal jurisdiction, labour boards can amend bargaining unit certificates where they are persuaded of the community of interest of the groups concerned. However a recent Ontario Tory government amended the Labour Act to give the employer an effective veto to any such initiatives: the employer must agree to the broadening of a bargaining unit for the certificate to be amended.[31]

Subsequently, two groups of academic librarians (Western and McMaster) have been forced to unionize as separate units, a move that is reported to have created a clear distinction between them and their faculty member colleagues and has weakened them in collective bargaining. However, the flip side of the coin is when librarians find themselves a minority group in a larger union, a situation which often gives rise to other difficulties. As Hovekamp writes,

> "[t]he inclusion of academic librarians in the same bargaining unit with faculty has not come without a price. Often cited is the librarians' minority status at the table of negotiations and the subsequent neglect of our own particular needs. Library professionals complain that they are frequently underrepresented and compromised during bargaining negotiations. Considering the sometimes significant differences in their job duties compared to other faculty, there is indeed the risk that librarians' special interests may not get enough attention."[32]

Echoed by Harris,

> "[I]n mixed units in which library workers are included with workers from a variety of different occupations, librarians often find that their interests are not particularly well looked after. In collective bargaining arrangements with universities, for example, librarians with faculty status are likely to comprise only a small percentage of the bargaining unit for academic employees . . . . As a result, their concerns are not likely to be taken up by the whole group."[33]

As described later in this chapter, this results in librarians finding themselves involved in two sets of negotiations when they participate in collective bargaining: one with the employer and another with their faculty bargaining team members.

Collective Bargaining Process—Practices, Strategies and Experiences

So, what does collective bargaining look like for academic librarians across Canada? Not surprisingly, the bargaining process varies from institution to institution. A collective bargaining survey was administered by the author in April 2013 to academic librarians via CAUT Librarians' listserv in an effort to "gather information regarding the structures and practices in place to support collective bargaining for academic librarians who are members of certified unions that include faculty members at universities in Canada," as well as to "better understand the issues faced by academic librarians relating to collective bargaining, the challenges academic librarians encounter as members of faculty bargaining teams, and what strategies have proven successful at the negotiating table." The survey was divided into two parts. The first part was comprised of 23 questions and was open to all respondents. The second part was comprised of 12 questions and was open to respondents who had served as members of their bargaining/negotiating team. A total of 140 responses were received. The majority of respondents (70.7%; n=53) reported having *academic* status (analogous terms and conditions of employment, including an equivalent system of ranks, and procedures for promotion and tenure as teaching faculty) as opposed to *faculty* status (same rights and privileges, ranks and salary as teaching faculty) (28%; n=21). Twenty six respondents indicated that they had served as members of their union's bargaining /negotiating team. Of these 26 respondents, 6 indicated that they had served twice and four indicated that they had served three times or more.

Librarian Bargaining Proposals

The development of strong librarian bargaining proposals that are included in the broader primary negotiating positions is a critical first step in securing improvements for librarians in bargaining. The survey revealed that librarian bargaining proposals are solicited through a variety of means, with consultation with librarians (68.9%; n=51) being the most common, followed by bargaining surveys (59.5%; n=44), and open calls for proposals (45.9%; n=34). The responsibility for approval of all proposals usually falls to the union's/association's Executive/Board (39.7%; n=27), followed by the entire union's/association's membership (23.5%; n=16), with approval by librarians themselves appearing to being the least frequent (14.7%; n=10). Librarians have mixed success with respect to getting their proposals included in the primary negotiating positions brought forward for bargaining, with 59.5% (n=44) reporting sometimes, 23% (n=17) reporting yes, and 4.1% (n=3) reporting no success. It is self-evident that it is next to impossible to achieve improvements for librarians when librarian proposals are not included in the primary negotiating positions. Survey respondents who had bargained reported that careful preparation of well thought out proposals, supported by strong arguments, and by all librarians, is critical to success in bargaining. All of this points to the need for organisation and preparation well in advance of the call for proposals. At York, librarians met over the course of a year, from 1990-91, with a senior member of the union staff to review the Collective Agreement with the view of identifying areas for improvement for librarians in the next round of bargaining where librarians saw significant gains.

Bargaining priorities for librarians appear to have changed over time. While salaries may have been one of the most important issues for academic librarians in the 1970s and 1980s (it certainly was at York), as illustrated in Table 1, survey results revealed that workload is now the most pressing issue, followed by pay equity/salary anomalies (indicating that salary is an ongoing concern). Other

Table 1 Most important bargaining priorities for librarians
Workload - 65.1% (n=41)
Pay equity/Salary anomalies - 50.8% (n=32)
Research leaves - 38.1% (n=24)
Continuing appointment and promotion (criteria, standards, process, etc.) - 34.9% (n=22)
Sabbatical leaves - 33.3% (n=21)
Hours of work/flexible work week - 25.4% (n=16)
Academic/faculty status - 22.2% (n=14)
Conference travel grants - 19% (n=12)
Research grants - 12.7% (n=8)
Vacation - 12.7% (n=8)

issues of importance mentioned that are not included in the table below were governance, academic freedom, and assignment of duties. These concerns reflect the importance of bargaining in protecting the values of academic librarianship.

At York, it took many rounds of bargaining to achieve salary improvements, beginning in 1985, the first year that librarians went to the bargaining table with a proposal asking for salary parity with faculty. York University President Macdonald had agreed to implement the recommendations of the Stewart Commission, which provided for salary parity upon the adoption of continuing appointment and promotion criteria—but this was never realized.[34] It wasn't until 1987, when the Ontario government passed Pay Equity legislation that was designed to "redress systemic gender discrimination in compensation for work performed by employees in female job classes"[35] that York librarians saw progress on this front. Directly as a result of the legislation, in 1995 the Employer finally agreed to a pay equity plan for librarians, which included a pool of funds to raise librarian salaries and to tie librarian salaries directly to faculty salaries with regularly mandated reviews.[36] In 1998, librarians were also successful in inserting themselves into the Salary Adjustment Funds Exercise, which was intended to address salary inequities by arguing the principles of pay equity which had the effect of raising librarian salaries even closer to the faculty line. By the early 1990s, a small librarian complement, with ever increasing student enrolments had also pushed librarian workload issues to the fore. Librarians went to the table with numerous demands over successive rounds of bargaining, with workload being the most pressing. During this decade they were able to secure stronger language relating to workload as well as 19 days research leave (in 1992) on top of regular sabbaticals, which was framed as a workload issue. One of the most important gains secured (in 1999) was language relating to librarian complement, which offered a measure of protection against any future reduction of professional librarian positions. As well, it protected against the replacement of those positions by paraprofessional or other type of staff such as post-doctoral fellows, something which has been taking place at other universities such as McMaster[37] despite increasing enrolments. It reads: "The Employer will approve, in a timely manner, a continuing stream position each time a professional librarian retires or resigns from employment during the term of the Collective Agreement, it being understood that the position need not necessarily be to replace the professional librarian who retired or resigned."[38]

Bargaining Team Selection and Composition

An important step in getting librarian proposals into collective agreements is to ensure that librarians are represented at the bargaining table as full members of the bargaining team. Survey respondents indicated that librarian proposals are, for the most part, bargained at the same time with faculty proposals (90.5%; n=67). A bargaining team appointed by the union/association Executive/Board is usually responsible for negotiating the agreement (75%; n=57), followed by bargaining team elected by the entire union/association membership (15.8%; n=12).

Table 2 Librarian membership on bargaining team
Librarian is included
Yes 43.1% (n=31)   Sometimes 44.4% (n=32)   No 9.7% (n= 7)   Don't know 2.8% (n=2)
Designated spot for librarian
Yes 25.7% (n=18)   n/a   No 52.9% (n=37)   Don't know 21.4% (n=15)

However, as demonstrated in Table 2, a librarian is not always included on the bargaining team.

Including a librarian on a team is the result of usual/past practice (41.2%; n=7), or required by the Constitution & By-laws or other document (29.4%; n=5). The most common method of selecting the librarian member is appointment by union/association Executive/Board (28.3%; n=17), followed by volunteer (26.7%; n=16), and then elected by union/association membership (13.3%; n=8). None of the respondents reported librarian members elected only by librarians. In the majority of cases, librarians participate in negotiating the entire agreement, with 8.8% (n=6) negotiating only librarian proposals. Most librarians indicated that having a librarian on the team influences the outcome of bargaining in a positive way (51.5%; n=34), followed by a significant number who did not know (40.9%; n=27), and then 7.6% (n=5) who indicated it did not. For those who have bargained, one of the most fundamental lessons learned is that it is virtually impossible to achieve improvements for a minority group in bargaining unless there is a member of that group at that table. It is also often the physical presence of that individual that prevents proposals from being abandoned or traded off in the final hours of bargaining. Securing a designated spot for librarians on the bargaining team is extremely important and may require proactive efforts on the part of librarians to modify existing union structures and governing documents.

Table 3 illustrates the areas where librarians believe they have benefited from collective bargaining.

Table 3 Areas that benefited from collective bargaining
Academic/faculty status - 78.9% (n=56)
Continuing appointment and promotion (criteria, standards, process, etc.) - 77.9% (n=53)
Sabbatical leaves - 75.4% (n=52)
Vacation - 68.1% (n=47)
Research leaves - 60.0% (n=39)
Pay equity/Salary anomalies - 58.8% (n=40)
Conference travel grants - 47.7% (n=31)
Workload - 38.2% (n=26)
Hours of work/flexible work week - 34.9% (n=22)
Research grants - 33.3% (n=20)
Reduced load - 27.7% (n=18)

For each of the questions posed in the first portion of the survey, there were a number of respondents who indicated that they did not know revealing a lack of understanding as well as a lack of engagement with the collective bargaining process. It is not uncommon for the same few individuals to share the burden of representing librarians at the faculty association/union level. While increased experience is very useful in bargaining, renewal is also important. There is a danger that too few will develop the necessary expertise to ensure that the interests of librarians continue to be represented when those experienced individuals retire or step back from union activities. Those newer to the institution may not fully understand what was involved in securing the terms and conditions of employment they currently enjoy. Succession planning, including mentoring, and the sharing of knowledge are critical to both achieving improvements for librarians as well as protecting those gains already achieved. There always needs to be a group of librarians who are looking out for the interests of the collective and seizing opportunities as they arise.

Bargaining Strategies and Experiences

A number of factors contribute to the success or failure of librarian bargaining proposals and these can be unpredictable. Not only does bargaining vary from institution to institution but it can also vary from one round to the next within the same institution. The librarian member can feel valued and respected in one round of negotiations and marginalized and excluded in another. Significant gains can be achieved in one round of negotiations and nothing in the one that follows. Ironically, there may be in some instances no correlation between how a librarian feels she or he has been treated and the gains that were secured. Similarly the style of bargaining between the parties can vary, ranging from a contest of wills, punctuated by raw debate or calm, infuriating stonewalling. Whether a "given negotiation is a combination of these or whether one predominates depends on the climate, personalities involved, and financial situation within which bargaining takes place."[39] Therefore, it is not uncommon for those who have served as a librarian member of a faculty bargaining team to have mixed feelings about the experience. The majority of the respondents who had bargained viewed it as positive (65.2%; n= 15), followed by mixed, both positive and not positive (30.4%; n=7), with only 1 respondent reporting not positive. Table 5 below illustrates how librarians viewed their experiences as members of the bargaining team.

Table 4 Experience as member of bargaining team
I was treated with respect and accepted as an equal member of the Bargaining/Negotiating Team Yes 84.0 % (n=21)   Sometimes 12% (n=3)   No 0.0% (n=0)   Not applicable 4.0% (n=1)
My contributions were valued by other members of the Bargaining/Negotiating Team Yes 79.2 % (n=19)   Sometimes 12.5% (n=3)   No 4.2% (n=1)   Not applicable 4.2% (n=1)
I felt free to speak my mind and express my views openly at the Bargaining/Negotiating table Yes 70.8 % (n=17)   Sometimes 16.7% (n=4)   No 4.2% (n=1)   Not applicable 8.3% (n=2)
I was treated with respect by the Employer/Administration at the Bargaining/Negotiating table Yes 70.8 % (n=17)   Sometimes 12.5% (n=3)   No 8.3% n=(2)   Not applicable 8.3% (n=2)

When asked to provide any additional comments relating to the experience of bargaining, much of what was offered reflects the experience and the lessons learned of others who have bargained. It is a rewarding exercise but one that is fraught with frustration and even anxiety, with the librarian often in a position of weakness. First, bargaining requires an incredible time commitment, which may be difficult to schedule within the structured work week of an academic librarian. As one respondent said, "[t]he time commitment is large since one serves in bargaining preparation twice as many hours as spent across the table. If bargaining is contentious spread over many months it takes an energy toll." Second, "[b]eing treated with respect by faculty on a negotiating team is something that has to be actively earned—a librarian does start from a position of 'inferiority'—i.e. an assumption of lower status—but if one works hard and offers good advice on THEIR issues, respect is earned, and once earned it is not lost." Experience gained by participating in other union positions and activities can serve librarians very well in bargaining by providing them with an understanding of faculty issues and concerns, in some cases better than some of their faculty member bargaining team colleagues. That said, there are concerns relating to the longstanding issues of both gender and status, which can put the librarian at a disadvantage. CAUT describes collective bargaining as "fundamentally a power relationship."[40] The librarian can feel powerless vis à vis the employer but also in relation to his/her bargaining team colleagues. One respondent said, "[a]s a female I wasn't always listened to, unless a male took up my point." Another responded, "[e]ven though professors are very willing to have a librarian on the team, they—just because of their personalities, ego, etc. . . . —take up way more space than I do. They talk more, argue more, everything more. It's just not my work style, so I feel as though I'm less respected because that's just not my style." And last, being in a minority on the team and representing a group that is a minority within a larger bargaining unit, one is confronted with the fact that the librarian issues may just not be that important to the membership. "[A] librarian issue was dropped to allow an agreement to be reached," reported one respondent. Those who have bargained will appreciate the difficult moment of realization and feeling of powerlessness when a librarian proposal is about to be dropped.

While 79.2% (n=19) respondents reported that librarian proposals were treated as seriously as faculty proposals, 12.5% (n=3) indicated that some were, and 8.3% (n=2) indicated that they were not. Again, respondents' comments provide valuable insights echoing the previous concerns.

- "On a number of occasions the librarians' concerns were traded off for something else. So it takes a number of years for [results] to be achieved."
- "There is a necessary weakness that results from people on both sides of the table knowing that the union as a whole will not go on strike for librarian issues. So, it is difficult to get full attention. If the librarians lobby the

union executive actively, persistently and noisily, however, the amount of attention paid can be increased markedly."
- "Librarians' issues were really only treated as seriously as other proposals when they were specifically tied to professors. For example, we proposed language re: Faculty : Student ratio AND Librarian : Student ratio. This was treated equally because it was part of the same proposal. If the issue was librarian-specific, it got a lot less attention from the group."

When asked if they felt pressure to settle too soon or for less than they had hoped for in bargaining, 69.6% (n=16) respondents said no, while 29.1% (n=6) replied yes they had. One respondent writes, "[the] President of [the] union let an inequity persist in order to reach an agreement." Fisher and Ury make reference to the persuasive "siren song" of "let's all agree and put an end to this" where "you may end up with a deal you should have rejected."[41] The librarian, being in a minority position, often feels pressured to just go along. Refusing to go along puts the librarian in a difficult position but may be what is required for improvements for librarians to be achieved at the bargaining table.

As is illustrated in Table 5, resistance on the part of Employers is perceived as to be the biggest obstacle to achieving improvements for librarians.

Table 5 Obstacles to achieving improvements for librarians
Resistance on the part of the Employer – 84.2% (n=16)
Lack of support from faculty members on the Bargaining/Negotiating Team – 21.1% (n=4)
Lack of support from librarian colleagues – 21.1% (n=4)
Lack of persistence on the part of the librarian on the Bargaining/Negotiating Team – 10.5% (n=2)
Lack of preparation in advance of bargaining – 10.5% (n=2)
Weak proposals – 5.3% (n=1)

Echoing the familiar theme of being a member of a minority group, another respondent cited as an obstacle, "[p]riorities on what can be achieved at any specific particular bargaining table. In other words, a change affecting all faculty members (approximately 900-1,000 members) versus something specific for librarians affecting only 35-40 people." In the context of total compensation (the cost of the entire package), it may be difficult to achieve significant gains if the cost of those gains is greater than the librarian proportional share of the package. This is something that plays out in the university at large, where the library often has to fight for its fair share of the "pie" in an environment of dwindling financial resources. It also appears that certain librarian proposals resonate more with faculty members, which may provide the conditions for gains to be achieved. One respondent reported, "our only controversial issue is vacation; librarians want more and faculty don't care (since they can take a full term free of teaching—something librarians don't have.)" Meanwhile, research leave was cited by several respondents as an issue that was supported by faculty members on the bargaining team. "The faculty members on the Team realized the necessity for Librarians to get research days." These proposals may resonate in the same way with employers. At York, increased vacation was met with stiff resistance during the same round of bargaining, in 2009, which saw librarians secure two additional research days (for a total of 22) as well as six half course releases (26 days/year) available annually on a competitive basis for librarians to pursue research and scholarship (on top of sabbaticals). The experience at York demonstrates that it is helpful to have more than one librarian proposal going into bargaining. It is impossible to predict which one may have success within any particular round. As respondents also relate, it can take many years to achieve progress with a particular issue.

With respect to the factors that contributed to achieving improvements for librarians at the bargaining table, as is illustrated in Table 6, support from faculty members on the Bargaining/Negotiating Team was cited as the most important factor.

Table 6 Factors contributing to achieving improvements for librarians
Support from faculty members – 81.8 % (n=18)
Persistence on the part of the librarian on the Bargaining/Team – 77.3% (n=17)
Preparation in advance of bargaining – 59.1% (13)
Strong proposals – 45.5% (n=10)
Support from librarian colleagues – 40.9% (n=9)
Willingness on the part of the Employer – 27.3% (n=6)

Strong support from faculty bargaining team members signals to employers the importance of librarian issues and the possibility that the lack of gains for librarians could prevent a settlement from being reached. Having a good chief negotiator was also cited as important. The style of the chief negotiator can vary considerably and can set the tone for bargaining. One chief negotiator may foster the notion of a team encouraging consensus in decision-making and where all, including the librarian, are seen as equal members. Another may adopt a bureaucratic efficiency, bestowing upon her- or himself executive powers and circumventing bargaining team members and even colluding with the employer. In some negotiations all members are encouraged to speak and participate; in others the chief negotiator acts as the principle spokesperson. The librarian can find her- or himself the spokesperson for all librarian issues or in a position of having to communicate with and convince the chief negotiator so that librarian proposals can be communicated effectively. Success may hinge on how effective that communication has been. When asked specifically what were the strategies that proved most successful with respect to achieving improvements for librarians at the bargaining table, as is illustrated below, the most frequently cited were preparation and organization.

- "We used a stepped bargaining strategy which allowed us to explore positions prior to official bargaining. This was helpful in articulating our proposal."
- "Having a member on the Bargaining team. Having a clear and consistent mandate from all Librarians over a number of years."
- "The technique of having librarian 'visitors' in negotiating sessions for librarian clauses, as described above. Holding education sessions with the librarians at intervals to make them more aware of their rights under the C/A and where improvements need to be made. Having a separate librarian-appointed 'proposals' committee to feed proposals to the union proposals committee. Always having at least one librarian on the union executive, proposals committee, negotiating committee, and grievance committee. Preferably more than one, but at least one, always. Getting librarians to union meetings to act as a visible voting block, so the union executive knows they need the librarians to stay elected."
- "Persuasive arguments and hard data."
- "Having the librarians' proposal or concerns well organized before the chief negotiator came to meet with the group."
- "Preparation, preparation, preparation, and having very well thought out arguments."
- "Our bargaining team was very willing to let the librarians on the team lead those discussions. We also consulted regularly with the entire librarian complement and were able to present well-grounded arguments in support of our position."
- "Maintaining equivalent status with faculty/curators."
- "Strong well written proposals/articles based on historical fact."
- "Good examples from other institutions; drafting the language for the team; doing research."
- "Bargaining alongside faculty seemed to result in more improvements. Previously librarians were always at a side table and we used to really get screwed there."
- "Having a strong negotiating team."
- "Made common proposal with members of other professions represented by the union."

When asked about the greatest challenges experienced at the bargaining table, in addition to employer intransigence, respondents frequently mentioned the minority status of the librarian on the bargaining team.

- "Understanding the process of negotiation."
- "Keeping my voice heard."
- "You spend more time negotiating your position with your faculty team members than with the administration. They assume you are just like them, only inferior. They do not understand our issues unless you take a lot of time educating them on every clause. It takes a lot of time and patience and persistence, and it has to be done with every new negotiating committee. When they vote you down, you come back the next day with more information, documents, letters from colleagues etc. Wear them down, if necessary. You have to polite but very strong."
- "Administration's apathy and unwillingness to compromise on some issues and use of questionable librarian/archivist salary data to justify its position on salary increases."
- "Trying to get 100% sabbatical pay for library department heads as is done for faculty chairs."
- "Employer dragging feet and not necessarily following the bargaining rules set up at the beginning of the bargaining process."
- "Because librarians had not brought forward proposals and we were not expecting administration to bring the sweeping changes they introduced (most of which we resisted successfully), we were initially unprepared to discuss librarians issues."
- "Chairs on both sides kept having chats and coming back having given more than I certainly wanted them to: thus bargaining did not occur at the table (administration chair refused to commit himself to anything at the table and kept retracting advances that had occurred at the table); not being listened to."
- "Outside of the discussions on the librarians' articles, I felt that I didn't have enough knowledge or experience to contribute very much to the issues surrounding faculty positions."
- "Employer intransigence."
- "So far, just being heard. Table dynamics as described above."
- "People doing their best when not qualified to do the job. Intransigence on the part of Administration."

The failure to see librarians as equals is a common refrain in the professional library literature. In their study of faculty perceptions of librarians at the University of Manitoba, Gaby Divas, Ada M. Ducas and Nicole Michaud-Oystryk found that "[o]verwhelmingly librarians were seen as "professionals" with a "service" function. Activities such as research, teaching, and management received low ratings."[42] "Separate but equal systems have never worked well in the professional world, nor do they seem to function any better in the academic environment," writes Stephen E. Atkin. "The teaching faculty has had difficulty according equality to academic librarians, and it will not—unless a clear distinction is made between professional and nonprofessional activities. Otherwise, the relationship is the one described by the president of a university: 'The teaching faculty view professional librarians as they do residence hall directors, counselors in the career center, or athletic coaches'."[43] Harris points out that "[l]ibrarians who work in academic settings have been particularly likely to emphasize the importance of research as the key to gaining respectability and status. However, despite their efforts members do not regard their colleagues in the library as true academics or 'real' faculty, regardless of the number of articles they publish or their status in collective bargaining arrangements."[44] Librarians find themselves in a catch-22 situation with respect to "class conflict." They need to negotiate provisions which will allow them to fulfill the criteria associated with faculty status, while simultaneously arguing that they are already meeting the criteria and are therefore entitled to the provisions. It is a paradoxical situation where librarians constantly need to prove themselves. This is the case despite it being true that, as Atkin points out, "[a]lthough the teaching faculty has the three responsibilities of teaching, research and service, significant portions of the faculty don't teach, don't conduct research, and don't perform any service for their profession or the university."[45] In addition, a significant portion of teaching faculty (i.e., those in studio based programs), do not hold PhDs, which is often what is used to distinguish faculty from librarians. The key is education of faculty through engagement and participation. As Garcha and Phillips point out, "involvement in union activities expands knowledge of work teaching faculty is doing but also provides faculty with more insight and understanding of the kind of work [librarians] do and how valuable it is to them and the teaching and research missions of the institutions."[46]

When asked about lessons learned, better preparation was a common response as well as increased confidence and assertiveness on the part of the librarian member of the team.

- "Having confidence in understanding how negotiations play out is key for future participation."
- "Better preparation. During the last round of bargaining some of our proposals were well thought-out and evidence based. But we could have done more. I thought that some of our proposals were so obvious and mutually beneficial that the Administration would readily agree to them. This was not the case."
- "The team should be tougher overall next time. Stand up more around dragging of feet."
- "Given that administration has signalled the likelihood that many of their previous proposals will come back in some form, we will be better prepared, perhaps with specific proposals of our own, or perhaps with counter proposals."

- "Need unanimity from librarian members on a particular issue; difficult to attain."
- "Actually asking team why they aren't listening to what I have to say; more intransigence along with explanation (on their part) as to why they think these moves are necessary; refuse to allow bargaining to NOT occur at the table."
- "I don't think I would do anything differently. Maybe take a valium or some other sedative before presenting librarians' issues to keep from getting all stressed out and taking things personally at the table."

An opportunity was provided at the end of the survey for additional comments, which were as follows.

- "As a Librarian I have been acclaimed as the Chief Negotiator in the upcoming collective bargaining session . . . a very positive example of faculty support for Librarians."
- "Participating on the bargaining team was a very interesting and rewarding experience, if a bit stressful at times."
- "ack. Horrendous process when administration is adversarial. There were 2 librarians on the Committee, one (male) was Chair of the Contract Committee and so appointed to Negotiating team where became co-Chair of Negotiating team."
- "We have a good contract in place. Other than funding merit awards, the main issues are to defend what we have."
- "Sometimes faculty aren't as interested in advocating for librarian issues, which is a bit discouraging."
- "I'm in a smaller institution and the librarians have been part of the faculty association since the mid-1990s. While we are certainly better off being in the association our small numbers mean we are not a priority at the negotiating table. Still for a small staff, about half are on the sunshine list so most members would say we do fine. We do not however, have sabbaticals or research leave, and I for one, would like to fight for that, but am in the minority on those issues. We have retirements coming up and I'm curious if younger newer librarians will decide these are priorities and fight for those clauses."
- "Bargaining is an interesting process whereby I feel that librarians can really prove themselves to faculty colleagues. It makes us partners, even though we are a tiny group in the union. I am enjoying negotiations this time for the most part and am hopeful for a positive outcome."
- "In one round of negotiations a librarian was chief negotiator for the union and the contract language was drafted by a librarian. In the cases where there hasn't been a librarian on the negotiating team, there was a librarian on the executive."

It is evident from the comments that, while librarians at some institutions are making progress on their issues, others are frustrated by the lack of support from faculty members. The number of respondents reporting that a librarian had served as chief negotiator, however, was an encouraging sign that demonstrates that librarians had, in some instances, not only secured an equal place at the table but also had earned a seat at the head of the table.

Conclusion

Catherine Coker, Wyoma van Duinkerken, and Stephen Bales offer the following strategies for academic librarians "seeking full citizenship" in the academy (these also emerged from the survey as being useful to librarians seeking to achieve improvements in collective bargaining).

> If you share the conviction that academic librarians are not clerks but scholars, and thus deserving of full academic citizenship, consider the following:
>
> *1) Organizing Effectively*: Become politically active through savvy organization . . . .
> *2) Educating Constantly:* Educating your teaching faculty colleagues, whether they consider you a colleague (yet) or not, as to the integral role of the librarian within the larger academic community . . . .
> *3) Participating Actively:* The previous steps may only be accomplished through consistent engagement in the life of the college or university . . . .[47]

Collective bargaining has proven a successful and powerful means of improving terms and conditions of employment for academic librarians. It requires proactive efforts on the part of librarians, including maintaining a high profile in union activities, organization and preparation, seizing opportunities when they arise, educating both faculty and librarian colleagues, changing union/association governing structures and documents (by-laws and constitutions), and a recognition that progress and gains may take many years. The importance of the stakes is posed by Spang and Kane:

> Perhaps then, the relevant questions for academic librarianship today are: How do academic librarians themselves . . . see their present situation? What are they, as a professional group, willing to do to improve it? How will library and institution management view such efforts? . . . Constructive resolution of these questions can help to shape the identity of academic librarianship in the next century. Until then, who speaks for academic librarians? Administrators do.[48]

And who speaks for librarians at the bargaining table?

Bibliography

Aby, Stephen H. "Library Faculty and Collective Bargaining: An Exploration." In *Advances in Library Administration and Organization*, Volume 28, edited by Delmus E. Williams, James M. Nyce, and Janine Golden, 283-321. Bingley, UK: Emerald, 2006.

Alberta Labour Relations Board, "Backgrounder: What Makes an 'Appropriate Bargaining Unit.'" http://www.alrb.gov.ab.ca/dp-002.html.

Applegate, Rachel. "Who Benefits? Unionization and Academic Libraries and Librarians." *Library Quarterly* 79, no. 4 (2009): 443-463.

Benjamin, Ernst. "Reflections." In *Academic Collective Bargaining*, edited by Ernst Benjamin and Michael Mauer, 384-86. Washington, DC.: American Association of University Professors; New York: Modern Language Association of America, 2006.

Canadian Association of University Teachers. *CAUT Collective Bargaining Manual*. Ottawa: CAUT, 2006.

Coker, Catherine, Wyoma van Duinkerken, and Stephen Bales. "Seeking Full Citizenship: A Defense of Tenure Faculty Status for Librarians." *College & Research Libraries* 71, no. 5 (2010): 406-420.

Collective Agreement Between the York University Faculty Association and The Board of Governors of York University, (2009-2015) http://www.yufa.ca/2012-15-ca.

Dekker, Jennifer. "A Rare Find: The Triumphs of York's Librarians" *e-LiS: e-prints in library and information science* (2009) http://eprints.rclis.org/13554/

Divay, Gaby, Ada M. Ducas, and Nicole Michaud-Oystryk, "Faculty Perceptions of Librarians at the University of Manitoba," *College & Research Libraries* 48, no. 1 (1987): 27-35.

Fisher, Roger and William Ury. *Getting to Yes: Negotiating Agreement Without Giving In*. New York: Penguin, 1991. 2nd ed.

Fleming-May, Rachel, and Kimberley Douglas. "Framing Librarianship in the Academy: an Analysis Using Bolman and Deal's Model of Organizations." *College & Research Libraries* 75, no. 3 (2014): 389-415.

Garcha, Rajinder and John C. Phillips, "US Academic Librarians: Their Involvement in Union Activities," *Library Review* 50, no. 3 (2001): 122-127.

Harris, Roma. *Librarianship: The Erosion of a Woman's Profession*. Norwood: Ablex, 1992.

Hovekamp, Tina Maragou. "Unions in Academic Libraries." In *The Successful Academic Librarian*, edited by Gwen Meyer Gregory, 111-124. Medford, NJ: Information Today Inc., 2005.

Irvine, Betty Jo. "Differences by Sex: Academic Library Administrators," *Library Trends* 34, no. 2 (1985): 235-257.

McMaster University Academic Librarians' Association, "MUALA Submission to the McMaster University Library Review Team." http://muala.ca/.

Pay Equity Commission. "A Guide to Interpreting Ontario's Pay Equity Act." (2010-2012) http://www.payequity.gov.on.ca/en/resources/guide/ope/ope_2.php.

Pritchard, Sarah. "Feminist Thinking and Librarianship in the 1990s: Issues and Challenges." (1999) http://www.libr.org/ftf/femthink.htm.

Shiflett, Orwin Lee. *Origins of American Academic Librarianship*. Norwood: Ablex, 1981.

Spang, Lothar and William P. Kane, "Who Speaks for Academic Librarians? Status and Satisfaction Comparisons between Unaffiliated and Unionized Librarians on Scholarship and Governance Issues." *College & Research Libraries* 58, no. 5 (1997): 446-462.

"The Status of Librarians at York University," Appendix E. n.d.

UWOFA Board of Directors. "Important Information Regarding Librarian Certification Drive." (2003) http://www.uwo.ca/uwofa/docs/lib_cert.pdf.

Winter, Michael F. *The Culture and Control of Expertise: Toward a Sociological Understanding of Librarianship*. New York: Greenwood, 1988.

York University, Presidential Committee on Professional Librarians. *Report to President H. Ian Macdonald, York University of The Presidential Committee on Professional Librarians*. Downsview: York University, 1976.

Part Four
Case Studies

From Certification to Strike – Academic Librarians & Archivists at The University of Western Ontario

Mike Dawes, Linda Dunn, and Aniko Varpalotai[1]

Part I – Certification

During the early 1990s, there was a move afoot to explore the unionization of librarians at The University of Western Ontario. Beginning as brief hallway discussions between a librarian and a faculty member, interest grew among a few librarians about what unionization had meant for faculty at Western. In 1998, the newly hired University Librarian, who came from a unionized environment, was asked to talk about the unionized librarian experience at a meeting of a loosely organized group of Western librarians. The negative aspects of unionization were clearly and overwhelmingly pointed out. Interest in unionization waned.

In 2002, librarians and archivists[2] began—once again—to seriously discuss alternatives to the existing terms of employment at Western under the Professional and Managerial Association, a non-certified body. It became evident to the group that, while librarians and archivists at most Canadian universities were members of their faculty associations and enjoyed academic freedom and status, those at Western were treated more like clerks. There was a growing dissatisfaction, especially within one of the largest libraries, The D. B. Weldon Library, that the administration handed prestigious projects out to only a few select individuals; the fires of discontent were being fanned by such favouritism. Led by two newly hired librarians who had previously worked in Canadian universities where librarians were unionized, small group discussions about unionization commenced. Communications were established with some faculty members at UWOFA who provided information and ongoing support. One librarian became established as the main communication conduit with faculty during these early days.

Discussion topics revolved around many issues and the opportunities to share experiences resulted in the growing realization that these concerns were being echoed across Western Libraries and were not simply one individual's problem with the system. Discussion centred on career advancement, which was attained only by assuming administrative positions. Ranks did not exist. Workload expectations of more than the formally designated 35 hours per week became a hot issue, especially in the two largest libraries. Librarians and archivists were expected to take the initiative and work as many hours as it took to get the job done—as professionals are expected to do. Opportunities to participate in study or research leaves did not exist. Many librarians and archivists were relatively newly hired and wanted opportunities to expand and hone their professional skills as had many of their unionized colleagues at other universities. Adding fuel to the fire was the fact that Western's average and median salaries were ranked the lowest amongst 114 research libraries for 2004-2005, as published by the Association of Research Libraries.[3] However, the most egregious aspect of working as a librarian or archivist at Western was that academic status and academic freedom were neither recognized nor enjoyed, as they were for colleagues at many other Canadian universities.

In December 2002, the University Librarian hosted a session where all librarians and archivists could discuss their discontent. They took the opportunity to expound on their grievances, which included issues of workload, non-existent research/study/professional development leaves, lack of recognition of the value they brought to the academic mission, lack of involvement in the academic process and governance of the University, promotion only upon assumption of administrative duties, and low compensation.

The Professional Practice Model

At a follow-up meeting in March 2003, the Acting Vice-President – Administration gave a verbal report that entry level salaries for librarians and archivists were competitive, but lagged behind other universities after five to seven years. She made a commitment to contracting a salary consultant to advise on appropriate salaries, and promised to report by September 2003. The other issues of discontent (workload, promotion, recognition and involvement in policy and governance) were handled by asking librarians and archivists to volunteer to serve on the Librarians and Archivists Steering Committee. The Steering Committee's administrative presence included the Acting Vice-President – Administration, the University Librarian, and three other administrative librarians, and the rank and file were represented by five librarians and two archivists. This Committee was charged with developing a new and more collaborative workplace that would bring Western in line with other universities. The Committee had the aims of recognizing "the value that academic librarians and archivists bring to the academic mission," involving "librarians and archivists in the academic process and governance of the University" and addressing an "appropriate compensation scheme that would recognize individual professional contributions throughout a career and that would rectify issues deriving from the current compensation scheme based on position classification."[4] The Committee studied models of work at other universities and conducted some information sessions with librarians and archivists, including soliciting feedback on issues on which the Committee was working. It became evident to the librarian and archivist members on the Steering Committee that Western Libraries administration would not accept any changes that did not fit their vision. It was the first, but alas, not the last time that administrators indicated—in no uncertain terms—that changes that did not fit the administration's vision would not work because they considered Western different from comparator universities; it was not the "Western Way."

The fall and early winter of 2003 saw the frustrations with the administrative Steering Committee colleagues grow to new heights, when after repeated requests for the promised consultant report on salaries, it was announced that it would not be available until January 2004. The Steering Committee continued to do its work and produced a document called the Professional Practice Model, in February 2004. Nothing very encouraging resulted.

Included in the document was a ranking scheme parallel to other universities, leaves for research, and promotion within the ranks without necessitating an administrative appointment. However, the report didn't include any agreed-upon details of how to operationalize any changes. The Steering Committee was unable to agree on the crucial issues of a grievance procedure, academic freedom, and academic status and absolutely nothing was said or agreed upon about a salary structure. Very few of the Steering Committee's goals were realized and librarian and archivist members did not accept it as a working document that would address their concerns. A concurrent external review (discussed later in this chapter) of Western libraries bolstered the resolve of librarians and archivists by recognizing their plight and noting the possible benefits of unionization. The aspirations of the members were clear, as was the entrenched repression and resistance to change on the employer's side. The stage was being set for a successful union drive.

It is to their credit that during the 10 months when the Steering Committee met, the librarians and archivists did not sit idle but gathered information and organized information sessions with members of the Faculty Association (UWOFA). Discussions ranged from the advantages of certifying to addressing the real fears some librarians and archivists had of leaving a familiar, yet problematic working environment. Many had previously never conversed with faculty members about, for example, academic freedom, which is often considered to be the lifeblood of an academic's existence. Through these discussions, the importance of having academic status and academic freedom for librarians and archivists became much clearer.

Joining UWOFA

Sessions with librarians from Queen's and Wilfrid Laurier Universities described how their unionized workplaces functioned. They provided information on how their ranking systems and promotion processes worked for librarians and archivists. They explained the appointment process with elected librarians participating fully in the hiring process. It was very helpful to hear what had been successfully implemented for librarians and archivists at other Canadian universities. A shot in the arm came in December 2003, when members of UWOFA, i.e., faculty members voted to approve the librarians and archivists joining the Association. The librarians and archivists felt accepted and supported.

The libraries' administration organized its own session on unionization with the main attraction being the Director of Faculty Relations forcefully expounding on the disadvantages of certifying and the difficulties of decertifying. There were insinuations that certification would lead to a loss of past benefits, including the existing relationship currently enjoyed with administration. Librarians and archivists were not used to such vehement statements and were stunned into silence and a feeling of insecurity. A faculty colleague, who had attended the meeting, just as forcefully reminded the Director of Faculty Relations that certification was a legal right under labour law. At that point, the value of the faculty-librarian and archivist relationship became apparent and that same faculty colleague led the fight for academic status and academic freedom for librarians and archivists during first contract negotiations. Many of the allegations made by the Director of Faculty Relations were more fully addressed in a 'frequently-asked-questions' document on certification that was distributed, along with union cards. Librarians and archivists were given the opportunity to meet outside of their library to ask any questions regarding the certification vote. Some librarians even requested to meet off-campus. Some had parents who had belonged to trade unions and were trying to understand what unionization meant for them as professionals. The momentum to join UWOFA as a certified bargaining unit intensified, and Western's administration inadvertently helped to convince people of the need to certify in order to protect their positions by firing a librarian with 20 years of service just a few weeks before the certification vote. One faculty member described it as constructive dismissal, after hearing how the administration had dealt with this employee. Another librarian, who was to retire later that same year, noted that he had been ambivalent about certifying but after the viciousness of the firing of this colleague, he realized the importance of signing. The certification vote, held in March 2004, saw an 80% turnout, with 88% voting in favour of joining UWOFA.

The very next day, signs went up in all the libraries telling the new union members how to go about de-certifying. In fact, those signs are still up in many of the staff rooms in the libraries at Western. The University did, however, prevent the librarians and archivists from joining the same bargaining unit as faculty members. One part of the former Premier Harris government's anti-union changes had removed powers of the Labour Board to decide that such a group could join an existing bargaining unit, essentially giving employers veto power. The existing faculty bargaining unit continued and a new one was created for the librarians and archivists, UWOFA-LA, the implications of which are discussed later.

The interim certificate from the Ontario Labour Relations Board was received in May 2004. The librarians and archivists of the University of Western Ontario were officially certified by the Ontario Labour Relations Board on September 15, 2004.[5] In June 2004, a contract committee was formed. Furthermore, the members ratified the composition of the negotiating team as three members from the new bargaining unit and three faculty members. This group would negotiate the first UWOFA-LA collective agreement.

Part II: First Contract and Beyond

Before certification, members in the bargaining-unit-to-be were in an anomalous position when compared with certified groups of librarians and archivists at other Canadian universities. Long before certification, they were considered academic staff, in the sense that their positions in the administrative hierarchy led through the Provost/Vice-President Academic. However, more than a decade before certification, they were moved to administrative staff status, reporting to the Vice-President Administration. With hindsight, it is clear that this structural anomaly informed the employer's positions and reactions to the union's proposals both latitudinally, i.e., over many dimensions, and longitudinally, i.e., persistent over time. The distinction between "administrative" and "academic" staff, and the corresponding reporting link through the V-P Administration rather than the Provost and V-P Academic is more than symbolic; it affects the conduct of negotiations. The employer's negotiating teams for bargaining with administrative staff consist of human resources and other management personnel. They have no particular knowledge of, nor sympathy with, academic concerns such as academic freedom, ownership of intellectual property, and support for research activity. In contrast, the employer's negotiating teams for academic staff include academics, who report to the Provost and V-P Academic, the academic leader of the University.

Terms and conditions of employment reflected the staff, rather than the academic, model: pay ranges were stringently capped; pension provisions were inadequate; career advancement and independence (including academic freedom and independence in structuring one's own work) were limited by a top-down hierarchy; and an external review[6] recommending transition to a more comparable status met with administrative reaction that was lukewarm at best. The then-Provost commented, in a November 18, 2004 letter, that ". . . although we value the input of these experienced external consultants, their view of the Libraries' operations is necessarily limited and is only one of many perspectives under con-sideration . . ." The contrast between staff and faculty models can be shown starkly in a side-by-side summary:

Librarians and Archivists at Western	Faculty Members at Western
Salaries capped.	Salaries not capped.
Limited career progress.	Performance-based career progress salary component, regular opportunities for promotion.
Starting salaries were competitive, but caps and low incremental raises quickly left members behind comparators.	Starting salaries comparable with other Canadian universities.
Average salary well behind comparators.	Average salary not too far behind comparators.
Low employee and employer pension contributions; particularly in the beginning years, this phase-in is very damaging in a Defined Contribution plan).	Employee/employer pension contributions more adequate.
Downward trend in salary relative to faculty, i.e., Ratio (LA salaries/Faculty salaries) declining.	

In spite of the split into two bargaining units, faculty members welcomed librarians and archivists to the union, and provided support and advice for the ensuing negotiations. The cooperation ranged from the obvious and practical (e.g., jointly analyzing which articles from the faculty collective agreement could be transferred with little modification), to organizational (e.g., recommending structure and procedures for producing and reviewing proposals for negotiations) to direct (e.g., several faculty members, including the faculty chief negotiator and deputy chief negotiator, were on the negotiating team). This cooperation was important, perhaps crucial, since the librarians and archivists had not had any real negotiating experience before certification.

Initial contact with the employer ran through the Vice-President – Administration. The union pointed out the unusual nature of this arrangement, and asked that librarians and archivists be properly treated as academic staff. By the time serious negotiations got underway (a year later!), the employer finally agreed to this change. Perhaps this was a matter of staffing or other administrative convenience, since it didn't result in any softening of their opposition to the core content of academic status: academic freedom; self-direction; space, time, and reward for academic activity (research); intellectual property; meaningful, fair, and transparent evaluation; career progress leading to promotion and tenure-like permanency; and participation in governance, including participation in appointments and defining and assigning workload.

Not surprisingly, negotiation of the first contract took a long time: from the first tentative meetings in June 2004 through the beginning of negotiations in June 2005 to eventual sign-off of a proposed collective agreement on August 11, 2006. This involved 68 negotiating sessions, many of which were full days. In addition to the academic-status concerns, some of the topics that required considerable time were grievance procedures, discrimination and harassment, employment equity, and of course, salary and benefits. For the latter, some progress was made, but given the extreme disadvantage of by some members, much remained to be done.

The First Contract in Application and Retrospect

Gains and compromises can be summarized as follows:

Gains	Compromises
Academic status, Academic freedom	
Removal of salary caps, establishment of ranks and salaries, larger increments	Salaries remain too low – well below established Ontario market value
Grievance & Arbitration, improved job security	
Academic Activity Leave (research)	Only a modest amount of Academic Activity Leave (compared to faculty Sabbatical Leave)
Pregnancy Leave salary 'top up' benefit increased	Little progress with most benefits, which are not on par with faculty; employer contributions to pension plan not on par with faculty
Increased input into decision-making (Unit Workload Plan; Promotion & Continuing Appointment Committee)	

One of the compromises was the employer's refusal to amalgamate the two bargaining units, or even to synchronize negotiations. Thus the length and expiry dates of the two units' collective agreements were out of sync (Librarians and Archivists: 2006-09; Faculty: 2006-10). This appears to be a straightforward divide-and-conquer approach; the employer's chief negotiator said several times that they see no benefit in amalgamation or synchronization. Of course, running negotiations for two bargaining units is a considerable burden for the Association, in terms of both expense and commitment of members, while the employer is merely spending other people's money. The pattern of employer insistence on staggered contract end dates has continued to the present. To date, this has not become sufficiently important to the Association to make it key to getting a settlement.

Second Contract

The negotiating team for the second contract continued to draw on the resources provided by faculty members, with chief negotiators drawn from faculty, as well as support and advice on issues such as salaries and benefits.

In review, some parts of the first contract were revealed as far too employer-friendly and subject to employer interpretation; for example, the process, criteria, and transparency of performance evaluations. And, as noted above, compensation remained a large concern. Negotiations did not take as long as the first contract had, but there were still numerous meetings, both in preparation and in direct negotiations. Many articles in the second contract were directly based on corresponding articles in the faculty contract. As well, the second contract incorporated many changes that faculty had negotiated. However, some employer proposals were impossible to swallow. On August 18, 2009, the union called for conciliation, responding to:

> Draconian positions taken by the Employer . . . the Employer has insisted on language in the Responsibilities of Members article that would essentially eliminate the job security of all UWOFA-LA Members. The proposed language in this article would also have deleterious implications for Reassignment and Workload. The Employer's position was discussed at length at the UWOFA-LA General Meeting, August 17. At that meeting, attended by close to 60% of the Bargaining Unit, members unanimously resolved that this article was "absolutely unacceptable." Peter Simpson, CAUT [Canadian Association of University Teachers] Assistant Executive Director, called it "the worst language we at CAUT have ever seen tabled for librarians and archivists in Canada.[7]

On September 9, the UWOFA Board of Directors unanimously authorized a strike vote. On October 30, the eve of the strike deadline, an agreement was finally reached. All union preparations were in place and strike and picket protocol had been worked out with the employer's team.

Some gains in the second contract included: improvements to the career progress plan; special increments for members whose long-standing problems were not adequately addressed by the first contract; average increase of floor salaries of 7.4% in the first year of the contract (but not many members were at the floor). We were unable to markedly reverse the deteriorating trend in librarians' and archivists' compensation relative to UWOFA faculty, nor relative to librarians and archivists at comparable Canadian universities.

Third Contract

Review of the second contract revealed two major areas to be improved: financial concerns and performance evaluations. In addition, members expressed strong concerns about the work culture in Western's libraries. Preparations for negotiations followed similar procedures to the previous two contracts, with much support from faculty members. As before, faculty members continued to fill key roles on the negotiating team including chief negotiator and financial analyst. Negotiations began on April 26, 2011, well before the June 30 expiry date of the second contract. The Contract Committee and negotiating team were well-prepared and made their case forcefully, calling for conciliation on the first day of negotiations. Matters proceeded smartly to the strike position and resolution described in the next section.

Part III: Strike

The UWOFA-LA strike in September 2011 was significant on a number of levels. It was the first strike in UWOFA's history, though both bargaining units had come close to strike deadlines during previous negotiations. The UWOFA-LA bargaining unit was very small relative to the Faculty bargaining unit (approximately 55 and 1500 members, respectively); and was composed of a majority (5:1) of women members. These factors, together with the provincial government's edict that public sector employers practice wage restraint set the stage for a David and Goliath show-down on one of Ontario's largest and most prestigious research-intensive university campuses.

Issues leading to the strike

One of the central issues that dominated previous UWOFA-LA negotiations was the increasing salary gap between Western's academic librarians and archivists and their counterparts at other comparable research universities. Despite achieving high rankings on national measures such as the *Maclean's Magazine* and the *Globe and Mail* newspaper annual university surveys, UWOFA-LA members were not only consistently at the bottom of the national and provincial pay scales but the gap was significant and growing over the years, notwithstanding unionization and formal recognition of their academic status. The predominantly female work force raised the question of pay equity, and a formal study was finally proposed during this third round of negotiations when all other efforts to improve compensation were to no avail. The issue of workplace climate also crystallized during the strike into a proposal for a workplace climate study, when language improvements relating to working conditions—workload, complement, appointments and promotions, etc.—similarly stalled. While climate issues were what led to certification, hopes that unionization would improve these relations had not fully materialized. A further concern related to the marginalization of the UWOFA-LA bargaining unit, and the employer's refusal to allow any form of merger with the Faculty bargaining unit, regardless of the increasingly similar language in the two collective agreements, common members of both negotiating teams, and a shared Joint Committee on the Administration of the Agreement between negotiations. During a time of publicly declared cost-saving measures, it made no sense to duplicate the time and human resources in two closely related sets of negotiations. Repeated efforts, during both Faculty and Librarian and Archivist negotiations, and various options presented by the union, were all rejected by the employer, who suggested each time that they might be considered at the next negotiations of either bargaining unit. Unified bargaining units are common practice at every other Canadian university where faculty, librarians and archivists are viewed collectively as academic staff and salary and contract language is adapted as necessary for each group and rank according to professional standards.

100% Strike Vote and Conciliation

Frustrations reached the tipping point just a few months into negotiations when it became clear that the employer had no intention of delivering on any of the union's central demands. Negotiations began on April 26, 2011 with UWOFA-LA tabling a comprehensive package of proposals, including compensation and benefits, and immediately filing for conciliation. The employer did not address the compensation aspects of the proposals until June 14, and following some back and forth, declared on June 28 that they had no interest in discussing or addressing the pay gap, the reality of which they had previously acknowledged. In debates over the extent of the gap, the employer's representatives said that they didn't have permission to share that data, that it should simply be accepted without evidence, and that the union's data was inaccurate. UWOFA-LA's analysis revealed that on average, Western's librarians and archivists were paid 20% less than the average salary at other Ontario universities—this was derived from data collected by the Association of Research Libraries and the Canadian Association of Research Libraries. It was further revealed that at every stage of a librarian's or archivist's career at Western, the pay was less than the average elsewhere. A librarian or archivist with an average salary of $72,169 in May 2011 was paid $18,000 less than the average salary at other Ontario universities. Western's 'final offer,' tabled on June 30 would have increased the gap to 23% after 4 years, raising the difference in pay to approximately $24,700. By contrast, UWOFA-LA's final offer would have reduced the gap to 11% after 3 years, which in dollar terms would have worked out to a difference of approximately $11,300. Meanwhile, the University was reporting an annual operating surplus estimated to be $29.8 million at April 30, 2011. Western's Strategic Plan[8] at this time proclaimed a commitment to competitive compensation across ranks of both staff and faculty, with a goal to enable Western to "recruit and retain the best." It went so far as to recognize "an excellent library" and an expressed desire to provide a "supportive workplace." As the team reported its lack of progress at regularly scheduled membership meetings, the need to have a strike vote and prepare for tougher bargaining became clear. An unprecedented 100% strike vote with almost 100% participation gave the negotiating team the unquestionable support it needed to continue pressing on the most central issues. With the facilitation of a Ministry of Labour appointed Conciliator, the team continued to work away at proposals where movement was needed if a strike was to be averted. Nonetheless, by the end of the summer, as the strike deadline neared, it was clear that the employer was not going to budge without more public pressure brought to bear on the issues so glaringly obvious at the table.

By the end of August, strike preparations were well underway, but there was still hope that issues would be settled before the September 8 deadline. The pay equity study would take several years to complete, and fundamental differences on complement, workload, and appointments remained. A No Board report was requested from the Ministry of Labour on August 15, setting in motion the countdown to a strike. Information pickets were organized during the students' Orientation Week, days ahead of the strike deadline. Faculty members joined the librarians and archivists as they handed out information to students, parents, and other university staff about the unresolved bargaining issues. The CAUT Defence Fund, consisting of a large reserve of money to assist any member association during a strike, had approved all necessary funding. The employer continued to insist that their final offer tabled on June 30 was unchanged, although there was flexibility in how the money could be allocated within the totality of the agreement. They argued that they had no more money to give, and that it was up to the librarians and archivists to decide if they wanted a strike. They insisted that their position would not change in the days leading up to or at any time during a strike, regardless of its duration. They were prepared to engage in the pay equity process but, given its uncertain outcomes, no other financial commitments were possible. The proverbial gauntlet had been thrown. Even though the employer's team advised that there was no point even meeting in the days leading up to the strike, meetings took place regardless. It was hard not to believe that this was the outcome the employer wanted right from the start—a trial run strike with UWOFA-LA before the 'big' bargaining unit came to the table again and challenged the administration to a strike that had been brewing for some years, but each time had been averted right at the very brink.

David and Goliath – the 'Tiny Perfect Strike'

At an emergency meeting on the eve of the strike deadline, members were informed that they would indeed be on the picket lines the following morning. Nervousness about the impact such a small bargaining unit might be capable of having on such a large campus, both geographically and in terms of the operations of the University, evaporated quickly. The local transit union had declared that its drivers would not cross the picket lines—thereby cutting all campus bus service. This alone heightened the visibility of the strike for students and others who may have missed the mounting tensions during the summer break. Faculty members, staff from other employee groups, graduate students, and union members from across the London community joined the small but strong contingent of librarians and archivists on the picket lines. Solidarity was palpable. As the two-week strike progressed, public rallies at the University gates drew supporters from across the country through the Canadian Association of University Teachers' Defence Fund's 'Flying Pickets.' Speakers and members from large union locals, including the Ontario Public Service Employees' Union, the Canadian Auto Workers, the teachers' federations, and others mobilized by the local Labour Council, all bolstered the spirits of the strikers. Messages of support poured in through social media; alumni and retirees joined the picket lines, supplied refreshments, and offered ongoing support. The University was called upon to answer to its poor treatment of a female dominated group of professionals.

Building Relationships with all Stakeholders – Within and Beyond the University Gates

It became clear that it would be central to a successful strike action to build and maintain relationships with all of the players: the negotiating team; administrators; members; union leadership; other campus employee groups; local labor organizations (including the Canadian Auto Workers, and teachers' federations); provincial and national associations; and bus drivers, among others. At the same time, important lessons were learned about roles and responsibilities within the union, particularly regarding the use of committees and resource people, and the need to resolve communication challenges. Given that this was a first strike for most of those directly involved, it is amazing in retrospect that it was resolved as quickly and successfully as was the case. In less than two weeks there was a tentative agreement that could be recommended to members. While one UWOFA board member coined the phrase, 'the tiny perfect strike,' issues had emerged behind the scenes. The union's negotiating policies had not envisaged a strike. Although everything up to and including preparations for a strike had previously been experienced, the actuality of a strike was a rather different and unprecedented event.

Outcomes and Analysis – Gains/Losses?

Was a strike necessary in this instance? Regrettably so, although much of what was achieved should have been attainable without a strike. Was it worth it? A resounding: 'Yes!' Gains can be grouped into three areas: financial, respect, and solidarity. Given that UWOFA-LA salaries were at the bottom and far behind other comparable institutions, fair and equitable compensation and benefits were at the top of the list, even at a time of government austerity measures. Pay equity had not been monitored for decades, despite legislation requiring that it be maintained. The gendered nature of the librarian work force heightened concern about the relatively low salaries and the employer's apparent disregard for equity. Low pay was equated with disrespect for the work of academic librarians and archivists and was further related to workplace climate issues that were contributing to poor morale and discontent. Agreement was reached during the strike to convene both a Pay Equity study and a joint Workplace Climate study, following ratification of the agreement. These were major victories with potentially far-reaching consequences. At the time of writing, the Pay Equity Committee is still at work, the Workplace Climate Committee has completed its report based on findings from surveys, focus groups and individual interviews and the implementation stage is ongoing.

There were three main gains on the salary side in the 2011-2015 UWOFA-LA Collective Agreement:

- An average 6.4% increase in salary floors across ranks in the first year of the contract.
- A one-time adjustment designed to compensate Members to some extent for the shortfall of their career increments in previous years. This came in the form of a Competitive Adjustment of $250 for each year of service. Average years of service were 11, so the mean amount received was about $2,750 (4% of the average 2010-11 salary).
- A large annual increase in the career increments. These rose from 54% to 102%, depending on salary level over the life of the agreement. The result is that an average career increment of $1081 in the lowest income group in 2010-11 will be replaced by one of $1,669 by 2014-15, and in the top income group the rise will be from $542 to $1097. Results of these changes are already apparent in the 2011-12 ARL salary data, which show increases of 5.1% and 6.2% in average and median salaries respectively of professionals in the UWO library system over the previous year. This is more than at any other ARL Canadian university except Saskatchewan. And the median is the highest in the table. The gap had been reduced from 20% to 16%. Western is no longer at the bottom in Ontario on mean salary. Furthermore, the deterioration of librarian and archivist salaries relative to faculty salaries at Western appears to have turned around.

UWOFA-LA had earned the respect of colleagues far and wide; and the bargaining unit had developed a strong bond and appreciation for solidarity which will hold them in good stead in future collegial and labour relations endeavours. Collectively, we learned that "although strikes are not the preferred way to complete a round of negotiations, it turns out that they are not necessarily an entirely bad thing, either."[9]

Lessons Learned/Recommendations

Given that there was no policy in place clearly articulating roles, responsibilities, and decision-making during a strike, both the negotiating team and the strike committee prepared reports and recommendations based on this experience and tabled these with the UWOFA Board of Directors for consideration and implementation in time for the next round of negotiations. Some of these reports' key recommendations and lessons learned include:

- Consistent and secure lines of communication among members of a bargaining unit as well as between members and the union are imperative. In this case, feedback and support from faculty was invaluable in the face of the backlash from library administration during pre-certification efforts and throughout each set of negotiations and ultimately the strike and its aftermath. Faculty support has been an invaluable source of strength and solace for this bargaining unit.
- It is important to cultivate those librarians and archivists who share the passion. Those who were involved at the beginning continue to be involved year-after-year. Igniting a passion in those who inherited what others have fought for and won is a challenge for unions. Communication and information remains a tried and true means to this end.
- Do not be deluded by stalling or scare tactics that are employed by the administration during certification drives or negotiations. Identifying and neutralizing such distractions saves time, strife, and effort for members and negotiators.
- Good governance and communication guidelines for Faculty Associations, adapted from CAUT guidelines, are under development for future negotiations. A framework for decision-making during negotiations and strikes is essential in order to build trust among union leaders, negotiators, and members.
- It is critical to develop collegiality and solidarity amongst faculty members and librarians and archivists. These groups share issues and need to routinely support one another, especially during bargaining. This is especially true as long as there remain two distinct bargaining units.

- Ongoing succession planning is essential, including mentoring and grooming negotiators to represent the diverse membership of each bargaining unit. It is critical to develop skill sets for writing contract language and costing proposals. Also critical is leadership development for those at the negotiating table as well as the board table. There is a need for empowering librarians and archivists to take control of their own bargaining unit and negotiations, with greater representation on the union board, executive, and all relevant union committees.
- Even a small bargaining unit within a very large organization can overcome the odds, achieve important gains, and build solidarity among its members in collaboration with other unions locally, provincially, and nationally.

Bibliography

Kyrillidou, Martha, and Mark Young. Table 14: Average, Median, and Beginning Professional Salaries in ARL University Libraries; Summary of Rankings, FYs 2001-02 to 2004-05 in *ARL annual salary survey 2004-05*, 2005. Retrieved from http://www.arl.org/storage/documents/publications/salary-survey-2004-05.pdf.

Professional Practice Model for the Librarians and Archivists of The University of Western Ontario. Prepared by the Librarians & Archivists Steering Team, in consultation with all librarians and archivists. For submission to Joyce Garnett, University Librarian, [and] Jane O'Brien, Acting Vice-President - Administration, 12 February 2004.

Re: The University of Western Ontario Faculty Association (Applicant) and The University of Western Ontario (Respondent), O.L.R.B. File No. 3846-03-R (certificate reproduced in Appendix A at http://www.uwofa.ca/collectiveagreements/). (Decision at [2004] O.L.R.D.. No. 2942).

Western University's Strategic Plan, Engaging the Future: Final Report of the Task Force on Strategic Planning, http://www.uwo.ca/univsec/strategic_plan/report/07.htm.

Varpalotai, Aniko, and Linda Dunn. "The first academic strike at Western." *Faculty Times, UWOFA Newsletter* Volume XIV, No. 3 (February 2012).

The Mouse that Roared: Finding Our Voice During the University of Western Ontario Librarians' and Archivists' Strike of 2011

Christena A. McKillop

Looking back at the relationship between Western librarians and archivists and the administration at the University, it would have been difficult to predict that negotiations in 2011 would end in a strike. Historically, the librarians and archivists had been able to secure contracts with limited labour unrest. Two collective agreements had been successfully negotiated with Western since 2004 by the University of Western Ontario Faculty Association - Librarians and Archivists (UWOFA-LA). A strike vote passed each time with strong support from the members. Both times, negotiations were difficult; however a settlement was eventually reached. Strike action had come close in 2010 with the University of Western Ontario Faculty Association's (UWOFA) agreement for professors being settled in a last minute deal dubbed "the almost strike." This negotiation set the stage for future bargaining to be challenging for UWOFA-LA in 2011.

Since certification, members of UWOFA-LA had shown an interest in union matters, especially those that pertained to workload, reduction of professional positions, and the ripple effect of budget cuts. Members regularly attended union meetings, participated on union committees, had large voter turnout for elections and other matters requiring voting, which reflected both a collective strength and engagement among members. This trend continued through the early days of preparations for the 2011 negotiations and was evidenced by close to 50% of the bargaining unit attending the first meeting of the contract committee.

Given the troubled climate for the 2010 faculty negotiations, librarians and archivists expected the same management response. A librarian colleague remarked, "It seemed that within Western's academic environment, respect for my professional expertise was being withheld until I could prove my value with some sort of assessment metric."[1] The union strategy of being well-prepared for negotiating was implemented. To that end, work began early so that UWOFA-LA would be ready when its Collective Agreement expired on June 30, 2011. An organizational meeting was called in July 2010 to apprise members of the steps involved and the work ahead needed in order for the bargaining unit to be prepared.[2] During this period, the chief negotiator and deputy chief negotiator were appointed, thus formalizing the process for the Contract Committee to begin its important work.

It is noteworthy that attendance remained high throughout the duration of the Contract Committee's work. Through this process, members became better informed not only about the Collective Agreement, but also about the issues facing the negotiating team. Contract Committee meetings proved to be a positive, mobilizing place and space for concerns to be discussed. Here, members were able to express opinions, thoughts and reflections about important issues and develop shared values. In this group, early signs of community began to emerge involving emotional safety, a sense of belonging and identification, personal investment and a common symbol system.[3] These meetings would become a significant conduit for information exchange for members, in addition to setting a firm foundation for moving forward. The high level of participation from UWOFA-LA members at this early stage of planning created a momentum where members became engaged and empowered through an evolving professional community.

Members of the Contract Committee and its sub-groups met regularly through the fall of 2010 and into the winter months of 2011. By preparing months in advance, there was time to conduct a survey to get a clear sense of members' priorities about specific issues such as workload, staffing complement, budget challenges and recent reorganizations. Information was also gathered from stewards and the professional officer.[4] Discussion, both formal and informal, was generated in the bargaining unit about what was important to members. This contributed to a stronger bargaining unit, characterized by a sense of purpose, direction and cohesion. UWOFA also consulted with colleagues across the province as well as with the Ontario Confederation of University Faculty Associations (OCUFA), which provided a broader context for important bargaining issues that members might face.[5] The chief negotiator and deputy chief negotiator shared this information so that members could see beyond local issues. Members could identify with colleagues across the country also experiencing similar issues. Again, this was a significant shift in how our membership began to understand itself as a community. Due to the nature of professional responsibilities and separate work locations across campus, members often felt disconnected and fractured rather than united and cohesive. Our conversations with each other now included references to these common issues. While the formal construct of the group was defined by union membership, shared social identification began to take hold when members' strong feelings emerged as a result of what was happening to UWOFA-LA. These feelings were determined by collective histories rather than personal histories, which contributed to shared social identification.[6] We had previously felt little if any of the momentum and cohesion that we were now experiencing as we became a more galvanized unit of political work action. By holding informational meetings through the winter and into the spring of 2011, members were informed about the work of the Contract Committee, as well as the preparations for negotiations thus adding to the collective history and shared identification.

Dates for negotiation had been proposed by the UWOFA-LA team in April of 2011 and members heard, via a *Bargaining Bulletin*, that only about half of them had been agreed to by the administration and not for full days but only for half days.[7] This was a signal to the membership that difficult times were ahead. Members were increasingly concerned that the substantive issues would be more complicated and difficult to resolve. A strike vote was held in mid-June 2011 and *UWOFA Matters* reported that members voted 100% in favour of a strike mandate with a voter turnout of 80%,[8] indicating strong support for the negotiating team's mandate.

UWOFA decided it would be beneficial to apply for a conciliator to meet with the negotiating team in late May and again in June 2011. The May issue of the *Faculty Times* reported that the full package of proposed articles, including Compensation and Benefits had been presented to administration. Core issues that remained unresolved for the membership included: job security, complement, salary and benefits as well as greater alignment with the Faculty Collective Agreement.[9] UWOFA also uncovered a Pay Equity study that was conducted 20 years earlier; it identified this employee group which then belonged to Western's Professional and Managerial Association (PMA) as a female dominated job category in need of pay equity adjustments. Adjustments were applied in 1990 but members were surprised and troubled to learn that the Pay Equity Plan was not maintained in the following years. UWOFA, along with the University of Western Ontario Staff Association (UWOSA), hired a pay equity consultant to further investigate.[10] This would eventually culminate in a Letter of Understanding for a Pay Equity Review for members, an important outcome of the strike.

The Strike Action Committee was formed during the months that led up to the expiration of the Collective Agreement. This Committee not only significantly contributed to the successful planning of the 2011 strike but was instrumental in creating a community. The formal construct of the Committee provided the framework for members' shared social identification, enabling them to act both harmoniously and productively.[11] A strong core of active people who are willing to do the necessary work and have experience in strike-related activities are key in making a successful committee.[12] Based on the Faculty Association's recent experience and lessons learned from the 2010 "almost strike," the UWOFA-LA

Strike Action Committee had the benefit of those members' experiences.[13] The Strike Action Committee recognized the pros and cons of a small bargaining unit. One of the advantages is that the small size of the unit makes getting information to and receiving information from members easy. However, there was concern that the bargaining unit might be too small to be effective. The Committee also realized the importance of morale, and headquarters became a clearinghouse for people to spend time relaxing, reading messages of support or viewing picket profiles and photos.[14] The librarian and archivist members demonstrated an active interest and support for strike planning by volunteering to serve on this Committee. A strong sense of community was built by the members who worked tirelessly on a myriad of planning and logistical efforts building up to the anticipated strike action.

Grass Roots Communication: Valuing the Undervalued

Contract negotiations continued through the summer of 2011. With prolonged discussions and mounting frustrations emerging out of the talks with the administration, the UWOFA Communications Committee launched more frequent communications with the membership of both bargaining units. The *Faculty Times*, a newsletter which covers a range of information, news and developments pertinent to both bargaining units, was instrumental to open and shared communication. It was published more often by the Committee in order to engage the membership in the latest developments. A second line of formal communication was the *UWOFA Librarians and Archivists Bargaining Bulletin*. As the name suggests, it is focussed on providing negotiating updates to the specific members of the UWOFA-LA bargaining unit. Thirdly, *UWOFA Matters* updates were posted on the UWOFA website (http://www.uwofa.ca/) in the format of news releases.

The May 2011 issue of the *Faculty Times* led with the article titled, "Academic Librarians and Archivists and the Struggle for Visibility." In this piece, the invisibility of librarians' and archivists' work was described in the context of evolving technology; ". . . the better academic librarians are at their job, the less visible they are to the people they help."[15] In his comments, James Compton, UWOFA president (2010-2011), articulated the challenges in the broader library world and the specific value of librarians and archivists to the academy. By 2012, The *Faculty Times* would become a venue through which the Librarian-Archivist membership would communicate its opinions. The February 2012 issue featured reflections about the UWOFA-LA strike. In terms of authorship, it drew heavily on librarians and archivists for content, whereas most *Faculty Times* issues contain content written by faculty members. But, the February issue signaled the importance of both the UWOFA-LA strike and members by featuring articles authored by librarians and archivists.

UWOFA's Communications Committee published three *Bargaining Bulletins,* providing the union's perspective on the issues. The first *Bulletin,* titled *Can a University Exist without Books?* highlighted a national report that indicated that the libraries on Western's campus were well run with good staff, services and collections. In 2010, Western Libraries was tied with McGill University and the University of Toronto-St. George for the being the best library as ranked in the Canadian University Report, but Western's librarians were the lowest paid academic research librarians in the nation.[16] A top ranking, which was boasted about by the administration, should have been equated with respect and fair wages, yet members' salaries were generally 20% lower than those at other Ontario university libraries. This disconnect rankled many members, who felt that Western's high performing track record was undervalued.

The second *Bulletin,* titled *Respecting the Golden Rule,* used language that informed members about mounting frustration at the negotiating table and reminded everyone that UWOFA-LA came to the table prepared for serious talks by presenting a full package of proposed articles to the employer. Members read that their negotiating team was pro-active and respectful of the negotiating process. In general the *Bargaining Bulletins* conveyed that the employer displayed a disregard for the bargaining process and thus disrespected the librarians and archivists. In the third *Bargaining Bulletin,* it was reported that UWOFA-LA members had voted 100% in support of a strike, which indicated strong support for the negotiating team and its mandate.

The formal communication to members during this time period was critical to keeping members apprised. Equally important was the frequency of the communication. Key messages were conveyed quickly with emails while complete coverage would wait for the paper-based *Bargaining Bulletins* and *Faculty Times*. During the strike, when information access was blocked from the University's infrastructure, including campus mail delivery and institutional email, members set up alternate email accounts as a main point of contact with the union. The UWOFA website remained a top source for information.

Labourers of Invisible Work

A shift within UWOFA-LA membership began in late summer. Although September 2011 arrived with the usual preparation for a new academic year, things were different for many librarians. The campus came to life with some students returning and others just finding their way around the University. It was the calm before the storm—the storm of teaching, providing tours, and instruction for many UWOFA-LA members. Yet, with the strike deadline of September 8th looming, many were giving faculty members notice that this academic year might be different and difficult. While many members prepared for library instruction sessions as usual, they also prepared for a strike.

Mounting frustrations and membership unrest were further captured in the growing need to articulate and name our professional roles within the larger academic community. We struggled to articulate what impact this strike would have in terms of what would *not* be done. For me, this was when the reality of the strike came home. It was the beginning of many conversations and explanations about the work I do and the contributions I make as an academic librarian. In the past, with few opportunities or reasons to name our roles to those beyond our own inner professional circle of colleagues, many of us struggled to explain what we do in jargon-free language.

I began to see how the librarian profession was viewed and understood by our students, faculty and others on campus as well as by the public. A colleague articulated the problem well: "We also came to a crisis as we faced the challenge of articulating our value as academic librarians and archivists, and of doing so in a way that would appeal to our university's administration."[17] Our relative invisibility in the University community, in many ways, had left us silent and without a language to define our central role as members of a larger academic community. Many factors contributed to this problem; technology connects users with information, reduced budgets have led to staff downsizing, and an increased reliance on outsourcing are but a few of the reasons.[18] While we were highly regarded as information professionals, what we do and the contributions we make continue to be poorly understood.[19] Many fumbled to tell me what they thought I did; namely, some of the stereotypical work of dealing with books. This was troubling, given that I thought we had moved beyond the findings published by Roma Harris and Christina Sue-Chen[20] and Judy Fagan.[21] Harris and Sue-Chen reported that university students perceived librarian work as consisting of traditional tasks such as cataloguing, or performing clerical tasks.[22] Fagan[23] similarly found that university students showed a lack of understanding of the professional nature of librarianship, with some respondents suggesting that librarians do excess teacher work or stay late to clean up after closing hours.[24] Beyond the physical side of libraries, even fewer users understood, for example, how the electronic research resources were made available for their use.[25] Users' lack of awareness, along with their inability to understand and explain the complicated and layered work of librarians and archivists, further highlighted the way we had become silent labourers of invisible work. While the services we provided were appreciated and the faces of librarians and archivists were seen, the actual work remained invisible, unspoken, and largely misunderstood. Our faculty and students appreciated many of us but they could not explain what we did and why it was important. It was increasingly clear to many of us that our absence from campus might be of little consequence.

Communicating effectively with our users in the University was critical. In early September, three information pickets were held, two on campus and one at a Labour Day picnic for local labour unions. Leaflets were titled, *Why have Western Librarians and Archivists Set a Strike Deadline?* Buttons read, *I Heart Western*

Librarians and Archivists. In addition, the Communications Committee provided members with talking points about the core issues of staff complement, compensation and benefits, as well as the long-standing 20% salary gap with other Ontario universities. These were used as conversation starters when distributing the leaflets. During an information picket held just outside of one of the larger libraries on campus, I distributed leaflets and had numerous students tell me that they did not use the library. When I inquired further about how they obtained their information for their papers and assignments, many replied that they got their information online. I took this opportunity to point out that all those top notch academic databases and online journals were selected and made available through UWOFA-LA members. The look of surprise on their faces was evident. This again illustrated the invisible nature of our work; the very fact that our work is both seamless and relatively misunderstood (by students, in particular) makes us so inconspicuous.

This notion of visibility was also explored in an article from the *Faculty Times* by James Compton titled, *Academic Librarians and Archivists and the Struggle for Visibility*. Compton cited other signs of de-professionalization in the larger environment, such as the appointment of a non-librarian or non-archivist to lead the prestigious Library and Archives Canada in 2009.[26] A UWOFA-LA colleague, Melanie Mills remarked on the relative invisibility of our work in libraries: "Paradoxically, the more fluid and intuitive an information search and retrieval experience we facilitate, the less visible the contributions of information professionals become."[27] During my time on the information picket line and while interacting with users prior to the strike, this was indeed my experience and it was sobering. When coupled with the fact that the librarians and archivists were a small bargaining unit of 50, many of us paused when considering the effect of a strike.[28] A further challenge during this time was the news that the libraries on campus would remain open. Staffed by library assistants and managers during this time, it was to be "business as usual" according to the administration. This caused concern for many members, who questioned how withdrawing the labour of our small bargaining unit would have any impact at all. By remaining open to users and maintaining access to resources and circulation functions, this effectively stripped away the common notion of what librarians do in a university library. It forced self-reflection and discussion among members about the core of librarianship, and its tenets and founding principles, which underpin our professional work. The articulation of these values by librarians and archivists on the information pickets and in campus conversations further increased the volume of the librarians' and archivists' voices.

Meanwhile a sense of community was being fostered by the members of the Strike Action Committee, who were hard at work finalizing a myriad of logistics. It was a huge task that members did not really appreciate until the strike actually began. The Committee's hard work paid off with schedules running smoothly and on-the-ground issues being quickly resolved. Teamwork was the key to success and contributed significantly to the strong community that was being fostered. Members felt a sense of belonging and personal investment, both of which are important elements in defining and creating community.[29] During this phase, internal communication increased so that members were well informed. Emails and membership meetings were frequent. With the reality of no further progress being made on key issues, *UWOFA Matters* reported that the decision was made to stage legal strike action with picket lines in place for 7:30 am on September 8th.[30]

A call went out for picket captain duty and I volunteered to take on this role during the strike. The yellow safety vests were our daily uniform, along with our UWOFA issued t-shirts and signs to carry. This meant that members were easily identifiable, which further contributed to a sense of belonging and personal investment—important attributes of a community.[31] The role of picket captain required that I reflect on the value and meaning of my work as an academic librarian. While normally there is little time for introspection, these were not normal times. I felt that articulating the value and meaning of librarianship was critical to making the case for professional and fair pay. Being a picket captain with leadership duties brought into sharp focus the need to both speak up and speak out.

Initially, the pickets had a nervous energy that came from something new, sprinkled with a degree of uncertainty. What would happen today on the shift, we wondered? Faculty members and both undergraduate and graduate students routinely joined us on the picket lines, along with staff and members of the public from time to time. Graduate students from the Faculty of Information and Media Studies (FIMS) program were regular participants. In fact, the FIMS students raised a banner stating that FIMS supported a fair deal for Western Librarians and Archivists on a campus building, indicating support for the UWOFA-LA prior to the strike. This bold message of support from the students created a social media buzz on campus and among UWOFA-LA members. The banner was removed, but the spirit of the FIMS student support remained strong throughout the strike period.

Information sheets were also made available for distribution on the picket line. These contained useful points for members when speaking about the issues. Prepared by the Communication Committee, they provided the context and framework for the job action and combined it with describing the work of the librarians and archivists in a way that clearly communicated value to students, faculty and the University community. They were employed on the picket line in a variety of ways by members: Some read from them, others paraphrased while others simply handed them out to passersby.

The buttons and stickers proved to be popular and it was gratifying to see them appearing on backpacks and jackets around campus. Posters were also produced and distributed. These could be found on faculty members' office doors, on hallway bulletin boards and on wall space throughout the libraries and campus.

This positive message was easily spotted and, for those who wore the buttons, it gave librarians and archivists an opener to say, "I see you already have one of our buttons; thanks for your support!" It also boosted morale to see all the buttons, stickers and posters as visible and tangible evidence of support for the strike and endorsement of the importance of the work of librarians and archivists.

Communication during the strike was critical and members wanted more information about the strike and negotiations. For many, there was a sense of being in another world when on picket duty or doing the work to support the picketers. In response, the Communication Committee increased its efforts and sent frequent email updates to members. Some members enjoyed sharing the more humourous side of being on strike and a members' only blog was created by a UWOFA-LA colleague Jennifer Robinson.[32] The blog featured pictures, text, a daily song and stories. Members regularly checked the blog as a way to wrap up the day on a more positive note. This also contributed to developing the strong sense of community among members and fostered a safe space for members to find their voices.

Rallies were held during the strike period, which were both invigorating and encouraging. Members of the Canadian Association of University Teachers (CAUT) Defence Fund Flying Pickets joined the picket lines and presented UWOFA with a cheque for $1,000,000, In *UWOFA Matters*, UWOFA President (2011-12) Bryce Traister, commented, "Our members know that academics across the country stand with them, lending their moral and material support to their effort to achieve a fair deal that gives them the respect they deserve."[33] While the financial support was appreciated, just as important to members was the moral support for the strike. One rally was attended by Sid Ryan, president of the Ontario Federation of Labour (OFL). Mr. Ryan not only joined the picket line but also spoke passionately for the cause. The rally was well-attended; media were present and reported on the strike. Jim Turk, then CAUT Executive Director, commented in *UWOFA Matters* that, "Western's librarians and archivists deserve this level of attention from one of Canada's top labour leaders. It demonstrates that their issues are national issues."[34] The financial support and CAUT's Flying Pickets were further evidence that academics across the country were paying attention and supported this strike. In addition, daily messages of encouragement were received and displayed at strike headquarters and many members made the time to read them.[35] These were often remarked on while travelling to and from the picket line and discussed while on picket duty. For a small bargaining unit, such as UWOFA-LA, external support was very important as it contributed to legitimacy of the strike and helped to validate the work of members. Librarians and archivists could see how they and their work were perceived by others in the field and across campuses nationally.

For nine days in September, UWOFA-LA members walked the picket line, volunteered for extra shifts, staffed the headquarters, drove shuttles to and from the picket line, and attended rallies, meetings and social events. It was exhausting but resolve remained solid. There was a strong sense of camaraderie throughout. A colleague noted, "In particular, we have benefitted from the sense of solidarity and community that was fostered on the picket lines, both among Western librarians and archivists, and among us and our colleagues at other institutions."[36] For many members, the strike provided an opportunity to come together for a common cause. "The solidarity, member participation, community support, and the determination to achieve a fair and equitable agreement, fuelled this small bargaining unit throughout the two week strike in September."[37] It was during this intense period that the voices of the librarians and archivists were raised as we spoke out on the picket lines and at rallies.

Loud and Clear

As a result of members being heard loudly and clearly, there came a breakthrough at the bargaining table. Negotiations resumed on September 20th, and a tentative agreement was reached. The deal was accepted by 84% of the UWOFA-LA members. Return to work was planned for early the following week. The UWOFA president commented, "In walking off the job, our librarians and archivists made a statement. In returning, they demonstrated grace."[38] In terms of outcomes of the strike, some are tangible and others are not. For example, modest financial gains were made but more importantly were the two Letters of Understanding, *Pay Equity Review* and *Workplace Climate*. That these two Letters were agreed to by both parties is significant to the issues of fairness and respect that were brought into sharp focus with the strike. These Letters were evidence that UWOFA-LA was being taken seriously by the employer. The chief negotiator and deputy chief negotiator observed, "If, in the end, our librarians and archivists are respected and fairly compensated for the expert work they do to support faculty and students at Western, it will all have been worth it."[39] The work of two joint committees began in the fall of 2012 and these committees will be operable until the expiration of the contract in June 2015. Members are hopeful that progress will be made on these important issues. Just as importantly, members will be actively involved in the process.

The fact that many students from FIMS joined the UWOFA-LA picket lines on a daily basis bodes well for the profession. As the FIMS students graduate and become our colleagues in libraries and archives across the country, they have already practiced using their voices to speak up for equity and the value of professional work. They have experienced firsthand the dismissiveness of Western's administration of academic librarians' and archivists' professional work. By becoming politically active and engaged in the profession as students, our new colleagues will be better able to communicate the value of our work, which is a benefit to libraries and archives everywhere.

A shift has occurred in the UWOFA-LA bargaining unit in that, post-strike, a new culture has begun to emerge. Membership participation and engagement continues to remain high, especially given the small number of members in the bargaining unit. Strong attendance at meetings, high voter turnout for ballot questions and participation on committees continues. Was the strike successful? Yes. "Without the thousands of hours committed by the determined librarians and archivists during this 18-day struggle, we could not have pulled it off."[40] A positive strike outcome that is more difficult to quantify includes the strong sense of community and camaraderie that was generated by UWOFA-LA members. In fact, many would point to this as being the best thing that came out of the strike. No retreat or facilitated workshop could ever have achieved the strong UWOFA-LA community that emerged. A UWOFA-LA colleague, Kristin Hoffmann, commented, "We learned, in a very tangible way, that when we are pro-active and work together, we can achieve great things."[41] The bargaining unit has been recognized for taking a stand on important issues, contributing to the sense of empowerment of members. "The resolve and resourcefulness shown by this small bargaining unit will continue to inspire both its members as well as the faculty in its sister bargaining unit"[42]. For UWOFA-LA members whose voices were once whispers they did indeed grow to a roar and were heard far and wide.

Looking into the future, UWOFA-LA members will need to not only monitor the Collective Agreement for trouble-spots and infractions but will also have to speak up about librarians' and archivists' concerns. Members must take ownership of their collective agreement and push for improvements. But most importantly, librarians and archivists will need to use their voices both collectively and as individuals to truly effect positive change for both the bargaining unit and the profession, today and into the future.

Bibliography

Compton, James. "Academic Librarians and Archivists and the Struggle for Visibility," *Faculty Times: a UWOFA newsletter*, May, 2011. http://www.uwofa.ca/publications/facultytimes/.

Dunn, Linda. "Librarians and Archivists Update," *Faculty Times: a UWOFA newsletter*, September, 2010. http://www.uwofa.ca/publications/facultytimes/.

Dunn, Linda and Elizabeth Bruton. "Update From the UWOFA-LA Contract Committee." *Faculty Times: A UWOFA newsletter*, February, 2011. http://www.uwofa.ca/publications/facultytimes/.

Fagan, Jody. "Students' Perceptions of Academic Librarians," *Reference Librarian* 78 (2002): 131-148.

Harris, Roma and Christina Sue-Chen. "Cataloging and Reference, Circulation and Shelving: Public Library Users and University Students' Perceptions of Librarianship," *Library & Information Science Research* 10 (1988): 95-107.

Harrington, Marni and Albert Katz. "Some of Our Observations on UWOFA's First Strike," *Faculty Times: A UWOFA newsletter*, February, 2012. http://www.uwofa.ca/publications/facultytimes/.

Hoffmann, Kristin. "Lesson in Solidarity from a Strike and a Symposium," *Faculty Times: A UWOFA newsletter*, February, 2012. http://www.uwofa.ca/publications/facultytimes/.

Horoky, Denise. "Strikes and Springsteen: Why My Graduate Students Expect Me to Be 'Better Than Google'," *Faculty Times: A UWOFA newsletter*, February, 2012. http://www.uwofa.ca/publications/facultytimes/.

Katz, Albert. "Almost a Strike: Lessons Learned," *Faculty Times: A UWOFA Newsletter*, February, 2011. http://www.uwofa.ca/publications/facultytimes/.

McMillan, David W. and David. M. Chavis. "Sense of Community: A Definition and Theory," *Journal of Community Psychology* 14 (1986): 6-23.

Mills, Melanie. "Information Workers in the Academy: The Case of Librarians and Archivists at the University of Western Ontario," *Ephemera* 10, no. 3/4 (2010): 532-536.

Mon, Lorri and Lydia E. Harris. "The Death of the Anonymous Librarian," *Reference Librarian* 52 (2011): 352-364.

Reicher, S., R. Spears and S. A. Haslam. "The Social Identity Approach in Social Psychology," in *Sage Handbook of Identities*, edited by M. Wetherell and C. Mohanty, 44-62. London: Sage Publications Ltd., 2010.

Seiss, Judith A. *The Visible Librarian: Asserting Your Value With Marketing and Advocacy.* Chicago: American Library Association, 2003.

Traister, Bryce. "A time to reflect," *Faculty Times: a UWOFA newsletter*, February, 2012. http://www.uwofa.ca/publications/facultytimes/.

University of Western Ontario Faculty Association. "Can a University Exist without Books?" *Librarians and Archivists Bargaining Bulletin*, June 13, 2011. http://www.uwofa.ca/documents/category:58.

———. "UWO librarians & Archivists Vote 100% in Favour of Strike Mandate," *UWOFA Matters*, June 20, 2011. http://www.uwofa.ca/uwofamatters/.

———. "Western Librarians & Archivists Set Strike Deadline for September 8," *UWOFA Matters*, August 19, 2011. http://www.uwofa.ca/uwofamatters/.

———. "Academics Rally For UWO Librarians & Archivists," *UWOFA Matters*, September 9, 2011, http://www.uwofa.ca/uwofamatters/.

———. "OFL President to Join UWO Librarians & Archivists," *UWOFA Matters*, September 13, 2011. http://www.uwofa.ca/uwofamatters/.

Varpalotai, Aniko and Linda Dunn. "UWOFA-LA Negotiating Update: UWOFA-LA Third Contract Negotiations Begin," *Faculty Times: a UWOFA newsletter,* May, 2011. http://www.uwofa.ca/publications/facultytimes/.

———. "The First Academic Strike at Western," *Faculty Times: a UWOFA newsletter*, February, 2012. http://www.uwofa.ca/publications/facultytimes/.

The Mouse That Didn't Roar: The Difficulty of Unionizing Academic Librarians at a Public American University

Stephanie Braunstein and Michael F. Russo

"I don't like Communism. I don't like to think that anyone's my equal. Nobody is. I'm superior to a great number of people and inferior to others, and for that reason I'm not at all sure that I'm in favor of democracy either...."

– from *The Mouse That Roared*

Introduction and Background

For nearly six days in August of 1973, the world's attention was focused on the Sveriges Kreditbank in Stockholm, Sweden. A lone gunman, with an accomplice who joined him later, took four bank employees hostage. By the end of the ordeal, two of the hostages had formed an emotional bond with their captors such that they defended their kidnappers and praised their humanity in public comments and in statements to authorities. This curious phenomenon was christened "Stockholm Syndrome." Though there are deep, psychoanalytic explanations for this reaction, in a nutshell, Stockholm Syndrome results when a hostage is treated respectfully by his or her captor. This humane treatment creates in the captive a debt of gratitude simply for not being harmed. Consequently, the person kidnapped tends to view the kidnapper with favour.[1]

While some may accuse us of hyperbole, we believe that the current employment situation in Louisiana higher education is analogous to a hostage taking.

Academic employees are essentially captives of the economic and political circumstances that dominate the employment landscape, and employees of publicly-funded institutions are especially vulnerable to the economic and political forces that affect their employment. Add to this the fact that public employees in Louisiana are not allowed to openly advocate in any official capacity for themselves with legislators; to do so would be a violation of ethics laws.[2] One would think that, under such circumstances, those who work in public universities in Louisiana would seek to advantage themselves in some form or fashion, if only for the sake of self-preservation. Unfortunately, one would be completely wrong.

Instead, the general reaction to budget cuts and layoff notices has been, anecdotally, to express *gratitude* to the state. At least, so the thinking seems to go, "*I still have a job.*" Thanks, in other words, for not hurting *me*. Stockholm Syndrome in the workplace.

A few years ago, before the economic downturn of 2008 became a rationale for the state of Louisiana to impose austerity on its public institutions—specifically, its public education system and its publicly-run healthcare system—the Faculty Senate of Louisiana State University (LSU) commissioned an *ad hoc* committee to look into representation options for faculty members, ways in which the faculty could have more of a direct impact on the decisions that were then being made for them by administrators. The issue then was faculty governance, not the more basic bread-and-butter issues of employment stability and salary stagnation. At the time the committee was established, faculty were faced with a situation in which they had been left out of major decisions that resulted in a complete reorganization of the campus structure. Faculty felt, at the time, that their representation was as essential to this process as it was overlooked by those in charge. This perception of being blind-sided by the University administration inspired a revolt among the faculty that resulted in a rather historical confrontation between an auditorium full of professors and the University Provost and Chancellor.[3]

Though issues of executive over-reach and administrative secrecy with respect to the LSU Board of Supervisors' decisions have continued to exist, the financial crash of 2008 and political trends in the Louisiana Legislature and Governor's Office changed some of the focus of concern. The faculty at LSU were no longer just distressed about governance or about having their voices heard; they also felt that their continued employment was being threatened.

Prompted by the threats of layoffs and/or furloughs, the Faculty Senate's *ad hoc* committee more vigorously continued its work, gathering information about the faculty's concerns and providing educational forums regarding those concerns. In the end, after over a year of research, consultation, and deliberation, the committee concluded that the only effective way the faculty could assert itself was through unionization. This conclusion was presented to the Faculty Senate; a union chapter affiliated with the Louisiana Association of Educators was established on campus; and the faculty—through a vote of the Faculty Senate—endorsed this organization, which was called LSUnited.

Even though the faculty, aggrieved as they were, now had a mechanism by which those grievances could be addressed, there was not a stampede to join the union. Though many spoke positively of the union and of the need for the faculty to act, few joined. Only about one hundred of approximately 1200 faculty members signed pledge cards. This reluctance extended to the ranks of librarians, who have faculty status at LSU; only a handful of librarians signed up.

Trying to determine what specifically was behind the reluctance of LSU's faculty to come together in an organization that could address many, if not all, of the problems experienced by rank and file teachers and researchers presented a conundrum. As librarians, we were especially curious to know what the issue was for our library colleagues. We were also curious to know if the attitudes at LSU were shared across the state by librarians at other institutions. Thus, we set out to examine Louisiana librarians' attitudes towards unions. As with any examination of cause and effect, we started with certain assumptions based on anecdotal or "common sense" theories; but, certainly, the examination was not conducted in order to prove those pre-conceived assumptions. Instead, it was conducted to better identify and ultimately understand whatever the results of our inquiry would be. The fact that several of our theories were substantiated by our inquiries is reassuring in an odd sort of positive/negative fashion; but we did not just prove ourselves right—we were also successful in finding some other areas we had not previously considered. All of these findings will be shared after giving some background via pertinent literature, both professional and popular.

Literature Review: General Publications Pertinent to Topic

While there is a reasonably substantial body of literature on the topic of librarians and unionization, this chapter will limit its literature review portion by observing three separate, but correlated filters: pertinence to academic librarianship, prominence of author(s)/source of publication, and currency.[4] In the language of information science research, the articles described below can be considered as fulfilling the two requirements of a successful search strategy: they reflect both adequate return and relevancy. As was just noted above, more recent articles (specifically, those published since 1990) are being given priority for discussion here. The reason for this decision is that this chapter does not aim to provide an historical overview of experiences with academic unions; rather, it does aim to prompt a discussion of if/how academic librarians view unionization as an option for addressing workplace problems.

An obvious additional consideration determining inclusion in this section of the chapter is geography. Based on the nature of the topic and the thesis being proffered, the authors decided to divide the literature review into two discrete sections based on whether the articles being referenced were from the United States or from Canada.

Publications from United States Sources

While the title of Deanna D. Wood's article from 1999 does not immediately alert the reader to the fact that she will be concentrating on academic librarians, her admission that she is "most familiar with the model of college and university faculty unions" and that "much of the discussion . . . [in her article] will draw on this experience"[5] promises a more focused perspective than what is claimed in the title, "Librarians and Unions: Defining and Protecting Professional Values." Because concern over maintaining professional values seems to be implied whenever librarians are asked about unionizing, this article seems an excellent starting point for research on our topic (and it will provide especially cogent information in the upcoming section where we discuss the findings from our survey).

For her thesis, Wood posits that "values embedded in the profession of librarianship . . . are affected and . . . complemented by collective action."[6] The term "collective action" is, of course, synonymous with unionization. Throughout her article, the author acknowledges the primary reasons that are associated with unionization—predominantly, compensation and benefits (what she terms as "process-based benefits"); but she takes the perspective that librarianship and its core values are especially well-suited to a unionized environment. Three of these values—collegial/cooperative decision-making, intellectual freedom, right of due process—she translates to "value-based benefits."[7] Her final point is that, in addition to the process-based benefits of salary, retirement programs, and vacation and sick leave policies, those three value-based benefits must also be protected by contract; and the logical way for that to happen is to unionize.

While Wood's article is, thus, generally partial to the idea of unionization, a 2009 article by Rachel Applegate is less enthusiastic. Applegate does acknowledge that "results show that compared to librarians at either private or nonunionized public colleges and universities, librarians at unionized public institutions are somewhat better off."[8] However, throughout her article—a complex statistical analysis of 1,904 academic libraries—she never convincingly endorses unions for academic librarians. In her own literature review, she makes references to studies that are, at best, ambiguous about showing any benefits for unionization of librarians:

> Tina Hovecamp's research showed no statistically significant relation between unionization and reported salaries, though more unionized librarians reported being in higher salary brackets.
>
> At some points (particularly when first organized) unions may have achieved higher salaries—hence studies from the mid-1970s, when unions were settling their first collective-bargaining agreements, tended to show a positive effect, while later ones did not.

At a single, large Midwestern university, Dean Elmuti and Yunus Kathawala surveyed faculty and found that a third believed that the union had no effect on compensation and another third were dissatisfied with (any) union influence on monetary factors.[9]

A third article, from 2006, essentially confirms Applegate's research. A study of American Research Libraries (ARL), taken annually over the period 1989-1998, indicates that when librarians first unionize, the resulting wage increases are notable; but after that initial wage hike, the following years show declining rates of increases until those increases are essentially non-existent. In other words, the "union wage gap for academic librarians . . . disappeared," and starting pay rates between unionized and nonunionized academic librarians were eventually equivalent.[10]

Publications from Canadian Sources

Examination of the articles from US sources shows at least two things: first, it shows that when focusing on the issue of salaries, a clear connection between wages and unionization is not easy to make. Of the three articles noted above, the one about working conditions (value-based benefits) reported more positively than did the two other articles about salary (process-based benefits). Leaving aside temporarily a deeper analysis of that observation, it must nevertheless be said that the Canadian literature most pertinent to our subject is also most positive when it reports on the effect of unions on securing academic freedom, fostering library faculty governance, and fighting deprofessionalization.[11] As we shall see, however, the Canadian literature is ultimately more positive concerning unionization no matter what the sub-topic benefits being discussed—value-based or process-based.

The travails of academics, including academic librarians, in Canada are not dissimilar from those that have affected academics in the US. Hiring trends—such as hiring part-timers, adjuncts, and staff to perform professional-level work—are as much a problem in the provinces as in the states. Such trends disadvantage all workers, including those who take the jobs. Arbitrary firings and attacks on academic freedom are common on both sides of the 49th parallel. The difference between Canadian librarians and their Acadian cousins in Louisiana seems to be the resolve—or lack thereof—with which these attacks on their profession are met.

As with the previously discussed literature from the US, the literature from Canada considers both the more material benefits of unionization and the more elusive benefits. In "Academic Freedom for Librarians: What is It, and why does It matter," a white paper publication from the Canadian Association of University Teachers (CAUT), the author first defines academic freedom and then makes the somewhat provocative statement that "academic freedom has mistakenly come to be understood as an individual right when, in fact, it is a professional right."[12]

Clearly, Turk is advocating for the value-based rationale for unionization of academic librarians; and his white paper is fleshed out with evidence of the intangible benefits being threatened and the actions various Canadian academic libraries took to respond to those threats. Examples of such Canadian libraries include the University of Western Ontario and McMaster University, in Hamilton, Ontario.

While the intangible benefits were most prominently highlighted in CAUT's white paper, indirect references to the tangible were made when reporting on the libraries mentioned above—libraries who moved to unionize as a result of both intangible and tangible threats. A report in a 2010 issue of *Library Journal* mentioned that the McMaster decision to unionize was at least tangentially related to librarian layoffs in 2009.[13] Over a year later, another *Library Journal* article reported the success of a strike by University of Western Ontario's Faculty Association of Librarians and Archivists (UWOFA-LA) that led to a salary increase of at least 1.5 percent per year over a period of four years.[14]

Shortly after the second *Library Journal* article was published, a one-day symposium on academic librarianship was held at the University of Toronto. One of the themes addressed by this symposium was labour issues ("the role of national and provincial labour organizations and local faculty associations"); in fact, the first session was entitled "Faculty Associations and National Labour Associations in Defense of Academic Librarianship."[15] One of the points made at this session was that "[i]n a unionized work environment grievances and collective bargaining can be used to effect change, and collective agreements can provide fairness, equity, a test of reasonableness as well as processes."[16]

After comparing and contrasting the literature focusing on value-based and process-based benefits, whether it be from the United States or Canada, one thing stands out: while process-based benefits—the bread-and-butter benefits of wages, health care, retirement, etc.—may not always be the most successfully addressed by academic unions, the value-based benefits—the intangibles of academic freedom, shared governance, etc.—make up for that lack. As a result, unionization of academics—librarians in particular—while not a panacea for everything wrong in the workplace, is a worthwhile endeavour and should not be dismissed before taking a close look at it as a remedy for at least some of the problems facing twenty-first century academic librarians in the United States and Canada.

Methodology of Study

In order to gather data about Louisiana academic librarians' attitudes about unionization, we developed a 29 question survey (see Appendix 1) hosted online by Qualtrics (http://www.qualtrics.com/). This free software allows for anonymous polling of selected communities of interest and gives basic statistical feedback on the responses.[17] Basic statistical feedback, rather than complex statistical analysis, was sufficient for our needs. Our questions allowed for targeted responses, making the answers relatively easy to connect to the purpose of our survey and not requiring intricate calculations of probabilities.

The population of 170 recipients invited to participate in the poll was drawn from three sources: first, from the email list of members of the Louisiana Chapter of the Association of College and Research Libraries (ACRL-LA); second, from the print version of the membership listing for the Academic Section of the Louisiana Library Association; and third, from library faculty listings found on Louisiana academic libraries' individual websites. These three sources were checked carefully to avoid duplicating invitees. Evaluating these sources from the opposite perspective, however, the authors may have missed some academic librarians in Louisiana. Nevertheless, based on the size of the total potential population and the familiarity of the authors with the Louisiana academic librarian community, the percentage of potential misses would be statistically irrelevant. After three weeks, the poll closed; 94 librarians had replied to the survey, a respectable response rate of just over 55 percent.

What the Survey Did—and Did Not—Tell Us

The librarians who responded to our survey would appear to be a stable and settled group of employees, satisfied with their work and with no major complaints against their employers. This conclusion is implied by the fact that most respondents (74 percent) enjoy academic ranks—librarian and associate librarian—that require tenure,[18] a process that usually takes a minimum of six years to complete. The majority (79 percent) have been working as academic librarians for longer than six years, and almost all of them work full-time. Additionally, our survey sample confesses to a certain chronological maturity: 64 percent admitted to being 46 years old or older. What does this mean in terms of how Louisiana's librarians view unionization? Does it mean that with stability and age come caution and a reluctance to disturb the *status quo*? Almost none of our respondents have lodged formal, job-related complaints, whether to the University ombudsman or to their personnel or human resources departments. Most librarians had no cause to file such complaints, further supporting the idea that most Louisiana librarians are quite satisfied with things as they are.

Interestingly, when we scratch the surface a little, we learn that, of the 67 respondents who said they were *not* looking for another job, 61 percent of these apparently satisfied librarians would jump at the offer of another job. Inasmuch as salary was cited as librarians' top concern (question 13), perhaps that is an explanation.

Salaries of public institutions of higher learning in Louisiana—and 82 percent of our respondents work in such institutions—have been frozen since 2008. Since then, state funding for higher education has been reduced by 80 percent.[19] With the cost of everything, including employer-provided healthcare benefits, increasing, naturally librarians in Louisiana are concerned about their salaries. This would seem to be an issue around which it would be easy to organize the state's librarians and higher education faculty generally.

To place the salary issue in some context, consider the microcosm of just Louisiana State University. LSU is a publicly-funded, Carnegie Research university within the Southeastern Conference, with an enrollment of just under 30,000. LSU's salaries for librarians put it last among ARL libraries in both median and average salary: that's 115th out of 115. . .*twice* (ARL). More telling is the fact that, in terms of how much it pays its librarians, LSU trails behind 11 of the 13 institutions it identifies as its peers. (Two of its peers are not included in the ARL salary survey). Perhaps even more embarrassing is the fact that LSU trails almost every rival school within the Southeastern Conference, according to ARL statistics. Forty-nine respondents indicated that salary was their most important issue. Second in importance were benefits, with 40 votes. Institutional support came in third, with 32 votes. Working conditions were a distant fourth. Two specifically academic issues—faculty governance and tenure—were lowest in priority for librarians. This is an indication that, in Louisiana, bread-and-butter issues trump all others, at least among librarians.

This assumption, based on the above listed responses from our survey, further complicates any analysis as to why Louisiana librarians are not embracing unionization. In this chapter's literature review, we made observations indicating that much of that literature pointed to academic unions as providing more satisfactory results when addressing working conditions and academic issues (faculty governance and tenure) rather than when addressing salary and benefits. Because the traditional perception of what a union can provide is linked more to salary and benefits (process-based benefits), the revelation that, for academics at least, the value-based benefits are the ones more successfully addressed by unions comes as something of a surprise.

Can we assume then that the relatively low interest by Louisiana academic librarians in joining unions comes from an *a priori* awareness that salaries and benefits will not substantially change upon joining a union? Based on the specific narrative responses in our survey, we doubt that an already existing knowledge of the findings of the literature is at the root of most Louisiana academic librarians' low union participation. Those narrative responses, coupled with the non-narrative responses that engendered them, point instead to a multiplicity of reasons that we cannot help but consider as having the end result of being self-defeating. Hopefully, the analysis that follows will support that opinion.

Why Not?

Since 68 percent of respondents said they didn't feel able to deal with these issues by themselves but would join an organization that could, why didn't they want to organize? Since only a small number of Louisiana librarians (17 percent) have actively negative views of unions, then why not create an organization of many to speak with one strong voice to the administration? The answers to the survey's open-ended questions provide some clues as to our colleagues' reluctance to represent themselves.

When survey responders, who said they were actively looking for another job, were asked to say why they were looking, most cited compensation, in some form, as their motivation. Budget cuts, salary reductions, and salary freezes were mentioned by 15 of the 27 respondents who chose to enlarge on their reason for wanting a change. The feeling of being over-worked was sometimes conjoined with the lack of compensation: "lack of pay for workload," for one example; "I am not being paid for the additional responsibilities I have acquired. . .," for another.

Others who were looking for work elsewhere cited the feeling of being stuck in place by an organizational structure that gave them no chance for advancement and thus no chance for a higher income. One despairing comment, "I've reached a dead end," epitomizes this circumstance.

A minority (38 percent) indicated that they would not join an organization that would help them resolve work-related issues. Why would someone choose to deny himself or herself such a resource, opting instead to fight Goliath without stones? The answers our colleagues from around the state provided can be roughly sorted into several categories.

Insufficient Awareness

While some respondents were openly hostile to unions in general, most who were not members indicated a general ignorance of whether their campus even had a union. Some thought unions were not allowed, but that is not true. Current law allows formation of labour unions, even within public entities.[20] The Right to Work law states, in part, "It is hereby declared to be the public policy of Louisiana that all persons shall have and shall be protected in the exercise of the right, freely and without fear of penalty or reprisal, to form, join and assist labor organizations or to refrain from any such activities".[21] In spite of being allowed, the union presence on higher education campuses in Louisiana amounts to a thimbleful of water in a vast ocean. According to the Louisiana Federation of Teachers' website, union chapters exist on only three campuses. The Louisiana Association of Educators presently has one campus chapter listed on its website. So, there may be a great deal of truth to the belief expressed by many librarians that there just is no union to join. This, of course, raises the question: Why don't they form one? That might be a question for another survey.

Unions Versus Professional Associations

There is another vein of thought among Louisiana librarians that unions simply have no place in academe. One respondent captured the essence of this thinking this way, "I do not think it's appropriate for a professional person in higher education." Others in the profession felt that the professional associations to which they belonged, such as the American Library Association (ALA), served the same function as a union, evincing a complete lack of understanding of the difference in the purpose of each. The ALA, as a professional organization, does a creditable job of articulating the principles of the profession, but it does not negotiate salaries and benefits, nor does it provide a mechanism for resolving grievances. The American Association of University Professors (AAUP), another professional association, does not negotiate salaries and benefits either. The AAUP articulates principles regarding, among other things, academic freedom; and most self-respecting universities in the United States honour those principles. The AAUP does have a mechanism for addressing grievances, but its judgments are not binding. Only a union can collectively bargain salaries, benefits, and grievance procedures that have a basis in law.

Too Costly

Cost is another reason some librarians give for not joining a labour union. School and academic librarians are generally included in one of the state's teachers unions. Currently, the dues for each of the two teacher unions are about $500 annually, a cost 97 percent of respondents said they were unwilling to pay. Our survey shows that 92 percent of librarians in the state would not pay more than $200 annually for membership. The majority—72 percent of the respondents—would not pay more than $100. Is this a consequence of salary stagnation? Are librarians in Louisiana paid so little they cannot afford to join an organization that might work to get them higher wages? If so, here is irony indeed.

Unions Don't Work

One respondent opined, "Faculty unions are ineffective and a waste of time." The paradox of this statement, coming from a Louisiana librarian, is that there really are no unions of which to speak in Louisiana higher education. The few chapters that currently exist are little more than organizations on paper. Membership is small and inactive. It would be hard to see how a union could be effective under those circumstances. Still, the respondent does have a point: a small union of inactive members would be a tremendous waste of time.

Against All Unions

Some respondents simply evinced a negative attitude towards all unions, not just faculty unions. This sentiment was succinctly stated by one respondent who wrote simply, "anti-union." Those who hold such views are perhaps unaware of the role of unions in the economic history of the US. In a 2007 hearing before the Senate's Committee on Health, Education, Labor, and Pensions, committee chairman Senator Edward M. Kennedy said, "Unions were fundamental in building America's middle class and they still have a vital role in preserving the American dream."[22] The Senator was referring to the not-coincidental growth, during the mid-twentieth century, of labour unions, the American middle class, and the more equitable distribution of income that accompanied both. This growth was steady from about 1940 to 1980. The years since have seen American union membership decline; consequently—and not surprisingly—the wealth created in the United States has gravitated disproportionately to the already-wealthy, while the wage earners who toil to create that wealth are getting less and less of it.[23] This seems to be a forgotten lesson.

To be anti-union in the United States is to be against the weekend, against the minimum wage, against overtime pay, against employer-supplied health insurance, against vacation with pay, against workplace safety. None of these things, which Americans now take for granted, would exist if unions had not. So, it remains a mystery why anyone who works for wages would be anti-union.

Regionalism

Is the explanation to be found in geography? Federal government statistics indicate that half of all union members in the United States live in just seven states, and none of those states are in the Deep South.[24] Speaking of unions in general and not specifically of faculty or librarian unions, "Louisiana union membership rates have never exceeded the US average."[25] All the states in the South Central regions of the US had membership rates that were below the national average.[26] Seven of the eight states that had memberships lower than 5 percent were in the Deep South.[27] These are generalizations, of course; these statistics cannot easily be extrapolated to our small sampling of librarians. Also militating against the regional theory is the fact that academic librarians in Louisiana come from all over the country, not just Louisiana or even the South. Even so, there is a regional culture that is hostile to organizations like labour unions; and, after years living in a place, it would be remarkable if some of that culture had not rubbed off.

Conclusion

So, what have we learned? The answer to why Louisiana's librarians have not banded together may be as varied as the librarians themselves. Ultimately, we recognize that there is not a culture of unionization in Louisiana, which has been a "Right to Work" state since the passage of Act 252 in 1954 (see prior section, "Insufficient Awareness"). The Right to Work law[28] seems to encourage labour organizing; but, in fact, this legislation has stripped away the power of organized labour by making participation in unions optional in workplaces where unions already exist. The law thus pits worker against worker, since each worker is basically on his or her own, with no organization for back-up. While it is clear the system within the state discourages unionization, unionization is not impossible, if there is the will to do it.

Most Louisiana librarians, while generally satisfied, know their situations are not ideal; and our survey results show that most would be interested in an organization that would help them navigate through their difficulties. Yet, through timidity or ignorance or lack of finances or apathy, that segment of the Louisiana library community which recognizes the value of unions has not taken the next logical step.

In our introduction, we stated that our main purpose for the survey was to satisfy our curiosity about why our specific campus did not wholeheartedly embrace the concept of a union as a remedy for perceived workplace problems. In order to broaden our scope and, as a result, eliminate bias pertinent to just one Louisiana university, we polled academic librarians from all Louisiana institutions of higher education. Our results did seem to bolster the anecdotal theories—that some academics see unions as inappropriate for professional workers and that other academics are philosophically or politically opposed to unions in any context.

In addition, our results did illuminate two other related reasons for lack of union participation—namely the misunderstandings about the roles of professional associations versus the roles of unions and about access to unions. This misinformation can lead to a negative response on our part—in other words, blaming someone or something for poor communication, whether it be the speaker or the one spoken to; or it can lead to a positive response on our part and the parts of groups who wish to be successful in unionizing academics, specifically librarians—using the data collected, not to blame, but to redirect and reinforce campaigns for academic unionization. Public relations campaigns must not assume that everyone understands the differences between various organizations in terms of what they can provide academic employees; those differences must be clear so that decisions about which group(s) to which one belongs can be made intelligently. It may seem evident that every worker should know his or her rights, but clearly that knowledge is not universal. Somehow that information is not being conveyed to Louisiana academics. The onus to remedy that lack of accurate information is on all Louisiana workers. Simply parroting the phrase, "Louisiana is a Right-to-Work state," is counter-productive. Each of us who works for wages in Louisiana, in academics or industry, should be aware of what that legislation actually says and not be intimidated by the limitations of the legislation but, rather, be emboldened by what the legislation does allow.

Postscript

Since the completion of this chapter, developments in the union movement on LSU's campus have occurred which magnify the difficulty of getting an academic union started in Louisiana. The fledgling union, LSUnited, has struggled for two years to catch on with faculty. In that time, the union has faced resistance from the University administration and apathy from the faculty. After an initial, modest surge in membership, membership numbers have declined and then plummeted.

We believe that two factors contributed to this downturn. The first factor was that would-be members did not see an obvious confluence of interests between themselves and LSUnited's parent organization, the Louisiana Association of Educators (LAE). When LAE was asked to help organize members at LSU, its only experience had been with K-12 schools. Thus, LAE's lobbying efforts were focused on its main constituency, whose interests were sometimes at odds with those of LSU's faculty.

The second factor was already addressed in the body of this chapter: many faculty members and librarians complained that union dues were more than they could afford. This complaint came mainly from the instructor-level faculty, those faculty members who generally have the lowest salaries. In consequence, the faculty members who stood to gain the most through collective bargaining were prevented from joining an organization that might have helped them get better income in the future because of their present inadequate incomes.

LSUnited attempted several times to negotiate the dues amount with LAE but was repeatedly told the dues could not be changed. The original strategy for organizing the campus was to get 300 faculty members signed up before requesting payroll dues deduction. However, LAE, because of the political climate, which included pending anti-union legislation, decided to request dues deduction when there were only 106 commitments. This request was denied by the administration, but LAE began collecting dues by other means nevertheless. This was when members who had previously signed pledge cards began to drop out, and the exodus has continued ever since.

Faced with continuing as a unit within LAE and having only a handful of members in consequence, LSUnited decided to disaffiliate from LAE and to become a stand-alone faculty advocacy group with the specific mission of advocating for faculty issues like salary and benefits. This focus will distinguish the organization from other faculty groups on campus, such as the AAUP, which focuses on academic freedom and other non-economic issues. The remaining members of LSUnited hope that by charging negligible dues, the organization will attract many more members and thereby have more of an effect on the economic conditions under which they all labour.

Bibliography

Addo, K. "Tax Break Cuts Pale Compared to Big Slashes." *Baton Rouge Advocate*, May 10, 2013. Retrieved from *NewsBank*.

Applegate, Rachel. "Who Benefits? Unionization and Academic Libraries and Librarians." *Library Quarterly* 79, no. 4 (2009): 443-463.

Blum, J. "LSU Unveils Realignment Plan: University Officials Describe Changes at Packed Faculty Forum." *Baton Rouge Advocate*, April 15, 2009. Retrieved from *Access World News*.

Eisenbrey, Roy, and Colin Gordon. "As Unions Decline, Inequality Rises." Economic Policy Institute, June 6, 2012. Retrieved from http://www.epi.org/publication/unions-decline-inequality-rises/.

Granfield, Diane, Mary Kandiuk, and Harriet Sonne de Torrens. "Academic Librarianship: A Crisis or an Opportunity?" *Partnership: The Canadian Journal of Library and Information Practice and Research* 6, no. 2 (2011): Special Section, 1-6.

Kelley, Michael, Lynn Blumenstein, David Rapp, and Bob Warburton. "New Agreement Ends UWO Librarian Strike." *Library Journal* 136, no. 17 (2011): 13.

Kyrillidou, Martha, and Shaneka Morris, eds. *ARL Annual Salary Survey 2010-2011*. Washington, DC: Association of Research Libraries, 2011.

Lee, Deborah O., Kevin E. Rogers, and Paul W. Grimes. "The Union Relative Wage Effect for Academic Librarians." *Industrial Relations* 45, no. 3 (2006): 478-484.

Louisiana Association of Educators. Retrieved from http://www.lae.org/home.aspx.

Louisiana Federation of Teachers. Retrieved from http://la.aft.org/.

LSA—R.S. 24:56.

LSA—R.S. 23:981, *et seq.*

Oder, Norman, Lynn Blumenstein, Josh Hadro, and Rocco Staino. "Union Vote for McMaster Librarians." *Library Journal* 135, no. 5 (2010): 13.

Pineville Police Officers' Association vs. City of Pineville, et al, 713 So. 2d 536 (La. Ct. App. 3d Cir.) 1998. http://www.library.mcgill.ca/mautlib/2010.08.25_McGill_Librarians.pdf.

Strentz, Thomas. *Psychological Aspects of Crisis Negotiation*. Boca Raton, FL: CRC Taylor & Francis, 2006.

Turk, James L. "Academic Freedom for Librarians: What is It, and Why Does It Matter?" Paper delivered by Executive Director of the Canadian Association of University Teachers. Retrieved from: http://www.library.mcgill.ca/mautlib/2010.08.25_McGill_Librarians.pdf.

US Congress. Senate. Committee on Health, Education, Labor, and Pensions. *Employee Free Choice Act: Restoring Economic Opportunity for Working Families, 2007.* 110th Cong., 1st sess., 2007.

US Department of Labor, Bureau of Labor Statistics. *Unions in Louisiana—2012.* Dallas, 2013. Retrieved from http://www.bls.gov/ro6/fax/union_la.htm.

———. *Union Members—2012.* Dallas, 2013. Retrieved from http://www.bls.gov/news.release/pdf/union2.pdf.

Wibberly, Leonard. *The Mouse that Roared.* New York: Bantam Books, 1959.

Wood, Deanna D. "Librarians and Unions: Defining and Protecting Professional Values." *Education Libraries* 23, no. 1 (1999): 12-16.

Appendix A

Thank you for agreeing to take this survey. The survey will take approximately 10 minutes. All responses are anonymous.

Demographics

What is your level of education? (Choose all that apply.)
- ☐ MLS/MLIS degree
- ☐ Additional Master's degree
- ☐ Doctoral degree
- ☐ Other

Your academic rank is
- ☐ librarian
- ☐ associate librarian
- ☐ assistant librarian
- ☐ general librarian

Is "faculty" (as opposed to "staff") the appropriate classification for academic librarians?
- ☐ Yes
- ☐ No

Are you employed on a full-time basis?
- ☐ Yes
- ☐ No

How many years have you been employed as an academic librarian?
- ☐ fewer than 3 years
- ☐ 3 to 6 years
- ☐ 6 to 10 years
- ☐ 10 to 20 years
- ☐ more than 20 years

How many years have you worked in the field of librarianship altogether, whether at an institution of higher education or elsewhere?

☐ fewer than 3 years
☐ 3 to 6 years
☐ 6 to 10 years
☐ 10 to 20 years
☐ more than 20 years

What is your age?

☐ under 25
☐ 26-35
☐ 36-45
☐ 46-55
☐ 56-65
☐ 66 or older

What is your annual salary?

☐ less than $30,000
☐ $30,000 to 49,999
☐ $50,000 to 69,999
☐ $70,000 or more

At which type of institution are you employed?

☐ Public
☐ Private

Your Job

Taking into account the things you like and those you don't like about your job as an academic librarian, overall, are you satisfied with your job?

☐ Yes
☐ No

Are you actively looking for or thinking about looking for another job?

☐ Yes
☐ No

If you answered "yes" to the previous question, why are you looking for or thinking of looking for another job?

If the opportunity presented itself, would you take a job somewhere else?

☐ Yes
☐ No

Issues in the Academy

	1-Not Important	2	3	4	5-Most Important
Salary					
Benefits					
Institutional support					
Tenure process					
Faculty governance					
Physical working conditions					

Please rank all the issues listed below in order of importance to you, 1 being not important, 5 being most important.

Do you feel that you are able to successfully address these issues on your own?

☐ Yes
☐ No

If your university employs an ombudsman, have you availed yourself of their services?

☐ Yes
☐ No
☐ My institution does not have an ombudsman.

If you have not availed yourself of the services of the university ombudsman, why haven't you?

☐ I was not aware of the service.
☐ I have not had a problem that might require the intervention of the ombudsman.
☐ I did not feel the ombudsman could help.

If you have availed yourself of the services of your institution's ombudsman, how many times have you done so?

If you have consulted with your institution's ombudsman, do you feel the ombudsman helped resolve your problem?

☐ Yes
☐ No

Have you lodged a formal complaint with your institution's human resource or personnel department against a supervisor?

☐ Yes
☐ No

If you have not lodged a formal complaint with your institution's human resource or personnel department against a supervisor, why haven't you?

☐ I did not know I could.
☐ I have not had a problem that would require the intervention of Human Resource Management.
☐ I did not feel filing such a complaint would resolve the issue.

If you have lodged a formal complaint with your institution's human resource or personnel department against a supervisor, how many times have you done so?

If you did file a formal complaint with your institution's human resource or personnel department against a supervisor, were you satisfied with the result?

☐ Yes
☐ No

Unions

If a faculty organization existed that would assist you in resolving work-related issues, would you join it?

☐ Yes
☐ No

If you answered No to the above question, please explain why you would not join such an organization.

Your feelings about unions are

☐ Generally positive.
☐ Generally negative.
☐ Neutral.

If you had the option to join a faculty union, what is the most you would be willing to pay in terms of annual dues? (Please select the maximum range you can afford.)

☐ $20-100
☐ $101-200
☐ $201-300
☐ $301-400
☐ $401-500

Does your institution have a faculty union that is affiliated with either LAE/NEA or LFT/NFT? [AAUP is not a union.]

☐ Yes
☐ No

If you are not a member of your institution's faculty union, please tell us why you have chosen not to join.

☐ I am a member.
☐ I am not a member because_____

Appendix B

Tables 1A & 1B: Indicating Categorization of Narrative Responses to Survey of Louisiana Academic Libraries

Categories are: Insufficient Awareness; Negative Attitude about All Unions; Negative Attitude about Professional Unions in Particular; Confusion about Differences among Various Professional Organizations (Not Understanding the Difference between a Union and a Professional Organization); Cost; Perceived Lack of Need; Other

Please note that in some cases the answers were corrected for spelling/basic grammar errors in order to facilitate better understanding on the part of the reader.

A. Questions 23/24—explanations for no interest in joining a "faculty organization . . . that would assist you in resolving work-related issues":

Explanation	Category
I have not had any experience that would require it, and it seems like a potential way to antagonize administration.	LN
I have not had a personal need for such an organization.	LN
I think that it pits professionals against professionals and is a poor model for collaboration	Neg Pro
I believe that Unions go too far on the side of the employee.	Neg All
Don't believe that unions are a constructive method for resolving work related issues	Neg All
I would have answered "maybe" if that would have been a choice. I don't have enough extra money to join a union, and I don't think employees should have to pay for those services that should be part of the job-but if the union was free, yes I would join.	Cost
I think I have other options for addressing these issues.	Conf
Anti-union	Neg All
I'm a member of the American Library Association and the Louisiana Library Association. I feel that those are my "unions."	Conf
I have tenure and have taken independent actions to solve my needs.	LN
Unions coupled with tenure are a bit much. I also find them to be shady, deceptive organizations.	Neg Pro & Neg All

Unions are not an appropriate for professionals or faculty	Neg Pro
Many personal reasons.	Other
I feel that the other methods and avenues of dealing with personnel and overall faculty issues are adequate.	Conf & LN
Do not feel it would help.	Other
Unions can serve a purpose. However in the academic university setting there are other items in place that can address the functions and purposes for a union.	Neg Pro & Conf
The question implied unions to me, and I would not join a union.	Neg All
I'm cheap, and I'm generally satisfied with my employment situation.	LN & Cost
I do not currently feel that librarians need to be classified as faculty, so I would have no need or desire to become a member of a faculty organization.	Neg Pro
Not necessary	LN
Not sure if that's something I need to be part of just yet as a fairly new librarian	Other
I don't think it would work.	Other
I don't feel that I need to at this time.	LN
Unions foster mediocrity and laziness	Neg All
I don't think such organizations are really effective.	Neg All
I am not really considered faculty and most of my concerns would not be addressed.	LN
Because there are many in company departments designed to help with various infrastructure issues.	LN
Not interested.	Other
Potential cons outweigh pros (ethical individuals, costs vs. benefits, potential political intervention, etc.)	Cost & Other
I would prefer to reconcile such problems myself	LN
Unions do not belong institutions of higher education	Neg Pro
It would get in the way here, I think. We are pursuing our grievance through proper channels.	LN & Other

B. Questions 27/28—explanation for no interest in joining "your institution's faculty union":

Categories are: Insufficient Awareness; Negative Attitude about All Unions; Negative Attitude about Professional Unions in Particular; Confusion about Differences among Various Professional Organizations (Not Understanding the Difference between a Union and a Professional Organization); Cost; Perceived Lack of Need; Other

Explanation	Category
As far as I know, there is no such group at my institution.	IA
I used to be so that I would have some teaching liability insurance: in general I do not feel that librarians have the same issues as teaching faculty.	Other
I don't know enough about it, and it has not been a particularly important concern for me.	IA & LN
As stated above, we don't have one and I believe that unions go too far on the side of the employee.	Neg All
We don't have one.	IA
Our institution does not have a union.	IA
We don't have one that I am aware of.	IA
Faculty union not available.	IA
I dropped my membership because with no raises, for 5 years I can't afford union dues (ironic, no?)	Cost
We don't have a union.	IA
Unions not allowed.	IA
I have not been invited to join.	IA
The mission of the Union is well documented, but specific goals and objectives have not been as readily publicized. The organization seems to be more reactive rather than proactive.	Other
Again, I feel LLA and ALA are my unions.	Conf
I do not know much about what it does and its activities.	IA
I was, but could use the money for other things.	Cost
Our institution does not have a faculty union.	IA
I do not believe in unions. Period.	Neg All
Doubtful about benefits of union in right-to-work state.	IA & Other
There is no union, Louisiana is a "right to work" state.	IA & Other
Faculty unions are ineffective and a waste of time.	Neg Pro
We do not have a faculty union.	IA
Do not think a union will help improve either the state's financial condition or its priorities, which is where the source of our problems lies.	Other
We do not have a faculty union.	IA
There is no organized union at my college. My mother is President of a parish chapter of LFT, and I support unions in general; however, my institution is rather small and most faculty consider it a good place to work, so no unionization effort has ever been made here.	IA
There is no union.	IA
We do not have a faculty union.	IA
There is no union.	IA
I do not think it's appropriate for a professional person in higher education.	Neg Pro
I am not aware of a faculty union on my campus.	IA
Refer to above answer.	Null

There is no faculty union.	IA
We don't have one.	IA
Option not available.	IA
There isn't a union.	IA
We don't have one to my knowledge.	IA
We don't have a union.	IA
None available.	IA
I have not made the time to join yet but I would like to be a member in the future.	Other
We are not unionized.	IA
We do not have a union.	IA
Unions have no place in academia.	Neg Pro
I don't think we have a union?	IA
There is no union.	IA
I feel that these unions have no real power or effectiveness.	Neg Pro &Other
No org.	IA
We don't have a union.	IA
We do not have a union.	IA
There is no union here.	IA
Deans do not have one on campus.	Other
I don't see the union having any strength in Louisiana.	Other
We do not have a faculty union.	IA
Not available.	IA
No such union exists.	IA
We don't have one.	IA
I haven't gotten around to it.	Other
My institution does not have one.	IA
No union.	IA
There is no union for faculty. The most-related association is Faculty-Senate.	IA
Don't have one.	IA
We don't have a union.	IA
One does not exist...that I am aware of.	IA
I have not seen where the Union has convinced faculty enough of the benefits to join.	Other
The union isn't strong and does not seem to have much influence.	Other
I feel I can deal with my work situation on my own.	LN
Unions do not belong in institutions of higher education.	Neg Pro
We do not have one.	IA
No union.	IA
We don't have one.	IA
We don't have one that I know of.	IA

Appendix C

Selected Additional Resources

Garcha, Rajinder, and John C. Phillips. "US Academic Librarians: Their Involvement in Union Activities." *Library Review* 50, no. 3 (2001): 122-127.

Garcha and Phillips, from University of Toledo, Ohio, report on the levels of involvement by librarians who belong to local or national unions. The authors developed a survey intended to determine, among other things, how active librarians were in their respective unions. The ultimate goal was to see if participation in union activity "contribute[d] to an understanding of how union membership and involvement for librarians are related to a better understanding and appreciation of the teaching faculty and vice versa" (pp. 122-123). Other information was gleaned via the survey, including salary data, academic ranking, and perceptions of faculty governance and workload fairness.

Hovekamp, Tina Maragou. "Organizational Commitment of Professional Employees in Union and Nonunion Research Libraries." *College & Research Libraries* 55 (1994): 297-307.

Tina Hovekamp has written several articles on research libraries and unions based on a dissertation done at University of North Carolina at Chapel Hill. This particular article addresses the question of dual loyalty—i.e., does the presence of a union adversely affect the commitment employees feel toward their employer? What stands out most in the article is the inability to determine causality. Does a negative attitude toward an employer come about as the result of unionization, or does unionization come about as the result of a negative attitude toward an employer? Both of these possibilities seem valid; and even more likely, both could be possible concurrently. A deleterious workplace environment could be the impetus for forming and joining a union; and unless (or until) that union made improvements in that workplace environment, the employees would continue to have negative attitudes toward their employer.

Hovekamp, Tina Maragou. "Unionization and Job Satisfaction among Professional Library Employees in Academic Research Institutions." *College & Research Libraries* 56 (1995): 341-350.

In this 1995 article, Hovekamp looks at factors contributing to the relationship between job satisfaction and union membership. While some studies report an inverse relationship between union membership and job satisfaction, others report the opposite. In the final analysis, her own study showed evidence that there was a correlation between union presence and job satisfaction; and the correlation was a negative one. However, just as in the article from 1994, it was impossible to determine which was the cause and which was the effect; in fact, she states that "there is no clear evidence that such attitudes [of lower levels of satisfaction] are a product of union culture" (p. 348).

Milton, Suzanne. "Librarians: Key Players in Faculty Unions." *Alki* 21, no. 3 (2005): 5-7.

This short article published in *Alki*, the journal of the Washington Library Association, is a brief case study of unionization by faculty at Eastern Washington University (EWU). The article is upbeat and indicative of a point of view that unionizing at academic institutions is a positive thing and something to strive to accomplish. Emphasis is placed on the involvement of librarians and how that involvement has shaped the success of the faculty union.

Spang, Lothar. "Collective Bargaining and Faculty Status: A Twenty-Year Case Study of Wayne State University Librarians." *College & Research Libraries* 54 (1993): 241-253.

Lothar Spang accomplishes a remarkable feat by documenting in depth most of the history of unionization successes and failures of librarians at Wayne State University (WSU) in Detroit, Michigan. The failures are notable because, according to Spang's analysis of the historical situation, they were primarily the product of a dysfunctional workplace—a workplace in which the employees were their own worst enemies. This sentiment is succinctly expressed in one highlighted quote from the article:

> And by the 1984 negotiations, librarians had become so mired in the issues of criteria for faculty status that they failed to adequately represent their bargaining position to the AAUP negotiating team. (249).

Reading this and other sections from the article, one gets a sense that this group's inability to show a united front gives new meaning to the phrase "shooting oneself in the foot."

Collegial Self-Governance for Professional Librarians:
The Establishment and Evolution of a Library Council at Brock University

Tim Ribaric

Collegial Governance & the Library Council

Most, if not all universities and colleges in North America practice some form of collegial self-governance. This is often instantiated through the development of various committee structures that serve to govern the academic function of the institution. In the case of the lives of traditional faculty members, this can include a departmental committee governed by a departmental chair, a faculty committee governed by a dean, or a committee matched to an appropriate organizational unit chaired by an administrator. In cases of unionized work environments these structures are almost always codified in Collective Agreements and are the result of collective bargaining between the institution's faculty association and its administration. The basic concept behind collegial governance is that the fundamental functions of the academic institution are split into a bicameral division where the management function of the institution rests in the hands of the administration, while matters involving the academic function fall in the hands of the faculty. For considerations that overlap between the two domains, joint committees are struck. The tradition of bicameralism traces its origins to British universities in the late 19th century and expanded to North America. As pointed out by Andrew M. Boggs, "the principles of bicameralism and lay governance became the norm in university governance across North America."[1] In the US, in 1996, the American Association of University Professors (AAUP) issued a formal statement on the importance of the development of shared governance. While not directly addressing the role of librarians in university governance, AAUP's statement does stress the division of duties amongst the different branches of universities. In particular, the statement stipulates the duties of the Governing Board, one important task of which is to ensure "the publication of codified statements that define the overall policies and procedures of the institution under its jurisdiction."[2] Contrast this to the role of faculty in governance: "The faculty has primary responsibility for such fundamental areas as curriculum, subject matter and methods of instruction, research, faculty status, and those aspects of student life which relate to the educational process."[3] It is through cooperation and communication between these two main bodies that effective university governance is possible. Guiding documents written by the AAUP in collaboration with the American Association of College and Research Libraries (ACRL) paint a much different set of criteria for American academic librarians. These documents, originally endorsed in 1972 and revised in 2013, place a different emphasis on the role of librarians in the governance of colleges or universities. In the AAUP & ACRL *Joint Statement on Faculty Status of College and University Librarians* it is stressed that librarians play a pivotal role in the development of the institution's educational policy but that this can only be accomplished by being granted faculty status and participating in committee structures in the exact way as do faculty members. Once full parity with faculty is achieved, governance comes next:

> With respect to library governance, it is to be presumed that the governing board, the administrative officers, the library faculty, and representatives of the general faculty will share in the determination of library policies that affect the general interests of the institution and its educational program. In matters of internal governance, the library will operate like other academic units with respect to decisions relating to appointments, promotions, tenure, and conditions of service.[4]

It is unfortunate that no particular guidance is given to what this library governance would look like from the perspective of AAUP and the ACRL. This leaves an even more heterogeneous landscape amongst American academic libraries. In this American context it in entirely possible for an institution to have nothing referred to as a 'Library Council' but instead a Faculty Council for the library or some other similarly named committee.

In Canada, the parallel national organization advocating for shared governance is the Canadian Association of University Teachers (CAUT). It has published several discussion papers and policy statements on the topic of governance including *CAUT Policy on Governance: Where Have We Been and Where Should We Go: A Discussion Paper* (2004). CAUT's position is that "academic staff should play a decisive role in making education decisions and setting educational policy."[5] CAUT believes that "final authority for administrative and financial matters should be the responsibility of the Board of Governors" and that "educational decisions and setting of educational policy should be the responsibility of a senior academic body."[6] CAUT has also directly addressed the topic of collegial governance and librarians in its *Discussion Paper on Governance and Librarians,* approved by CAUT Council in 2000. The CAUT statement stresses that "librarians must also be able to participate fully in academic affairs and, to that end, must be eligible for membership on all governing bodies of the university."[7] The CAUT statement then adds additional carriage as compared to the AAUP statement in that it clearly states that librarian members should be included specifically in the bicameral decision-making process.

This process of collegial governance has been well exercised by faculty members but is less commonly exercised by professional librarians. In fact, the complicated interplay of the working conditions and faculty status of professional librarians vary from institution to institution, which directly impacts collegial governance. The role of professional librarians in the academy is influenced by many factors, such as relationship with the faculty, traditions of the institution, and inclusion in the faculty association/union, to name but a few, which serves to complicate the participation of librarians in governance activities.

However, similar to faculty there is a body that creates a collegial governance structure for the librarians at academic institutions—a 'Library Council,' not unlike the Faculty Councils that exists at many universities. In the most basic formulation the Library Council is a committee run by and comprised of the librarians (both administrative and non-administrative) of the institution.[8] Depending on the rules used to govern the Council, its charge is to provide high level direction, including planning and policy-making, and discussion of the affairs of the library. In some instantiations (in particular in the United States) it is also the parallel to the departmental/faculty committee. There is a wide spectrum of differences in how Library Councils conduct their affairs. An attempt to normalize the definition and structure of the Library Council is therefore important. In the Canadian context, this is seen in the policy statements that are written and endorsed by CAUT. CAUT maintains a series of policy statements, endorsed by their Council, that outline best practices for a number of topics. Of particular note is *Academic Status and Governance for Librarians at Canadian Universities and Colleges.* It stipulates in section 3.1: "As academic staff, librarians have both a right and a duty to participate in collegial governance of the academic institution"[9] and further in section 3.3:

> All librarians should be members of a library council. The library council should have the responsibility for the development of policies and procedures for the operation of the library. As with faculty councils, discussion at the library council should include any issue which has an impact on librarians, the library, or the academic institution as a whole. The library council should be empowered to make recommendations on such issues to the relevant body. The library council should be responsible in turn to the institution's senior academic body or its equivalent. The mandate and structure of the library council should be negotiated and defined in relevant Collective Agreements.[10]

CAUT also offers a more specific pronouncement within a policy document entitled, "Library Councils". Therein it is stressed that: "The Library Council shall be mandated as a planning and policy-making body, not merely as an information-sharing committee. Discussion at the council shall include any issue which has an impact on the librarians, the library, or the post-secondary educational institution as a whole."[11] The CAUT position paper also makes a series of recommendations concerning the operation of the ideal Library Council: it should be a policy-making body, the membership should include all librarians (both administrative and not) as peers, and the composition and function of the Library Council should become enshrined in the Collective Agreement. Further consideration should also be given to what status the University Librarian has in relation to the Library Council. Two main distinctions include having the University Librarian attend meetings as guest, or having the University Librarian attend as an *ex-officio* member of the committee. In the latter case, it is stressed that the University Librarian sits as a peer and, according to the CAUT statement, can either be a voting or non-voting member. It is also cautioned that the University Librarian not Chair the Library Council, as this would have the effect of stifling the collegial nature of the committee.

A Look at the Structure and Function of Library Councils

Little in the way of published material is available that studies the structure and function of Library Councils. Most literature is devoted to the evaluation of job satisfaction of librarians, including the analysis of faculty status and the ability to participate in committee work. An unpublished report about a survey conducted by Leona Jacobs of Canadian academic librarians in 2007 sheds light on the Canadian context. The author presents the results of a survey conducted through two email lists: the CAUT Librarian list, and the Canadian Association of College and University Libraries (CACUL). The data collected represent 28 responses from 25 Canadian academic libraries and attempts to explore characteristics of Library Councils in Canadian universities to examine their perceived effectiveness. While some of the data are inconclusive, a reliable conclusion that can be made is that most respondents did not perceive the Library Council to be an effective body. Reasons behind this were dependent on a few key factors: the relationship between the Council and the University Librarian, the railroading of meetings by members, and most tellingly the general notion that there was a lack of support for the validity of the body itself and the decisions being made.[12]

Case Study: the Library Council at Brock University

To understand how a Library Council functions in practice, it is worth looking at a well-established example of such a body. Enter Brock University and its Library Council, which has as its roots the certification of faculty members and librarians and the drafting of the first Collective Agreement. Right from the outset, librarians at Brock were involved in all activities relating to inclusion in the bargaining unit, defining terms of work, as well as negotiating the Collective Agreement. From the beginning, Brock's librarians were treated as colleagues and equal partners with faculty, which placed them in a position of strength. Instead of the librarians having to demonstrate their work as comparable to that of faculty, they were able to band together with faculty and demonstrate their value to the Administration during the process of negotiating a Collective Agreement. Furthermore, Brock's Library Council is enshrined in the Collective Agreement and in language that describes its function and structure in a manner that very closely adheres to the best practices outlined by the previously mentioned CAUT policy documents. The Brock University Library Council includes all librarians at the University as members; as well, the University Librarian is included on the Council as an *ex-officio* voting member. The Brock instantiation of Library Council does not have representation from any other staff group within or external to the Library. The CAUT policy documents are silent on whether there should be inclusion of any members external to the librarian complement of the institution as members of the Council. However, survey respondents found that inclusion of external members had the effect of "frustrating full and open discussion of the issues brought before the council."[13] Brock's Library Council, then, is intended to function as a policy-making body, at least *prima facie* although not always in practice.

Keeping these two considerations in mind—the strong historical connection of librarians at Brock to faculty members and the close correspondence of the Library Council to suggested guidelines from CAUT—the effectiveness and the impact of the Library Council has had on the working lives of librarians at Brock University will be examined.

The Formation of the Brock University Faculty Association

On November 26, 1996 faculty members at Brock University voted in favour of unionization. At this unionization vote alongside the group of faculty members stood Brock's professional librarians, who were also casting ballots. In fact, on that important day faculty members voted 64 percent in favour of unionization while the librarian contingent present voted 75 percent in favour.[14] This demonstrates that even from the very early days of the Brock University Faculty Association (BUFA), librarians had been actively involved in its activities. This spirit of inclusion was seen during the lead up to this certification vote. In literature produced by BUFA to build the case for certification three important points were repeated: "1. The administration must bargain; 2. Librarians can be defined as part of the bargaining unit; and 3. Members will have the protection of the law."[15]

Founded in 1964, the history of Brock University is relatively short when compared to other universities, the faculty association was created. While not a certified union at the time, BUFA strove to create a collegial atmosphere with Brock's Administration. This was accomplished through a variety of means but was explicitly stated with a document meant to articulate an agreement of working conditions. Entitled *An Agreement on the Terms and Conditions of Employment for Faculty between the Brock University Faculty Association and Brock University; 13 September 1990-30 June 1997*, the document was a 57 page handbook of suggested practices. It included processes for assessing workload, salary details, and promotion and tenure guidelines. The major problem with this agreement, at least from the perspective of librarians, was that it didn't stipulate any similar rights and responsibilities for librarians. In fact, the first article in the *Agreement* specified explicitly that its contents were meant for faculty members only.[16] The quasi-legal status of the document was also a significant impediment to its fair implementation. The administration was not legally bound to honour it.

Librarian Self-governance is Recognized at Brock University through the Establishment of the Library Council

In that Collective Agreement, there was an article, number 17, entitled, "Library Council." A mere half page in length, it laid out the prerequisites of what would become one of the few methods, obtained through collective bargaining, of collegial self-governance professional librarians at Brock University would have. It consisted of only four sections:

17.01 - There shall be a Library Council which shall establish its own rule of procedure, a copy of which shall be furnished to each member of the Council and to the Union.

17.02 - The Library Council shall be composed of:

   a) All professional Librarian members of the Bargaining Unit.
   b) The University Librarian and the Associate University Librarian(s) as ex officio members.

17.03 - The members of the Council will elect a chair and a secretary at the first meeting of Council in the fall term and the terms of those offices shall be for one (1) year.

17.04 - Library Council shall meet at least once in each Fall and Winter Term:

   a) to establish the Appointments and Promotion committee which shall consist of the Associate University Librarian and (3) professional librarians of the Council for staggered three (3) year terms . . .
   b) to consider any matters it deems relevant to the administration and policies of the Library.[17]

In a few words, section 17.04 enshrined two important mechanisms for the professional librarians of BUFA. It established an Appointments and Promotion Committee and secondly it explicitly stated that the Library Council would become the body where matters relating to the Administration of the library were to be discussed. While the rest of the Collective Agreement created stipulations on the difference between work responsibilities of faculty and librarians, it provided the first legally binding indication that faculty and librarian work is at least parallel in purpose. That is to say the Collective Agreement did not (at this point in time) mention the term 'Research/Scholarly Activity' or 'Sabbatical,' in reference to librarian members. Being officially allowed to conduct scholarly activity was negotiated into the Collective Agreement in 2006[18] as the culmination of discussions initiated through Library Council. Similarly, librarians were first able to enjoy 'sabbatical leaves' instead of 'professional leaves' after the negotiation of the 2011 Collective Agreement. Once again, this gain was a direct result of Library Council making efforts to increase the capacity of librarians at the University. Nevertheless, the 1997 Collective Agreement represented a very significant accomplishment for librarians at Brock University for many reasons but particularly owing to the establishment of a recognized Library Council. As such, the librarians at Brock University had explicitly created a mechanism for collegial self-governance that closely resembles suggested best practices outlined by CAUT. A further positive aspect of the composition of Library Council was that it was empowered to create its own rules of procedure to suit its own needs. Also of interest is that other sections of the Collective Agreement specifically called upon the Library Council to render verdicts in the adjudication of library matters. This is seen particularly in article 25, "Workload for Professional Librarian Members"[19] and will be examined later in this chapter. It should be noted that while composition and function of departmental/centre committees were specified, there were no provisions in the BUFA Collective Agreement for faculty councils which do not, and have never, existed at Brock. The inclusion of language for a Library Council can be perceived as recognition of the need for a specific structure for collegial governance in the library, which was understood in other parts of the University.

The Impact of Library Council on Librarians at Brock University

Many themes rise and ebb when investigating the trajectory of BUFA librarians as they interact on Library Council. One dominant theme that recurs without fail, however, is the open and constructive exercise of collective discussions of staffing which involve formulating job descriptions/positions that reflect the changing environments in which libraries and librarians find themselves. This comes hand-in-hand with another observed theme, that of collegial review. Year after year the conduct and activities of Library Council demonstrate a strict adherence to policy regarding 'special meetings' of Council to discuss colleagues being reviewed for permanence or promotion as well as the discussion of candidates who have been brought in to interview for vacancies. What can be inferred from the existence of these discussions is that every librarian on staff has had some form of input into the professional progression of all of their colleagues from the point they are hired by Brock Library. This supports what has been previously alluded to as one of the tenets of collegial governance. If the librarians are to be regarded as part of the faculty side of the bicameral governance structure, then they have the purview of being able to perform some form of assessment of their colleagues, without administrative interference, as faculty members do. The duty of Library Council to perform reviews of appointments appears to be a unique characteristic not seen in other instantiations of Council. In fact, comparing this function to results from the Jacobs survey, it would appear that Brock's Library Council is the only body that makes such determinations. There is a certain amount of gravitas with these recommendations as well. In the case of appointments, the procedures stipulate that the members of the Appointments and Promotion Committee conduct the interview process and with written feedback from the remaining non *ex-officio* members of Library Council make a final recommendation to the University Librarian. The University Librarian then takes the recommendation and either agrees to it or, if not, must specifically communicate back to the Appointments and Promotion Committee articulating concerns with the proposed appointment. If a resolution cannot be reached in this back-and-forth, the resolution must be determined through consultation with the Provost. Members of Library Council, then, have certain weight in the appointment process—one that echoes very strongly of the faculty model of appointments; that is to say, the bulk of the appointment is made upon the work of collegial determination. A similar situation occurs when a librarian member is applying for promotion. The Appointments and Promotion Committee, with input from the rest of the Library Council, makes a final recommendation to the University Librarian and a parallel process of accepting or denying the recommendation commences, as is seen with the appointment process.

The number of Library Council meetings held each year has been volatile. The waxing and waning of meeting frequency can be seen as both problematic and a sign of success. The more cynical would state that, outside of special meetings for appointment and promotion related issues, the Library Council has ceased to be an effective body where real decisions and procedures develop. Much of the business first seen as being within the jurisdiction of Library Council has moved slowly to *ad hoc* working groups struck to complete individual projects. These working groups have membership that extends beyond Library Council members and typically includes staff from all departments within the Library. Indeed if only factoring in the years when the 'Special Meeting' was an option, the distribution of special to regular meetings is over 50%. The more enthusiastic would say that Library Council is successful as demonstrated by its lack of need for frequent meetings. As the role of the professional librarian at Brock began to

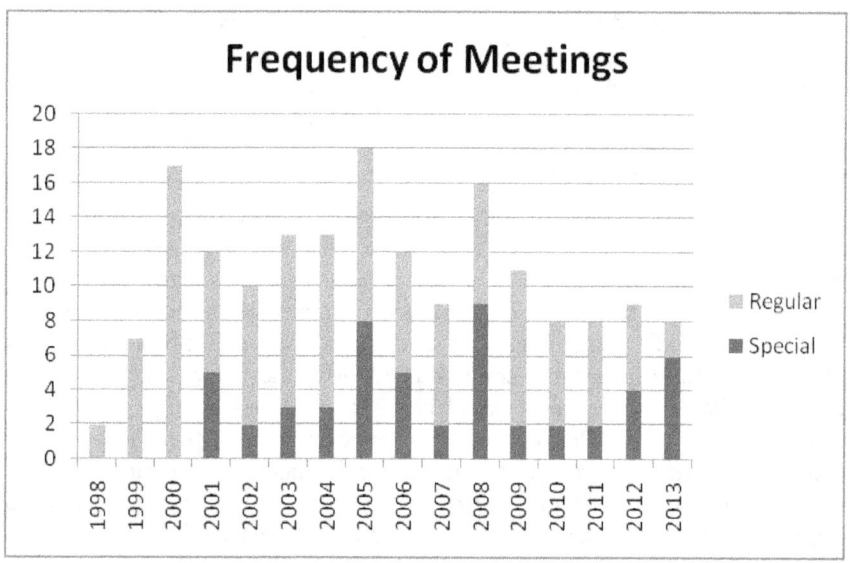

Figure 1 – Frequency of Library Council Meetings per year.

expand through subsequent Collective Agreements so too did the opportunity to participate in other University-wide planning committees outside of Library Council. It might be suggested that these other committees have been assigned mandates that have slowly eroded some of what initially had been Library Council business. Librarians serving on those committees would be contributing to the planning of library and university activities in different forums instead of through official Library Council business. For example, librarians had a nebulous presence on the University Senate in the early days. They could serve as staff representatives but definitely were not counted as members of the 'teaching faculty,' which Senate rules stipulate must be the bulk of the membership. Recently in 2013 Senate rules were changed to officially provision a seat for a librarian member. Here specifically an option is created for a librarian to be included on the most influential governance body within the institution. In a similar vein, the BUFA Executive Committee created the position of Professional Librarian Representative in 2009, thus allowing a librarian to always be a member of the BUFA Executive Committee. In a sense there has been a slow erosion of the governance function of Library Council that has been made up for by other opportunities across campus.

In early years, the lion's share of Library Council time was spent creating equitable procedures relating the logistical function and structure of Council proceedings to satisfy article 17.01, as seen above. This is understandable, of course, as formalizing collegiality requires some give-and-take between the Administration and librarians. However, once these rules of procedure became second nature,

Library Council could focus its attention on professional issues and the pursuit of parity with the faculty side of the house. As alluded to earlier, librarians were not officially enabled to conduct research and scholarly activity under the auspices of the Collective Agreement until 2006. This allowance for scholarly pursuit was very rigidly defined in what was referred to as a 'release day'.[20] In this scenario, a librarian would need to apply ahead of time to garner the permission to conduct other business not relating directly to professional practice. Library Council conducted several discussions on the efficacy of such a system and how difficult it was to articulate when the situation called for a 'release day'. Through the insistence of these discussions the 'release day' was removed from the Collective Agreement in the 2008 round of bargaining. This hard fought effort might be all for naught when compared to the larger picture. Studies have indicated that the presence of a Library Council or formal library planning group do not greatly contribute to perceived job satisfaction of the typical academic librarian. In the Brock environment, the consensus seems to be that Library Council is a necessary entity but could be one that could be more effective. Returning to this idea of assessing job satisfaction, there is evidence in both American[21] and Canadian[22] contexts to support this claim. In fact, both of these studies accumulated evidence that reveals that participation in library/university planning has only a mild positive correlation to perceived job satisfaction. One of the strongest measures of satisfaction amongst academic librarians surveyed in both studies is academic status and its impact on other responsibilities, i.e., working conditions and opportunities for professional participation.[23] In fact, the opportunity to participate in university/library planning is not a significant indicator of satisfaction amongst academic librarians. This is consistent with the experience of Library Council at Brock University. The bulk of business conducted by Library Council is not participation in library planning but that of collegial review. The largest portion of the activities of Library Council at Brock is devoted to considering applications for permanent placement, and assessing potential new hires. This supports the results found in the two previously mentioned studies. It is interesting to note that the frequency of meetings held by Library Council over the years is primarily influenced by hiring practices. In the anomalous years of 2005 and 2008, this is clearly seen. In 2005, there was a flurry of hiring activity that necessitated Library Council meetings. That year, two librarians and one Associate University Librarian were added to the staff complement. Similarly, in 2008, many meetings were necessary to determine the successful candidate for a newly created position, that of head of Liaison Services. No other single activity besides the discussion of potential candidates creates so many occasions for Library Council to meet.

Not so surprising as what is in the history of Library Council meetings is what is not. The answer to the obvious question of where some important decisions get made if not Library Council is difficult to articulate. The most concise answer is that these decisions are made directly by the administration in cases of high level considerations. For example, seen in the course of the history of Brock's Library Council is a more opaque treatment of the collection and acquisition budgets. In fact, no specific details or figures have been presented on this topic to the body of Library Council at any time, thus giving the impression that these matters are instead within the sole purview of the administration. This stands in contrast to CAUT's suggested guidelines for the function and structure of Library Councils, in particular, section 2.1: "While not limited to the following, Library Councils shall consider and vote on issues and policies affecting librarians and the library, including: . . . library budget proposals, prior to submission to senior administration."[24] Indeed, however, the actions of Library Council as instantiated at Brock University never had in its mandate any specific mention of dealing with the acquisitions budget as articulated in the previously described article 17 of the Collective Agreement.

That is not to say that the Library Council has never been able to participate in meaningful conversation on high level considerations such as planning. In fact, the current *Library – Strategic Plan*[25] on the Provost's website found its genesis in numerous meetings of the Library Council and drew much of its scope and detail from deliberations conducted by the Council.

As the years have progressed, the text of the Collective Agreement regarding the Library Council has changed but not in any substantive way. Through this text and through activities conducted during meetings of Library Council, librarians at Brock continue to exercise a form of collegial self-governance that has a strong emphasis on peer evaluation. Even if the Library Council at Brock fails to demonstrate a tradition of positively affecting general library policy, the gains it has achieved in the realm of collegial self-governance are notable in and of themselves.

Bibliography

American Association of University Professors (AAUP). "1966 Statement on Government of Colleges and Universities." *American Association of University Professors*. http://www.aaup.org/report/1966-statement-government-colleges-and-universities.

———. "Joint Statement on Faculty Status of College and University Librarians." *American Association of University Professors*. http://www.aaup.org/report/joint-statement-faculty-status-college-and-university-librarians.

Boggs, Andrew M. "Understanding the origins, evolution and state of play in UK university governance." *The New Collection* 5 (2010): 1 – 10.

Brock University. *An Agreement on the Terms and Conditions of Employment For Faculty between the Brock University Faculty Association and Brock University, 13 September 1990 - 30 June 1997*. St. Catharines: Brock University, 1990.

———. *Collective Agreement between Brock University and the Brock University Faculty Association, July 1, 1997 to June 30, 2000*. St. Catharines: Brock University, 1997.

———. *Collective Agreement between Brock University and the Brock University Faculty Association, July 1, 2000 to June 30, 2003*. St. Catharines: Brock University, 2000.

———. *Collective Agreement between Brock University and the Brock University Faculty Association, July 1, 2003 to June 30, 2006*. St. Catharines: Brock University, 2003.

———. *Collective Agreement between Brock University and the Brock University Faculty Association, July 1, 2006 to June 30, 2008*. St. Catharines: Brock University, 2006.

———. *Collective Agreement between Brock University and the Brock University Faculty Association, July 1, 2008 to June 30, 2011*. St. Catharines: Brock University, 2008.

———. *Collective Agreement between Brock University and the Brock University Faculty Association, July 1, 2011 to June 30, 2014*. St. Catharines: Brock University, 2011.

Brock University. "Library – Strategic Plan, 2012." http://www.brocku.ca/webfm_send/23579.

Brock University Faculty Association. *Why certify?* St. Catharines: Brock University, 1996.

Canadian Association of University Teachers (CAUT). "Academic Status and Governance for Librarians at Canadian Universities and Colleges." http://www.caut.ca/about-us/caut-policy/lists/general-caut-policies/policy-statement-on-academic-status-and-governance-for-librarians-at-canadian-universities-and-colleges, 2010.

———. "CAUT Librarians' Committee Discussion Paper on Governance and Librarians," 2000.

———. "CAUT Librarians' Committee Discussion Paper on Library Councils," 2007.

———. "Governance." http://www.caut.ca/about-us/caut-policy/lists/general-caut-policies/caut-policy-statement-on-governance, 2008.

———. "Library Councils." http://www.caut.ca/about-us/caut-policy/lists/general-caut-policies/policy-statement-on-library-councils, 2008.

Horenstein, Bonnie. "Job Satisfaction of Academic Librarians: An Examination of the Relationships between Satisfaction, Faculty Status and Participation." *College & Research Libraries* 54, no. 3 (1993): 255-269. http://crl.acrl.org/content/54/3/255.

Jacobs, Leona. "Library Councils in Canadian Academic Libraries: A summary of responses." 2008. https://www.uleth.ca/dspace/handle/10133/564.

Leckie, Gloria J., and Jim Brett. "Job Satisfaction of Canadian University Librarians: A National Survey." *College & Research Libraries* 58, no. 1 (1997): 31-47. http://crl.acrl.org/content/58/1/31.

Savage, Larry, Michelle Webber, and Jonah Butovsky. "Organizing the Ivory Tower: The Unionization of the Brock University Faulty Association." *Labor Studies Journal* 37, no. 3 (2012): 293-310. doi: 10.1177/0160449X12463077.

Notes

Introduction
Dekker & Kandiuk

1. CAUT, *Librarian Salary and Academic Status Survey, 2012 Part I: Salaries, Salary Scales and Academic Status, Dec. 2012* http://www.caut.ca/docs/default-source/librarians/2012-lsass---part-i-revised.pdf. This number includes colleges from British Columbia as represented by the Federation of Post-Secondary Educators of BC; from Alberta as represented by the Alberta Colleges Institutes Faculty Associations; and from Ontario as represented by the Ontario Public Services Employees Union.

2. United States Department of Labor, Bureau of Labor Statistics, *Union Members Summary 2013*, (Jan. 2014), 1, http://www.bls.gov/news.release/union2.nr0.htm.

3. Kathleen de la Peña McCook, "Unions in Public and Academic Libraries," Adopted from *Encyclopedia of Library and Information Sciences* (3rd ed. New York: Taylor and Francies, 2010), 2013 http://www.academia.edu/5665510/_Unions_in_Public_and_Academic_Libraries_.

4. Roma M. Harris, *Librarianship: the Erosion of a Woman's Profession* (Norwood, N.J.: Ablex, 1992): xiv – xiii.

5. HRSDC calculations based on Statistics Canada. *Table 282-0078 - Labour Force Survey Estimates (LFS), Employees by Union Coverage, North American Industry Classification System (NAICS), Sex and Age Group, Annual (Persons)*, CANSIM (database); United States Department of Labor, *Union Members*; Sarah Barriage, "Library Workers Will Not be Shushed: 2012 Union Review," *Progressive Librarian* 41 (2013): 86.

6. Association of Universities and Colleges of Canada, "Our Universities," http://www.aucc.ca/canadian-universities/our-universities/.

7. Bruce Barry, *Speechless: The Erosion of Free Expression in the American Workplace* (San Francisco: Berrett-Koehler, 2007): 64.

8. Henry Giroux, "Public Intellectuals Against the Neoliberal University," *Truthout* (Oct. 29, 2013) http://www.truth-out.org/opinion/item/19654-public-intellectuals-against-the-neoliberal-university.

9. With a contribution by Francesca Holyoke.

Chapter 1
Jacobs

1. The author wishes to acknowledge, with much appreciation, the assistance of Rosemary Howard, Judy Vogt, and Mark Sandilands for their support and assistance.

2. Canadian Association of College and University Libraries and Canadian Association of University Teachers, *Guidelines on Academic Status for University Librarians* (Ottawa, ON: Canadian Library Association, 1979), 1.

3. Although the phrase "academic librarians" typically refers to librarians working in both college and university settings, the use of the term in this chapter is in the context of universities only.

4. Joan Mount, "Faculty Status at Laurentian-Two Years Later," *Canadian Library Journal* 35, no. 6 (1978); Ashley Thomson, "Five Years Later: Faculty Status at Laurentian," *Canadian Library Journal* 38, no. 4 (1981).

5. For the purposes of this chapter, the word "tenure" is used to describe those employment contracts for academic staff that may only be terminated as a result of some demonstrated cause.

6. "Association of College and Research Libraries Joint Statement on Faculty Status of College and University Libraries," American Library Association, http://www.ala.org/acrl/standards/jointstatementfaculty.

7. Susan Kroll, ed., *Academic Status: Statements and Resources* (Chicago, IL: Association of College and Research Libraries, 1994), 9-10.

8. "ACRL History," American Library Association, http://www.ala.org/acrl/aboutacrl/history/history.

9. Hazel Bletcher, "On the Formation of a Canadian Library Association: Paper Given before the Alberta Library Association,"*Canadian Library Council Bulletin* 2, no. 2 (1945): 19.

10. Ibid.

11. Canadian Library Association, "Library Associations of Canada, 1900-1946," *Canadian Library Association Bulletin* 11, no. 6 (1955): 270-71; Elizabeth Hulse, *The Morton Years:The Canadian Library Association, 1946-1971* (Toronto, ON: Ex Libris Association, 1995), 2.

12. Commission of Inquiry, *Libraries in Canada: A Study of Library Conditions and Needs* (Chicago, IL: American Library Association, 1933), 3.

13. Ibid.

14. Ibid., 4.

15. Ibid.; Hulse, *The Morton Years*, 3.

16. Commission of Inquiry, *Libraries in Canada: A Study of Library Conditions and Needs*, 144.

17. Hulse, *The Morton Years*, 3.

18. Ibid., 4.

19. Ibid.

20. Ibid., 4-5; Canadian Library Association, "Library Associations of Canada, 1900-1946," 271-72; Kathleen Jenkins, "Review of the Association's Constitutional Structure, Traditions, Inter-Relations with Sections and Committees, with Critical Comment," *Canadian Library Association Bulletin* 7, no. 3 (1950): 91.

21. Hulse, *The Morton Years*, 9.

22. Ibid., 8.

23. Ibid., 9; Jenkins, "Review of the Association's Constitutional Structure," 91.

24. News-Herald (Vancouver), "The Canadian Library Council," *Canadian Library Council Bulletin* 1, no. 2 (1944): 17.

25. Hulse, *The Morton Years*, 9-10.

26. Canadian Library Association, "From Council to Association," *Canadian Library Association Bulletin* 3, no. 1 (1946): 17.

27. Canadian Library Association, "Committees: 1 September 1955 [to] 31 August 1960," *Canadian Library: the Bulletin of the Canadian Library Association - le Bulletin de l'Association canadienne des Bibliothèques* 17, no. 6 (1961): 344.

28. Canadian Library Association, "Annual Meeting: Reports of Meetings, Colleges and University Librarians," *Canadian Library Association Bulletin* 6, no. 2 (1949): 101.

29. Jenkins, "Review of the Association's Constitutional Structure," 92.

30. Canadian Library Association, "Committees: 1 September 1955 [to] 31 August 1960," 344.

31. Edna Hunt, "Why Join the Research Libraries Section of CLA?," *Canadian Library Association Bulletin* 16, no. 3 (1959).

32. Canadian Library Association, "Conference Reports: Summary Reports of Sections, Research Libraries," *Canadian Library* 17, no. 3 (1960): 145.

33. Douglas G. Lochhead, "The Research Libraries Section and the Canadian Library Inquiry," *Canadian Library: the Bulletin of the Canadian Library Association - le Bulletin de l'Association canadienne des Bibliothèques* 18, no. 6 (1962): 258.

34. Ibid.

35. "Elizabeth Morton (Executive Director, Canadian Library Association) to John Wilkinson (Chair, Colleges and Universities Committee, Canadian Library Association)," 18 June 1962, Canadian Library Association Papers, MG28 I197 v17, Library and Archives Canada.

36. "Minutes," 27 June 1962, Canadian Library Association, College and University Committee, Canadian Library Association Papers, MG28 I197 v2, Library and Archives Canada.

37. Ibid., 2.

38. Ibid., 3.

39. Canadian Library Association, "Annual Reports of Officials, Project, Sections, Committees for 1959-1960," *Feliciter* 5, no. 9 (Part 2) (1960): 19; Canadian Library Association, "Committees: 1 September 1955 [to] 31 August 1960," 344-45.

40. "ACRL History," http://www.ala.org/acrl/aboutacrl/history/history.

41. Arthur M. McAnally, "Status of the University Librarian in the Academic Community," in *Faculty Status for Academic Librarians: A History and Policy Statements* (Chicago: American Library Association, 1975), 10; C. James Schmidt, Introduction to *Faculty Status for Academic Librarians: A History and Policy Statements* (Chicago, IL: American Library Association, 1975), v; Association of College and Research Libraries, University Libraries Section, Committee on Academic Status, "Status of College and University Librarians," *College & Research Libraries* 20, no. 5 (1959): 399.

42. "Elizabeth Morton (Executive Director, Canadian Library Association) to John Wilkinson (Chair, Colleges and Universities Committee, Canadian Library Association)," 14 July 1962, Canadian Library Association Papers, MG28 I197 17, Library and Archives Canada.

43. Canadian Library Association, "The CLA-ACB Committees 1960-1967: College and University Libraries Committee," *Canadian Library: the Bulletin of the Canadian Library Association - le Bulletin de l'Association canadienne des Bibliothèques* 24, no. 6 (1968): 595; Elizabeth Morton, "Winnipeg Conference," *Canadian Library: the Bul-*

letin of the Canadian Library Association - le Bulletin de l'Association canadienne des Bibliothèques 20, no. 2 (1963).

44. Canadian Library Association, "Library Standards for Salaries," *Canadian Library Association Bulletin* 3, no. 1 (1946): 19.

45. "Report of the Salary Committee, 1946-1947," n.d., Canadian Library Association Papers, MG28 I197 v61, Library and Archives Canada.

46. Canadian Library Association, Committee on Salaries, "Report of the Committee on Salaries, 1947-1948," *Canadian Library Association Bulletin* 5, no. 1 (1948): 47-48.

47. Canadian Library Association, Salaries Committee, "Annual General Meeting of the Corporation: Committee Proceedings, Salaries Committee," *Canadian Library Association Bulletin* 9, no. 2 (1952): 50-51.

48. Canadian Library Association, Salaries and Personnel Committee, "Annual General Meeting: Summary Reports of Committees, Salaries and Personnel Committee," *Canadian Library Association Bulletin* 10, no. 7 (1954): xvi-xvii.

49. Canadian Library Association, "Association Activities," *Canadian Library Association Bulletin* 11, no. 6 (1955): 277.

50. Canadian Library Association, Committee on University Libraries Salaries and Personnel, "CLA-ABC Committee on University Libraries Salaries and Personnel: Summary of Replies to Questionnaires, 1955 and 1956," *Canadian Library Association Bulletin* 12, no. 6 (1956).

51. Canadian Library Association, Committee on University Salaries and Personnel, "Salaries and Personnel (University Libraries)," *Feliciter* 1, no. 3 (1956): 30.

52. Ibid., 32.

53. Ibid.

54. Ibid.

55. Ibid., 33.

56. Canadian Library Association, Standards and Salaries Committee (University Libraries), "Report of the Standards and Salaries Committee (University Libraries)," *Feliciter* 3, no. 11-12 (1958): 1.

57. Ibid.

58. Ibid., 1-2.

59. Canadian Library Association, "Annual General Meeting, 1958: Standards and Salaries," *Canadian Library Association Bulletin* 15, no. 2 (1958): 68.

60. Canadian Library Association, Standards and Salaries Committee (University and College Libraries), "Sub-Committee on Standards and Salaries (University and College Libraries)," *Feliciter* 4, no. 10 (1959): 58.

61. Canadian Library Association, "Report of the Standards and Salaries Committee (University Libraries)," 2.

62. Canadian Library Association, "Sub-Committee on Standards and Salaries (University and College Libraries)," 57.

63. Ibid.

64. Canadian Library Association, "Report of the Standards and Salaries Committee (University Libraries)," 2.

65. Ibid.

66. Canadian Association of College and University Libraries, Salary Survey Committee, "Report of the CACUL Salary Survey Committee," *CACUL Newsletter* no. 2 (1964): 9.

67. Dominion Bureau of Statistics, "DBS Daily Bulletin: Thursday, December 3, 1964," *CACUL Newsletter* no. 3 (1964): [6].

68. Canadian Association of College and University Libraries, "Annual Meeting and Workshop, Halifax: Report from the Secretary [9 June 1964]," *CACUL Newsletter* no. 3 (1964): 14.

69. D. C. Appelt, "From the President of CACUL: Executive Meeting [25 October 1966]," *CACUL Newsletter*, no. 7-8 (1967): 14.

70. Canadian Association of College and University Libraries, Salary and Budget Survey Committee, "Salary and Budget Survey," *CACUL Newsletter* no. 7-8 (1967).

71. Les Fowlie, "The National Conference of Canadian Universities and Colleges and the Canadian Universities Foundation," *Canadian Library* 19, no. 5 (1963): 351. The CUF was an executive arm of the NCCUC.

72. Robert Blackburn, "Report of the President," *CACUL Newsletter* no. 1 (1963): 3.

73. Appelt, "From the President of CACUL: Executive Meeting [25 October 1966]," 13.

74. For example, see: Canadian Association of College and University Libraries, "General Meeting [Minutes, 26 June 1963]," *CACUL Newsletter* no. 2 (1964); F. Dolores Donnelly, "The National Library in the Library Community: Current Developments and Trends," *Archivaria* 15 (1982-1983); Doris E. Lewis, "CACUL as of October 1964: Excerpts from CACUL President's Report to the Fall Meeting of the Canadian Library Association," *CACUL Newsletter* no. 3 (1964); Doris E. Lewis, "Report of the President," *CACUL Newsletter* no. 4 (1965); Gurdial S. Pannu, "The Downs' Survey: A Summary and a Review," *Canadian Library* 24, no. 6 (1968).

75. Pannu, "The Downs' Survey," 640.

76. Robert B. Downs, "Resources of Canadian Academic and Research Libraries: Summary of Recommendations," *CACUL Newsletter* no. 10 (1968): 43.

77. Canadian Association of College and University Libraries, Position Classification & Salary Scales, "A Draft Report on Position Classifications and Salary Scales in Canadian Academic Libraries," (Calgary, Alberta: CACUL, 1966), 2.

78. Ibid., 4.

79. Ibid., 15-16.

80. Canadian Association of College and University Libraries, *Position Classification and Principles of Academic Status in Canadian University Libraries* (Ottawa, ON: Canadian Library Association, 1969).

81. Canadian Association of College and University Libraries, "Annual General Meeting [Minutes, 10 June 1969]," *CACUL Newsletter* 2, no. 4 (1970): 401.

82. Canadian Association of College and University Libraries, "Committee on Academic Status: Terms of Reference," *CACUL Newsletter* no. 9 (1967): 30.

83. Canadian Association of College and University Libraries, "Annual Meeting 1967 [Minutes, 17 June 1967]," *CACUL Newsletter*, no. 9 (1967): 20.

84. Canadian Association of College and University Libraries, Committee on Academic Status, "CACUL Committee on Academic Status: Report, June, 1968," CACUL Newsletter, no. 10 (1968): 10-11.

85. Ibid., 12-14.

86. Ibid., 15.

87. CACUL Committee on Academic Status, "Principles of Academic Status in Canadian University Libraries: Draft Report [24 June 1968]," *CACUL Newsletter* 2, no. 1 (1969): 12-13.

88. Canadian Association of College and University Libraries, "CACUL Committee on Academic Status: Report, June, 1968," 10.

89. Ibid., 10-11.

90. CACUL Committee on Academic Status, "Principles of Academic Status in Canadian University Libraries: Draft Report [24 June 1968]," *CACUL Newsletter* 2, no. 1 (1969): 12-13.

91. CACUL Committee on Academic Status, "Principles of Academic Status in Canadian University Libraries: Revised Draft May 1969," *CACUL Newsletter* 2, no. 2 (1969): 93-94.

92. Canadian Association of College and University Libraries, "Annual General Meeting [Minutes, 10 June 1969]," *CACUL Newsletter* 2, no. 4 (1970): 401-02.

93. Canadian Association of College and University Libraries, *Position Classification and Principles of Academic Status*, 23.

94. Ibid.

95. Canadian Association of College and University Libraries, "Annual General Meeting [Minutes, 10 June 1969]," 402.

96. I. F. Bell, "President's Mid-Year Report," *CACUL Newsletter* 2, no. 5 (1970): 458.

97. Canadian Association of College and University Libraries, "Minutes of the CACUL Annual General Meeting at Hamilton, Ontario [24 June 1970]," *CACUL Newsletter* 2, no. 6 (1971): 590.

98. Donald Redmond, "Annual Report of the President to CACUL-ACBCU for 1969-1970," *CACUL Newsletter* 2, no. 6 (1971): 594.

99. Canadian Association of College and University Libraries, Committee on Academic Status, "Committee on Academic Status Report," *CACUL Newsletter* 2, no. 6 (1971): 609.

100. Ibid.

101. Ibid., 617.

102. Canadian Association of College and University Libraries, "CACUL Annual Meeting [Draft Minutes, 1971]," *CACUL Newsletter* 3, no. 1 (1971): 14.

103. Calvin D. Evans, "Librarians and CAUT: Historical Overview and Future Directions," *CAUT Bulletin* 24, no. 5 (1976): 12.

104. Donald C. Savage, "*A Historical Overview of Academic Status for Librarians*," Canadian Library Journal 39, no. 5 (1982): 287. The title for this document also underwent revision with the final version approved being *Guidelines on Academic Status for University Librarians*.

105. Evans, "Librarians and CAUT," 12.

106. Donald C. Savage, "73-74 Reports: Report from the Executive Secretary," *CAUT Bulletin* 22, no. 6 (1974): 25-26.

107. Craig Heron, *The Canadian Labour Movement: A Short History*, 3rd ed. (Toronto, ON: James Lorimer & Company Ltd., Publishers, 2012), 94-98.

108. Ibid.

109. *Post-Secondary Learning Act, RSA 2003, c. P-19.5 s. 90*. A current example of this situation is the author's home province of Alberta, Canada where academic staff are excluded from the *Employment Standards Code* and the *Labour Relations Code*, as noted in Section 90 of the Province's *Post-Secondary Learning Act*.

110. Savage, "73-74 Reports: Report from the Executive Secretary," 25.

111. Julie Schroeder, "The Bargaining Unit for the Academic Librarian," *Canadian Library Journal* 32, no. 6 (1975): 463.

112. Ibid., 464.

113. Ibid.

114. Savage, "A Historical Overview," 287.

115. Don White, "Academic Status: Right or Rite?," *Canadian Library Journal* 26, no. 4 (1969): 289.

116. Elizabeth Ward, "Libraries and Unions: The Saint Mary's University Experience," *Canadian Library Journal* 31, no. 3 (1974): 240.

117. Elizabeth Ward, "The Community of Interest and Academic Status," *Canadian Library Journal* 31, no. 6 (1974): 543.

118. Ruth Hafter, "Academic Status - the Wrong Name, the Wrong Game," *APLA Bulletin* 39, no. 1 (1975): 9.

119. Ibid.

120. Savage, "A Historical Overview," 288.

121. Canadian Association of College and University Libraries, *Position Classification and Principles of Academic Status*, 23.

122. John Wilkinson, "Letters: Faculty Status," *Canadian Library Journal* 36, no. 1-2 (1979): 52.

123. Savage, "A Historical Overview," 290.

124. Ibid.

125. Mount, "Faculty Status at Laurentian," 428.

126. David Fox, "Finding Time for Scholarship: A Survey of Canadian Research University Librarians," *portal: Libraries & the Academy* 7, no. 4 (2007): 452.

127. Ibid., 457.

128. Mount, "Faculty Status at Laurentian," 78.

129. Savage, "A Historical Overview," 290.

130. Ibid.

131. Thomson, "Five Years Later," 222.

132. Ibid.

133. David Fox, "The Scholarship of Canadian Research Librarians," *Partnership: The Canadian Journal of Library & Information Practice & Research* 2, no. 2 (2007): 9-10.

134. Steven Horn, "The Professional Ladder," *Canadian Library Journal* 27, no. 3 (1970): 200-02.

135. Canadian Association of College and University Libraries and Canadian Association of University Teachers, *Guidelines on Academic Status for University Librarians*, [8].

136. Margaret Beckman, "Library Governance," *CAUT Bulletin* 24, no. 5 (1976): 22.

137. Donald C. Savage, "Letters: Library Governance," *CAUT Bulletin* 25, no. 1 (1976): 14.

138. Savage, "A Historical Overview," 290.

139. Leona M. Jacobs, "Library Councils in Canadian Academic Libraries: A Summary of Responses" (unpublished report, University of Lethbridge, 2008), http://www.uleth.ca/dspace/handle/10133/564.

140. William Watson, "Professional Status and Professional Responsibilties," *CACUL Newsletter* 2, no. 4 (1970): 417.

141. Ibid.

142. Savage, "A Historical Overview," 287.

143. Canadian Association of College and University Libraries and Canadian Association of University Teachers, *Guidelines on Academic Status for University Librarians*.

144. Canadian Association of University Teachers, "Librarian Salary Survey and Academic Status Survey. Part 1: Salaries, Salary Scales and Academic Status," (Ottawa, ON: Canadian Association of University Teachers, 2012).

145. Savage, "A Historical Overview," 288.

146. Canadian Association of University Teachers, "Librarian Salary Survey and Academic Status Survey."

Chapter 2
Dekker

1. Toni Samek, "Library Workplace Speech, a Modern Irony! The Push for Library Workplace Speech," Concerned Librarians of British Columbia, http://concernedlibrarians.blogspot.ca/2009/02/library-workplace-speech.html; Andrew Lockhart, "The Canadian Library Association's Failure to Advocate for Librarians and Libraries," Progressive Librarians Guild London Chapter, http://plglondon.wordpress.com/2012/01/27/the-canadian-library-associations-failure-to-advocate-for-librarians-and-libraries/; Lisa Sloniowski, "Who Speaks for Libraries and Librarians (1/2)," Progressive Librarians Guild Toronto Area Chapter, http://plggta.org/archives/113; Jennifer Dekker, "Who Speaks for Libraries and Librarians (2/2)," Progressive Librarians Guild Toronto Area Chapter, http://plggta.org/archives/154.

2. CAUT (Canadian Association of University Teachers), "CAUT Withdraws Consideration of Censure of McGill University," Canadian Association of University Teachers, http://www.caut.ca/issues-and-campaigns/librarians-and-libraries/2012/11/26/

caut-withdraws-consideration-of-censure-of-mcgill-university; Penny Stewart, "Academic Librarians are Under Attack," *CAUT Bulletin* 56, no. 10 (2009), May 23. http://www.cautbulletin.ca/en_article.asp?articleid=2958.

3. CAUT, "Canada's Past Matters," CAUT, http://www.canadaspastmatters.ca/.

4. Lockhart, *Canadian Library Association's Failure.*

5. Robin Sutton Harris, *A History of Higher Education in Canada, 1663-1960.* (Toronto: University of Toronto Press, c1976).

6. Paul Douglas Axelrod, *Scholars and Dollars : Politics, Economics and the Universities of Ontario, 1945-1980.* (Toronto: University of Toronto Press, 1982).

7. Neil Tudiver, *Universities for Sale: Resisting Corporate Control Over Canadian Higher Education.* (Toronto: J. Lorimer; Canadian Association of University Teachers, c1999).

8. Philip A. Massolin, "Modernization and Reaction: Postwar Evolutions and the Critique of Higher Learning in English." *Journal of Canadian Studies* 36, no. 2 (Summer 2001), 130-163.

9. David M. Cameron, "The Challenge of Change: Canadian Universities in the 21st Century," *Canadian Public Administration/Administration Publique du Canada* 45, no. 2 (2002), 145-174.

10. Harris, *History of Higher Education.*

11. Axelrod, *Scholars and Dollars,* 77-99, 141-178.

12. Ibid., 77-99.

13. Association of Universities and Colleges of Canada, Robert Oliver Berdahl, Canadian Association of University Teachers, James Duff, *University Government in Canada: Report of a Commission Sponsored by the Canadian Association of University Teachers and the Association of Universities and Colleges of Canada* (Toronto: University of Toronto Press, 1966), 5.

14. Ibid., 8-10.

15. Harry Crowe Foundation, "Harry Sherman Crowe (1922-1981)," https://www.crowefoundation.ca/about/harry-crowe.asp; Michiel Horn, *Academic Freedom in Canada: A History* (Toronto: University of Toronto Press, 1999).

16. Massolin, *Modernization,* 137.

17. James Turk, "History of CAUT," Canadian Association of University Teachers, http://www.caut.ca/pages.asp?page=1021.

18. American Association of University Professors, "History of the AAUP," http://www.aaup.org/about/history-aaup.

19. University and College Union, "About UCU: Our History," http://www.ucu.org.uk/index.cfm?articleid=2176.

20. See: James Gibson Murray, "Power and Politics in Academe: Faculty Unionism in Ontario," (Educat.D, University of Toronto, 1985); Gérard Bélanger, "La Syndicalisation des Professeurs d'Université," *Relations Industrielles/Industrial Relations* 29, no. 4 (October, 1974), 857-864; Joseph H. Chung, "Le Syndicalisme des Professeurs d'Université—Quelques Réflexions," *Relations Industrielles/Industrial Relations* 28, no. 2 (April, 1973), 325-342; John William Knox, "Trade Unionism in Canadian Universities: An Empirical Study of Unionised and Nonunionised Academic Staff at Canadian Universities" (Ph.D. University of Bradford (UK), 1987); Roland Penner, "Faculty Collective Bargaining in Canada: Background, Development and Impact," *Interchange* 9, no. 3 (1978), 71-86; Mark Thompson, "The Development of Collective Bargaining in Canadian Universities," *Proceedings of the 28th Annual Meeting of the Industrial Relations Research Association, December 1975*, (Vancouver: University of British Columbia Institute of Industrial Relations, 1975); B.L. Adell and D.D. Carter, "Collective Bargaining for University Faculty in Canada," (Kingston: The Industrial Relations Centre, Queen's University, 1972).

21. See: Jack Riley, "Collective Bargaining in Illinois State Universities: A Study of Faculty Attitudes" University of Illinois at Urbana-Champaign, 1976); John C. Smart, "Professors and Unions: A Study of Collective Bargaining in the Academic Profession. Presented at the Annual Meeting of the American Educational Research Association." (San Francisco, American Educational Research Association, April 23, 1976); Everett Carll Ladd and Seymour Martin Lipset, *The Divided Academy: Professors and Politics* (New York: McGraw-Hill, 1975); Frank R. Kemerer and J. Victor Baldridge, *Unions on Campus*, 1st ed. (San Francisco: Jossey-Bass, 1975); James Walter Driscoll, "Determinants of Faculty Attitudes Towards Collective Bargaining for the Faculty at Cornell: Participation and Trust in the Decision-Making Process" (PhD, Cornell University, 1975); G. Gregory Lozier, Kenneth P. Mortimer and Pennsylvania State University, *Anatomy of a Collective Bargaining Election in Pennsylvania's State-Owned Colleges* (University Park, Pa: Center for the Study of Higher Education, Pennsylvania State University, [1974]); E.D. Duryea and Robert S. Fisk, *Faculty Unions and Collective Bargaining* (San Francisco: Jossey-Bass, 1973); Joseph W. Garbarino, "Faculty Unionism: From Theory to Practice," *Industrial Relations: A Journal of Economy and Society* 11, no. 1 (1972), 1-17.

22. Tudiver, *Universities for Sale*, 84.

23. Gordon Arnold, "The Emergence of Faculty Unions at Flagship Public Universities in Southern New England," *Labor Studies Journal* 22, no. 4 (Winter 1998), 62-87.

24. Tudiver, *Universities for Sale*, 84-85.

25. "Salary Scale Recommended for College and University Libraries in Canada." *Feliciter* 2 (11, 1956), 23.

26. Sub-Committee on Standards and Salaries (University and College Libraries), CLA, "Report on the Standards and Salaries Committee (University Libraries)," *Feliciter* 2, no. 10 (June-July 1957), 57.

27. University and College Libraries. Sub-Committee on Standards and Salaries. "Salaries of Librarians in Academic Institutions,"*Feliciter* 4 (June 1959), 57-59.

28. Edith Adamson, Chief, Adult Education Section, Education Division, Dominion Bureau of Statistics to Mrs. E. Southwell, CAUT. 4 October 1961. M G28 I 208 vol. 64 Library and Archives Canada; Elizabeth Hulse, *The Morton Years: The Canadian Library Association, 1946-1971* (Toronto: Ex Libris Association, 1995), 37-42.

29. J.P. Zweig, "CAUT Survey of Salaries in Canadian Universities, 1959-1961." M G28 I 208, Vol. 64, Library and Archives Canada.

30. Gwendolyn Marie Stiggins Cruzat, "Collective Bargaining in Academic Librarianship" (PhD, Wayne State University, 1976), 104.

31. Zweig, "CAUT Survey of Salaries in Canadian Universities, 1959-1961." M G28 I 208, vol. 64, Library and Archives Canada.

32. Ibid., 9.

33. Hulse, *Morton Years*, [1].

34. Marion C. Wilson, "Reminiscences, 1994" quoted in Hulse, *Morton Years*, 49.

35. J.H. Stewart Reid to Margaret Evans, 3 May 1961. M G28 I 208, vol. 64, Library and Archives Canada.

36. Robert Bingham Downs et al., *Resources of Canadian Academic and Research Libraries* (Ottawa: Association of Universities and Colleges of Canada, 1967), 5, 9.

37. CACUL (Canadian Association of College and University Libraries) and Commission on the Cost of Higher Education, *Forecast of the Cost of Academic Library Services in Canada, 1965-1975; a Brief to the Bladen Commission on the Cost of Higher Education* (Waterloo, Ont: University Press, 1964).

38. Downs et. al., *Resources of Canadian Academic and Research Libraries*, 9-11.

39. Ibid., 125.

40. Ibid.

41. Hulse, *Morton Years*, 39.

42. Robert Bingham Downs, ed., *The Status of American College and University Librarians* (Chicago: American Library Association, 1958), 25.

43. Ibid., 26.

44. Author translation.

45. "L'Étude sur les Membres qui Constituent l'Association Locale des Professeurs—1969-1970." MG 28 I 208, vol. 137, Library and Archives Canada.

46. Greg Linnell, "The Institute of Professional Librarians of Ontario: On the History and Historiography of a Professional Association." *The Canadian Journal of Information and Library Science/La Revue Canadienne des Sciences de l'Information et de Bibliothéconomie* 30, no. 3/4 (2008): 175-199; Hulse, *Morton Years*, 45.

47. "The Birth of COWCUL." *Feliciter* 14, no. Dec./Jan./Feb. (1968): 25.

48. "L'Étude sur les Membres qui Constituent l'Association Locale des Professeurs—1969-1970."

49. Please note that the data presented here are uncorrected and have been transcribed exactly as they appeared in the original record.

50. "L'Étude sur les Membres qui Constituent l'Association Locale des Professeurs—1969-1970."

51. "L'Étude sur les Membres qui Constituent l'Association Locale des Professeurs—1969-1970"; Mario F. Bognanno and Edward L. Suntrup, "Occupational Inclusions in Faculty Bargaining Units," *Industrial Relations* 14, no. 3 (October, 1975): 358-363.

52. Lewis Capers Branscomb, ed., *Case for Faculty Status for Academic Librarians,* (Chicago: A.L.A, 1970); Robert Bingham Downs, "Status of Academic Librarians in Retrospect," *College & Research Libraries* 29 (July, 1968): 253-258; Bruce Thomas, "Status, and all That," *Library Journal* 89 (June, 1966): 2275-2280; John Marshall, "Search for Status," *Library Journal* 91 (November, 1966): 5556-5563; Robert Bingham Downs, "The Current Status of University Library Staffs," in *The Status of American College and University Librarians*, ed. Robert Bingham Downs (Chicago: American Library Association, 1958) 13-27; Robert Hans Muller, "Faculty Rank for Library Staff Members in Medium-Sized Universities and Colleges," *Bulletin of the American Association of University Professors* 39 (September, 1953): 421-431.

53. Edward Monahan to M.O. Morgan, 25 June 1970. MG 28 I 208 vol. 137, Library and Archives Canada.

54. "Terms and Conditions of Employment for Librarians: Survey." (1974). M G28 I208, vol. 274, Library and Archives Canada.

55. Willard Allen to Donald Savage, 7 May 1975. M G28 I208, vol. 274, Library and Archives Canada.

56. CAUT, "Guidelines on Academic Status for University Librarians." (1976) M G28. I 208, vol. 366, Library and Archives Canada.

57. Donald C. Savage, "Memorandum from Donald Savage to Local and Provincial Associations, Feb. 27, 1976." M G28 I208, vol. 274, Library and Archives Canada.

58. Ibid., 2.

59. Ibid. This item is the first and only that clearly points to contemporary divisions between rank and file academic librarians and senior library administrators. In earlier documents, such as the Membership Survey, Chief Librarians were considered col-

leagues of rank and file librarians, though clearly Chief Librarians had higher status in the university since, in several cases, they were the only librarians who were also faculty association members (See note 54). Given the time period, this is unsurprising, as a wave of collective bargaining was beginning to sweep Canadian universities, and decisions regarding who was included or excluded in bargaining units might have polarized librarians.

60. Robert P. Haro, "Collective Action and Professional Negotiation: Factors and Trends in Academic Libraries," *ALA Bulletin* July-August (1969): 995.

61. Tom Eadie, "Remembrances of Things Past," in *Critical Issues in Library Management: Organizing for Leadership and Decision-Making: Papers from the Thirty-Fifth Allerton Institute*, Eds. Bryce L. Allen and Terry L. Weech (Urbana-Champaign, Ill.: Graduate School of Library and Information Science, University of Illinois at Urbana-Champaign, 1995), 76.

62. "Minutes of CAUT Committee on Professional Librarians Meeting, August 20." (1976) M G28 I208, vol. 274, Library and Archives Canada.

63. Ron D. Lowe to Tom Eadie, 23 January 1978. M G28 I208, vol. 274, Library and Archives Canada.

64. Systems and Procedures Exchange Center and Academic Collective Bargaining Information Service, *SPEC Kit on Collective Bargaining* (Washington, D.C.: Systems and Procedures Exchange Center, 1974).

65. ARL (Association of Research Libraries), "Review of Collective Bargaining Activities in Academic and Research Libraries," *ARL Management Supplement* 1, no. 3 (1973).

66. University of Toronto and UTFA, "Memo of Agreement between the Governing Council of the University of Toronto and the UTFA (1976)."

67. "U of T Faculty, Librarians Vote. Librarians at the University are Eligible for Membership in the Faculty Association." *Feliciter* 23, no. 1 (1977).

68. "Equal Pay for Work of Equal Value." *Athenaeum* 40, no. 20 (1978).

69. Donald C. Savage, "A Historical Overview of Academic Status for Librarians," *Canadian Library Journal* October (1982), 287-291.

70. Ibid., 287.

71. Ibid.

72. MUFA Librarians, "Statement of the MUFA Librarians regarding the Firing of Donna Millard and Barbara McDonald April 27, 2009," http://www.mcmaster.ca/mufa/LibrarianDismissal2009.pdf; Susan K. Roll, "Library & Librarian Crisis at St. Paul University," http://apuobibliolib.wordpress.com/2013/05/25/library-librarian-crisis-at-st-paul-university/.

Chapter 3
Attridge Bufton

1. This article is based on research conducted for the author's Master of Arts in history. The author would like to thank Ian Bufton, Sean Bufton, Christina Turnbull, Dominique Marshall, Frances Montgomery, Pamela Walker and John Walsh for their invaluable comments and contributions to earlier versions of this chapter. In addition, it would have been impossible to tell this story without the oral histories of Andrew Brook, Susan Jackson, Frances Montgomery, Valerie Swinton and Jill Vickers as well as the documents contained in personal files provided by Susan Jackson and Frances Montgomery.

2. Charlotte R. Mudge, "Collective Bargaining of Librarians in Canada: Issues and Concerns," *Argus* 11, no. 3/4 (1982), 94.

3. Susan Jackson, retired librarian, Carleton University, in oral history interview with the author, April 2011.

4. Valerie Swinton, retired librarian, Carleton University, in oral history interview with the author, May 30, 2011. Although Swinton's last name was McDougall at the time of unionization, her current last name will be used for this analysis except in the reference list, where all documents authored by her in the 1970s will be cited using Valerie McDougall. Her attitudes are consistent with those noted by Carl Garry in the overview of the opinions of Canadian professional librarians on unionization in his chapter, "The Unionization of the Profession," in *Canadian Libraries and Their Changing Environment*, eds. Lorraine Spencer Garry and Carl Garry (Toronto: York University, Centre for Continuing Education, 1977), 499–501. Garry notes that librarians had "an anathema for unionization which was regarded as working class".

5. CUPE: Canadian Union of Public Employees.

6. CUASA: Carleton University Academic Staff Association.

7. PIPSC: Professional Institute of the Public Service of Canada.

8. Jackson, oral history.

9. W.E. Beckel to Hilda G. Gifford, November 7, 1982, ACC 1996—97, PINFO-28, Fall Convocation, Hilda Gifford File, Carleton University Library Archives, Ottawa, Ontario, 1.

10. Hilda Gifford, "Function and the Library Building," *Royal Architectural Institute of Canada Journal* 36, no. 4 (1959): 104.

11. Ibid.

12. C.C. Gibson, Secretary to the Board of Governors, Minutes of the Thirty-Eighth Meeting of the Board of Governors of the Ottawa Association for the Advancement of Learning, Carleton College, June 2, 1958, 2, http://www6.carleton.ca/records/ccms/wp-content/ccms-files/OAAL-INC-Carleton-College-BOG-Minutes-1948-06-0238S.pdf. Hilda Gifford's starting salary was $2,800.

13. Kathryn Hubbard, e-mail message to author, April 25, 2012. Regarding the sex of chief librarians in Canadian academic libraries, see *Survey of Libraries in Canada* (1936 to 1948), produced by the Dominion Bureau of Statistics for the Minister of Trade and Commerce. See also *Library Work as a Profession for Canadian Women*, Mabel Dunham's 1920 Ontario Library Association presidential address.

14. David Farr, unpublished tribute to Hilda Gifford, Hilda Gifford File, A294 2004-17, Carleton University Library Archives.

15. Direct faculty involvement in acquisitions was standard practice in Canadian academic libraries at this time.

16. Ben Jones, Honorary Degree Citation for Hilda Gifford. Public Relations and Information Services fonds, University Communications, ACC 1996-17 PINFO-28 Convocation Fall 1982. Carleton University Library Archives, Ottawa, Ontario, 1982, 1.

17. Canadian Association of College and University Libraries, *Guide to Canadian University Library Standards. Report of the University Library Standards Committee of the Canadian Association of College and University Libraries 1961–1964*, (1965) 5. For example, Gifford was a consultant to the University Library Standards Committee of the Canadian Association of College and University Libraries (ibid., iii).

18. Jackson, oral history.

19. Robert B. Downs, *Resources of Canadian Academic Research Libraries*, (Ottawa: Association of University and Colleges of Canada, 1967), 107.

20. The history of the gendered nature of American librarianship has been studied extensively. One of the most oft-cited studies is *Apostles of Culture: The Public Librarian and American Society, 1876–1920*, by Dee Garrison, which typically is the primary historical source for the feminization of librarianship in North America as Canadian historical literature on this topic is scarce. However, both *Professionalization, Gender and Librarianship in Ontario, 1920–75*, by historian, Lorne Bruce, and Nina Milner's master's thesis, "Lady Librarian: The Feminization of Librarianship in Canada, 1880–1920" provide historical accounts of this process in Canada.

21. Downs, *Resources* 119. Salary comparisons between institutions are difficult to produce. The national median salary reported in the Downs study excludes librarians in managerial positions, while the Carleton figure includes all librarians except the chief librarian. However, apparently there were only two librarians in the "department and division heads" category (i.e., managerial staff) so the Carleton median may not be excessively inflated.

22. Pat Armstrong and Hugh Armstrong, *The Double Ghetto. Canadian Women and Their Segregated Work,*, (Don Mills, Ontario: Oxford University Press, 1978).

23. Hon. W.D. Euler, Minister of Trade and Commerce, *Survey of Canadian Libraries. Being Part III of the Biennial Survey of Education in Canada, 1936–1938*, (Ottawa: J.O. Patenaude, I.S.O, 1939), 14; Hon. C.D. Howe, Minister of Trade and Commerce. *Survey of Libraries 1948–1950. Part III of the Biennial Survey of Education in Canada, 1948–1950*, (Ottawa: Edmond Cloutier, Queen's Printer and Controller of the Stationary, 1952), 19.

24. The *Survey of Libraries in Canada, 1936–1938* reported that in university, college and professional libraries, between 1936 and 1938, of the 199 full-time librarians who reported their income, all of those in the highest salary bracket were men, while female librarians dominated the lower salary categories. A Canadian study, done in the 1970s, confirmed that salaries for female librarians in Canada had continued to be lower, on average, than those of their male colleagues (see Sherrill Cheda, Linda Fischer, Mary Ann Wasylycia-Coe and Phyllis Yaffe, "Salary Differentials of Female and Male Librarians in Canada," *Emergency Librarian* 5, no. 3 (Jan./Feb. 1978): 3–13.

25. References to the low salaried nature of North American librarianship can be found dating back to the late 1800s. See, for example, an untitled editorial in *The American Library Journal* 1, no. 1, September 1876 (this editorial is unauthorized but could have been written by journal editor, Melvil Dewey); W.E. Henry's 1922 article *Recruiting for College and University Libraries*; the 1927 *Report of the Bureau of Public Personnel Administration to the Committee on the Classification of Library Personnel of the American Library Association* which proposed a set of universal job classifications and pay scales that would improve compensation for librarians in both the United States and Canada; *Salary Scales Recommended for Public Libraries, College and University Libraries in Canada* approved by the Canadian Library Association in 1957; Kenneth D. Shearer and Ray L. Carpenter's 1976, *Public Library Support and Salaries in the Seventies. The Survey of Libraries in Canada, 1944–1946* article. The book refers to a recent increase in salaries that would make librarianship more competitive, as a profession, while the survey published for 1948 –1950 mentions the low pay of academic librarians relative to that of public librarians. While the majority of librarians worked in public libraries—in both Canada and the United States—until the 1970s, librarians in all sectors appear to have been concerned about salary levels.

26. W.E. Henry, "Recruiting for College and University Libraries," *Bulletin of the American Library Association, Papers and Proceedings of the Forty-Fourth Annual Meeting of the American Library Association* 16, no. 4 (July 1922): 124–25.

27. Olga B. Bishop, *The Use of Professional Staff in Libraries: A Review 1923–1971*, CLA Occasional Paper No. 81, (Ottawa: Canadian Library Association, 1973).

28. Swinton, oral history.

29. Ibid. Librarians across North America were concerned about the "task redistribution" (i.e., competition) from professional librarians to "paraprofessionals" in the 1970s. For example, the Systems and Procedures Exchange Centre (SPEC), a division of the Association of Research Libraries, conducted a survey of the use of non-professional library assistants in academic libraries across the United States and published the SPEC Kit on Paraprofessionals in October 1975 in a document entitled, *Paraprofessionals in ARL Libraries*. The kit was designed to assist library administrators in assessing the use of paraprofessionals in their libraries.

30. Downs, *Resources*.

31. Ibid., 110.

32. Ibid., 113.

33. Academic collegiality can be defined as the practice of professors acting together as peers and jointly making the decisions—at the departmental, faculty and senate levels—related to all academic matters at a university, based on the tradition of self-government at British universities, such as Oxford and Cambridge (See Sandra Rastin, "Organizing Tactics in a Faculty Unionization Drive in a Canadian University," *Labor Studies Journal* 25, no. 2 (2000): 105–6; John H. Van de Graaff, Burton R. Clark, Dorothea Furth, Dietrich Goldschmidt and Donald F. Wheeler, *Academic Power. Patterns of Authority in Seven National Systems of Higher Education*, (New York: Praeger Publishers, 1978), 2 and 83. More broadly, however, collegiality is commonly referred to as the collaboration between, and shared experiences of, colleagues—both of which Hilda Gifford tried to promote amongst librarians.

34. Susan Jackson and Frances Montgomery, retired librarians, Carleton University, in oral history interview with the author, April 24, 2012.

35. The expression "to play mother" can be used to refer to the role of the person who pours tea for others in a social setting. For a discussion about the sexual division of labour within Canadian society, see, *But can you type? Canadian Universities and the Status of Women*, by Jill McCalla Vickers and June Adam as well as Pat Armstrong's and Hugh Armstrong's *The Double Ghetto*.

36. Jackson, oral history, 2011.

37. Ibid.

38. Ibid.

39. Ibid.

40. Ibid.

41. Ibid.

42. See, for example, Joan Sangster, *Transforming Labour: Women and Work in Postwar Canada*, (Toronto, Buffalo, London: University of Toronto Press, 2010), 233.

43. The growth in Canadian unionization during this period was driven by the formation of public sector unions, provincially and federally. Carleton support staff were acutely aware of both the job opportunities and higher salaries to be found in the federal public service; salary differentials, in particular, fuelled some of their dissatisfaction and facilitated their unionization, which took place during the same period. However, there is no evidence that such comparisons led to discontent amongst Carleton librarians.

44. For example, the 1973 Canadian Library Association (CLA) conference featured two speakers, who addressed women in librarianship and library unionism, respectively. Sherrill Cheda, a librarian at Ontario's Seneca College in the 1970s, made an impassioned plea for equity in libraries in her conference presentation entitled, *That Special Little Mechanism*. Her argument was simple: as a woman and as a librarian without a penis, she was battling a "heritage of sex discrimination" in which men were rewarded with leadership roles and women were assigned "to the lower paying housekeeping duties". She suggested that librarians had a duty to alleviate workplace unfairness in a

number of ways, such as creating more part-time jobs for working mothers and ensuring that women got promoted into senior leadership positions. Sherrill Cheda, "That Special Little Mechanism," *Canadian Library Journal* 31, no. 5 (1974): 422-432.

Also presenting, at the 1973 CLA conference, was Jack Hughesman, the director of education for the prairie region of CUPE. Hughesman's goal was to encourage librarians to assert their professionalism by joining a union. As he pointed out, CUPE represented approximately 80% of the unionized library staff in Canada (most in public libraries) and although the overall percentage of library workers in unions was significantly lower than the national average at a time when librarians' with collective agreements could make as much as 25% more than their non-unionized peers. Jack Hughesman, "Union Representative Looks at Librarians," *Canadian Library Association Conference 1973 Proceedings*, (Ottawa: Canadian Library Association, 1973). In addition, from the early 1960s to the mid-1970s, the Institute of Professional Librarians of Ontario (IPLO) attempted to regulate the profession. The IPLO was a federation of librarians established during a period when Ontario librarians were actively discussing the possibility of unionizing and its mandate was to create a professional identity for librarians as an alternative to unionization, which organizers believed would complicate the process of professionalization. A key organizational goal was to attain legal status as the professional regulatory body that would effectively allow it to function as a bargaining agent for its members. However, ultimately these efforts failed and the IPLO was disbanded in 1976. Greg Linnell, "The Institute of Professional Librarians in Ontario: On the History and Historiography of a Professional Association," http://eprints.rclis.org/12214/ For a brief overview of this period, see Garry, "The Unionization of the Profession," in *Canadian Libraries in Their Changing Environment*, 499–521.

45. Valerie McDougall, Letter to Professor R.H. Crowther, Canadian Association of University Teachers, May 9, 1974, 1, in the author's possession. Neil Brearley, Martin Foss and Valerie Swinton conducted a salary survey of professional librarians in March, 1974. According to Susan Jackson, the survey revealed "phenomenal" variations between librarians' annual salary increases: "You might have got 1% or you might have got 8% . . . . And so at that point it was kind of an ah-ha moment . . . there was no equity . . . . It was a personal relationship thing and if you were a favoured person, you got a good amount of money. If you were not a favoured person . . . you might be invited to move along." Jackson, oral history, 2011.

46. McDougall, Letter to Professor R.H. Crowther, 1.

47. Swinton, oral history.

48. McDougall, Letter to Professor R.H. Crowther, 1.

49. Ibid.

50. Swinton, oral history.

51. Martin Foss, Memorandum to Geoffrey Briggs, July 15, 1974, 1, in the author's possession.

52. McDougall, Letter to Professor R.H. Crowther, 1.

53. Professional Staff Committee, Carleton University Library, Report of York University Meeting of University and College Librarians in Ontario, September 1974, in the author's possession.

54. Cal Evans, Report on York Meeting, (n.d.), in the author's possession.

55. Professional Staff Committee, Report of York University Meeting.

56. Jill Vickers, Letter to Martin Foss and Valerie McDougall, in the author's possession, October 10, 1974, 1–2.

57. Ibid., 2.

58. *CUASA News* (October 1974): 2, http://www.cuasa.ca/services/newsletter.php.

59. Membership in the Association of Professional Librarians of Carleton University (APLCU) was voluntary.

60. Jackson, oral history, 2011.

61. Ibid.

62. Ibid.

63. Ibid.

64. APLCU, Minutes of Meeting, December 4, 1974, in the author's possession, 1.

65. Ibid.

66. Frances Montgomery, retired librarian, Carleton University, in oral history interview with author, June 11, 2011.

67. APLCU, Collective Bargaining Committee, Report, February 1975, in the author's possession.

68. APLCU, Minutes of Meeting, March 14, 1975, in the author's possession, 1.

69. Ibid.

70. APLCU, Minutes of Meeting, April 15, 1975, in the author's possession, 1; APLCU, Minutes of Meeting, April 25, 1975 in the author's possession, 1. On April 25, the APLCU minutes showed that 365 voted in favour of CUASA as bargaining agent and 93 against. It is unclear how many professional librarians worked at Carleton University that year but, at the same meeting, it was reported that 29 out of 31 librarians had responded to an earlier 1975 salary survey.

71. Swinton, oral history.

72. Jackson, oral history, 2011.

73. Case for Excluding Library Staff from Bargaining Unit, March 3, 1975, Office of the President Fonds, Acc. #1997-21, PRES-232-12, Collective Bargaining CUASA

Correspondence, Part I, Carleton University Corporate Archives, Ottawa, Ontario. In this document, the case for excluding librarians is based on a perceived lack of a "community of interest" between faculty members and librarians.

74. Jackson, oral history, 2011.

75. Michael K. Oliver, "Forum", *This Week Times Two* Special Edition (April 10, 1975), Archives and Research Collections, Carleton University Library Ottawa, Ontario, 6.

76. Jill Vickers, Distinguished Research Professor, Carleton University, in oral history interview with the author, May 4, 2011.

77. Geoffrey Briggs, e-mail message to the author, November 1, 2011.

78. Ibid. According to the late Don McEown, Secretary Emeritus to the Carleton University Board of Governors, Oliver had a different leadership style from his predecessor, the charismatic A. Davidson Dunton and was very unpopular with professors (Don McEown, Secretary Emeritus, Carleton University, in oral history interview with the author, March 14, 2011). Former CUASA President, Jill Vickers, has described Oliver as "threatening" (Vickers, oral history).

79. Ibid.

80. Ibid.

81. Jackson, oral history, 2011.

82. Catherine Shanley, "The Library Employees' Union of Greater New York, 1917–1929," *Libraries and Culture* 30, no. 3 (1995): 235–64.

83. Mudge, "Collective Bargaining of Librarians in Canada."

84. Montgomery, oral history, 2011.

85. Calvin D. Evans, "Librarians and CAUT: Historical Overview and Future Directions," *CAUT Bulletin, Special Report,* Canadian Association of University Teachers, March, 1976, 12–3; William H. Nelson, *The Search for Faculty Power. The History of the University of Toronto Faculty Association 1942–1992* (Toronto: The University of Toronto Faculty Association and Canadian Scholars' Press, 1993), 100.

86. See example, Cal Evans and Tom Eadie, *AALO Elaboration of the Fourteen Points in Answering the Question "What is it We Want as University Librarians?"* in the author's possession, (n.d.).

87. Neil Brearley and Valerie McDougall, Librarians and CUASA: A Statement to the Sub-Committee Exploring the Membership of Librarians in CUASA, 1975, in the author's possession. In particular, the AALO (the Association of Academic Librarians of Ontario), the Association of College and Research Libraries (ACRL) and the CAUT/Canadian Association of College and University Libraries (CACUL) all produced documents that included statements about academic status. The AALO seems to have been formed by librarians who attended the original "York" meeting in October 1974.

88. Ibid., 2.

89. Andrew Brook, retired professor, Carleton University, in oral history interview with the author, April 17, 2011.

90. Swinton, oral history.

91. Vickers, oral history.

92. Ibid.

93. Swinton, oral history.

94. Vickers, oral history.

95. Ibid.

96. Ibid.

97. APLCU Collective Bargaining Committee, Report.

98. J.A. Brook, B. Wand, V. McDougall, and N. Brearley, CUASA Report of the Sub-Committee on Membership of Librarians, Carleton University Academic Staff Association (n.d.), in the author's possession, 1.

99. APLCU, Minutes of Meeting, July 11, 1975, in the author's possession.

100. APLCU Collective Bargaining Committee, Report.

101. Jackson, oral history, 2011.

102. Ibid.

103. Brook, oral history.

104. Jackson and Montgomery, oral history. According to Andrew Brook, the increase in salaries alone was spectacular: "in the end, the [Chief] Librarian was not willing to cap salaries . . . let alone reduce salaries of his favourites. And so the librarians, as a whole, got an average 28% increase to bring everybody else up to the level that his chosen few were earning." (Brook, 2011)

105. Jackson, oral history, 2011.

106. Theodore L. Guyton, *Unionization: The Viewpoint of Librarians* (Chicago: American Library Association, 1975), 174.

107. Ibid. 1.

108. Vickers and Adam, *But can you type?*; The Chilly Collective, eds., *Breaking Anonymity. The Chilly Climate for Women Faculty*, (Waterloo, Ontario: Wilfrid Laurier University Press, 1995).

109. United Nations, 2013, http://www.un.org/womenwatch/feature/iwd/history.html.

Chapter 4
Sonne de Torrens

1. I would like to express my gratitude to Mary Kandiuk and Jennifer Dekker for undertaking this much needed project and inviting me to participate; a note of gratitude to Chris Penn, at the UTFA office, for her on-going assistance in helping me locate relevant documentation and to the archivists at the UTARMS for their help in locating materials.

2. This chapter is very much the result of a collective effort on the part of many. I would like to thank my colleagues (Gale Moore, Kent Weaver, Ken Lavender, Rea Devakos and Jeff Newman), who have offered their support and shared their personal memories and archives with me over the past year or more. This chapter is dedicated to the commitment, courage and perseverance of those who participated in the *Reference Revolution* and the years of work before and after, paving the way for colleagues today. A special thank you to those who agreed to be interviewed for this article: Liz Avison (June 2013), Anne Foster Worlock (March 2013), Susan Johnston (August 2013), Gale Moore (April 2013), Mary-Jo Stevenson (July 2013) and Anne Woodsworth (July 28, 2013).

3. The U of T librarians viewed themselves as academic professionals, who had rights pertaining to participation in the governance of the University, equity in the workplace with respect to salaries, promotions and the academic right to speak openly without fear of reprisal. The concept of librarianship, as a "profession," has had a long history. In 1876, Melvil Dewey noted, "[t]he time has at last come when a librarian may, without assumption, speak of his occupation as a profession," see M. Dewey, "The Profession." *American Library Journal* I (1876): 5-6. The last quarter of the nineteenth century was when library work was professionalized, with the visible signs of library schools opening (first in 1887) and organization of the American Library Association in 1876, see Joanne E. Passet, "Men in a Feminized Profession: The Male Librarian, 1887-1921." *Libraries & Culture* 28, no. 4 (Fall, 1993): 385-402, 386. The Canadian Library Association was not established until 1946. In more recent times, for librarians at Ontario post-secondary institutions, the idea of a profession had been reinforced by the work of the *Institute of Professional Librarians in Ontario* (IPLO) from 1954-1975. The impact of this on U of T librarians is discussed in greater deal in the section entitled, "Graduate Studies and Academic Librarianship" later in this chapter, but the annual reviews of the UTL system from the 1960s and 1970s shows that many U of T librarians were active members.

4. Higher educational standards and graduate programs in library science supported by faculty, in the 1960s, resulted in librarians being hired with advanced degrees, and, hence, librarians conscious of being part of the academic community.

5. Dubbed the *Reference Revolution*, the title of the event originated from within the group of librarians seeking reform. It is recalled as being a fitting term and was quickly adopted by colleagues in the central system, reflecting a collective consciousness that was rooted in the times. The 1970s was a pivotal decade of social and political change, ushering in the *Sexual Revolution*, the feminist movement, the *Silent Revolution* and the *Quiet Revolution* in Quebec, which had included, among many changes, the secularization of education and a new labour code (Code du Travail), the rise of the FLQ

in Quebec, the *Islamic Revolution of Iran*, the *Cultural Revolution of China*, the *Black Power Movement* and many more.

6. Discussion between librarians in LAUT and UTFA began in 1974. In 1975, at the UTFA annual general meeting, the membership approved librarians as members, see William H. Nelson, *The Search for Faculty Power: The History of the University of Toronto Faculty Association 1942-1992* (Toronto: Canadian Scholars' Press, 1993, reprinted 2006), 100.

7. For some of the more notable accounts, see Claude Bissell, *Halfway up Parnassus: A Personal Account of the University of Toronto 1932-1971* (Toronto: University of Toronto Press, 1974); Martin L. Friedland, *The University of Toronto: A History* (Toronto: University of Toronto Press, 2002, revised edition 2013); W. Stewart Wallace, *A History of the University of Toronto 1827-1927* (Toronto: University of Toronto Press, 1927); Robert H. Blackburn's *Evolution of the Heart: A History of the University of Toronto Library Up to 1981* (Toronto: University of Toronto Press, 1989) provides a detailed history of the various aspects of managing a large library system. He mentions the restlessness, within the library, but does not discuss these developments within the profession of librarianship. The focus is on the growth of the UTL system and the men who were University Librarians from 1843-1981; literature on the labour history of faculty, from the perspective of UTFA, see William Nelson, *The Search for Faculty Power: The University of Toronto Faculty Association 1942-1992* (Toronto: Canadian Scholars Press, 1993).

8. The Association of Research Libraries ranked the UTL system third in the 2012 North America rankings.

9. For more reading on this subject, see Roma Harris's section on "Keeping Silent About Women" in Roma M. Harris, *Librarianship: The Erosion of a Woman's Profession* (Norwood, N.J.: Ablex Publishing Corporation, 1992), 12-14; Bertha Bassam, *The Faculty of Library Science University of Toronto and its Predecessors 1911-1972* (Toronto: University of Toronto Press, 1978).

10. The documentation consulted for this article is from UTARMS, personal archives, the archives at UTFA, as well as interviews with librarians who were employed in the UTL system at that time. Every effort has been made to ensure that the fullest account of what transpired is documented and recounted in a manner that is fair to all concerned.

11. For a study of women employed at U of T, see Alison Prentice, "Bluestockings, Feminists, or Women Workers? A Preliminary Look at Women's Early Employment at the University of Toronto." *Journal of the Canadian Historical Association/Revue de la Société historique du Canada* 2, no. 1 (1991): 231-262.

12. Similar trends are reflected at other post-secondary institutional libraries. In 1970, 92% of the chief administrators of large academic libraries were male, see Michael D. Cooper, "A Statistical Portrait of Librarians: What the Numbers Say." *American Libraries* 7:6 (Jun. 1976): 327-330, 328.

13. University of Toronto, *Facts & Figures* (Toronto: University of Toronto Press, 1991-2010).

14. The role of the male librarian dominates the historiography of the profession in the public libraries of Rome, the monastic libraries of the Middle Ages, the princely and municipal libraries in the Renaissance, the national, state and university libraries of the Enlightenment. For similar gender tendencies in the development of the Ivy League collections in the US, see Thomas F. O'Connor, "Collection Development in the Yale University Library 1865-1931." *The Journal of Library History (1974-1987)* 22, no. 2 (Spring, 1987): 164-189.

15. *General Regulations for the Management of the King's College Library* (written by John Strachan, President of King's College) states the library was under the management of the Vice-President and was allocated six assistant librarians, who at that time were male, see Blackburn, *Evolution*, 9-10.

16. A similar trend existed in the United States; for an overview, see Robert Bingham Downs, "Status of Academic Librarians in Retrospect." *College and Research Libraries* 29 (1968): 253.

17. University of Toronto, *Minutes of the Library Committee* (May 9, 1898), 322. UTARMS.

18. Blackburn, *Evolution*, 103.

19. Blackburn, *Evolution*, 103-104.

20. University of Toronto, *Minutes of the Library Committee* (May 9, 1898), 322. UTARMS.

21. Blackburn, *Evolution*, 104.

22. This was relatively late in comparison to what had been happening in the US, where the formal education of librarians began in 1887 when Melvil Dewey, Chief Librarian of Columbia College (later Columbia University) founded the first School of Library Economy, see Mary Biggs, "Sources of Tension and Conflict between Librarians and Faculty." *The Journal of Higher Education* 52, no. 2 (Mar. – Apr. 1981): 182-201,184; at McGill University, in 1904, three to four week courses ran in the summer, the first formal program in librarianship in Canada, see Elaine Adele Boone, "Professional Education for Librarianship in Toronto 1882-1936" Ph.D. University of Toronto (1997), 26.

23. Bertha Bassam, *The Faculty of Library Science University of Toronto and its Predecessors 1911-1972* (Toronto: University of Toronto Press, 1978).

24. Passet, "Men in a Feminized Profession," 386.

25. For discussions about stereotypes and spinster librarians, see Rosalee McReynolds, "A heritage dismissed." *Library Journal* 110, no. 18 (1985): 25-31; and Roma M. Harris, Librarianship*: The Erosion of a Woman's Profession* (Norwood, N.J.: Ablex Publishing Corporation, 1992), 72.

26. At U of T, the "feminine professions" included nursing, household science, occupational and physiotherapy, dental nursing, child study, education, physical education, social work and the arts. The "masculine professions" were applied science and engineering, dentistry, medicine, law and forestry, see N. Kiefer, *The Impact of the Second*

World War on Female Students at the University of Toronto 1939-1949 (Toronto: University of Toronto, 1984), 13-14, 126.

27. For further discussion of similar patterns in the United States, see Anne E. Burgh and Benjamin R. Beede, "American Librarianship," in *The Role of Women in Librarianship 1876-1976: The Entry, Advancement, and Struggle for Equalization in One Profession,* eds. Kathleen Weibel and Kathleen M. Heim (Phoenix, AZ: The Oryx Press, 1979), 275.

28. For the theoretical foundations in the nineteenth century religious context of education at U of T and in the British heritage, see Sara Z. Burke, *Seeking the Highest Good: Social Service and Gender at the University of Toronto 1888-1937* (Toronto: University of Toronto Press, 1996).

29. University of Toronto, *Minutes of the Board of Governors* (December 10, 1931). UTARMS.

30. Blackburn, *Evolution,* 104.

31. Bassam, *Faculty of Library Science,* 42-43.

32. "Women Still Outnumber Men in the Library Science Programs." *The Globe and Mail (1936-Current).* May 31, 1979, http://search.proquest.com/docview/1239261631?ac countid=14771.

33. References to Carol Moore in the archival documents, from the 1970s, use her previous surname, Weiss. For the sake of continuity, "Moore" is used throughout this chapter.

34. Lorna Marsden was involved with an equity study, comparing librarians' salaries with those in engineering.

35. Wanda Auerbach, "Discrimination Against Women in the Academic Library." *University of Wisconsin Library News* 17 (February, 1972): 1-11; and Anita R. Schiller, *Characteristics of Professional Personnel in College and University Libraries.* Research Series no. 16 (Springfield: Illinois State Library, 1969), 76.

36. Blackburn, *Evolution,* 335-339.

37. For further reading, see E.O. Wright, J. Baxtor and G.E. Birkelund, "The Gender Gap in Workplace Authority: A Cross-National Study." *American Sociological Review,* 60 (1995): 407-435.

38. In May 1964, the Ontario legislature passed the *Act to Establish the Department of University Affairs* with the growth of government support in post-secondary education. This name was changed, in 1972, to the Ministry of Colleges and Universities. In the early 1960s, the province was supporting 14 universities and affiliated colleges and 22 colleges of applied arts and technology. For the impact on the Collection Department at the UTL system, see this brief history, UTL, Collection Department, http://onesearch.library.utoronto.ca/collection-development-history.

39. Bassam, *Faculty of Library Science,* 83.

40. Ontario University Presidents' Research Committee, *The Supply of Librarians: A Report to the Presidents of the Provincially Assisted Universities of Ontario from the Presidents' Research Committee* [n.d. 1964], 1.

41. Ontario University Presidents' Research Committee, *The Supply of Librarians*, 3-4.

42. University of Toronto. President's Committee on the School of Graduate Studies, *Graduate Studies in the University of Toronto: Report of the President's Committee on the School of Graduate Studies 1964-1965* (Toronto: University of Toronto Press, 1965), 107.

43. Members of this committee were John C. Cairns, Harry C. Eastman, Kenneth C. Fisher, H. Northrop Frye, A.C.H. Hallett, Charles S. Hanes, Robert F. McRae, John C. Polanyi, Ernest Sirluck, William C. Winegard. The committee was chaired by Bora Laskin and the secretary was Frances Ireland, see B. Bassam, B. *The Faculty of Library Science, University of Toronto and its Predecessors 1911-1972* (Toronto: University of Toronto Press, 1978), 83.

44. University of Toronto, *Report of the President's Committee on the School of Graduate Studies* (Toronto: University of Toronto Press, 1965), 107.

45. University of Toronto, *Report of the President's Committee on the School of Graduate Studies*, 108-109.

46. The chart in the annual report noted that, in 1973-1974, the turnover rate was 9.8% for librarians; in 1972-1973, the turnover rate was 13% for librarians; 1969-1970 rate of librarians terminated 12%; 1965-1966 rate of librarians terminated 16.2 %, see University of Toronto Libraries, *Annual Report of Chief Librarian 1974-1975*, UTARMS P78-0537.

47. University of Toronto, *Report of the President's Committee*, 109.

48. Ibid., 107.

49. Ibid., 109.

50. Ibid., 110.

51. The IPLO worked on behalf of librarians from 1954-1975, see L. Houser, *The Institute of Professional Librarians of Ontario: An Analysis, 1954-1975* (Toronto: Institute of Professional Librarians, 1975).

52. The *Annual Reports of the Chief Librarian* in the UTL system, from 1965 to 1973, would list staff, their positions and professional memberships. UTARMS P78-0537.

53. Bassam, *Predecessors*, 79.

54. Brian Land prepared a brief for the Spinks Commission on graduate programs in Ontario, see Bassam, *Predecessors*, 103.

55. Three librarians went on leave to complete higher degrees, in 1967-1968, see *Annual Report of the Chief Librarian*. UTARMS P78-0537; three librarians were listed as

having completed their MLS degrees as part of a general up-grade happening in the library in 1970-1971, see *Annual Report of the Chief Librarian*, UTARMS P78-0537; two librarians, Joyce Sowby and Michael McCahill, completed their MLS degrees in 1971-1972, see *Annual Report of the Chief Librarian*, UTARMS. P78-0537.

56. Richard Landon (1942-2011) joined the library in 1967, and later became the Director of the Thomas Fisher Rare Books Library.

57. Accounts of these clandestine meetings were relayed in interviews with Mary-Jo Stevenson, Gail Moore, and Anne Foster Worlock.

58. Robert H. Blackburn wrote to James Feeley, President of LAUT, on February 20, 1970, concerned about LAUT's organization of an open forum for the librarians and notes, "Frankly I am puzzled by your eagerness to make the Association into a public news agency or forum or to run a publicity campaign without having (as far as I know) agreed on a point of view or objective for such a campaign. And I am uneasy about the authority which such a news agency or campaign could derive, in the minds of the public . . ." UTARMS A1988-0034.

59. James Feeley left the U of T Library in May 1970 to become Head Librarian at Algonquin College in Ottawa, see LAUT *Report #3* April 13, 1970. Richard Landon, of the Rare Books department, became President of LAUT, following James Feeley's departure, see LAUT *Report* #4 August 13, 1970; for members of the LAUT executive, see LAUT, *Report* #1, November 28, 1969, UTARMS, B72-1105.

60. LAUT, *Constitution*, November 4, 1969 and May 1977. UTARMS, B1975-1032.

61. LAUT, *Report* #5, February 1971. UTARMS, B72-1105.

62. LAUT, *Report* #4, August 13, 1970. UTARMS, B72-1105.

63. As part of the bibliography prepared, there were several articles from the *IPLO Quarterly*, for example, Jennifer Arbuckle, "A Professional Librarian Views Library Unions," *IPLO Quarterly* 15 (January 1974): 109-116; Joanna B. Curtis, "Professionals Form a Union," *IPLO Quarterly* 15 (January 1974): 89-100. Another journal which was influencing readers at the time was the *California Librarian*, from which the following articles were recommended, Darryl Mleyner, "Professional Unions," *California Librarian* 31 (April 1970): 110-118 and Martha Boaz, "Labor Unions and Libraries," *California Librarian* 33 (April/July 1971): 104-108. In terms of the faculty status, in addition to the ACRL publications cited, they referenced Virgil F. Massman, *Faculty Status for Librarians* (Metuchen, N.J.: Scarecrow Press, 1972) as being the most comprehensive text available on faculty status, at that time.

64. LAUT, *Unionization or Faculty Status*, [n.d.], [1974], UTARMS, B75-1032. Prepared by Pat Fysh and Jane Clark, 3.

65. In 1974, CAUT stated that its priorities were "academic freedom and tenure, collective bargaining and the establishment of local offices," see Israel Cinman, "CAUT Enters New Era: Structure Aimed at Strengthening CAUT's Role in Collective Bargaining and Lobbying Governments." *CAUT Newsletter* (1974).

66. ACRL survey results conducted among academic librarians, see R. Hyman and G. Schlachter, "Academic Status: Who Wants It?" *College and Research Libraries: News* (Sept. 1972): 209-210.

67. LAUT, *Unionization*, 6.

68. See earlier discussion on the history of librarianship in section entitled "The 'Feminine Profession' at the University of Toronto".

69. A similar trend existed in the United States, for an overview see Robert Bingham Downs, "Status of Academic Librarians in Retrospect." *College and Research Libraries* 29 (1968): 253.

70. Blackburn, *Evolution*, 230.

71. The CUG was not a public commission evoked by the government; it was an internal enquiry.

72. University of Toronto, Commission on the Government of the University of Toronto, *Toward Community in University Government* (Toronto: University of Toronto Press, 1970).

73. University of Toronto, *Toward Community*, 11-15, 56-63.

74. The membership of the UWC included 160 persons, including the Chair of UTFA, Presidents of the Graduate Student Union, Students' Administrative Council and representatives from faculty, students, academic and non-academic staff.

75. Martin L. Friedland is the author of *The University of Toronto: A History* (Toronto: University of Toronto Press, 2002, revised edition 2013).

76. LAUT, *Report* #3 (April 13, 1970). UTARMS B72-11005/002.

77. UTARMS A85-0031/006.

78. Ibid., 6.

79. Ibid.

80. Association of the Teaching Staff. *Brief to the Commission on University Government.* Section IV: The University Library, 16. May 19, 1969. UTARMS B1985-0031/006.

81. Commission of University Governance Briefs, UTARMS A1985-0031/006.

82. Commission of University Governance Briefs, UTARMS A75-0048/001.

83. Ibid.

84. Ibid.

85. Ibid.

86. UTARMS B72-1105. Richard Landon also submitted a brief, as an individual, on July 18, 1969, UTARMS B73-1025.

87. Michael Rosenstock in Collections was later Head of Collections Development at Robarts Library.

88. UTARMS B72-1105.

89. Ibid.

90. Ibid.

91. J.B. MacDonald, *The Governing Council System of the University of Toronto: A Review of the Unicameral Experiment* (Toronto: University of Toronto Press, 1977), 78.

92. UTFA Archives, letter from Sack, Charney & Goldblatt to Prof. Jean Smith, President of UTFA, Feb. 21, 1979.

93. Blackburn, *Evolution*, 309.

94. The librarians who signed this memo were Jane Clark, Anne Foster, Pat Fysh, Susan Johnston, David Jones, Mary McTavish, Pat Norman, Chester Carsten, Jana Prokop, Judith Sheppard, Sophia Skoric, Mary-Jo Stevenson, Carol Weiss, Peggy White, and Joan Winearls. UTARMS, A1985-0034/002 and Blackburn, *Evolution*, 307.

95. Blackburn, *Evolution*, 307.

96. UTARMS, A1985-0034/002, 2.

97. Blackburn, *Evolution*, 307.

98. The 14 librarians who signed were Chester Carsten, Jane Clark, Anne Foster, Pat Fysh, Susan Johnston, David Jones, Mary McTavish, Jana Prokop, Judith Sheppard, Sophia Skoric, Mary-Jo Stevenson, Carol Moore, Peggy White and Joan Winearls. UTARMS A1990-0024/007.

99. UTARMS A1990-0024/007.

100. See previous list of names who signed the memo to Robert H. Blackburn. Of these, two were male and 12 were female, resulting in 86% being women.

101. The late 1960s brought many American academics into Canada following the civil rights movements and during the Vietnam War; it was a time of international campus unrest and youth movements. In 1972, a radical student movement led by future NDP leader, Bob Rae, included sit-ins at Robarts Library; this resulted in undergraduate students being allowed access to the Robarts Research Library, which had been intended for graduate students only, see University of Toronto, http://www.greatpast.utoronto.ca/bios/history10.asp.

102. The *Reference Brief* is appended to the *Meincke Report*, UTARMS 0416.

103. A complete list of the correspondence concerning this event formed part of the background reading for the *Miencke Report* UTARMS 0416.

104. Blackburn, *Evolution*, 305-306.

105. For an early discussion of librarians acquiring academic status, see Robert Bingham Downs, "Academic Status for University Librarians—A New Approach" [n.d., 1946]. Reprinted from *College and Research Libraries* (January 1946). See also Robert Bingham Downs, "Status of Academic Librarians in Retrospect." *College and Research Libraries* 29 (1968): 253.

106. American Library Association, ACRL, Association of American Colleges, Association of American University Professors, "Statement on Faculty Status of College and University Librarians," *College and Research Libraries News* 35 (Feb. 1974): 26 and "Standards for Faculty Status for College and University Librarians," *College & Research Libraries News* 32 (Feb. 1971): 36-37.

107. Here are some examples with year of certification: University of Manitoba (1973), Cape Breton University (1974), Bishop's University (1975), Ottawa University (1975), Carleton University (1975), Acadia University (1976), Moncton University (1976), Regina University (1977), York University (1977), Windsor University (1978), Queen's University (1995) and the list continues, see CAUT, *Librarian Salary and Academic Status Survey 2010*, Table C, p. xxiv.

108. Blackburn, *Evolution*, 306.

109. UTARMS 0416. See memo to H.C. Scholler.

110. *Emergency Librarian* was also the name of a new Canadian library journal with a feminist perspective that was widely read and supported by U of T librarians. The co-editors were Phyllis Jaffe and Sherrill Cheda, who were radical Toronto librarians who inspired colleagues. For information on Sherrill Cheda, see http://section15.ca/features/reviews/2008/09/01/emergency_librarian/ and www.thestar.com/news/obituaries/2008/06/10/sherrill_cheda_72_arts_activist_loved_books.html Accessed June 16, 2014.

111. Memo to H.C. Sholler, Associate Librarian, Director of Readers' Services, dated May 24, 1973. UTARMS 0416.

112. UTARMS, A1985-0034.

113. Anne Woodsworth acquired a Ph.D. in Higher Education Administration, University of Pittsburgh (1987), and MLS, University of Toronto, 1969, a Bachelor of Library Science, University of Toronto (1964) and a Bachelor of Fine Arts, University of Manitoba (1962). Woodsworth married into the J.S. Woodsworth family that founded Woodsworth House, later to be called Woodsworth College at U of T. In an interview with Woodsworth, on July 28, 2013, she recounted discovering that the Head of Cataloguing, Jack Cain, who only had a BA, was making a higher salary. This discover led to an enquiry between male and female managers.

114. These events were conveyed in the author's interview with Anne Woodsworth on July 28, 2013.

115. UTARMS A1990-0024/007.

116. Letter to Jean Yolton from Robert H. Blackburn, February 26, 1974. UTARMS A1990-0024/007.

117. University of Toronto, *Report of the President's Committee on the School of Graduate Studies*, 112.

118. Members of the committee were John Volinska (non-union technical staff), Carol Moore (Reference Department), Susan Cozzi (Technical Services), Mary E. Murray (Book Selection), David Esplin (Associate Librarian, Director of Reader Services), Sheila Laidlaw (Head Librarian, Sigmund Samuel Library), Brian Land (Director, Faculty of Library Science), Judith Gelmon (Graduate Student), Dean Robert A. Greene (Faculty of Arts & Science), Prof. J.P. Siegel (Faculty of Management Studies), Susanne Hynes (union staff), see *Meincke Report*, UTARMS 0416.

119. *Meincke Report*, UTARMS 0416.

120. The *Reference Brief* (p.4) is appended to the *Meincke Report*, UTARMS 0416.

121. Members of the MRAP Working Group were announced in the MRAP Newsletter of October 4, 1974: Adele Annett, Rick Bebout, Robin Braithwaite, Jane Cooper, Martin Evans, Janet Mortimer, Michael Rosenstock and Sylvia Salo.

122. UTARMS A1990-0024/009.

123. The *Policy for Librarians* is still used at U of T; only articles relating to remuneration and research days have changed in the last 35 years.

124. The Working Group to formulate a *Policy for Librarians* included the following faculty, librarians and two library administrators: Donald Smith (Personnel Librarian) and David Esplin (Associate Chief Librarian); librarians participating were Marietta Chadwick (Engineering), Liz Avison (Media Centre), Harriet Velazquez (UTLAS), Jane Cooper (Robarts) and Gale Moore (Robarts); members of the faculty were professors Peter Silcox (Political Economy, Erindale), David Smith (French) and Hal Smith (S.G.S. and Engineering).

125. UTARMS B83-1132.

126. The *Haist Rules* were used to write the policies for tenure, promotion and appointments for faculty at U of T. Physiologist, R.E. Haist, and members of a presidential committee appointed in 1964, authored these guidelines, which were approved by the Governing Council in 1967. Michiel Horn, *Academic Freedom in Canada: A History* (Toronto: University of Toronto Press, 1999), 305.

127. UTARMS B83-1132.

128. Ibid.

129. Ibid.

130. Ibid.

131. Two prominent US Supreme Court cases put into question tenure, the *Board of Regents of State Colleges v. Roth* 408 US 564 (1972) and *Perry v. Sindermann*, 408 US 593 (1972).

132. UTARMS B83-1132.

133. UTFA Newsletter to Members, May 15, 1978.

134. Ibid.

135. University of Toronto. Governing Council. Minutes. June 15, 1978. UTARMS.

136. Article 3, *Memorandum of Agreement*, University of Toronto.

137. Librarians and faculty at St. Michael's University College formed a union in 2011. "UTFA appealed to the Provincial Labour Board and was recognized as an appropriate union and eligible to represent their interests. USMC faculty and librarians with continuing and contractually limited term appointments are represented by the University of Toronto Faculty Association (UTFA), and constitute a certified bargaining unit within the ambit of the Ontario Labour Relations Act. The UTFA-USMC unit certified in February of 2011 and negotiations on a first contract began about one year later in 2012" see UTFA, News Release, October 9, 2012.

138. UTFA Archives. SJAC Report #1 (Dec. 11, 2012).

Chapter 5
Inskip & Jones

1. David L. Jones and Robin Inskip, *Ontario Community College Librarians' Equality Campaign (1973-1975)* (Brampton: Information and Research Services, 1975).

2. CAAT Academic Bargaining Team, *Submission to the Estey Arbitration Between the Civil Service Association of Ontario (CSAO) Academic Bargaining Unit and the Council of Regents for the Colleges of Applied Arts and Technology* (Toronto: CSAO, 1974).

3. Bentley, Lynne. Unpublished transcript of presentation to the CTCL Section, CACUL at the CLA Annual Conference, (Edmonton, 1989).

4. E.M. Rogers, *Diffusion of Innovations* 4th ed. (New York: The Free Press, 1995).

5. Malcolm Gladwell, *The Tipping Point: How Little Things Can Make a Big Difference*. (Boston: Little Brown, 2000), 7.

6. Malcolm Gladwell, quoted in Danielle Sacks, "Fifty Percent of 'The Tipping Point' is Wrong." Jonah Berger Shows You Which Half," *Fast Company*, March 18, 2013, http://www.fastcompany.com/3006693/fifty-percent-of-the-tipping-point-is-wrong-jonah-berger-shows-you-which-half.

7. Rogers, *Diffusion of Innovation*, 15.

8. Ismali Sahin, "Detailed Review of Rogers' Diffusion of Innovations Theory and Educational Technology-Related Studies Based on Rogers' Theory," *The Turkish Online Journal of Educational Technology—TOGET* 5, no. 2 (2006): 18. http://www.tojet.net/articles/v5i2/523.pdf.

9. Fred Emery and Eric Trist, "The Causal Texture of Organizational Environments," *Human Relations*, 18 (1965).

10. Eric Trist, Fred Emery, and Hugh Murray, eds., *Social Engagement of Social Science: A Tavistock Anthology* (Philadelphia: University of Pennsylvania Press, 1990-1997).

11. Barbara Gray, "Cross-sectoral Partners; Collaborative Alliances Among Business, Government and Communities," in *Creating Collaborative Advantage*, ed. C. Huxham (London: SAGE Publications, 1996, 57-80). Under "Theoretical Overview of the Success Factors," http://dx.doi.org/10.4135/9781446221600.

12. Ibid.

13. John D. Dennison and Paul Gallagher, *Canada's Community Colleges: A Critical Analysis*. (Vancouver, University of British Columbia Press, 1986); William Gerald Fleming, *Ontario's Educative Society, Vol. 4, Post-secondary and Adult Education*, (Toronto: University of Toronto Press, 1971).

14. Gray, *Collaborating*.

15. Michael L. Skolnik, "The Evolution of Relations Between Management and Faculty in Ontario Colleges of Applied Arts and Technology," *Canadian Journal of Higher Education* 18, no. 3 (1988): 83-11.

16. Michele Landsberg, *Writing the Revolution* (Toronto: Second Story Press, 2011).

17. Ann H. Stromberg. "Women in Female-dominated Professions," in *Women Working: Theories and Facts in Perspective*, ed. Ann H. Stomberg and Shirley Harkness (2nd ed.) (Mountain View, CA: Mayfield Publishing, 1988), 207-208.

18. Canada. Royal Commission on the Status of Women in Canada, *Report of the Royal Commission on the Status of Women in Canada*, 1970: 396.

19. Ibid.

20. Ibid., 397.

21. Ibid., 367

22. Ontario. Provincial Secretariat for Social Development, *Equal Opportunity for Women in Ontario: A Plan for Action, June 1973*, ([Toronto]: Provincial Secretariat for Social Development, 1973), 4-5.

23. Ibid., 50-52.

24. CAAT Academic Bargaining Team, *Submission to the Estey Arbitration Between the Civil Service Association of Ontario (CSAO) Academic Bargaining Unit and the Council of Regents for the Colleges of Applied Arts and Technology* (Toronto, CSAO, 1974), 88-96.

25. CAAT Academic Bargaining Team, *Submission*, 63-64; M.J. Qureshi, "Academic Status, Salaries and Fringe Benefits in Community College Libraries in Canada," *Canadian Library Journal* 28, no. 1 (1971): 41-45.

26. Stromberg, "Women in Female-dominated Professions"; Roma Maria Harris, *Librarianship: The Erosion of a Woman's Profession*, (Norwood, NJ: Ablex Publishing Corporation, 1992).

27. A "sweetheart union" is a union that participates in sweetheart contracts: [a] "term of derision for an agreement negotiated by an employer and a union with terms favourable to the employer" (Teamsters, *Definitions of Common Labor Terms*, 2013).

28. Skolnik, "Evolution of Relations."

29. Harris, *Librarianship*; Stromberg, "Women in Female-dominated Professions."

30. CAAT Academic Bargaining Team, *Submission*, 125.

31. Ibid., 130-131.

32. Ibid., 133.

33. Laura Sabia ... played an important part, as National Chair of the Committee for the Equality of Women, in the creation of the Royal Commission on the Status of Women called by Prime Minister Lester B. Pearson in February 1967. She was a founding member and, from 1969 to 1973, the first President of the National Action Committee on the Status of Women." (Wikipedia). Wikipedia contributors, "Laura Sabia". (2013) http://en.wikipedia.org/wiki/Laura_Sabia, Retrieved August 27, 2013.

34. CAAT Academic Bargaining Team, *Submission*, 145.

35. Ibid., 150.

36. Landsberg, *Writing the Revolution*, 259.

37. Robin Inskip and David L. Jones, "Community College Librarians—A Dispatch from the Front," *IPLO Quarterly* 16 no. 3 (1975): 146-149.

38. Robin Inskip, "Building Consensus and Power in the Library Community: the Marketing of School Library Services by a Provincial Library Association," *Emergency Librarian* 11, no. 4 (1984): 9-13; Robin Inskip, *Marigold System: A Case Study of Community Networks and Community Development* (Halifax: Dalhousie University School of Library and Information Studies Occasional Papers, 1987); Robin Inskip, "Planning and Facilitating Interorganizational Collaboration" (unpublished doctoral dissertation, University of Toronto, 1992).

39. Inskip, "Building Consensus and Power."

40. CAAT Academic Bargaining Team, *Submission*, 2.

41. Jones and Inskip, *Ontario Community College Librarians' Equality Campaign*, Appendix QF.

42. Mary Cornish and Fay Faraday, "Litigating Pay and Employment Equity: Strategic Uses and Limits—the Canadian Experience," Paper presented to the International Pay and Employment Equity for Women conference held by the New Zealand Advisory Council on the Employment of Women (Wellington, New Zealand June 28-29, 2004); Landsberg, *Writing the Revolution*.

43. Rosalie Silberman Abella, *Equality in Employment: A Royal Commission Report*, (Ottawa: Minister of Supply and Services Canada, 1984), 2. http://worthwhile.typepad.com/files/abella1984-part1-eng.pdf.

44. Canada. *Constitution Act, 1982, Part 1, Section 15* http://laws-lois.justice.gc.ca/eng/const/page-15.html.

45. Cornish and Faraday, "Litigating Pay."

46. Bentley, Unpublished transcript.

47. Ibid.

Chapter 6
Raven, Holyoke & Jensen

1. Detailed in the collective agreements of Memorial University of Newfoundland, Mount Saint Vincent University, Northern Ontario School of Medicine, University of Guelph, University of Toronto, and University of Saskatchewan.

2. Adam Balcziunas and Larissa Gordon, "Walking a Mile in their Shoes," *College & Research Libraries News* 73, no. 4 (2012): 192-195; Catherine Coker, Wyoma van Duinkerken and Stephen Bales, "Seeking Full Citizenship: A Defense of Tenure Faculty Status for Librarians," *College & Research Libraries* 71, no. 5 (2010): 406-420; David Fox, "The Scholarship of Canadian Research University Librarians," *Partnership: The Canadian Journal of Library and Information Practice and Research* 2, no. 2 (2007b): 22; Janet Swan Hill, "Wearing Our Own Clothes: Librarians as Faculty," *Journal of Academic Librarianship* 20 (1994): 71-76; Denise Koufogiannakis and Ellen Crumley, "Research in Librarianship: Issues to Consider," *Library Hi Tech* 24, no. 3 (2006): 324-340.

3. Martha Fallahay Loesch, "Librarian as Professor: A Dynamic New Role Model," *Education Libraries* 33, no. 1 (2010): 31-37.

4. Howard L. Simmons, "Librarian as Teacher: A Personal View," *College & Undergraduate Libraries* 6, no. 2 (2000): 41-44.

5. Heidi Julien and Shelagh K. Genuis, "Librarians' Experiences of the Teaching Role: A National Survey of Librarians," *Library & Information Science Research* 33, no. 2 (2011): 103-111.

6. Jane Kemp, "Isn't Being a Librarian Enough? Librarians as Classroom Teachers," *College & Undergraduate Libraries* 13, no. 3 (2006): 3-23.

7. R.N. Johnson, "Faculty Status for Academic Librarians: What do Nonteaching Faculty Teach?" *Tennessee Librarian: Quarterly Journal of the Tennessee Library Association* 49 (1997): 8-9.

8. Pauline Wilson, "Librarians as Teachers: The Study of an Organization Fiction," *Library Quarterly* 49 (1979): 146-162.

9. Fred P. Borchuck and Bernice Bergup, *Opportunities and Problems of College Librarians Involved in Classroom Teaching Roles,* ERIC Document No. ED134216 (1976).

10. J.H. Shera, "Library-Instructional Integration on the College Level," in *ACRL Monographs, no. 13: Report of the 40th Conference of Eastern College Librarians,* ed. H.G. Bousfield, Vol. 13 (Chicago: Association of College and Reference Librarians, 1955), 7-8, 13.

11. Julien and Genuis, *Librarians' Experiences of the Teaching Role,* 103-111; Kemp, *Isn't Being a Librarian Enough?* 3-23; Loesch, *Librarian as Professor,* 31-37; Brendan A. Rapple, "The Librarian as Teacher in the Networked Environment," *College Teaching* 45, no. 3 (1997): 114; Stephen C. Weiss, "The Origin of Library Instruction in the United States, 1820-1900," *Research Strategies* 19, no. 3 (2003): 233-243.

12. Keith Devlin, "The Difference between Teaching and Instruction," http://devlinsangle.blogspot.ca/2012/03/difference-between-teaching-and_01.html.

13. Hill, "Wearing Our Own Clothes," 71.

14. Canadian Association of University Teachers. Librarians' Committee. *Discussion Paper on the Expanding Role of Teaching by Librarians in Post-Secondary Institutions,* (Ottawa: Canadian Association of University Teachers, 2009); Heidi Julien, "A Longitudinal Analysis of Information Literacy Instruction in Canadian Academic Libraries," *Canadian Journal of Information & Library Sciences* 29, no. 3 (2005): 289-313.

15. Angie Gerrard and Jessica Knoch, "Trial by Fire: New Librarians as Team Teachers." *Academic Exchange Quarterly* 8, no. 4 (2004): 14.

16. R. Newhouse, "Professional at 28," *Library Journal* 131, no. 7 (2006): 34-36.

17. Kemp, *Isn't Being a Librarian Enough?* 10.

18. Julien and Genuis, *Librarians' Experiences of the Teaching Role,* 103-111.

19. Kemp, *Isn't Being a Librarian Enough?* 3-23.

20. CAUT (Canadian Association of University Teachers), *Model Clause on the Scholarly Activity of Academic Librarians.* (Ottawa: Canadian Association of University Teachers, 2003).

21. Ibid.

22. Ibid.

23. AAUP (American Association of University Professors) and ACRL (Association of College and Research Libraries), *Joint Statement on Faculty Status of College and University Librarians.*, http://www.aaup.org/file/faculty-status-of-librarians.pdf.

24. Rebecca Watson-Boone, "Academic Librarians as Practitioner-Researchers," *Journal of Academic Librarianship* 26, no. 2 (2000): 85; Charles B. Lowry, "Research and Scholarship Defined for portal: Libraries and the Academy," *portal: Libraries and the Academy* 4, no. 4 (2004): 449-453; Koufogiannakis and Crumley, *Research in Librarianship*, 324-340; Marie R. Kennedy and Kristine R. Brancolini, "Academic Librarian Research: A Survey of Attitudes, Involvement and Perceived Capabilities," *College & Research Libraries* 73, no. 5 (2012): 431-448.

25. For a more detailed analysis, see Judith M. Nixon, "Core Journals in Library and Information Science: Developing a Methodology for Ranking LIS Journals," *College & Research Libraries*. Forthcoming. A Google search for "librarians as researchers," as an example, generates thousands of results; "librarian as researcher" figures prominently as a topic in librarians' blogs; examples include the CARL Research Institute referred to later in this section.

26. Koufogiannakis and Crumley, *Research in Librarianship*, 324-340; Fox, *Scholarship of Canadian Research University Librarians*, 22.

27. Charles R. Hildreth and Selenay Aytac, "Recent Library Practitioner Research: A Methodological Analysis and Critique," *Journal of Education for Library and Information Science* 48, no. 3 (2007): 236-258.

28. The Academic Workload clause from the Collective Agreement between LUFA and Laurentian reads as follows: "Clause 5.40.2 The academic workload of a full-time Member during the academic year includes: (a) teaching/professional librarianship/ archives management, including the supervision of graduate and undergraduate students; (b) scholarly activity, including commitments to external granting agencies; (c) University governance, administrative duties, and other contributions to the University. The normal guideline for the distribution of the workload among the three main workload components is: forty percent (40%) teaching/professional librarianship/archives management, including the supervision of graduate and undergraduate students; forty percent (40%) scholarly activity, including commitments to external granting agencies; and twenty percent (20%) University governance, administrative duties, and other contributions to the University." http://laurention.ca/webfm_send/71.

29. Fox, *Scholarship of Canadian Research University Librarians*, 22.

30. Vic Catano et al., "Occupational Stress in Canadian Universities: A National Survey," *International Journal of Stress Management* 17, no. 3 (2010): 232-258.

31. Martin A. Kesselman and Sarah Barbara Watstein, "Creating Opportunities: Embedded Librarians," *Journal of Library Administration* 49, no. 4 (2009): 383-400. David Shumaker defines embedded librarianship in his 2012 book *The Embedded Librarian*, as moving librarians out of libraries and emphasizing a strong working relationship between the librarian and a group or team of people who need the librarian's expertise.

32. Lars Christiansen, Mindy Stombler and Lyn Thaxton, "A Report on Librarian-Faculty Relations from a Sociological Perspective," *Journal of Academic Librarianship* 30, no. 2 (2004): 118.

33. Ibid.

34. Paul Alan Wyss, "Library School Faculty Member Perceptions regarding Faculty Status for Academic Librarians," *College & Research Libraries* 71 (2010): 375.

35. "CARL is the leadership organization for the Canadian research library community"; "CARL has 29 university library members and two federal government libraries." Its members are represented by their library directors/university librarians. http://www.carl-abrc.ca/en/about-carl/.

36. Selinda Adelle Berg, Heidi LM Jacobs and Dayna Cornwall, "Academic Librarians and Research: A Study of Canadian Library Administrator Perspectives," *College & Research Libraries* 74, no. 6 (2013): 560-572.

37. Heidi LM Jacobs, Selinda Adelle Berg and Dayna Cornwall, "Something to Talk About: Re-Thinking Conversations on Research Culture in Canadian Academic Libraries," *Partnership: The Canadian Journal of Library and Information Practice and Research* 5, no. 2 (2010): 11; Necia Parker-Gibson, "Library Mentoring and Management for Scholarship," *Library Philosophy and Practice* (March, 2007): 1-8.

38. Heidi L.M. Jacobs and Selinda Adelle Berg, "By Librarians, for Librarians: Building a Strengths-Based Institute to Develop Librarians' Research Culture in Canadian Academic Libraries," *Journal of Academic Librarianship* 39 (2013): 227-231.

39. Fox, *Scholarship of Canadian Research University Librarians*, 6.

40. In the US, the Association of Research Libraries (ARL, www.acrl.org) and ALA's Association of College and Research Libraries Division (ACRL, www.ala.org/acrl) are primary sources of such information. In the UK, among many documented research efforts is the three-year Library and Information Science Research Coalition (lisresearch.org).

41. ACRL, *A Guideline for the Appointment, Promotion and Tenure of Academic Librarians*, American Library Association, http://www.ala.org/acrl/standards/promotiontenure.

42. Scott Walter, "The 'Multihued Palette' of Academic Librarianship," *College & Research Libraries* 74 (2013): 224.

43. California State University. Academic Senate. Faculty Affairs Committee, "Faculty Service in the California State University (CSU): An Integral Component in the Retention, Tenure, and Promotion of Faculty," California State University, http://www.calstate.edu/AcadSen/Records/Reports/serviceFinalreport.pdf.

44. Candace R. Benefiel et al., "Service to the Profession: Definitions, Scope, and Value," *Reference Librarian* 35 (2001): 368.

45. Concordia University and Concordia University Faculty Association, *Tentative Collective Agreement for 2012-2015*, http://www.cufa.net/collective_agreement/2012-2015.html.

46. Ibid.

47. David Fox, "Finding Time for Scholarship: A Survey of Canadian Research University Librarians," *portal: Libraries and the Academy* 7 (2007): 451-462.

48. Tina M. Neville and Deborah B. Henry, "Support for Research and Service in Florida Academic Libraries," *Journal of Academic Librarianship* 131, no. 7 (2007): 76.

49. Wyss, Library School Faculty Member Perceptions, 375-388.

50. Ibid., 384.

51. Ibid.

52. Deborah B. Henry and Tina M. Neville, "Research, Publication, and Service Patterns of Florida Academic Librarians," *Journal of Academic Librarianship* 30 (2004): 435-451.

53. Rachel A. Fleming-May and Kimberly Douglass, "Framing Librarianship in the Academy: An Analysis Using Bolman and Deal's Model of Organizations," *College & Research Libraries* 75, no. 3 (2014): 389-415.

54. Fox, *Finding Time for Scholarship*, 456.

55. Jeanne M. Brown, "Time and the Academic Librarian," *portal: Libraries and the Academy* 1, no. 1 (2001): 59-70.

56. Parker-Gibson, *Library Mentoring and Management for Scholarship*, 5.

57. Deborah Lee, "On the Tenure Track: Strategies for Success," *C&RL News* 68 (2007): 629.

58. Michelle A. Massé and Katie J. Hogan, eds., *Over Ten Million Served: Gendered Service in Language and Literature Workplaces*. (Albany, NY: State University of New York Press, 2010).

59. Kirsten M. Christensen, "The Value of Desire: On Claiming Professional Service," in *Over Ten Million Served*, eds. Massé and Hogan, 131.

60. Valerie Lee, ""Pearl was Shittin' Worms and I was Supposed to Play Rang-Around-the-Rosie?" An African American Woman's Response to the Politics of Labor," in *Over Ten Million Served*, eds. Massé and Hogan, 269.

61. Phyllis van Slyck, "Welcome to the Land of Super-Service: A Survivor's Guide ... and Some Questions," in *Over Ten Million Served*, eds. Massé and Hogan, 200.

62. McGill University Senate, "Minutes," http://www.mggill.ca/senate/sites/mcgill.ca.senate/files/minutes_march_21_2012.pdf.

63. Christensen, *Value of Desire*, 123-138.

64. Myriam J.A. Chancy, "Outreach: Considering Community Service and the Role of Women of Color Faculty in Diversifying University Membership," in *Over Ten Million Served*, eds. Massé and Hogan, 150.

65. Ibid.

66. Christensen, *Value of Desire*, 129.

67. Alvin M. Schrader, Ali Shiri, and Vicki Williamson, "Assessment of the Research Learning Needs of University of Saskatchewan Librarians: A Case Study," *College & Research Libraries* 73 (2012): 147-163.

68. Ibid., 147.

69. University of Saskatchewan, "University Library Standards for Promotion and Tenure," http://library.usask.ca/employment/files/Library%20Standards%20-%20July%201%202011.pdf, 15.

70. Fleming-May and Douglass, *Framing Librarianship in the Academy*.

71. Benefiel et al., *Service to the Profession*, 362.

72. University of Saskatchewan, *University Library Standards for Promotion and Tenure*, http://library.usask.ca/employment/files/Library%20Standards%20-%20July%201%202011.pdf, 14-15.

73. Christensen, *Value of Desire*, 128.

74. Paula M. Krebs, "Not in Service," in *Over Ten Million Served*, eds. Massé and Hogan, 163.

75. Ibid., 169.

Chapter 7
Harrington & Gerolami

1. David Camfield. *Canadian Labour in Crisis: Reinventing the Workers' Movement* (Halifax: Fernwood Publishing, 2011).

2. McCook, Kathleen de la Peña. "Collective Bargaining is a Human Right: Union Review for 2011," *Progressive Librarian* 38/39 (2012): 69-90.

3. Tina Maragou Hovekamp. "Unions in Academic Libraries," in *The Successful Academic Librarian*, edited by Gwen Meyer Gregory (Medford, NJ: Information Today Inc., 2005), 111-24.

4. Laurence Dickter. "Empowering Library Workers through Collective Bargaining," *Public Libraries* 41, no. 3 (2002): 141-2.

5. Suzanne Milton. "Librarians: Key Players in Faculty Unions," *American Libraries* 21, no. 3 (2005): 5.

6. American Library Association, "American Library Association President Roberta Stevens on proposed collective bargaining legislation", http://www.weac.org/blue/Legislative/ALA-letter.pdf.

7. Association of College and Research Libraries, *Joint Statement on Faculty Status of College and University Librarians* (1972), last modified October 2012, http://www.ala.org/acrl/standards/jointstatementfaculty; Canadian Association of University Teachers, *Academic Status and Governance for Librarians at Canadian Universities and Colleges* (1993), last modified September 2010, http://www.caut.ca/about-us/caut-policy/lists/general-caut-policies/policy-statement-on-academic-status-and-governance-for-librarians-at-canadian-universities-and-colleges.

8. Michael R. Brundin and Alvin M. Schrader. "National Statistical Profile of Canadian Libraries," (2012), http://www.cla.ca/AM/Template.cfm?Section=Advocacy&Template=/CM/ContentDisplay.cfm&ContentID=13785.

9. David Fox, "A Demographic and Career Profile of Canadian Research University Librarians," *The Journal of Academic Librarians* 33, no. 5 (2007): 546.

10. Rachel Applegate. "Who Benefits? Unionization and Academic Libraries and Librarians," *Library Quarterly* 79, no. 4 (2009): 443-463.

11. Deborah Lee, "Faculty Status, Tenure, and Compensating Wage Differentials Among Members of the Association of Research Libraries," *Advances in Library Administration and Organization* 26 (2008): 151-208.

12. Gwen Meyer Gregory and Mary Beth Chambers, "Faculty Status, Promotion, and Tenure- What are You Getting Into?" in *The Successful Academic Librarian*, edited by Gwen Meyer Gregory (Medford, NJ: Information Today Inc., 2005), 57-66; Gillum, Shalu, "The True Benefits of Faculty Status for Academic Librarians," *Reference Librarian* 51(2010): 321-8.

13. Bill Crowley, "The Dilemma of the Librarian in Canadian Higher Education," *Canadian Journal of Information and Library Science* 22, no. 1 (1996): 1-18; Horowitz, Stephanie A., "Faculty Status and the Publication Impact of ARL Librarians." (2007): 21-22.

14. Gloria Leckie and Jim Brett, "Job Satisfaction of Canadian University Librarians: a National Survey," *College and Research Libraries* 58, no. 1 (1997): 37.

15. Alan Bernstein, "Academic Librarians and Faculty Status: Mountain, Molehill or Mesa," *Georgia Library Quarterly* 46, no. 2 (2009): 12–15.

16. Hovekamp, *Unions in Academic Libraries*, 111.

17. Gloria Leckie and Jim Brett, "Academic Status for Canadian University Librarians: an Examination of Key Terms and Conditions," *Canadian Journal of Information and Library Science* 20, no. 1 (1995): 1-28.

18. Roma Harris and Juris Dilevko, "Bargaining Technological Change in Canadian Libraries," *Canadian Journal of Information and Library Science* 22, no. 3 (1997): 20-36.

19. Deanna Wood. "Librarians and Unions: Defining and Protecting Professional Values," *Education Libraries* 23, no. 1 (1999): 12-16.

20. Association of Universities and Colleges in Canada. *Listing of Universities in Canada*. (2013), http://www.aucc.ca/canadian-universities/our-universities; Canadian Association of University Teachers. *Member Associations* (2013), http://www.caut.ca/about-us/member-associations.

21. *Directory of Libraries in Canada* (Toronto: Greyhouse House Publishing, 2012).

22. Leckie and Brett, "Job Satisfaction."

23. Canadian Association of University Teachers, *Academic Status and Governance for Librarians at Canadian Universities and Colleges*.

24. Heidi L.M. Jacobs, Selinda Berg and Dayna Cornwall, "Something to Talk About: Re-thinking Conversations on Research Culture in Canadian Academic Libraries," *Partnership: The Canadian Journal of Library and Information Practice and Research* 5, no. 2 (2010); John A. Camp, David G. Anderson, and Anne Page Mosby, "In the same boat together: Creating an environment for research and publication," in *Building on the First Century: Proceedings of the Fifth National Conference of the Association of College & Research Libraries* (Chicago: Association of College and Research Libraries, 1989), 9-11; Jill Cirasella and Maura A. Smale, "Peers Don't Let Peers Perish: Encouraging Research and Scholarship Among Junior Library Faculty," *Collaborative Librarianship* 3, no. 2 (2011): 98–109.

25. Leckie and Brett, "Job Satisfaction."

26. Canadian Library Association, *Code of Ethics of the Canadian Library Association* (1976), last modified June 1979, http://www.cla.ca/AM/Template.cfm?Section=Position_Statements&Template=/CM/ContentDisplay.cfm &ContentID=3035; American Library Association, *Code of Ethics of the American Library Association* (1939), last modified January 2008, http://www.ifmanual.org/codeethics.

27. Applegate, "Who Benefits?" 461.

Chapter 8
Wheeler, Graebner, Skelton & Patterson

1. Blaise Cronin, "The Mother of all Myths," *Library Journal*, 126 no. 3 (2001): 144.

2. David Fox, "A Demographic and Career Profile of Canadian Research University Librarians," *Journal of Academic Librarianship* 33, no. 5 (2007): 545, doi: 10.1016/j.acalib.2007.05.006.

3. CAUT (Canadian Association of University Teachers), *Academic Status and Governance for Librarians at Canadian Universities and Colleges*, http://www.caut.ca/about-us/caut-policy/lists/general-caut-policies/policy-statement-on-academic-status-and-governance-for-librarians-at-canadian-universities-and-colleges.

4. Mary K. Bolin, "Librarian Status at US Research Universities: Extending the Typology," *Journal of Academic Librarianship* 34, no. 5: 416. doi: 10.1016/j.acalib.2008.06.005.

5. ACRL (Association of College and Research Libraries), *Standards for Faculty Status for Academic Librarians*, http://www.ala.org/acrl/standards/standardsfaculty.

6. Gloria J. Leckie and Jim Brett, "Job Satisfaction of Canadian University Librarians: A National Study," *College & Research Libraries* 58, no. 1 (1997): 37.

7. Laurie-Ann M. Hellsten et al., "Women on the Academic Tenure Track: An Autoethnographic Inquiry," *International Journal for Cross-Disciplinary Subjects in Education* 2, no. 1 (2011): 271.

8. Lynn Bosetti, Colleen Kawalilak and Peggy Patterson, "Betwixt and Between: Academic Women in Transition," *The Canadian Journal of Higher Education* 38, no. 2 (2008): 99.

9. Carolyn Ellis, "Heartful Autoethnography," *Qualitative Health Research* 9, no. 5 (1999): 674. doi: 10.1177/104973299129122153.

10. Bosetti et al., "Betwixt and Between," 98.

11. Arthur van Gennep, *Rites de passage* [The Rites of Passage] (Chicago: University of Chicago Press, 1960).

12. Victor W. Turner, "Passages, Margins and Poverty: Religious Symbols of Communitas," in *High Points in Anthropology*, Eds. P. Bohannan and M. Glazer, (New York: Knopf, 1988), 504.

13. Terry Plum, "Academic Libraries and the Rituals of Knowledge," *RQ*, 33 no. 4 (1994): 496; Mark Dressman, "Congruence, Resistance, Liminality: Reading and Ideology in Three School Libraries," *Curriculum Inquiry* 27, no. 3 (1997): 267-315.

14. Pamela J. Bettis et al., "Faculty in a Liminal Landscape: A Case Study of a College Reorganization," *Journal of Leadership & Organizational Studies* 11, no. 3 (2005): 47-61.

15. Bosetti et al., "Betwixt and Between," 98.

16. Ibid., 100.

17. Ibid., 101.

18. Carolyn Ellis, Tony E. Adams and Arthur P. Bochner, "Autoethnography: An Overview," *Forum Qualitative Sozialforschung/Forum: Qualitative Social Research* 12, no. 1 (2011): paragraphs 33-35. http://www.qualitative-research.net/index.php/fqs/article/view/1589.

19. Erica Firment, "Why You Should Fall to your Knees and Worship a Librarian," *Librarian Avengers* (blog), [2007?] http://librarianavengers.org/worship-2/.

20. Ibid., paragraph 5.

21. Bharat Mehra, Kevin S. Rioux, and Kendra S. Albright, "Social Justice in Library and Information Sciences," in *Encyclopedia of Library and Information Sciences*, ed. Marcia J. Bates and Mary Niles Mack, 3rd ed., (Boca Raton, FL: CRC Press, 2010): 4820. doi:10.1081/E-ELIS3-120044526.

22. Joseph Campbell, *The Hero with a Thousand Faces*. (New York: Pantheon Books, 1949), 30.

23. Mireille Vézina and Susan Crompton, "Volunteering in Canada," *Canadian Social Trends* 93 (2012): 43.

24. Carol C. Kuhlthau, "Inside the Research Process: Information Seeking from the User's Perspective," *Journal of the American Society for Information Science* 42, no. 5 (1991): 366.

25. Campbell, "The Hero," 30.

Chapter 9
Vaisey

1. Canadian Association of University Teachers (CAUT) Grievance Handling Workshop, Participants' Manual.

2. Windsor University Faculty Association, *Faculty Association Handbook for Grievance Officers*, http://www.wufa.ca For the range of possibilities, see p. 5.

3. See, for example, Lanigan v. Eastern School District, 2013 PESC 12, http://www.canlii.ca/.

4. Patti Ryan, (2011), Quoting Peter Simpson in conference report from the CAUT Librarians' Conference, October 2011, http://www.yufa.org/external/ConferenceReports/CAUTLibrarians2011_Ryan.html.

5. CAUT Grievance Handling Workshop, Participants' Manual.

6. Andrew Richard Albanese, "Take This Job and Love It," *Library Journal* 133, no. 2: 36-39; J.N. Berry III, "Great Work, Genuine Problems," *Library Journal* 132, no. 6: 26-29.

7. Tina Maragou Hovekamp, "Unions in Academic Libraries," in *The Successful Academic Librarian*, ed. Gwen Meyer Gregory (Medford, NJ: Information Today Inc., 2005); Rajinder Garcha and John C. Phillips, "US Academic Librarians: Their Involvement in Union Activities," *Library Review* 50, no. 3 (2001).

8. Kreitz, Patricia A. and Annegret Ogden, "Job Responsibilities and Job Satisfaction at the University of California Libraries," *College and Research Libraries* 51, no. 4: 297-320; Joan M. Leysen and Jeanne M. K. Boydston, "Job Satisfaction Among Academic Cataloguer Librarians," *College and Research Libraries* 70, no. 3: 273-293; Ilene F. Rockman, "Job Satisfaction Among Faculty and Librarians: A Study of Gender, Autonomy, and Decision Making Opportunities," *Journal of Library Administration* 5, no. 3: 43-56.

9. Albanese, 36.

10. The research was carried out under Saint Mary's University Research Ethics Board File 11-172. The initial approval covered the September-October 2011 period with a further extension to address collegiality (December 2011-February 2012).

11. Some collective agreements express "tenure" as permanency of employment or continuing appointment. Because "tenure" is widely understood as a concept, I have used it to express all three notions.

12. Loraleigh Keashly and Joel H. Neuman, "Faculty Experiences with Bullying in Higher Education: Causes, Consequences and Management." *Administrative Theory and Praxis* 32, no. 1 (2010): 60.

13. Ibid., 61.

Chapter 10
Kandiuk

1. Canadian Association of University Teachers, *CAUT Collective Bargaining Manual* (Ottawa: CAUT, 2006), 1.

2. Roger Fisher and William Ury, *Getting to Yes: Negotiating Agreement Without Giving In* (New York: Penguin, 1991; 2nd ed.), xix.

3. Fisher and Ury, 6.

4. Canadian Association of University Teachers, 3.

5. Roma Harris, *Librarianship: The Erosion of a Woman's Profession* (Norwood: Ablex, 1992), xiv.

6. Orvin Lee Shiflett, *Origins of American Academic Librarianship* (Norwood: Ablex, 1981), 222.

7. Harris, 25.

8. Ibid., 1.

9. Rachel A. Fleming-May and Kimberley Douglas, "Framing Librarianship in the Academy: an Analysis Using Bolman and Deal's Model of Organizations," *College & Research Libraries* (in press), 1.

10. Michael F. Winter, *The Culture and Control of Expertise: Toward a Sociological Understanding of Librarianship* (New York: Greenwood, 1988), 15.

11. Winter, 25.

12. Ernst Benjamin, "Reflections" in *Academic Collective Bargaining* ed. Ernst Benjamin and Michael Mauer (Washington, DC.: American Association of University Professors; New York: Modern Language Association of America, 2006), 384.

13. Rajinder Garcha and John C. Phillips, "US Academic Librarians: Their Involvement in Union Activities," *Library Review* 50, no. 3 (2001): 124.

14. Stephen H. Aby, "Library faculty and collective bargaining: An exploration," in *Advances in Library Administration and Organization*, Volume 28, ed. Delmus E. Williams, James M. Nyce, Janine Golden (Bingley, UK: Emerald, 2006), 284.

15. Aby, 285.

16. Benjamin, 384.

17. Tina Maragou Hovekamp, "Unions in Academic Libraries," in *The Successful Academic Librarian*, ed. Gwen Meyer Gregory (Medford, NJ: Information Today Inc., 2005), 121.

18. Lothar Spang and William P. Kane, "Who Speaks for Academic Librarians? Status and Satisfaction Comparisons between Unaffiliated and Unionized Librarians on Scholarship and Governance Issues," *College & Research Libraries* 58, no. 5 (1997): 448.

19. Canadian Association of University Teachers, 3, 5.

20. Rachel Applegate, "Who Benefits? Unionization and Academic Libraries and Librarians," *Library Quarterly* 79, no. 4 (2009): 443-463.

21. Garcha and Phillips, 124.

22. "The Status of Librarians at York University," Appendix E. [accessed July 20, 2013] n.d.

23. Jennifer Dekker, "A Rare Find: The Triumphs of York's Librarians" (2009), http://eprints.rclis.org/13554/.

24. York University, Presidential Committee on Professional Librarians. *Report to President H. Ian Macdonald, York University of The Presidential Committee on Professional Librarians.* (Downsview: York University, 1976), 20.

25. Betty Jo Irvine, "Differences by Sex: Academic Library Administrators," *Library Trends* 34, no. 2 (1985): 235.

26. Sarah Pritchard, "Feminist Thinking and Librarianship in the 1990s: Issues and Challenges" (1999), http://www.libr.org/ftf/femthink.htm.

27. Harris, 17.

28. "The Status of Librarians at York University." n.d.

29. Ibid.

30. Alberta Labour Relations Board, "Backgrounder: What Makes an 'Appropriate Bargaining Unit'" (1996), http://www.alrb.gov.ab.ca/dp-002.html.

31. UWOFA Board of Directors, "Important Information Regarding Librarian Certification Drive" (2003), http://www.uwo.ca/uwofa/docs/lib_cert.pdf.

32. Hovekamp, 112.

33. Harris, 112.

34. York University, Presidential Committee on Professional Librarians. 20.

35. Pay Equity Commission, "A Guide to Interpreting Ontario's Pay Equity Act" (2010-2012), http://www.payequity.gov.on.ca/en/resources/guide/ope/ope_2.php.

36. Collective Agreement Between the York University Faculty Association and The Board of Governors of York University, "Appendix E: Pay Equity" (2009-2015), http://www.yufa.ca/2012-15-ca.

37. McMaster University Academic Librarians' Association, "MUALA Submission to the McMaster University Library Review Team," http://muala.ca/.

38. Collective Agreement, "Appendix I," http://www.yufa.ca/2012-15-ca.

39. Hovekamp, 117.

40. CAUT, 4.

41. Fischer and Ury, 98.

42. Gaby Divay, Ada M. Ducas, and Nicole Michaud-Oystryk, "Faculty Perceptions of Librarians at the University of Manitoba," *College & Research Libraries* 48, no. 1 (1987): 27.

43. Atkin, 178.

44. Harris, 37-38.

45. Atkin, 178.

46. Garcha and Phillips, 124.

47. Catherine Coker, Wyoma van Duinkerken, and Stephen Bales, "Seeking Full Citizenship: A Defense of Tenure Faculty Status for Librarians." *College & Research Libraries* 71, no. 5 (2010): 417-18.

48. Spang and Kane, 461.

Chapter 11
Dawes, Dunn & Varpalotai

1. Acknowledgements: The authors wish to acknowledge the contributions of their colleagues: Elizabeth Bruton (Co-Chair of the UWOFA-LA Contract Committee), Jim Davies (Chair of the UWOFA Salary Committee), and Bernd Frohmann (member of UWOFA and UWOFA-LA negotiating teams). Special thanks and acknowledgement are due to Archivist, Bev Brereton, for her extensive contributions to the historical background for the pre-certification period.

2. The first archivists were hired in December 2001.

3. Martha Kyrillidou and Mark Young, Table 14: Average, Median, and Beginning Professional Salaries in ARL University Libraries; Summary of Rankings, FYs 2001-02 to 2004-05 in *ARL annual salary survey 2004-05* (2005), 34. Retrieved from http://www.arl.org/storage/documents/publications/salary-survey-2004-05.pdf.

4. Professional Practice Model for the Librarians and Archivists of The University of Western Ontario. Prepared by the Librarians & Archivists Steering Team, in consultation with all librarians and archivists. For submission to Joyce Garnett, University Librarian, [and] Jane O'Brien, Acting Vice-President - Administration, 12 February 2004.

5. Re: The University of Western Ontario Faculty Association (Applicant) and The University of Western Ontario (Respondent), O.L.R.B. File No. 3846-03-R (certificate reproduced in Appendix A at http://www.uwofa.ca/collectiveagreements/). (Decision at [2004] O.L.R.D.. No. 2942).

6. Carole Moore, Carolynne Presser, and Michael Ridley, *Western Libraries, University of Western Ontario: External Review: Carole Moore, University of Toronto: Carolynne Presser, University of Manitoba: Michael Ridley, University of Guelph: Report.* October 3, 2004.

7. *UWOFA Librarians and Archivists Bargaining Bulletin* 3, no. 2 (August 2009). http://uwofa.ca/@storage/files/documents/215/labb3_2.pdf; *UWOFA Librarians and Archivists Bargaining Bulletin* 3, no. 3 (September 2009). http://uwofa.ca/@storage/files/documents/227/labb3_3.pdf.

8. University of Western Ontario, *Engaging the Future: Final Report of the Task Force on Strategic Planning.* http://www.uwo.ca/univsec/strategic_plan/report/07.htm.

9. Aniko Varpalotai and Linda Dunn, "The First Academic Strike at Western," *Faculty Times: A UWOFA Newsletter* XIV, No. 3 (February 2012): 3-4.

Chapter 12
McKillop

1. Denise Horoky, "Strikes and Springsteen: Why My Graduate Students Expect Me to Be 'Better Than Google'," *Faculty Times: A UWOFA Newsletter* (February 2012): 6. http://uwofa.ca/@storage/files/documents/428/ftvolxiv3.pdf.

2. Linda Dunn, "Librarians and Activists Update," *Faculty Times: A UWOFA Newsletter* (September 2010): 11. http://uwofa.ca/@storage/files/documents/319/ftvolxiii3.pdf.

3. David W. McMillan and David M. Chavis, "Sense of Community: A Definition and Theory," *Journal of Community Psychology* 14 (January 1986): 6-23.

4. Linda Dunn and Elizabeth Bruton, "Update From the UWOFA-LA Contract Committee," *Faculty Times: A UWOFA Newsletter* (February 2011): 8, http://uwofa.ca/@storage/files/documents/339/ftvolxiv1.pdf.

5. Ibid.

6. Stephen Reicher, Russell Spears and Alexander Haslam, "The Social Identity Approach in Social Psychology," in *Sage Handbook of Identities*, ed. Margaret Wetherell and Chandra Talpade Mohanty (London: Sage, 2010), 45-63.

7. University of Western Ontario Faculty Association. "Can a University Exist Without Books?" *Librarians and Archivists Bargaining Bulletin* (June 2011): 1-2, http://uwofa.ca/@storage/files/documents/367/labb3_01.pdf.

8. University of Western Ontario Faculty Association, *"UWO Librarians and Archivists vote 100%* in Favour of Strike Mandate," *UWOFA Matters* (June 2011) http://www.uwofa.ca/uwofamatters/.

9. Aniko Varpalotai and Linda Dunn, "UWOFA-LA Negotiating Update: UWOFA-LA Third Contract Negotiations Begin," *Faculty Times: A UWOFA Newsletter* (May 2011): 2-3, http://uwofa.ca/@storage/files/documents/363/ftvolxiv3.pdf.

10. Ibid.

11. Riecher et. al., *The Social Identity*.

12. Aniko Varpalotai and Linda Dunn, "The First Academic Strike at Western," Faculty Times: A UWOFA Newsletter (February 2012): 3-4, http://uwofa.ca/@storage/files/documents/428/ftvolxiv3.pdf.

13. Marni Harrington and Albert Katz, "Some of Our Observations on UWOFA's First Strike," *Faculty Times: A UWOFA Newsletter* (February 2012): 7-8, http://uwofa.ca/@storage/files/documents/428/ftvolxiv3.pdf.

14. Ibid.

15. James Compton, "Academic Librarians and Archivists and the Struggle for Visibility," *Faculty Times: A UWOFA Newsletter* (May 2011): 1, http://uwofa.ca/@storage/files/documents/363/ftvolxiv3.pdf.

16. UWOFA, *"Can a University Exist Without Books?"*

17. Kristin Hoffmann, "Lesson in Solidarity from a Strike and a Symposium," *Faculty Times: A UWOFA Newsletter* (February 2012): 5, http://uwofa.ca/@storage/files/documents/428/ftvolxiv3.pdf.

18. Judith A. Seiss, *The Visible Librarian: Asserting Your Value With Marketing and Advocacy* (Chicago: American Library Association, 2003).

19. Lorri Mon and Lydia E. Harris, "The Death of the Anonymous Librarian," *Reference Librarian* 52 (2011): 352-364.

20. Roma Harris and Christina Sue-Chen, "Cataloging and Reference, Circulation and Shelving: Public Library Users and University Students' Perceptions of Librarianship," *Library & Information Science Research* 10 (January 1988): 95-107.

21. Jody Fagan, "Students' Perceptions of Academic Librarians," *Reference Librarian* 78 (2002): 131-148.

22. Harris and Sue-Chen, *Cataloging and Reference.*

23. Fagan, *Students' Perceptions of Academic Librarians.*

24. Ibid.

25. Seiss, "*The Visible Librarian*".

26. Compton, "*Academic Librarians and Archivists*".

27. Melanie Mills, "Information Workers in the Academy: The Case of Librarians and Archivists at the University of Western Ontario," *Ephemera* 10, no. 3/4 (2010): 532-536.

28. Hoffman, "Lesson in Solidarity."

29. McMillan and Chavis, *Sense of Community.*

30. UWOFA, "Western Librarians & Archivists."

31. McMillan and Chavis, *Sense of Community.*

32. Hoffman, "Lesson in Solidarity."

33. University of Western Ontario Faculty Association, "Academics Rally For UWO Librarians & Archivists," *UWOFA Matters* (September 2011): http://uwofa.ca/uwofamatters/id:58.

34. University of Western Ontario Faculty Association, "OFL President to Join UWO Librarians & Archivists," *UWOFA Matters* (September 2011) http://uwofa.ca/uwofamatters/id:57.

35. Hoffman, "Lesson in Solidarity."

36. Hoffmann, "Lesson in Solidarity," 5.

37. Bryce Traister, "President's Column: A Time to Reflect," Faculty Times: A UWOFA Newsletter (February 2012): 3-4, http://uwofa.ca/@storage/files/documents/428/ftvolxiv3.pdf.

38. Bryce Traister, "A Time to Reflect." *Faculty Times: A UWOFA Newsletter* (February 2012): 2, http://uwofa.ca/@storage/files/documents/428/ftvolxiv3.pdf.

39. Varpalotai and Dunn, "*The First Academic Strike at Western,*" 4.

40. Harrington and Katz, "*Some of Our Observations,*" 7.

41. Hoffmann, "*Lesson in Solidarity,*" 5.

42. Varpalotai and Dunn, "*The First Academic Strike at Western*", 4.

Chapter 13
Braunstein & Russo

1. Thomas Strentz, *Psychological Aspects of Crisis Negotiation*. (Boca Raton, FL: CRC, 2006).

2. LSA—R.S. 24:56.

3. J. Blum, "LSU Unveils Realignment Plan: University Officials Describe Changes at Packed Faculty Forum," *Baton Rouge Advocate*, April 15, 2009.

4. A list of additional resources will be appended to the end of the chapter so that the reader can do further research into articles older and more contingently relevant to our thesis.

5. Deanna D. Wood, "Librarians and Unions: Defining and Protecting Professional Value," *Education Libraries* 23, no. 1 (1999): 13.

6. Ibid., 12.

7. Ibid., 13, 15-16.

8. Rachel Applegate, "Who Benefits? Unionization and Academic Libraries and Librarians," *Library Quarterly* 79, no. 4 (2009): 443.

9. Ibid., 447.

10. Deborah O. Lee, Kevin E. Rogers, and Paul W. Grimes, "The Union Relative Wage Effect for Academic Librarians," *Industrial Relations* 45, no. 3 (2006): 483.

11. "Deprofessionalization" is used here to describe a current trend in academic libraries to reduce the duties of and number of professional librarians, replacing them with support staff, adjuncts, and student workers (Turk, 2010).

12. Ibid., 4.

13. Norman Oder, Lynn Blumenstein, Josh Hadro, and Rocco Staino, "Union Vote for McMaster Librarians," *Library Journal* 135, no. 5 (2010): 13.

14. Michael Kelley, Lynn Blumenstein, David Rapp, and Bob Warburton, "New Agreement Ends UWO Librarian Strike," *Library Journal* 136, no. 17 (2011): 13.

15. Diane Granfield, Mary Kandiuk, and Harriet Sonne de Torrens, "Academic Librarianship: A Crisis or an Opportunity?" *Partnership: The Canadian Journal of Library and Information Practice and Research* 6, no. 2 (2011): Special Section, 1-6.

16. Ibid., 3.

17. Values calculated include minimum value, maximum value, mean, variance, standard deviation, and total responses.

18. The term "tenure" is being used to cover all of the variations in semantics for the concept of a continuing or permanent appointment for a faculty member in an institution of higher education.

19. K. Addo, "Tax Break Cuts Pale Compared to Big Slashes." *Baton Rouge Advocate*, May 10, 2013.

20. *Pineville Police Officers' Association vs. City of Pineville, et al.*, 713 So. 2d 536 (La. Ct. App. 3d Cir.) 1998.

21. LSA—R. S. 23:981.

22. US Congress. Senate. Committee on Health, Education, Labor, and Pensions, *Employee Free Choice Act: Restoring Economic Opportunity for Working Families, 2007*, 110th Cong., 1st sess., 2007: 2.

23. Ross Eisenbrey and Colin Gordon, "As Unions Decline, Inequality Rises," Economic Policy Institute, June 6, 2012, http://www.epi.org/publication/unions-decline-inequality-rises/.

24. US Department of Labor, Bureau of Labor Statistics, *Unions in Louisiana—2012*, Dallas, 2013. Retrieved from http://www.bls.gov/ro6/fax/union_la.htm.

25. Ibid.

26. US Department of Labor, Bureau of Labor Statistics, *Union Members—2012*, Dallas, 2013. Retrieved from http://www.bls.gov/news.release/pdf/union2.pdf.

27. Ibid.

28. LSA—R.S. 23:981, *et seq.*

Chapter 14
Ribaric

1. Andrew M. Boggs, "Understanding the Origins, Evolution and State of Play in UK University Governance," *The New Collection* 5 (2010): 5.

2. American Association of University Professors, "1966 Statement on Government of Colleges and Universities," 138. http://www.aaup.org/report/1966-statement-government-colleges-and-universities.

3. Ibid., 139.

4. American Association of University Professors, "Joint Statement on Faculty Status of College and University Librarians," 2. http://www.aaup.org/report/joint-statement-faculty-status-college-and-university-librarians.

5. Canadian Association of University Teachers, "Governance," http://www.caut.ca/about-us/caut-policy/lists/general-caut-policies/caut-policy-statement-on-governance, 2008.

6. Ibid.

7. Canadian Association of University Teachers, *CAUT Librarians' Committee Discussion Paper on Governance and Librarians*, 2000, 1.

8. Ibid., 3.

9. Canadian Association of University Teachers, "Academic Status and Governance for Librarians at Canadian Universities and Colleges, 2010," http://www.caut.ca/about-us/caut-policy/lists/general-caut-policies/policy-statement-on-academic-status-and-governance-for-librarians-at-canadian-universities-and-colleges, 2010.

10. Ibid.

11. Canadian Association of University Teachers, "Governance," 2.

12. Leona Jacobs, "Library Councils in Canadian Academic Libraries: A Summary of Responses." 2008, 13. https://www.uleth.ca/dspace/handle/10133/564.

13. Ibid., 5.

14. Larry Savage, Michelle Webber, and Jonah Butovsky, "Organizing the Ivory Tower: The Unionization of the Brock University Faculty Association." *Labor Studies Journal* 37, no. 3 (2012): 305.

15. Brock University Faculty Association, *Why Certify?* (St. Catharines: Brock University, 1996).

16. Brock University, *An Agreement on the Terms and Conditions of Employment For Faculty between the Brock University Faculty Association and Brock University, 13 September 1990 - 30 June 1997* (St. Catharines: Brock University, 1990), 1.

17. *Collective Agreement between Brock University and the Brock University Faculty Association, July 1, 1997 to June 30, 2000* (St. Catharines: Brock University, 1997), 21.

18. Brock University, *Collective Agreement between Brock University and the Brock University Faculty Association, July 1, 2006 to June 30, 2008* (St. Catharines: Brock University, 2006), 137.

19. Brock University, *Collective Agreement*, 1997, 57.

20. Brock University, *Collective Agreement*, 2006, 105.

21. Bonnie Horenstein, "Job Satisfaction of Academic Librarians: An Examination of the Relationships between Satisfaction, Faculty Status and Participation," *College & Research Libraries* 54, no. 3 (1993): 255-269.

22. Gloria J. Leckie and Jim Brett, "Job Satisfaction of Canadian University Librarians: A National Survey," *College & Research Libraries* 58, no. 1 (1997): 31-47.

23. Ibid., 37.

24. Canadian Association of University Teachers, "Library Councils," 2008.

25. Brock University, "Library – Strategic Plan, 2012," http://www.brocku.ca/webfm_send/23579.

Contributors' Biographies

Stephanie Braunstein is an Associate Librarian and the Head of Government Documents/Microforms at Louisiana State University (LSU) Libraries and, as such, also serves as the coordinator of one of the state's two Regional Libraries participating in the Federal Depository Library Program. She is currently serving on the Depository Library Council for the United States Government Printing Office and is active in state and national library associations, especially their Government Documents Roundtables. From 2010 to 2013, she represented the LSU Libraries to the Faculty Senate and sat on that body's Executive Committee for the last two years of her tenure.

Martha Attridge Bufton, BBA (Hons), MA, is a full-time subject specialist in Reference Services at the Carleton University Library where she is a member of CUPE 2424, Carleton's support staff union. She is actively involved in her local and represents the support staff on the university pension committee. She has recently completed her Master of Arts in history at Carleton and her areas of interest include oral history as well as gender and labour history. Martha is also the editor-in-chief of *InsideOCULA*, the official publication of the Ontario College and University Library Association.

Mike Dawes is a Professor Emeritus of Mathematics at the University of Western Ontario (UWO). He has served on the Board, on Committees, and as President of the UWO Faculty Association. He has a decades-long involvement and interest with salaries and benefits, and in negotiations with the UWO Administration regarding those and also language concerns. He has also served as Chair of the OCUFA Collective Bargaining Committee. During his 40 years at UWO both the faculty (1997) and the librarians & archivists (2005) at Western certified UWOFA as their bargaining agent, and he was Chief Negotiator for the first contract for each of these bargaining units, for subsequent contracts for the faculty (2002, 2006, 2010), and for the 2009 contract for librarians & archivists. He has been granted the OCUFA (Lorimer) and the CAUT (Don Savage) Awards for collective bargaining, in 2010 and 2012 respectively.

Jennifer Dekker is the History, Philosophy and Religious Studies Librarian at the University of Ottawa. Previously she was an Adjunct Librarian at York University's Glendon College. She has served for three terms on the Executive Committee of the Association des Professeur(e)s de l'Université d'Ottawa (APUO), most recently as 2nd Vice President. She has been active on the APUO's Board of Directors, Collective Bargaining Committee, and is a trustee of the Canadian Association of University Teachers Defence Fund. Jennifer also created and maintains the University of Ottawa unionized academic librarians' website, *Les bibliothécaires de l'APUO/APUO Librarians*. For the past six years, she has served on the Ontario Library Association's Editorial Committee and is a regular columnist.

Linda K. Dunn is a research, instructional and collections librarian specializing in supporting the scientific disciplines at The University of Western Ontario. She actively participated in the successful certification drive for Western's librarians and archivists culminating in the formation of the UWOFA-LA (University of Western Ontario Faculty Association-Librarians and Archivists) bargaining unit. She has been a negotiating team member for all three collective agreements, serving as Deputy Chief Negotiator for the last two collective agreements of UWOFA-LA.

Natasha Gerolami is Head Librarian at Huntington University, a federated partner with Laurentian University, holds a faculty appointment in the department of Communication Studies and is currently a Union Steward. Her research interests include information ethics and the political economy of information/librarianship.

Carla Graebner is the Liaison Librarian for Economics and Government Information and Project Manager for Data Curation at Simon Fraser University. She has served as President for the Simon Fraser University Faculty Association, Economic Benefits Advisory Committee and is currently a member of their Bargaining Committee. Carla is a member of the CAUT Librarians' Committee.

Marni R. Harrington is an Associate Librarian in the Faculty of Information and Media Studies at the University of Western Ontario. She is a Faculty Association Board Member (UWOFA), and was Co-chair of the Strike Action Committee for the librarian and archivist 18-day strike in September 2011. Other research interests include collecting controversial materials, and mentoring in academic libraries.

Francesca Holyoke is the Head of Archives and Special Collections at the University of New Brunswick Libraries (2011-). She was previously an Information Services Librarian, then Head of UNB Libraries' Science & Forestry Library (1993-2011). Prior to that she worked as a consultant, project librarian and co-ordinator of a distance delivered library assistant training program. In 1999 she became involved with her faculty union, the Association of the University of New Brunswick Teachers. She has served on many bargaining support committees, joint employer-employee committees and the Executive having been Secretary, VP and President. Most recently she has co-chaired the Grievance Committee. She is a past chair of the CAUT Librarians' Committee (2008-2012) and in that capacity was a member of the CAUT Executive. She has presented on issues relating to academic librarianship at CAUT Conferences, Faculty Association Western Regionals, the Ontario Library Association Super Conference, and the 2011 Academic Librarianship Symposium hosted by librarians from the University of Toronto, Ryerson University, and York University Faculty Associations.

Robin Inskip received a B.A. from UWO (political science, 1967), an M.L.S. from U of T (1972), and an Ed.D. from U of T (1992). She developed a new library at Seneca College, King Campus 1972-1978. She was Manager (and President) C.L.S.I. (Canada) 1978-1979 (a Circulation systems vendor), researcher and writer (contracts) for such people as Hugh Faulkner, federal Cabinet Minister, and John Sheppard, Vice Chairman, Science Council 1979-1980. She was a Professor, School of Library and Information Studies, University of Alberta, from 1980-2010.

Leona Jacobs has been a librarian at the University of Lethbridge since 1989. During this time she has served in a number of roles relating to systems and technology, to public service supervision, to assessment and to collections coordination. Since 2011, Leona has been assigned as the subject liaison librarian to the Sciences. The continuing thread through all of this has been her abiding interest in the role(s) the university library plays (and can play) within the academy and the resulting roles, relationships and working conditions for academic librarians working within this culture and community.

Karen Jensen, Associate Librarian, was appointed Head, Bibliographic Access in the Collection Services division of the Concordia University Libraries in January 2011. Karen was first appointed as a librarian at McGill University in 1988 and held the title of Science Cataloguing Librarian from 1990-2010. Karen was a lecturer in Concordia University's Library Studies Program during 1993 and 1994 and is now a trainer for two Catalogers Learning Workshop courses (managed by the Program for Cooperative Cataloging, Library of Congress, and the American Library Association). Karen is a member of the CAUT Librarians' Committee and served on the McGill Association of University Teachers (MAUT) Librarians' Section Executive in 1996-1997 and from 2006-2010.

David L. Jones, Librarian Emeritus, entered librarianship in 1970/71 with an MLS from UWO after undergraduate and graduate studies in Biology and Chemistry. His first career position was at Humber College (1971-1980) where he became involved in professional activities through Canadian Library Association (CLA), the Canadian Association of College & University Libraries (CACUL), the Community and Technical College Libraries Section (CTCL) and the Humber College Local of the CSAO/OPSEU where he was an active advocate for Colleges of Applied Arts and Technology (CAAT) librarians. In 1980 he moved to the University of Alberta's Science and Technology Library as Assistant Science Librarian and later Collections Coordinator. In the mid-1990s he became Map Librarian, a position he maintained until his recent retirement. As Map Librarian his professional involvement focused on map library related activities through the Association of Canadian Map Libraries and Archives (ACMLA) and other map related groups. He has also been a presenter at University of Alberta's School of Library and Information Studies (SLIS) and an active mentor of students and early-career librarians.

Mary Kandiuk is the Visual Arts, Design and Theatre Librarian and a Senior Librarian at York University in Toronto. She has been actively involved in the York University Faculty Association for many years, has served in numerous Executive positions including four terms as Vice-President Internal, and as a member of three collective bargaining teams. She was a member of the Canadian Association of University Teachers Librarians' Committee from 2005-2008 and was the recipient of the 2005 Canadian Association of University Teachers Academic Librarians' Distinguished Service Award.

Christena A. McKillop is an Associate Librarian and the Director of Western Libraries' Education Library located at the University of Western Ontario's Faculty of Education. Previous roles included being the Director of a public library and an Acting Director at a corporate information centre. Christena obtained her MLIS from Western and a BA from the University of Toronto. Christena is active in numerous library and university committees. She has been Chief Steward for UWOFA-LA and member of the UWOFA Executive Committee (2011-13) as well as the Secretary of the Ontario Teacher Education Library Association (2009-2014).

Dr. Margaret (Peggy) Patterson is a full-time faculty member in the Werklund School of Education at the University of Calgary. Dr. Patterson's research focuses on various aspects of the post-secondary environment including, but not limited to, creating healthy campus environments; teaching and learning in higher education; leaders, leadership and governance in higher education, and the evolution of the forms and functions of the higher education in Canada. Dr. Patterson has previously published research using autoethnographic methodology.

Meg Raven practices librarianship at Mount Saint Vincent University in Halifax, NS where she coordinates library reference and instructional services, and where librarians teach credit courses. Her research interests include investigating the role academic librarians play within the academy, and the divergent research expectations of professors and first-year university students. She is a firm believer that teaching and scholarship are key components of the academic librarians' workload portfolio. Meg has served on her Faculty Association's Executive and Bargaining Committees, and she served two terms on the CAUT Librarians' Committee.

Tim Ribaric is the Digital Services Librarian at Brock University. His duties include administration of the Brock University Digital Repository, infrastructure development, and metadata support. He has been actively involved with the Brock University Faculty Association (BUFA) since starting at Brock in 2006. He has served as the Professional Librarian Representative on the BUFA executive council, has been a member of the Collective Agreement Negotiation Team, and has served as BUFA Observer on a variety of University and Senate committees.

Michael F. Russo is an Associate Librarian for LSU Libraries. He has worked at LSU a total of thirteen years and has served as Instruction Coordinator the past eleven. While at LSU, he helped to found LSUnited, a faculty union affiliated with the National Education Association. He was born and raised in New Orleans, where he also lived until being flushed out of the city by Hurricane Katrina. He now lives in Baton Rouge, Louisiana.

Michael Skelton is a recently retired reference and collections librarian. Prior to retirement Michael worked at Wilfrid Laurier University (WLU). During his tenure at WLU, Michael was actively involved in the faculty association. Notably, he is the first part-time librarian to serve as president of the Wilfrid Laurier University Faculty Association.

Harriet M. Sonne de Torrens, MA., MISt., Ph.D., L.M.S., is a medievalist and an academic librarian at the University of Toronto Mississauga. She is a member of the University of Toronto Faculty Association (UTFA) Executive, chair of the UTFA Librarians Committee, and a member of the Steering Committee of the Canadian Association of Professional Academic Librarians. Publications and research interests can be viewed at https://utoronto.academia.edu/HarrietSonnedeTorrens.

Douglas Vaisey, in his 39 years at Saint Mary's University in Nova Scotia, was active in the faculty union as an early negotiator for librarians, bargaining unit representative and later as chair of the union's grievance and arbitration committee. His day job was as a reference librarian in the Patrick Power Library, one of the most gratifying of all library positions.

Aniko Varpalotai, is a Professor Emerita of Education, Western University (London, Ont.). She is a former President of the University of Western Ontario Faculty Association (UWOFA) and has served on every negotiating team since Faculty, and subsequently Librarians & Archivists, certified at Western. Most recently, she was Chief Negotiator for UWOFA-LA during their 2011 negotiations which led to the first strike of academic staff at Western. She also served as Chair of OCUFA's Collective Bargaining Committee and Status of Women Committee.

Justine Wheeler is a librarian at the University of Calgary. She is the Head of the Business Library and Downtown Campus Library. Justine is currently serving her third term on the University of Calgary Faculty Association (TUCFA) Board of Directors. Her work for the Board has included representing the Faculty Association on numerous committees including promotion, tenure, and academic review committees and General Faculty Council. Currently, Justine is also a PhD student in the field of educational leadership.

Index

academic freedom, 3-4, 21, 42-43, 137-39
    collective agreements and, 151-52, 164-65, 222-27
academics
    librarians as, 89-90, 93, 99-102, 132-137
    librarians' role in, 279-80, 284
    reforms in. *See* education: reforms in
    role of library in, 82, 137-40, 175-76
    service and, 140-41
ACRL. *See* Association of College and Research Libraries
affirmative action. *See* employment equity
American Association of University Professors (AAUP), 133
    AAUP and ACRL *Joint Statement on Faculty Status of College and University Librarians*, 95, 133, 278

Association of College and Research Libraries (ACRL), 14, 87-88, 133
associations, faculty
    development of, 87-89, 281-84
    gender bias and, 88-93
    membership in, 176-81, 259-60
autonomy. *See* governance
Canadian Association of Research Libraries (CARL), 135-36, 139, 153, 158t2, 162, 330n35
collection development
    faculty involvement in, 85-86, 92
    scholarship and, 134-36
    teaching and, 128
collective agreements. *See also* contracts
    definition of, 197
    grievances and, 185-87
    salary and, 153-58
    self-governance through, 282-84
collective bargaining, 197-98, 203. *See also* unions
    strategies, 207-15

contracts. *See also* collective agreements
    negotiating conditions of employment, 225-29, 237-40
de-professionalization. *See also* status of librarianship, 83, 155, 255-56
economic conditions
    salary inequality and, 73
    unionization and, 252-53
education. *See also* graduate studies
    reforms in, 65
    requirements for librarians, 83, 84-85
employment equity, 67-71, 96-97, 109-11, 117, 227
feminism
    campaigns for equality, 109-11
    rise of, 81
freedom, academic. *See* academic freedom
gender. *See also* women
    inequality and, 83-84, 88, 109-11
    salary parity and, 112-15
governance. *See also* representation
    college and university, 277-79
        librarians and, 89-93, 285-86
        library council role in, 284
        faculty role in, 278
    library, 163, 252-53, 278-80
        council formation, 281-82
    tenets of, 284
graduate studies. *See also* education
    academic librarianship and, 84-87
Institute of Professional Librarians of Ontario (IPLO), 68, 86, 310n45, 314n3
labour movements, 24-26, 152-53, 200-202. *See also* strikes
librarianship, marginalization of, 198
library management. *See* governance: library

marginalization of librarianship, 197-98
parity. *See* status
recognition. *See* status
    librarians and, 64-67, 89-93, 225-29, 282-84
Reference Revolution, 81, 93-98
representation
    librarians in university leadership, 91-93
research, 134-36
    librarians as researchers, 132-37
    MLS as preparation for, 135
salary
    bargaining, 225-29, 233-35
        female parity, 112-15
    collective agreements and, 153-58, 254-55
    contract negotiations for parity, 116-19
    inequalities, 225-29, 258
scholarly work of librarianship, 134-36
social ecology theory, 108-9
social justice, 176-77
standards
    professional, 64-65
    tenure and, 26-30
status. *See also* de-professionalization. *See also* tenure
    academic, 171-72,
    definition of, 171-72
    gender and, 63-65, 89, 96-98, 109-11
    occupational, 67, 137-40
    professional, 86-87, 89-90, 222-23
    recognition of, 64-67, 90-92, 240-43, 246-47
    salary and, 65, 85-86
    unionization and, 67-70
strikes. *See also* labour movements

execution of, 241-46
University of Western Ontario Faculty Association, 151-52, 221-22, 229-31
teaching
   instruction vs., 129-130
   librarians as teachers, 128-132
   workload of, 130-32
tenure. *See also* status
   definition of, 171-72
   impact on salaries, 154
   labour movement and, 24-30
   requirements, 141-43
unionization
   conditions of employment and, 185-87, 224-28
   faculty status and, 154, 200-203
   grievances and fear, 190-91
   Louisiana State University, 257-59
      surveys, 266-70, 271-75
   professionalization vs., 67, 71-72
   public libraries and, 72
   purpose of, 74-75, 153-55, 198-200
   question of, 88, 254-56
   social justice and, 176-77, 233-35
   York University, 200-203
unions. *See also* collective bargaining
   professional associations vs., 259-60
universities
   role of librarians in, 89-93
University of Western Ontario Faculty Association (UWOFA)
   strike at. *See under* strikes
visibility. *See* status: recognition
women. *See also* gender
   discrimination, 109-11, 117-18, 227
   in leadership, 64, 88, 98
   librarianship and, 64, 83, 197-98
   salaries, 65, 96, 111
   status. *See* status: gender and working conditions
   collaborative alliances, 108-9
   discrimination. *See under* women
   employment equity, 67-71, 96-97, 109-11, 117, 227
   filing complaints and grievances, 187-89
      assistance with, 191-92
      fear of, 190-91
   professional practice, 222-23
   respect, 189-90
   unionization, 224-25, 258-62
workload
   autonomy and, 163
   issue of, 137-41
   library council membership, 285-87
   research and scholarship, 132-37, 160-62, 286
   service responsibilities and, 142-43, 153-55, 158-60
   teaching responsibilities and, 130-32, 162-63

www.ingramcontent.com/pod-product-compliance
Lightning Source LLC
Chambersburg PA
CBHW051349290426
44108CB00015B/1936